Life Below Stairs
in the twentieth century

Life Below Stairs
in the twentieth century

PAMELA HORN

AMBERLEY

First published 2001
This revised edition published 2010

Amberley Publishing Plc
Cirencester Road, Chalford,
Stroud, Gloucestershire, GL6 8PE

www.amberleybooks.com

British Library Cataloguing in Publication Data.
A catalogue record for this book is available from the British Library.

ISBN 978 1 84868 812 4

Typesetting and Origination by FONTHILLDESIGN.
Printed in Great Britain.

CONTENTS

Domestic work is the oldest, the largest and most unorganised form of women's employment. Service between master and man and mistress and maid is an age long relationship stretching far back into history. It is associated in some minds with a slave tradition of which an echo lingers in the opprobrious term 'slavery'. . . . It is not far fetched to hazard that this distant heredity still counts for something in the modern situation and is a subconscious element in the dislike with which the 20th century girl views domestic work.

Report on Post-War Organisation of Private Domestic Employment
by Violet Markham and Florence Hancock,
Parliamentary Papers, 1944-45, Vol. V, 3.

Shillings and Pence Conversion Table

Old Money	Decimal	Old Money	Decimal
1d	1/2p	1s 8d	8 1/2p
2d or 3d	1p	1s 9d or 10d	9p
4d	1 1/2p	1s 11d	9 1/2p
5d	2p	2s	10p
6d	2 1/2p	2s 6d	12 1/2p
1s	5p	3s	15p
1s 1d	5 1/2p	5s	25p
1s 2d or 1s 3d	6p	10s	50p
1s 6d	7 1/2p	20s	100p, i.e £1

ACKNOWLEDGEMENTS

I should like to thank all who have helped with the preparation of this book, either by providing photographs and documents or in other ways. I am especially grateful to the many people who responded so generously to my appeals for reminiscences of domestic servant life in the twentieth century; their contributions are acknowledged in the notes. However, I should particularly like to thank Arthur R. Inch, Mrs Mary Cocking and Mrs Sheila Whiting for their patience in responding to my many queries. Anne Jüssen of the Frauen Museum, Bonn, also devoted much time to transcribing the fascinating and lengthy correspondence between herself and her friend, Adele, in 1969-70, when Adele was an *au pair* in England.

Others have given permission for the use of documents and photographs and to them also my thanks are due. They include Mrs Anne Monk of the Girls' Friendly Society, David Ball of *myhome*, John Kirkham of Barnardo's Photographic Archive, Jim Garretts, Director of Manchester Jewish Museum, David J. Brazier of Studley College Trust, William Weber of Mrs Hunt's Agency, London, the Guardian and Observer Syndication, and Rosie Cox of Coventry University, who provided details of her own researches into modern domestic service in London. Miss Eileen R. Hawkins kindly gave permission for the use of the Young Women's Christian Association records kept at the Modern Records Centre at the University of Warwick. Stirling Smith Art Gallery provided photocopies of servant reminiscences in their possession.

I have received much efficient help and guidance from staff in the libraries, record offices, museums and university archives where I have worked and to them, too, I should like to express my gratitude. They include the Archival Resource Centre, University of Essex; the Bodleian Library, Oxford; the British Library; the British Library Newspaper Library, Colindale; the British Library of Political and Economic Science, London School of Economics; Cardiff Local History Library; the Women's Library at the London Metropolitan University; the Imperial War Museum Photograph and Sound Archives; Leicestershire Record Office; the London Metropolitan Archives; Maidenhead Reference Library; Margate Local History Library; Market Harborough Museum; the Modern Records Centre, University of Warwick; the National Archives, Kew; the Rural History Centre, University of Reading; Staffordshire County Council Arts and Museum Service, especially Helen Ruthven at Shugborough; the TUC Library at the London Metropolitan

University and its librarian, Christine Coates; the University of Reading Archives and the former archivist, Michael Bott; and the Wiener Library, London, and its head librarian, Colin Clarke.

Finally, as always, I owe a great debt to my late husband for his unfailing help and advice, and for his company on many research 'expeditions'. Without him this book could not have been written.

PAMELA HORN, April 2001 and 2010

PREFACE

The twentieth century saw a transformation in the scale and nature of paid household employment. At the beginning of the century domestic service was still the largest single, female occupation, as it had been during the reign of Queen Victoria. For vast numbers of middle- and upper-class householders, the employment of resident servants was an accepted part of family life. Although recruitment problems were already emerging before 1914, it was the First World War which witnessed the first real changes in that well-established pattern, as many domestics seized the opportunity to pursue other careers.

High unemployment in the 1920s and 1930s forced numerous women, in particular, to make a reluctant return to household work, but the seeds of a new order had already been sown. Recruitment drives were undertaken and government training programmes were provided, while female refugees fleeing persecution in Nazi Germany found, often enough, that their only hope of entering Britain was to become a maid. But despite these efforts, domestic labour was never again to be freely available in the way it had been in the nineteenth century.

After the Second World War this was even more clearly apparent. State initiatives to boost domestic work, including the widening of the home help service, were again a feature of the years after 1945. However, overall the second half of the twentieth century saw a decline in the use of paid household labour. Only in the final decades of the century did that alter, as a new demand for cleaners and childcare providers arose from comfortably off, working couples and as older people living alone looked for help with household chores. Professional cleaning firms grew up to satisfy some part of this need. Also important were foreign domestic workers, particularly from the Philippines, Portugal and Spain. Their role was especially significant in the larger cities, including London.

The course of this process of change in domestic employment and the way it impinged upon the growth of the hotel and catering trades are discussed, as is, for the first time, the development of household service for the whole of the twentieth century. Whereas once the recruitment of a maid was, at least in part, a status symbol as well as a useful adjunct to family life, by the 1990s the employment of a cleaner or a nanny was seen primarily in functional terms, to meet a particular need or to resolve a domestic problem. Only a comparatively few wealthy families still employed staff for reasons of prestige, rather than purely out of necessity. Even in these cases their requirements were often met by the recruitment of a married couple, with the husband acting as butler and his wife as cook-housekeeper. Additional workers were brought in on a daily basis to carry out cleaning duties or to provide extra help when important social functions were held.

The way in which this has affected the relationship between employer and worker is assessed. After all, domestic service is unlike any other occupation, as it involves bringing outsiders into the home where they may witness the intimacies of family life at close quarters including the tensions and the pleasures, the quarrels and the celebrations. Such a situation calls for a degree of discretion and diplomacy on the part of the worker to complement his or her skills in performing the household duties required, and respect from the employer for the feelings of the servant. That was as true at the end of the 1990s as it had been a century earlier, even if at both dates those high personal standards were not always met.

Part one

1900-1920

CHAPTER ONE

FROM PEACE TO WAR

One of the commonest subjects of general and plaintive discussion at the present day is the difficulties of the 'servant problem'. . . . The girl who goes out to service goes away for the most part from home and friends. She enters a household of the personalities composing which she knows nothing and has no opportunity of learning anything before making the experiment at her own risk. Other occupations now opened up to young women of the poor offer them a release from this difficulty.

The Lancet, 20 January 1912

SERVANT-KEEPING BEFORE 1914

In the early twentieth century the ability to employ a maid was a potent symbol of respectability and status, as well as one of necessity, given the labour-intensive layout of most middle- and upper-class homes. At the same time, in society at large it was widely accepted that a working-class girl with domestic skills would be properly equipped to deal with future family responsibilities. As Lady Willoughby de Broke wrote in 1916: 'A well-trained domestic servant is of real value to the nation, she makes the best possible wife and mother, as she has acquired a good knowledge of housewifery and habits of cleanliness, punctuality, and, to some extent, of hygiene.'[1]

When in 1901 Seebohm Rowntree published his social survey of the people of York, he made the 'keeping or not keeping of servants' the dividing line between the working classes and 'those of a higher social scale'.[2] At that date he estimated 28.8 per cent of the York population fell into this 'superior' stratum. In the nation at large domestic work was by far the largest single female occupation, with over a quarter of working girls so employed in the years before 1914. However, as we shall see, within that overall picture there were sharp regional differences.

In many places, particularly in southern England, families of relatively humble means struggled to keep a maid, even if at its lowest level this meant employing a girl from an orphanage, poor law school, or reformatory to whom they paid a shilling or two a week. In 1911 of 611 girls leaving London's poor law institutions, no less than 595 went into service, with five of the remainder becoming dairy maids and a further five going into laundries.[3] Not surprisingly, the industrial training they were given prior to leaving school concentrated on domestic work, and a number of institutions even ran commercial laundries to boost funds. Pupils

Maid-of-all-work in London, early twentieth century. (*Author's collection*)

were widely employed on household chores within the schools themselves, to economise on paid staff. In 1915, the chief inspector of reformatory and industrial schools in Great Britain complained of the heavy tasks many little girls were expected to carry out, including 'scrubbing and cleaning floors'. This was work 'fitted for a strong healthy charwoman, but not at all suitable for the little child for whom the Industrial School is supposed to take the place of home, but for whom I have sometimes a qualm that it becomes the abode of soulless drudgery'.⁴ Despite this protest, children in these institutions continued to be 'trained' for household duties into the 1920s and 1930s and to enter domestic service when they left. The occupation had the merit of providing them with a roof over their heads, as well as food and a small wage, but they were vulnerable to exploitation by unscrupulous mistresses, since few had a family to whom they could turn for help in time of need. Often they had to rely on charitable assistance, provided by organisations like the Metropolitan Association for Befriending Young Servants (MABYS) and the Girls' Friendly Society (GFS).

One unfortunate case in 1913 involved a Miss Ada Nixon of Rusholme, who starved a youngster she had recruited from Runcorn workhouse. When she took up the position the girl had weighed 5 stone 6 lb. A year later, when she returned to the workhouse after her plight came to public attention, her weight had dropped to 4 stone 5 lb. Nor had her mistress paid the meagre 2s a week wages promised. She claimed that the girl was not worth this sum 'until she had learned a little'. For the mistreatment Miss Nixon was fined £5 with costs or, in default, one month's imprisonment.⁵ But such punishments did not deter sadistic mistresses from bullying and beating their young maids.⁶

Other employers at the lower end of the servant-keeping scale included Winn Anderson's father, who was a Bristol Channel pilot based in Cardiff. Money was tight and years later his daughter expressed surprise that 'quite ordinarily-placed families like ours were never without a servant'.⁷ Among those they recruited was fourteen-year-old Kate from an orphanage. She had never known family life and virtually 'adopted' Winn's baby brother, 'carrying him around with her and spending all her spare time playing with him and taking him for walks'. There was a warm relationship between the family and their maid and when Kate developed tuberculosis after being with them for six years, they continued to keep in touch. Every other Sunday Winn's mother, armed with a parcel of cakes, fruit, sweets, or something similar, would make the lengthy rail journey to visit her in the sanatorium in North Wales where she was being treated. She continued to do this until Kate died. [8]

Often, as with Lilian Westall in Palmers Green, these humbler employers wanted their servant to assume a variety of roles, so as to impress friends and neighbours. In 1908, at the age of fifteen, Lilian became nurse-housemaid for a clerk, his wife and their three children. For this she received 2s a week:

> In the morning I did the housework; in the afternoon I took the children out; in the evening I looked after them and put them to bed. My employers didn't seem to have much money themselves . . . but they liked the idea of having a 'nurse-maid' and made me buy a cap, collar, cuffs and apron. Then the mistress took me to have a photograph taken with the children grouped around me. Perhaps someone still has that photo of themselves when children, showing the nanny with her charges. [9]

Lilian remained at this place until she was nearly seventeen and then left 'to better myself, mum', as she put it.

Girls heard of job vacancies in various ways. Sometimes it was through the recommendation of a family member or of friends. One Brighton girl became housemaid for a well-to-do family when her aunt, who was already working for them, 'spoke for her'. [10] In another case a fourteen-year-old Norwich girl followed her neighbour's daughter into a Beckenham household: 'she sort of recommended me'. The youngster was to be one of three maids and set off with her belongings packed in a wicker hamper. Her uniform was purchased by the mistress and she had to refund the cost on an instalment system at so much a month.

> When I got to Liverpool Street [station] the lady of the house met me and I was so poverty stricken she nearly put me on the next train back again, 'cos I must have looked a proper little urchin (big hat, long skirt to look older). I quite expected a Rolls-Royce to meet me at the station. Instead of that it was the gardener with the wheelbarrow. [11]

She was desperately homesick and pleaded with her mother to be allowed to return. 'I wouldn't mind what I done at home, if only she would let me come. She wrote back and said be thankful you've got a bed to lie on and a good meal'. The girl never asked again, and out of her small wage of 8s a month she managed to send 2s 6d home. [12]

Where personal contacts failed, then advertising in a newspaper or application to a servant registry office were other options. Such appeals as 'Wanted, for Country Rectory near Cowbridge, strong General, able to milk', or 'Wanted, experienced House-Parlourmaid . . . good plate-cleaner, lamps; valet gentleman; good needlewoman; wages £22', which both appeared in the *Western Mail* in September 1913, give a flavour of what was expected. *The Times*, too, encouraged servants to use its advertisement columns, by arguing that it was to their advantage to take a situation with employers who purchased an expensive newspaper.

Servants employed by the Meakin family at Creswell Hall, Creswell, Staffordshire, *c*. 1914. The chauffeur is standing in the centre of the photograph and the gardener, wearing leggings, is on the far right. (*Arts and Museum Service, Staffordshire County Council*)

> A family which pays 3*d* for a daily paper (which is the price of *The Times*) instead of 1*d* or ½*d*, is evidently a family of the best class, keeping a number of servants, so that they are company for each other. These families are just the people to offer a comfortable & permanent situation, & to appreciate good service. . . . They are not cheap, commonplace people, but good families having fine establishments & too anxious to have everything of the best not to keep plenty of servants for the work to be done.[13]

As a further inducement it offered to insert advertisements free of charge for servants. Only when an engagement had been secured would payment be expected.

For socially ambitious employers, the size, composition and appearance of domestic staff were important factors in establishing their personal standing. Although in 1911 only a fifth of the 800,000 families who employed servants had a staff of three or more, while almost three-fifths boasted a single domestic only, those who could join that elite group hastened to do so. As Lady Cynthia Asquith drily observed, there was never 'any virtue other than economy, in keeping only one instead of several servants'.[14] The recruitment of male servants in livery was regarded as particularly prestigious, with special attention paid to the height of the man concerned. Eric Horne was one who admitted ruefully that he could 'never hope to attain the very top of the tree' as a butler because he was 'three inches short of six feet'.[15]

Even among maids height was important. The Norwich girl who moved to Beckenham commented sadly that she was unable to rise above a house-parlour maid 'because I wasn't tall enough. You had to be tall to be a parlour maid', since that involved ceremonial roles performed in wealthier households by footmen. When she helped to serve at table she had to wear white gloves, because her hands were so 'common looking. . . . The water was very hard and me hands used to be raw with chaps and whatnot, so I had to wear white gloves.'[16] Her employers preferred not to be reminded of the discomfort the duties they expected from her were causing.

The Edwardians judged the amount of a man's income by the size of his house and the number of his servants. Loelia, Duchess of Westminster, recalled that although her parents moved in exclusive social circles they were regarded as 'dreadfully badly off' because their limited finances meant they could only employ five maids, a manservant, a boy and two gardeners. Their friends were 'mostly people who had too many servants to count and who owned stately homes'.[17] Lady Cynthia Asquith, too, remembered the lives of the well-to-do being 'benevolently ordered' by a large staff 'often there would be as many as three for the housework, three in the kitchen and three in the [butler's] pantry.'

Within these households the position of employers and servants in the social hierarchy was clearly defined, with a firm line drawn between 'Upstairs' and 'Downstairs':

> No one from Upstairs was expected to lend a hand at the sink – not even once a week. Indeed, no such invasion of the Staff's territory would have been tolerated. In some really well-ordered households it was even the rule that no housemaid should be seen broom or duster in hand. Except for the bedrooms all the housework had to be done before any of the family or their guests came downstairs.[18]

Books of advice to young girls entering service reinforced the message, as in *A Few Rules for the Manners of Servants in Good Families*, published by the Ladies Sanitary Association in 1895 and widely distributed early in the new century. Its strictures included such warnings as:

> Do not walk in the garden unless permitted or unless you know that all the family are out, and be careful to walk quietly when there, and on no account to be noisy . . .
> Never sing or whistle at your work where the family would be likely to hear you. . . .
> When meeting any ladies or gentlemen about the house, stand back or move aside for them to pass.
> When you have to carry letters or small parcels to the family or visitors do so upon a small salver or hand-tray.
> If obliged to take anything in the hand, or to lift it off the salver, do not give it to the person to whom it belongs, but lay it down on the table nearest to him or her.[19]

There were many other 'do's and don'ts' of a similar kind – all intended to emphasise the servant's inferiority in relation to his or her employer. Only in the case of the children of the household might there be some relaxation. That was true not only of the nursery staff who looked after them and for whom they might develop a good deal of affection, but of other staff members. Lady Cynthia Asquith remembered her 'thrilled awe' when as a little girl she visited the kitchen 'ruled over by Her Unserene Highness The Cook'. There she was allowed to whisk an egg or plaster her face all

Page in a London club in the early twentieth century carefully passing on a message to one of the members using a silver salver. (*Author's collection*)

over with dough. Still more enjoyable were visits to the butler's pantry where 'men in green baize aprons smoked cigarettes and however busy they might seem setting trays or spitting on the silver [as part of the cleaning process], were yet always able to spare time to show me a card-trick and hospitable enough to open a bottle of fizzy lemonade'.[20]

Sometimes when she stayed in other country houses, Lady Cynthia enjoyed similar contacts. Years later she remembered the sight and aroma of the housekeeper's cupboard at one large house. In reality the cupboard was a small room 'to which the bustling little housekeeper conducted me the morning after my arrival. I can still hear the jingle of the clustered keys worn at her waist, and savour the fragrance of crystallised apricots, lumps of ginger and almonds, raisins, and a hundred other delectabilities.'[21]

However, even with children these relationships were carefully regulated. That was indicated in one woman's memories of her own family's servants at this time: 'Despite the great social differences we were genuinely fond of them, in a special sort of way, of course. I remember my brother and I pleading with mother to allow us to have tea in the kitchen with the maids. This privilege was granted us only about once a month.'[22]

In general, the well-to-do with a large staff found it easier to recruit servants than those keeping one or two domestics only. That was especially true in the years immediately before 1914 when the rising demand for servants outstripped the supply. Not only did those in large establishments have a more clearly defined work routine than applied in humbler homes, where (as with Lilian Westall) a wide range of duties might be expected, but there was companionships from fellow servants and some reflected glory from the employer's elevated social status. As an Essex lad remembered, when he went as groom to St Osyth Priory, 'I suppose I thought I was going there to be a gentleman as well.'[23] Albert Thomas, who became third footman to a well-known sporting duke, similarly thought this was 'a lovely job . . . to be sure, hard work and plenty of it, but nice work, elevating work, and instead of being looked down upon we were respected by the townsfolk.'[24] Membership of prestigious households could also help to secure further promotion for those anxious to make a career in service, rather than merely take it up until they married (in the case of the womenfolk) or until they moved on to something else (in the case of the men). According to Loelia, Duchess of Westminster, her mother excelled as a chatelaine and even wrote a popular cookery book. 'Under her tuition any cook became a star and none needed further recommendation than having "been with Lady Ponsonby"'.[25]

In prosperous middle-class families too, like that of Edward Hopkinson, a leading Manchester businessman, the ownership of a substantial house and garden and the employment of several servants were 'an emblem of success'. Wives confined their domestic role to ordering the meals, 'captaining the staff', dealing with the shopping and carrying out various social and charitable duties. The Hopkinsons lived in Alderley Edge, Cheshire, and had a number of similarly well-to-do business people as neighbours. Their daughter, Katharine, later claimed that the 'poor people' in the community were 'almost exclusively the personal retainers of the Edge houses, the gardeners, the coachmen and later the chauffeurs'.[26] In this socially competitive environment, status might be affected by such apparent trivialities as the way in which the parlourmaid greeted guests:

> There were no butlers but the maids were excessively trim, clad in starched print of a morning and in black or brown with finely woven aprons in the afternoon and always, of course, wearing a cap as a badge of office . . . those few houses which produced untidy maids gave an impression of a slatternly home. . . . [The] trimmer the maid and the more distant her manner the more intimidating the formality of one's entrance.[27]

Apart from contributing to their employers' social standing and helping to promote their own careers by the contacts they made and the experience they gained, many servants in affluent households enjoyed handling beautiful objects. A former maid described as the happiest time in her life the period between the ages of fourteen and twenty-two when she worked 'in the stately homes of England before the decline of the real gentry and noblemen set in. . . . I feel that I was privileged to have lived in such mansions and to have seen and touched the wonderful treasures they contained.'[28] Her feelings were shared by Frederick Gorst, who became an under-footman to Squire Leache at Carden Park, Cheshire, around the turn of the century. Not only did he relish wearing his smart plum-coloured livery with matching vest trimmed with silver buttons, but he took pride in the display of the silverware which he had to clean. Under the butler's supervision, the dinner table was laid with a white damask cloth and in the centre was a large bowl of dark red geraniums grown especially in one of the hothouses:

> Two silver baskets of fresh fruit and two pairs of five-branch candlesticks, with each candle covered by a fringed silk shade, made a lavish setting. Then the flat silver, and the Crown Derby china with insets of the Squire's crest, the same lush red as the geraniums, were arranged.[29]

In such households the strict division between employers and servants was matched by the hierarchical structure below stairs. The senior staff – the butler, housekeeper, cook, nurse, and lady's maid not only had their own duties to carry out, but they supervised the work of subordinates. Ernest King, who went as a hall boy to the

Chichesters of Bishop's Tawton, north Devon, soon discovered that his real 'lord and master' was the butler:

> I suppose I first learnt to be a servant by being a servant to the servants: the table in the servants hall to lay, the staff cutlery to clean and the staff meals to put on the table. In the butler's pantry I spent most of my time at the washing-up tub.[30]

As a result, his hands and arms became chapped up to the elbows during the winter. He also had to clean the windows in the house, all the knives, and the boots, including the family's, the butler's and those belonging to any visitors. At meal-times in the servants' hall silence had to be observed when the senior staff were present. Only when the main course of the mid-day dinner had been consumed did the head servants retire to the housekeeper's room to eat their pudding. Then the rest of the staff were free to talk. 'We lower servants had to walk the chalk-line. Obey, or else.'[31]

High quality service continued to be enjoyed in these households up to the outbreak of the First World War and, indeed, beyond. But for most servant-keeping households, with one or two maids, recruitment difficulties were already being experienced. In many respects the period from 1900 to 1914 was a transitional one, spanning the years between the Victorian era, when the main domestic debate had been about the quality of the staff, and that after 1918, when the prime concern was their quantity or, more accurately, their scarcity. Although indoor servant totals continued to rise between 1901 and 1911, reaching over 1.4 million at the later date in England and Wales (of whom males made up 54,260 and females 1,359,359), they did not keep pace with the increase in families seeking domestic help. In 1881 there had been 218 female servants to every thousand families and even in 1901 the figure had been 189 per thousand. However, by 1911 that had fallen to 170 per thousand. The difficulty was most apparent among younger maids, whose numbers dropped sharply by over 62 per cent for those under fourteen years of age between 1901 and 1911, and by 17.2 per cent for those aged fourteen. All age groups up to twenty-five registered a decline, even though the majority of female servants remained young, with around 54 per cent of maids in the age range fifteen to twenty-five in 1911 (compared to around 56 per cent in that age group in 1901). However, the largest proportionate increase over the period occurred among women aged between thirty-five and fifty-five.[32]

Much of the shortfall among the youngest girls could be attributed to a general raising of the school-leaving age to fourteen, but for those above that age other explanations had to be sought. These included the widening of employment opportunities for women in factories, shops and offices, which gave greater freedom for leisure activities and for continued contacts with family and friends than was possible in residential service. Few servants had more than one afternoon and evening off per week and as Mrs Dence remembered of her own spell in 'gentleman's service' around 1906, limits were placed on other outings: 'one must ask to post a letter although the post office was just outside one of the entrances.

Two footmen and a coachman at Caerhays Castle, Cornwall, *c.* 1907. All three are dressed in breeched livery. The footman on the left was Richard Edwin Inch. He eventually became a butler. (*Arthur R. Inch*)

If you had shopping to do you must ask and say where and what for. We were not allowed to speak in the corridors or to the menservants, although we were often working in the same room.' Like many maids at that time, she and the other domestics were expected to attend Church on Sunday, 'wearing bonnets and black, no "feathers, flowers, veils, furs or shining jewellery", this was stated in these words in the letter answering my application for the post'.[33] Girls unwilling to accept such restrictions simply looked around for other employment.

Another factor limiting servant supply was the change in population distribution. Country girls were more likely to go into service than their urban counterparts, because of the shortage of alternative jobs in villages. They were also more popular with employers, who considered them cleaner, harder working and less likely to have undesirable family connections than youngsters from the poorer districts of large towns, which also provided maids in these years. Yet, by the early twentieth century, under a quarter of the population lived in rural districts. Hence, the potential supply of servants was curtailed.

Many town girls, especially the daughters of skilled craftsmen, looked down on maids as mere 'skivvies' or 'slaveys', but the country girls countered by condemning factory work as rough and 'common'. 'I never did work in a factory, never; no, I shouldn't have wanted to. There was nothing to do, only domestic service', remembered a woman from the Leicestershire village of Medbourne. She went as a maid to a nearby vicarage in about 1914.[34] Nevertheless, this did not prevent her from feeling nervous when she first went there:

> Sitting, . . . looking bewildered at the big dresser in the kitchen, I thought I shall never be able to work here. . . . There was a big high wall and I thought 'oh dear, oh dear, it looks like a prison'.[35]

She was paid 4s a week and for that she had to clean the bedrooms, prepare vegetables and scrub the house and the entrance steps. Staff prayers were conducted daily in the vicar's study and there was one half-day off a week, between 3 p.m. and 6 p.m. This she spent visiting her family in Medbourne: 'I really and truly wished I could be ill to go home, because I was really worked hard, nothing but hard work . . . . But that's how life was lived, those days. You were down there and they were up there.'[36] Later she admitted to being sensitive about her status as a maid: 'I really didn't like telling people I'd been in service.'

Her ambivalence towards domestic employment reflected the perception of growing numbers of men and women that it was a demeaning occupation, with long hours, little liberty and often enough low and irregular pay. Mrs Dence was not alone in receiving her wages just once every quarter: 'Can you imagine having only £2 four times a year to provide all one needed. Perhaps it was just as well we had no free time.'[37]

With the benefits of better education and a cheap press, youngsters could learn of events in the wider world and they were less willing to accept the rules and restrictions associated with household service. The petty distinctions employers imposed were widely resented, including their insistence on the wearing of a special uniform; most maids particularly disliked having to wear a cap. Within the house, they were restricted to certain rooms except when they were cleaning the others and they had to use different entrances and staircases from the family when going to and from the house, or moving around within it. They were also used as 'gatekeepers' to ward off unwelcome visitors when answering the front door by, if necessary, declaring their mistress was 'not at home'.

Even in the comfortable surroundings of landed households, the demarcations were an irritant. A kitchenmaid, for example, was not only excluded from the luxurious 'front' rooms of the house, where the family lived, but she might never see her mistress at all, except perhaps at Christmas when she

Nurse Abberley, a young nanny employed by the Irving family in Wales, *c.* 1904. Nannies often enjoyed close relations with the families they served and these could continue even when the children became adults. (*Mr. E. J. B. Irving*)

was given a length of print material as a present, to be made up, at her own expense, into a working dress. Margaret Thomas, who worked in the kitchen of a large Yorkshire country house, saw her mistress once only, when she was told that the family would be going to Scotland for the shooting and she was not to accompany them because she was not strong enough for the heavy duties there. 'I was upset as I had been looking forward to the visit, for the others had told me the castle was on an island .... But I appreciated the fact that the Lady told me herself'.[38]

There were also differences in food. A London maid remembered being allowed half a pound of cheese a week. 'But I mustn't use their cheese, I had the cheaper cheese.'[39] In this house there was an old-fashioned bellows type vacuum cleaner for the carpets and the mistress used to weigh the dirt when she had finished, to see that the job had been done thoroughly:

> in the end I used to save the bigger dirt. .... So if I had not enough dirt I used to add a bit and she thought it was wonderful! In the pot house I had one or two bags of different colour with dirt in so I could make my weight up. What was the weight she wanted? About a cup and a half of dirt for each room.[40]

Another girl, one of three servants employed by an elderly widow in Shetland, recalled that while the mistress had a three-course dinner in the evening, the maids were only supposed to have two courses for their main meal in the middle of the day. 'We were always allowed the meat course but either soup or pudding. . . . And . . . she went into the storeroom every morning and gave out the stuff that had to be cooked and she would count the prunes.'[41] However, the two other maids, who were older, learned to circumvent the restrictions and made sure that the staff had three courses as well. They discovered where the key to the store room was kept and when the opportunity offered they slipped in and supplemented the supplies that had been allocated.

Other much-resented actions by employers included hiding pennies under the carpets or down the side of upholstered chairs to test the servant's honesty or her diligence. Names were changed as well. Margaret Thomas, who worked in a number of large households, recalled there was 'always a general name for footmen. In one house they were William and another Henry.'[42]

Although the parental home of these young servants might be far more uncomfortable than the conditions they experienced in service, it was the blatant drawing of distinctions that led to resentment. As Frank Dawes has noted,

> a housemaid making her mistress's comfortable feather bed could compare it with her own lumpy flock mattress. As her feet sank into the thick pile of the carpet in the drawing room she could hardly fail to notice the difference between that and the bare boards, or the thin strip of threadbare rug in her own room.[43]

Furniture shops even sold servants' beds, which were 2 ft 6 in wide, instead of the customary 3 ft, while a suite for a maid's bedroom, comprising toilet table, washstand, chest of drawers, towel-horse, and chair, could be purchased for about £3 to £4.[44] Small wonder that some of the more spirited girls took pleasure in outwitting their employer. Florence Hancock, later a leading figure in the trade union movement, began her working life as a kitchen maid. From an early age she rebelled against the class differentiation: 'I took every opportunity of blending together the two qualities of food so that dining-room and kitchen shared and shared alike.'[45]

It was in such circumstances that independent-minded servants like Eric Horne railed against the 'vast abyss' that separated master and servant:

> Servants are looked upon as a part of the furniture of the house; live furniture, nothing more. If the live furniture is in the town house and is wanted in the country house, or vice versa, it is simply moved there. If a piece of the live furniture gets broken in body and health, the gentry simply say: 'Chuck it out and get another.'[46]

That these factors contributed to the unpopularity of domestic service in the Edwardian era was confirmed in a government report published just after the end of the First World War. Among the points it mentioned as particularly causing offence was the practice of addressing workers by their Christian or surname, rather than adding a Miss or Mr. This was considered one reason for the 'superior attitude adopted' by other people, including those from the same, or even a lower, social stratum, towards maids:

> Further, the attitude adopted by the Press and the stage is usually an unfortunate one, as servants are frequently represented as comic or flippant characters, and are held up to ridicule. . . . The limited hours off duty render any social life outside the employer's house a difficulty, and within it restriction is often placed on the reception of visitors of either sex.[47]

To ease the burden of domestic work and to make it more palatable to potential maids, advertisers began to offer labour-saving products. The makers of Sunlight soap, for example, boasted it could do 'Double Work in Half the Time', while the virtues of new polishes and convenience foods were similarly extolled.[48]

Gas lighting replaced lamps and candles in some homes, while in the most modern electricity was installed, especially for lighting. One contributor to *The Times* in 1914 saw the advent of cheap electricity as pointing the way to a long-term solution of the 'servant question'. By the use of electric power, such chores as sweeping, dusting, washing and heating could be carried out with half the existing amount of labour. As a consequence,

> we can create anew the time when servants rejoiced in their calling and took some pleasure in it, even to the extent of becoming friends with their masters. Not till that time returns will the servant question disappear . . . and the human element will get a fairer chance.[49]

Telephones obviated the need to send servants out with messages. Instead staff were trained to take telephone calls on behalf of their employer. To be 'good at the telephone' was considered an 'indispensable talent for modern footmen'.[50]

Unfortunately, despite these innovations, the most important labour-saving device of all was still lacking, a sensibly designed house. Although basements were less common in Edwardian houses than in their Victorian predecessors, few middle-class dwellings were built to be run without domestic help. Even newly constructed flats in London had servants' quarters, though *The Lancet* in 1905 condemned the cramped and dark condition of many of them. It expressed surprise that properties which were rented for such relatively high sums as £150 or £250 a year and which were located in the most fashionable parts of the capital, nonetheless housed servants in rooms where they could never enjoy direct sunlight and where 'diffused light is but a matter of a few hours daily even in midsummer. In flats such as these there are good, even imposing, reception rooms and, perhaps, two well-lighted bedrooms. For the rest the rooms . . . are almost in darkness and but very imperfectly ventilated.' It was this, *The Lancet* claimed, which accounted for the anaemic appearance of so many servants employed in affluent homes. 'It is difficult to understand how the well-educated classes . . . can allow themselves to take flats

Kitchen staff at the Carlton Hotel, London, in the early twentieth century. There was a growing trend for the well-to-do to dine out at hotels and restaurants in the Edwardian years. (*Author's collection*)

where they themselves are housed in comfort but where the servants live under conditions which, to say the least of them, must be eminently depressing.'[51]

A small number of well-to-do householders, tired of coping with the 'servant problem', decided to move into service flats, where help was provided along with the accommodation. The first service block was built around this time by the Savoy Company, near to its luxurious hotel off the Strand, and was christened Savoy Court. Each unit was lavishly decorated and there were telephones and electrical sun baths. A touch on the bell brought meals from the property's own kitchens. Among those who took a suite at Savoy Court was the actress Lily Langtry, who paid £50 a year for accommodation and an extra £30 for the services of a personal maid, valet and chambermaid.[52] Soon other properties were built on the same lines. In April 1914 one advertiser in *The Times* claimed encouragingly: 'Servant Worries Avoided' by renting a 'residential suite' in De Vere Gardens, adjoining Hyde Park. 'Rent £125. Full attention from Housekeeper.'[53]

But such innovations only contributed in a small way to solving the difficulties of would-be servant-keepers. Sometimes a solution was found by reducing home entertaining and inviting friends to eat out in luxury hotels like the Savoy, the Carlton, the Ritz and others in London and elsewhere which catered for this new trend.[54] On a typical Sunday evening at the Savoy the restaurant was so full that tables spilled out into the palm lounge.

The degree of unpopularity of domestic service did, however, vary from one part of the country to another. Maids were thinnest on the ground in industrial counties like Lancashire, the West Riding of Yorkshire and Durham, where not only were the predominantly working-class families unlikely to be able to afford paid assistance, but where even among the better-off it was common for daughters or other female members of the household to lend a hand, supplemented perhaps by the help of a 'daily' to do the heaviest work or the washing. In both Lancashire and the West Riding there were opportunities for girls to work in the textile mills, while for those wishing to take domestic posts there were openings in the seaside resorts along the Lancashire coast.

In 1908 the annual exodus of domestic servants from Manchester to Blackpool was blamed for aggravating the 'servant problem' in the former city. The attraction of spending the summer in Blackpool 'below stairs' might be social rather than financial, but there was always the hope of boosting basic pay with tips. Among the non-cash benefits were the opportunities to meet a variety of guests in hotels and boarding houses, and to enjoy the entertainments of the resort itself. 'High wages were not needed to attract the relatively limited number of servants Blackpool's landladies required', comments John Walton.[55]

In 1911, servants were estimated to average 97 per thousand families in Lancashire and 100 per thousand in the West Riding of Yorkshire, compared to a national average of 170 servants per thousand families. At the other end of the servant-keeping scale were non-industrialised counties in southern England like Surrey, where in 1911 the proportion was 353 female servants to every thousand families, and East Sussex, where it was 331 per thousand. Likewise, among towns with a population of 50,000 or more, there were places like Burnley, with 45 servants per thousand families and Rochdale, with 49 per thousand, on the one hand, and affluent Bournemouth, with 415 servants per thousand families and Eastbourne with 408, on the other.[56] Large concentrations of servants were also found in certain parts of London, with Hampstead, Harrow, Chelsea and Westminster recording very high figures.

In Scotland similar variations were apparent. The city of Edinburgh alone, with its commercial, professional and academic interests, contained more than one eighth of Scotland's 135,052 female indoor servants in 1911, while industrial Dundee had just over one seventieth of the total. According to the population census, female domestics comprised 5.3 per cent of the entire population of Edinburgh; in Dundee they compromised 1.4 per cent.[57]

The tensions to which the 'servant problem' gave rise were seen clearly in 1911, when the Liberal Government introduced its National Insurance bill. This was designed to give sickness benefit and free medical treatment to manual workers, including domestic servants. In the case of the females, that took the form of a contribution of 3d per week from the mistress and 3d per week from the maid, with the mistress collecting the servant's contribution and purchasing stamps to be stuck on the insurance card. To some employers that was an intolerable interference by the state in domestic life and an insult to mistresses, implying that they neglected their servants when they were ill. Lady Hawarden, for example, expressed vehement hostility to the measure, adding darkly: 'Woe betide the country which invades women's own domain and forces obnoxious legislation upon it.' Widespread petitions and demonstrations against the bill were organised, with the *Daily Mail* playing a leading part in fomenting opposition

WHY MISTRESSES AND SERVANTS OPPOSE THE BILL.

Because it creates a new tax of 26/- a year for every servant.

Because it makes every woman who pays wages a tax-collector in her own house.

Because it will destroy happy domestic relations in hundreds of thousands of homes.

Because it draws 3d. a week from the earnings of the servant and 3d. a week from the slender housekeeping resources of struggling middleclass families.

Because the sick benefits it promises are absurdly small in comparison with the yearly tax.

Because it confers no benefit at all, except the services of an underpaid and overworked State doctor, when the mistress provides board and lodging for the sick servant.

Because mistress and servant are paying the equivalent of four weeks benefits when the average "expectation of sickness" in the case of a servant is one week.

The *Daily Mail* was a strong opponent of the inclusion of domestic servants in the health insurance provisions of the 1911 National Insurance Act. (Daily Mail, 20 November, 1911)

to an initiative which made 'every woman who pays wages a tax collector in her own home'. David Lloyd George, who had introduced the measure in the Commons, referred to the 'hundreds of thousands of mistresses' who had proclaimed they would never allow their servants to join the scheme.[58]

Some maids who had, perhaps, enjoyed good treatment from their employer when they were ill and did not see why they should contribute 3d per week to a scheme they did not need, or who thought it tactful to share their mistress's indignation, signed petitions against the proposed legislation. However, many others welcomed the idea of receiving 7s 6d a week benefit for twenty-six weeks when they were sick, as well as free medical treatment, rather than relying on an employer's goodwill. One young maid who refused to sign a petition remembered the vicar telling her she was a 'very wicked girl' because she would not change her mind. She also had 'plenty of black looks from the mistress and master'.[59]

After some weeks, the agitation died down and the bill became law, with 'the stamp' accepted as a normal feature of domestic service life. When the scheme was implemented in July 1912, every insured female worker became entitled to medical attendance from a doctor of her own choice; free treatment in a sanatorium or other institution 'when suffering from tuberculosis'; a weekly sickness benefit of 7s 6d for twenty-six weeks; and a disablement benefit of 5s a week, should she be unable to work after this period had elapsed. Male servants were covered on similar terms, save that for them the weekly contribution was 4d and the sickness benefit amounted to 10s a week for twenty-six weeks.[60]

Some organisations sought to induce loyalty towards employers by offering maids long-service awards. The Young Women's Christian Association was one such body.

From 1905 it awarded certificates to girls under twenty-one years of age who had been members of the Association for two years and had also held their current post for two years; girls who had been ten years in the same job and had belonged to the YWCA for five years were to be awarded a special bar to their membership badge. By June 1905 there were said to have been almost seven hundred bar brooches awarded. The arrangement continued until 1918 when lack of funds and a falling off in demand due to the war led to its demise.[61] Reformatories and industrial schools also offered rewards to girls who remained in their first post for at least a year. In 1912, at Sale Industrial School, near Manchester, six silver watches were presented to former pupils who had achieved 'three years' good service' in their first place; a further ten girls received a reward of 10s for completing one year's good service in their first place.[62]

Even in this period, strong bonds of affection and mutual regard existed between some families and their domestic staff. Nurses, lady's maids and valets were particularly likely to enjoy the confidence of their employers. Lady Astor described Nannie Gibbons, her children's nurse, as 'my strength and stay and the backbone of my home. . . . She was with us for forty years, until she died. She had, I often think, every virtue, and added to them one that is not always found in Nannies – she was utterly and absolutely loyal to me'.[63]

In humbler households similar warm links were forged. Sarah Dallaston entered service on a Leicestershire farm when she was thirteen. Like her father, her new employers were devout Baptists and she soon settled in happily. She learnt to churn the butter and to make pork pies, while at haymaking time tea and food were taken to the men in the fields. In summer, she picked strawberries and in the autumn there were apples and nuts to gather. Each week she accompanied her employers to Market Harborough market and although her health had been delicate before she went to the farm, with the good food and fresh air she soon grew strong. 'We used to go to chapel on Sunday mornings . . . Mr. Glover'd sit and read the Bible every night, just to himself. Read a passage to Mrs. Glover and I before we went to bed. . . . They were happy days they were.' However, after she had been there four years, her father said she ought to be earning higher wages, and so she had to move to another farm with a larger staff. 'I didn't want to leave. . . . The Glovers didn't want me to leave. Ever so upset they were.'[64]

Seventy years later Sarah recalled this period of her life with nostalgia. 'They were very kind to me. It was a lovely life.' However, such sentiments were shared by comparatively few early twentieth-century maids.

Mistresses, for their part, complained that girls were becoming too proud to do housework. *The Sphere* sympathised with that sentiment, declaring:

> The present condition of friction between mistress and maid is one totally destructive to domestic peace. . . . The servant who takes an interest in her work seems no longer to exist, and in return for high wages we get but superficial service. . . . Every sort of contrivance now lessens labour, carpet sweepers, knife machines, bathrooms, lifts, in spite of these the life of a housewife is one long wrestle and failure to establish order. [65]

There were even those who claimed, not very convincingly, that the current fashion for the well-to-do to spend months on the Riviera and in Egypt was due to the 'difficulty of getting good servants' in Britain.[66] With the outbreak of war in August 1914 such complaints became a good deal louder and more insistent.[67]

THE IMPACT OF THE FIRST WORLD WAR

Between 1914 and 1918 almost 400,000 servants are estimated to have left domestic work for positions in the armed forces or in various areas of war production, including metalwork, engineering, transport, commerce, and agriculture.[68] Women began to be recruited for the munition factories in the spring of 1915, with around a million of them eventually employed in that sector.[69] A contemporary claimed that perhaps a quarter of the females in the industry came from domestic service.[70]

Whatever the precise total, it is clear that many maids welcomed the opportunity to leave what they regarded as the drudgery of household work for the greater freedom and higher wages of industrial production. That did not necessarily mean that their advent was welcomed by male colleagues or the trade unions, but under the pressures of war, traditional working practices were temporarily relaxed in a number of industries. Women and unskilled males carried out tasks normally reserved for skilled or semi-skilled men. However, although the women were supposed to be paid the same piece rates as male colleagues, providing they carried out similar work, that did not apply to time rates. As a result, employers often arranged production processes so that it could be claimed the females were not performing the same tasks as the men. They were thus paid at only about half or two-thirds of the male rate.[71]

Nevertheless in a wide range of industries (and in the Women's Auxiliary Army Corps from 1917) former servants carried out tasks that would have seemed impossible before the war and they earned sums well in excess of their pre-war pay. Significantly, even in 1921 the number of female domestics in England and Wales was still around 200,000 below what it had been a decade earlier; in Scotland it had fallen by over 5,000.

However, when the war broke out, it was male servants who first came under pressure to enlist. On 12 August 1914, less than a fortnight after hostilities began, *The Times*, in a leader, called on those employing 'men in unproductive domestic occupations, both in and out of doors' to encourage them to join up:

> There are large numbers of footmen, valets, butlers, gardeners, grooms, and gamekeepers, whose services are more or less superfluous and can either be dispensed with or replaced by women without seriously hurting or incommoding anybody. . . . The well-to-do classes are, as a whole, responding finely to the call . . . but many of them may not perhaps have realised yet how large a reserve of the national manhood is represented by those who serve their personal comforts and gratifications.

In January 1915, *Country Life* was even blunter when it posed five questions to be answered by those still keeping male staff:

Domestic skills in use on the Western Front. Women's Auxiliary Army Corps cooks are seen working at an army camp at Abbeville in France, 15 September 1917. (*Imperial War Museum Photograph Archives*)

1. Have you a Butler, Groom, Chauffeur, Gardener, or Gamekeeper serving you who, at this moment should be serving your King and Country?
2. Have you a man serving at your table who should be serving a gun?
3. Have you a man digging your garden who should be digging trenches?
4. Have you a man driving your car who should be driving a transport wagon?
5. Have you a man preserving your game who should be helping to preserve your Country?

A great responsibility rests on you. Will you sacrifice your personal convenience for your Country's need? Ask your men to enlist TO-DAY [72]

Even in April 1918, more than two years after conscription had been introduced for men aged from eighteen to forty-one, the issue was still being debated in parliament. One MP complained of families with only two or three members who employed six to ten servants. He was assured that under a recent order, all certificates of exemption granted on occupational grounds to male domestic indoor or outdoor servants had been withdrawn, provided the men concerned fell within the requisite limits of age and medical grade.[73]

A number of families cut staff, however, partly on economy grounds, as prices and taxes rose, or to meet changes in their style of living, rather than merely for patriotic reasons. In other cases, estate owners prompted men to enlist by promising to guarantee an income to the wives and families of married volunteers while they were away and to keep a job open for all of them when they returned. This was done by the Earl of Ancaster on his Lincolnshire and Rutland estates, with the added incentive of a £5 bonus for every man when he enlisted.[74] At Welbeck Abbey, all building, planting and general improvements were brought to a standstill so that the hundreds of men employed by the Duke of Portland might be free to join up.[75] Game preservation was cut back, in order to release keepers for the war effort and at noted sporting estates like Elveden in Suffolk the Game Department was broken up, with those keepers and warreners who were unable for some reason to join up being transferred to other parts of the estate.[76] *Country Life* quoted one correspondent who claimed that eight of his underkeepers had enlisted and the ninth was about to follow suit. 'I have still two left, one of them too old for the khaki and the other too young.' Within months, on many large estates over two-thirds of the staff had 'exchanged the shot-gun and the traps for the service rifle and the bayonet.'[77]

Gardens lost their immaculate appearance, as workers left and lawns were turned over to potato growing. At Aynho Park, Northamptonshire, the gardeners were reduced from nine in mid-1915 to four two years later. Of these, three were too old to serve and the fourth, aged sixteen, was too young. Despite his inexperience he was given charge of the greenhouses. Early in 1918 his efforts were supplemented by a gardener invalided out of the army who gave the youngster some much-needed instruction.[78]

A number of men took the initiative themselves. Edwin Lee, who worked for the Astor family at Cliveden as a footman, joined up soon after the war began after talking it over with Mr Astor. He was assured that a job would be waiting for him when he returned and his action was symptomatic of what happened to other Cliveden workers. Except for a few elderly retainers, all the male staff left the house, stables and gardens. According to Lee, many who enlisted in 1914 never returned. They included three of the footmen, the 'odd man' from the London house, and several gardeners, stablemen, electricians and night watchmen. One footman became a commissioned officer and of him Mrs Astor wrote: 'He came to see me, and told me that living with us has been a great help to him in his military career. "I know good manners", he said.'[79]

Like many other large country houses during the war, part of Cliveden was converted into a convalescent home, while vegetables were grown in the gardens instead of flowers, to aid the food production campaign. Much of the work both indoors and outdoors on the estate was carried out by females, ranging from the housekeeper and the maids to members of the Women's Land Army.[80]

Advertisements for servants reflected the new situation. Not only were there fewer of them, but where male staff were asked for, emphasis was laid on the need for them to be ineligible for enlistment on grounds of age or poor health. Typical of many was an appeal in *The Times* in February 1915 for a 'Single-handed Footman under Butler, for Herefordshire'. He must be under eighteen or 'ineligible for Army', and was to be paid £18 a year, with livery and morning suit supplied. In another case, where there was a vacancy for a 'Working Butler', a foreigner was preferred '(Swiss or Italian).' Female substitutes were also recruited, as with the 'Lady Chauffeur', who offered her services, 'experienced; RAC certificate; running repairs'.[81] Violet Firth was a middle-class volunteer who became a 'lady gardener' and found the experience deeply disillusioning:

to be a servant is very painful to one's self respect, and no amount of money will compensate that injury to anyone who has independence of spirit; education fosters independence of spirit, and therefore reduces the number of those willing to be humiliated. . . . It offends the innate self-respect of a man or woman to be treated as an automaton.[82]

The substitution of female staff for male was encouraged by leading socialites like Mrs Cornwallis-West, the former Lady Randolph Churchill, who publicly expressed a preference for women servants.[83] One *nouveau riche* hostess described by Sir Edward Hulton even employed a set of 'handsome, strapping "foot girls," who wore blue livery jackets, striped waistcoats, stiff shirts, short blue skirts, black silk stockings and patent leather shoes with three-inch heels', to replace her footmen.[84] But most mistresses chose the discreet alternative of parlourmaids.

Clubs and hotels followed suit. In March 1915 *Country Life* noted with approval that the Athenaeum Club had substituted waitresses for male waiters and that the policy was also adopted by the United Services Club.[85] According to that club's historian, they remained stolidly at their posts even when an air-raid was under way in the neighbourhood.

Many hotels were affected not only by the loss of English staff but by that of German and Austrian waiters and kitchen staff, who were now enemy aliens. Even the prestigious Savoy in London suffered, with 'spy scares' sweeping through the hotel. Later on food shortages added to the difficulties and in the 'huge, half-empty kitchen with a skeleton staff of clumsy boys and tired old men, the maître-chef cursed the Boche and tried to somehow camouflage his rissoles'.[86]

Other establishments were similarly affected for, as the 1911 population census had shown, out of 23,054 males classed as 'waiters (not domestic)', over one-eighth were of German extraction.[87] Dorothy Haigh, who worked at the Grand Hotel, Bournemouth, before the war, remembered that virtually all the waiters were German. The day before hostilities began she and other members of staff saw them off at the railway station: 'We never knew where they went.'[88] Dorothy herself stayed on for a few months until the government requisitioned the property and the staff had to leave. She took several other hotel jobs before getting married and then taking a post as a crane driver in a rolling mill, in 1917.

As a result of the changes, even large households were female-dominated. Rosina Harrison, who became a young lady's maid to the daughters of Lady Ierne Tufton in 1917, remembered the atmosphere was less formal than was the case after the war when the male servants had returned:

although we were all kept working we were a happy lot, and we'd break off at any time to make our own fun. . . . There was a cook and two others in the kitchen, four parlourmaids, three housemaids, two lady's maids . . . and a chauffeur; we didn't even have an odd job man. Nor was there a butler; his duties fell on the head parlourmaid, and Major Tufton's valeting was done by the second parlourmaid. . . . It was very much a time of women's lib below stairs.[89]

Lady's maid learning hairdressing skills in London, early twentieth century. (*Author's collection*)

Even so, many women servants were anxious to join in the war effort and leave the restrictions of domestic life. One girl, who had been employed as a housemaid for 5s a week and who was engaged to be married, seized the chance to move when she saw an advertisement for munition workers at Woolwich Arsenal. She had found her mistress 'very old and very crochety, she was always moaning about I didn't do this, I didn't do that', so the change was welcome. So also was the better pay and the companionship of her fellow workers. 'You never had many friends when you were in service you were never out, only one evening a week'. But in the Arsenal there were opportunities to gossip with colleagues on the journey to and from the factory. After the war she stayed on, getting a job dismantling cartridges. She never returned to domestic service.[90]

Her feelings were shared by Elsie Bell, who got a wartime job at Pirelli's cable works. She enjoyed the greater freedom and the fact that 'you were amongst more people', to say nothing of the higher wages. These amounted to £3 a week compared to her previous 2s 6d.[91]

With Annie Edwards, a young Sussex cook, it was the chance to join the Women's Land Army which led her to abandon domestic work. She had grown up on a farm and had always enjoyed the life, but at the age of about sixteen she had been sent into service. She was promoted from kitchenmaid to cook, and then took a post in Pulborough, not far from where she was born. She was there when the war broke out and was soon helping her mistress at the local Red Cross centre. She made slings, cut up bandages and did knitting and sewing. She went there every day, in between her domestic duties and it was when she was returning to prepare dinner for the family one afternoon that she saw posters appealing for volunteers for the Land Army. It meant she could go back to farming and that evening when her mistress returned, she went to the drawing room to ask whether she could apply. The mistress was somewhat reluctant but agreed, telling her that as she had been born on a farm 'I think you will be of use'.[92] Annie then went to Worthing to join up. After being accepted and passing a medical examination she went for six weeks' training before going to work full-time with horses. When the war was over and she was released from the Land Army, she stayed on at the same farm and remained there for around thirty years.

The outflow of girls from domestic service to the war effort and the increased recruitment of female staff by the well-to-do, seeking to replace men who had joined up, created particular difficulties for middle-class housewives. Significantly, even in 1921, it was the commuter areas of London, rather than the affluent West End, which showed the sharpest relative fall in servant numbers compared to pre-war. Thus, in six West End boroughs, including Chelsea, Kensington, Westminster and Hampstead, the proportion of domestics per 100 families had fallen by not much more than a quarter, from 57.4 in 1911 to 41.3 in 1921; but in four middle-class boroughs, including Lewisham and Wandsworth, the figure had virtually halved, from 24.1 servants per 100 families at the earlier date to 12.4 at the later. [93]

Outside the capital similar trends could be discerned, with wide regional differences in the availability of maids in 1921. The population census of that year recorded 1.1 million women and girls employed as servants (or 22.6 per cent of the employed female population). They were in the proportion of thirty servants to every thousand of the *total population*, compared to thirty-eight per thousand recorded in 1911. However, the ratio, as before the war, varied considerably according to the nature of the area. Thus the nation's county boroughs averaged twenty-two female domestics per thousand of the population, while in an aggregate of rural districts the figure was thirty-nine per thousand. Among the counties, the top positions were held by affluent East Sussex (sixty-seven maids per thousand) and West Sussex (sixty-two per thousand), while, as in 1911, Lancashire came at the bottom of the servant-keeping table, with just seventeen female domestics per thousand of the population, closely followed by Staffordshire, with eighteen per thousand. In Wales, Glamorgan, with its important iron, steel and coal industries, registered just twenty maids per thousand persons. [94] In the 1920s and 1930s counties like Glamorgan and Lancashire, with little tradition of household service, suffered severe unemployment and many women were drawn into the government's domestic training programme.

Most employers seeking to recruit staff during the war years pinned their hopes on private registry offices or press advertisements. *The Times*, in particular, encouraged mistresses and servants to use its advertising and registry office facilities. 'For the convenience of ladies', it announced in February 1915, 'facilities have been provided in various establishments in London whereby Servants who reply to their advertisements in *The Times* may be interviewed by appointment. A Lady Expert is in attendance from 10 to 6 o'clock daily . . . to advise and assist in drafting Servants Wanted . . . and other private announcements.' Among the eight venues listed were the department stores of John Barker & Co. Ltd of Kensington High Street and Harvey Nichols & Co. Ltd of Knightsbridge. [95]

The servants' book of Mrs Collier, a clergyman's wife from Theydon Bois, Essex, indicates the problems in one middle-class household at this time. In the eleven years before the war she had had just two house-parlourmaids, one nurse (who had stayed for seven and a half years) and nine cooks, including three temporary workers. But in the four war years there were seven different nurses, nine cooks, and four house parlourmaids, plus at least four different charwomen, employed temporarily when it was impossible to find a house-parlourmaid. Over that period wages also increased, so that the nurse in 1918 was earning £40 a year, compared to £29 paid to her predecessor in 1914, while the wages of the house-parlourmaid had jumped from £16 a year in 1914 to £24 or £25 in the last months of the war. The cook's earnings, too, had risen from £23 in 1914 to £30 in 1918, even though the girl employed in the latter year was not very satisfactory. Entries in the servants' book indicate some of Mrs Collier's difficulties:

1918

22 June: Received an application for cook's place from C. Hayden . . . age 44. Wages £30, engaged her to come on June 26th.

Edith Easter who is now doing cook and partly h.p. maid will try & take h.p. maid's place. Has been a general, so requires much teaching.

26th June: C. Hayden arrived, paid her fare from Cold Norton 12/9d. (& return).

27th June: C. Hayden announced she thought she had better leave. Her eyes are bad, she feels run down, needs a rest etc.!!! Left by the 3.30 p.m. train.

Sept.: After many struggles & employing a variety of charwomen, I heard Annie Strange would be shortly requiring a situation as h.p. maid, engaged her to come on Sept. 24 at £25-a-year to be raised to £26 in January 1919.

24th Sept.: Annie Strange arrived rather slow & wonderfully ugly.

Edith Easter (cook) a rather flighty, & not too honest girl announced she wished to leave on Oct. 7th.

Oct.1st: Edith Easter, on consideration of receiving £30 a year, said she wd. stay as cook, for which I was thankful, gave her a little talking to & so it was settled.

Oct.11th: Annie Strange announced she felt she could not settle in Theydon & would leave when I am suited. Heard of Alice Seymour, interviewed her & engaged her to come on Oct. 29th at £24.[96]

Small wonder that with this kind of rapid staff turnover, some mistresses preferred to dispense with resident maids, and to rely instead on the help of 'dailies' and on labour-saving appliances. *The Ideal Servant-Saving House*, published in 1918, included various examples of the latter, including the 'O-Cedar Mop' polisher, which 'Cleans as it Polishes'. According to its manufacturer it was the 'Greatest Labour Saver

Three rather dishevelled maids employed at Blakeshall, Worcestershire, during the First World War. (*Arts and Museum Service, Staffordshire County Council*)

of Modern Times'. The British Commercial Gas Association likewise advised
housewives how to be 'Happy though Servantless': 'The ideal servantless home
is the all-gas house. . . . In the all-gas house convenience, cleanliness, economy,
efficiency, and comfort, without unnecessary labour, are signs of progress which no
woman can afford to disregard. Dirt and drudgery depart with the disappearance
of smoky fuel.'[97]

While some women with modern homes welcomed the opportunity to run their
household as they thought fit, without taking into account the sensibilities of a
maid, most housewives longed for an end to the war so as to return domestic life
to its accustomed routine. However, even before the Armistice was signed, some
commentators were warning that girls who had enjoyed independence as wage-
earners in factories, workshops and offices would be reluctant to return to the
restrictions of household service. On 8 November 1918, Ward Muir, in an article
entitled 'Why Mary Won't Come Back' dismissed the idea that his 'Aunt Matilda's'
former maid would wish to return. Not only had she lost the 'respectfulness',
which had made her accept that it was a natural and proper fate for her to wait on
a mistress who had been 'too stupid ever to earn a penny in her life', but

> as for the comforts which Mary lacks by having left Aunt Matilda's roof I have
> had glimpses of those comforts. . . . I have seen Mary's bedroom, furnished with a
> 'servant's set'. I have seen the bare little kitchen in which Mary wasn't allowed to
> receive admirers (not even the jolly young motor-bicycle repairer), but in which
> she was supposed to sit very contentedly for six evenings a week. And I don't
> think that Mary will come rushing back to these havens of luxury.[98]

Events were to confirm the correctness of Muir's assessment, even though females were
speedily dismissed from the war-related industries once hostilities ended in November
1918. There was an immediate reduction in the range of employment opportunities
open to women, while gender divisions at work were largely re-established. The process
was speeded up by initiatives like the 1919 Restoration of Pre-war Practices Act, under
which women were expected to vacate posts they had occupied as substitutes for men.
Those who did not respond rapidly were criticised and the Press, which had praised
female patriotism during the war, was equally robust in condemning those who sought
to hang on to their new careers. At the end of December 1918, the *Daily Telegraph*
commented scathingly on girls who since they had been 'in munitions' had acquired
'a remarkable . . . taste for factory life. Many of them, of course, might return at once
to the domestic service from which they came, but, for the moment at any rate, they
literally scoff at the idea'.[99] The following month the *Daily News* complained of a
shortage of female servants in Bristol, with women said to be refusing 'good wages'
and large houses standing empty for lack of domestic help.[100]

As unemployment levels rose, the government offered all demobilised workers
an out-of-work donation or 'dole' to tide them over until they could find fresh jobs.
The donation was 20s a week for women, to last for thirteen weeks. In the event,
because of the dislocations of the war and its aftermath, this non-contributory

Women's Auxiliary Army Corps waitresses in an Officers' Club at Abbeville, 15 September 1917. (*Imperial War Museum Photograph Archives*)

scheme carried on in various forms until the end of 1919. The following year a new Unemployment Insurance Act was introduced to cover all manual workers, except for agricultural workers and domestic servants. Servants were allegedly omitted on the grounds that they did not experience prolonged unemployment, but doubtless it was a partial sop to a middle-class electorate outraged that potential maids were being 'paid to do nothing' through the dole. Despite repeated protests over the years, indoor domestic servants of both sexes remained outside the protection of national unemployment insurance until 1946.[101]

By March 1919 over half a million women were officially recorded as unemployed, but the real total was undoubtedly higher, since employment exchanges were expected to exercise 'extreme strictness' when accepting female applicants for unemployment benefit. Any applicant whose right seemed doubtful was to be rejected. Although those refused had a right of appeal against the decision, relatively few were successful. Another difficulty was that those offered work by the exchanges, no matter how low the pay or unsatisfactory the working conditions, could be excluded from benefit if they refused.[102] Inevitably, with the demand for servants, many of the vacancies were in poorly paid domestic work. In one case, a woman was offered non-resident kitchen work at a wage of 16s a week, with 1s 6d deducted for food. Her fares would have cost a further 3s 6d a week, leaving just 11s to cover all her other outgoings. When she refused the position because the wage was inadequate, her unemployment benefit was reduced.[103]

Despite their reluctance to take up domestic employment, therefore, more and more women were forced to do so. As Gail Braybon comments, placements of maids through the labour exchanges remained 'low from November 1918 to February 1919, then shot up, so that they were 40 per cent higher in the succeeding six months than they had been during the corresponding period of 1918'.[104]

Residential employment was particularly unpopular and yet it was this which householders most demanded. In May 1919, a 'glut' was reported among those offering themselves as charwomen at the employment exchanges. They had come forward in the proportion of ten applicants to every vacancy reported; almost the same preponderance of 'day girls' appeared, with eight day servants available for each vacancy. But there were just two applicants for every three vacancies notified for resident domestic service.[105]

To try to persuade potential servants to take up domestic work, meetings were organised in some towns so that mistresses and maids could negotiate acceptable working conditions. In March 1919, one such gathering in Harrogate led to an agreement limiting maids to a maximum ten-hour working day and allowed the wearing of the much-disliked cap (which many regarded as a symbol of domestic bondage) to be optional.[106] In Bromley later in the month still more detailed arrangements were drawn up. They included an acceptance of the principle of trade unionism among servants, the allowing of one half-day and evening off per week, plus a half-day on Sunday, one full day a month and an annual paid holiday. Servants were to be allowed to take baths in the bathroom, like members of the family, once a week rather than having to resort to tin or hip baths in their room and they were to have two free hours each day for rest and relaxation. If they were resident they were not to be expected to go out on errands at night and they were to have meal breaks of half-an-hour for breakfast and tea and one hour for the mid-day dinner.[107]

At Kingston-on-Thames a joint meeting led to an agreement on minimum wages for all grades of servant, plus a programme of breaks for meals and for leisure similar to those accepted in Bromley. Assurances were also to be given that satisfactory sleeping accommodation would be provided. The manager of the local employment exchange was requested to take account of the agreement, so that any girls who refused situations on these terms would have their out-of-work donation stopped.[108]

The *Labour Woman*, which was published by the Labour Party, put forward similar proposals. In February 1919 it published a Domestic Workers' Charter of Emancipation to cover minimum wages, working hours, dress, holiday entitlement and what it called 'social questions'. These included a requirement that workers should be addressed as 'Miss' or 'Mrs' as the case might be, rather than being called by their Christian or surname only, since this was considered demeaning.[109]

Other suggestions for solving the 'servant problem' included the formation of a War Workers' Reserve, along the lines of the Corps of Commissionaires. It would be professionally organised and would vouch for the integrity, efficiency and reliability of the workers that it sent out and for the suitability of the employers recruiting them.[110] However, in the end, nothing came of the proposal.

By a mixture of carrot and stick, therefore, increasing numbers of women were persuaded either to return to domestic service or to take it up for the first time. Day posts were most popular among the maids, since these enabled them to live at home or to stay in lodgings, thereby allowing them to spend their leisure hours as they thought fit. But this process of assimilation into the labour force did not take place rapidly enough for some. The unemployed were repeatedly accused of preferring to live on the dole rather than work. The *Evening Standard* referred scathingly to 'Slackers with State Pay', while the *Southampton Times* in March 1919 commented that several months after the Armistice,

> women still have not brought themselves to realise that factory work, with the money paid for it during the war, will not be possible again. . . . Women, for instance, who left domestic service to enter the factory are now required to return to the pots and pans.[111]

As late as April 1923, the *Daily Mail* ran a series of 'Scandals of the Dole' in which it described as the 'most flagrant scandal connected with the dole' the existence 'of the thousands upon thousands of women who are now drawing it when they ought to be in domestic service':

> Houses are shut up in every direction, housewives are being endlessly inconvenienced and social life is being hopelessly dislocated, just because the government will not do the one perfectly obvious thing and make it illegal for women to draw the dole when they are capable of domestic service.[112]

Members of Parliament joined in too. In November 1919, Mr Macquisten, MP for Glasgow Springburn, claimed that from the day the Armistice was signed, there had been work for all the women in the country. 'Of course, it was not the work they wanted. . . . There are hundreds of thousands of positions as domestic servants open to women to-day, and they will not accept them. . . . I should like every working woman to go to a Labour Bureau and commandeer a servant. . . . The female allowance should never have been granted at all, because . . . there was plenty of work for females in this country.'[113]

However, the debate largely ignored the fact that many unemployed women, for example in the textile and mining areas, had never been domestic servants and were unsuitable for such positions. As Ray Strachey wrote scathingly, they had neither the necessary clothing for the job nor the necessary experience. 'They were rough, and often wild, and if they had been taken into an ordinary house they would have been turned out again very promptly amid a smash of broken crockery.'[114] The only solution was to provide a domestic training programme, the solution the government eventually adopted.

Meanwhile, male servants, too, were leaving the armed services to return to civilian life. For some, the restraints of private domestic work were no longer acceptable. A few, like Albert Thomas, took related employment – in Thomas's case as a club steward.[115] There was also an increased demand for waiters; in 1921 it was estimated that out of a total of 61,006 male indoor servants recorded in the Census, only 48 per cent were in private service. The rest were in institutional or commercial employment. A further 15,390 men were classed as waiters.[116]

There was also a campaign to persuade demobilised, out-of-work soldiers to take household employment. The *Daily Mail*, for example, pointed out that men who had been batmen during their service life were well fitted for domestic duties.[117] But although some soldiers did take up the occupation, with batmen perhaps accompanying their demobilised masters into private life, 'the loyalty which had flourished in a shared danger sometimes failed to survive the transfer into a world of unshared privilege'.[118]

Even Edwin Lee, who returned to Cliveden and was to remain with the Astor family until 1963, admitted to finding his war service an enlightening experience. 'I got to know men from all walks of life. . . . It gave me a broader understanding. . . . It took me a little time to shake down [at Cliveden] for there was a new staff with new ways.'[119]

Ernest King was another pre-war servant who returned to his former post. He had entered the Royal Navy early in the war, on the strength of a brief period as a steward on board a passenger liner some years earlier. Eventually, he was discharged on health grounds and at once rejoined his pre-war employer, Lord de Vesci, in the army as the latter's soldier servant. After the war he became Lord de Vesci's butler once more and remained in the position for about two years. Much of that time was spent in Ireland, where de Vesci's country estate was, and where King found himself in the midst of the fight for Irish independence. Many of the household servants were members of Sinn Fein or sympathisers with its cause. 'As an Englishman and an ex-Serviceman I knew I was a possible target.'

Eventually the situation became so serious that Lord de Vesci closed his Irish home and moved to London. But for King this had undesirable financial implications. Not only did he lose his free house on the estate and the generous allowance of coal, logs, milk and vegetables he and his Irish-born wife had received, but he also lost his tips, since in London no guests stayed overnight. In Ireland there had been large house parties and the tips had almost doubled his pay.[120] He decided to ask for an increase in wages and was offered only a miserly £12 a year, or about 5s a week, so gave in his notice. At this point Lady de Vesci intervened, offering to increase his pay by £1 10s a week out of her own pocket and to allow him a flat rent-free. But he had made up his mind to move. 'I wanted to break out into something entirely new to me, the world of the rich. Not the old rich, but the new rich.' To that end he obtained a post with Mrs de Wichfeld, the heiress to an American meat-packing fortune and one of the richest women in the world.[121]

Some older male servants, however, had difficulty in getting employment at all. In the post-war world, landed families, in particular, were hit by rising taxation and falling income from their land, as a result of a severe agricultural depression. Many reduced their domestic establishments or substituted cheaper and more biddable parlourmaids for the butlers and footmen they had previously employed. Eric Horne worked for one such family. As a result of their financial difficulties they cut their domestic establishment from twenty-five indoor servants to three. He was not one of those who stayed on. He then tried to find a new post. The first he obtained was as a single-handed butler, which meant in effect that he was a general utility man, working a sixteen-hour day, including meal breaks. He began at 6.30 a.m. by opening up the house, sweeping and dusting the front hall, cleaning the dining room grate and cleaning the boots. He also had to do valeting. His day ended when he closed up the house and completed any necessary valeting duties. He was expected to answer all the bells, be smart and clean in his appearance and be ready to take letters to the post. No private visitors were allowed and smoking was forbidden. [122]

Despite his dissatisfaction with the post, he stayed for two years, before looking for something better. Unfortunately, he soon discovered there was a glut of unemployed butlers. He advertised in the *Morning Post*, searched the clubs in the West End of London and went to 'all places where butler's places are likely to be heard of, but to no effect'. Except for occasional temporary work, he had still found no employment by the time he published his autobiography in 1923. 'Everywhere it is parlourmaids, and married couples that are wanted. The married couples having to do the work of perhaps four servants that were kept previously.' [123]

However, it is to the experience of those who, unlike Eric Horne, were able to find posts in the inter-war years that we must now turn.

Part two

1920-1939

CHAPTER TWO

SERVANT LIFE
BETWEEN THE WARS

Cheerful and Willing Maid; modern and considerate home; own room; h. & c.;
Staples bed; good wages and outings; Altrincham dist.
    'Domestic Servants Wanted' column, Manchester Guardian, 7 February 1939

SERVANT ROLES AND RECRUITMENT

Despite the reluctance of many men and women to enter household service after the First World War, the pressures created by industrial depression and high unemployment led to a steady rise in the number of domestic workers throughout the inter-war period. For some new recruits, like Jean Rennie, the experience was galling. Jean, who was the daughter of a Greenock riveter, was prevented by family poverty from taking up a scholarship at Glasgow University. Instead, in 1924 she became third housemaid at a country house in Argyllshire. As she subsequently wrote: 'My greatest horror was the knowledge that I would now have to submit to the badge of servitude – a cap and apron.'[1] However, when Mrs Fugill realised in 1926 that she would have to be a servant, she resolved to avoid private employment. Instead she became a scullery maid at the Monmouth Training College for Teachers, where she 'would be serving my own kind and not . . . people with money to buy service. The young men training as teachers there, were from the same background as myself.' Throughout her career she always worked in institutions, moving to a London hospital in 1929.[2]

Between 1921 and 1931 the total of female servants in England and Wales climbed from about 1.1 million to 1.3 million and continued to rise thereafter, reaching perhaps 1.4 or 1.5 million at the end of the 1930s, according to contemporary estimates.[3] Among the menfolk, the increase was from 61,006 in 1921 to 78,489 a decade later, although unlike the position among the women, where the vast majority worked in private homes, around half of the males were employed in hotels, clubs and other establishments rather than in private service. However, the number of householders grew even more rapidly. Between 1921 and 1931 the total of separate families (including both servant-keepers and non-servant-keepers) jumped by over 17 per cent while that of female servants, including those in hotels, hospitals, and the like, rose by about 16 per cent. In Scotland the increase in the number of maids was still smaller, growing from 122,248 in 1921 to 138,679 a decade later – a rise

"Servant to the Home"

For all the ages man has monopolised Science. Always the male has bent invention to his purposes, to make easier his work ; and woman, the worker in the home, has toiled with implements that have changed not from the days of Pharaoh—labour-wasting, inefficient.

So, to the woman it serves, the Hoover is far more than a labour-saving device. To her it means recognition of her needs. Invention, so long a servant to man's activities, has at last produced a "Servant to the Home."

And the Hoover replaces the most inadequate of all her tools, the dust-stirring, ineffectual broom. It simplifies her most difficult household task, the thorough cleaning of carpets. In one easy, rapid

operation, the Hoover beats out all the germ-harbouring dirt and destructive, embedded grit from her carpets, sweeps them electrically, and cleans by air suction.

And because it cleans dustlessly, the Hoover has realised for her the joy and pride of an ever clean home.

To-day the Hoover comes to you in a new, improved model. Lighter, made even more durable, this new Hoover will more than ever justify its description of "Servant to the Home."

Only £3. 19s. down and 31s. a month for a short time pays for the Hoover while you use it. There is also a larger model for hotels, clubs, offices and large residences. Write for illustrated booklet and names of nearest Hoover dealers.

Hoover, Limited, 286, Regent Street, London, W.1, and at Birmingham, Manchester, Leeds and Glasgow

The HOOVER
It BEATS.... as it Sweeps   as it Cleans   Reg. TRADE MARK

Before replying to advertisements refer to page 91.   73

Labour-saving appliances came into wider use after the First World War. They included this Hoover vacuum cleaner advertised in 1923 as 'Servant to the Home'. (Good Housekeeping, *September 1923*)

of 13.4 per cent.[4] By 1931 perhaps five households in every hundred in England and Wales kept a resident maid, compared to around seventeen per hundred in 1911. About three-quarters of the 1931 servant-keepers (or 375,000) kept one servant only.[5]

Also, the age range of the servants themselves had changed, compared to the pre-war years, with the proportion of those over thirty-five increasing markedly. In 1911 workers in that age group had comprised 20.5 per cent of the maids in England and Wales, but twenty years later they formed 33.2 per cent. So, although two-thirds of maids were still under the age of thirty-five, it was very different from the situation in 1911, when almost four-fifths had been in this category.

The fact that servants were, on average, older than before 1914 affected their approach to their work and their employers. Although they might be better able to take responsibility than younger girls, thereby easing the employers' supervisory role, they were also more self-assured and less willing to be controlled by mistresses, especially in their leisure hours. They were more expensive, too, than the under-twenties who had comprised nearly a third of female domestics in 1911. That particularly affected families of modest means living in the suburbs, since it was they who had commonly recruited cheap school-leavers before the war. Many either began employing charwomen for a few hours a week, or did their own housework. It was to meet their needs that advertisements stressed the labour-saving aspects of new appliances that were coming on to the market, be they gas fires, vacuum cleaners, or, in a small way, refrigerators and washing machines. Specialist workshops and factories also carried out tasks formerly performed in the home, with a rise in the number of commercial laundries and bakeries, as well as canning, bottling, preserving and pickling factories. There was a proliferation of small restaurants too, especially in the large cities, as middle-class families began to eat out more often.

Even more than at the beginning of the century, younger girls regarded service as an occupation of last resort. Many moved from job to job very frequently, in search of better conditions. In the small university town of Bangor, in Wales, one inhabitant described them as playing 'a sort of musical chairs, changing from one place to another and praising or condemning their old mistresses to the new'.[6] Similarly, a survey of 468 householders in London at the beginning of the 1930s found that over one third of their servants had been in the post for under a year, while more than two thirds had been there for less than four years. Just one ninth had remained for ten years or over.[7] It was in these circumstances that *The Times* began publishing obituaries extolling the virtues of 'Faithful Servants' who had remained with the same family for many decades.[8]

Among the young maids who moved from place to place very rapidly was Miss G. J. Goff from near St Austell, in Cornwall. She began her career working for an auctioneer and estate agent, but left after a year to 'better' herself:

> I was in 10 places in 12 years, but never did succeed, in fact I always 'worsened myself'. . . . I was usually terrified to give notice because of getting a good reference. One would apply for a post, go for an interview, and then wait for the letter telling one the post was filled or you were not suitable. Then you knew you had not been given a very good 'reference'. 'So-and-So has been in my employ for such a time. I find her honest, truthful, a good worker – but'. Nine times out of ten that 'but' damned you.[9]

Sometimes, as with Edith Hall, who grew up near Hayes in Middlesex, the advent of light industry in an area enabled girls to intersperse spells in service with work in factories. Edith held some posts for just a few days or weeks. She later claimed that between the ages of fourteen and seventeen she had about seventeen different jobs. Unlike Miss Goff, she did not worry about references either. At one house when her mistress refused to give this all-important document, she merely wrote one out for herself, giving a friend's name who was in service at a big house. The friend then sent it off. 'No-one ever discovered that she was the maid and not the mistress. After that, some of my in-service friends used to ask me for references when their employers would not give one if they considered the maid had left for no valid reason.'[10] Eventually, at the age of nineteen and by judiciously editing her previous work record, Edith began a nursing career by becoming a probationer in an isolation hospital.

A growing proportion of girls who entered domestic service chose to be day workers rather than resident maids, because of the greater personal freedom this permitted. For less well off householders the change also offered advantages. They no longer had to provide accommodation for staff on the premises, so they were able to move into smaller, more modern homes. Savings were also made in lighting, heating and food.[11] As Alan Jackson points out, few suburban dwellings – constructed after 1920 contained provision for resident servants, although families still hired a daily maid for reasons of prestige, as well as out of necessity. Jackson mentions middle-class householders in Golders Green, London, who ensured that the day servant was in attendance for the evening meal, 'which would be taken at the front of the house, with curtains drawn well back and lights blazing'. In this way the neighbours could see what was happening.[12]

In England and Wales as a whole it was estimated in 1931 that 40 per cent of women servants were non-resident, compared to about 24 per cent of their male counterparts.[13]

The relative scarcity of domestic help between the wars led to some improvement in working conditions and in employers' attitude towards their staff. Nevertheless, the pace of change was slow and the social divide between mistress and maid remained clear. Many employers clung to pre-war ideas of deference. Daphne Robinson, who grew up in Bangor in the 1920s and 1930s, remembered that servants were 'not the same as us. They were a different species, and not to be classed in the same category as ourselves. They were "common", a word widely used in those days.'[14] Even Violet Markham, who was closely involved in organising the government's domestic training programme, nonetheless complained of the maids in her own household. 'Oh my dear', she wrote to a friend, 'my path has been so encumbered by odious servant worries & a procession of damsels through this house who arrive with wonderful testimonials & reveal the standards of a lodging house.'[15]

Religious prejudice also survived, although less intensely than in the Victorian years. Even at the end of the 1930s advertisements for domestic staff in *The Times* and the *Manchester Guardian* sometimes included the phrase 'Protestant preferred'. An appeal for a cook general in the Manchester Guardian during February 1939 contained the proviso: 'Church of England; reference from clergyman.'

In an occupation untouched by such regulations as the factory and workshop legislation, which applied in manufacturing industry, working conditions depended on the personal relationship between mistress and servant. There was none of the commercial spirit and profit motive which applied to employer – employee relations in business or in hotels and catering. For that reason, some girls, particularly those made redundant from factories and shops, preferred to take posts in hotels and guest houses, where landladies rarely looked for the deference expected from workers in private employment. As a seasonal occupation, it also offered a temporary change of career, rather than a permanent switch for girls who hoped to return to their original situations when times improved.

The issue of status was certainly important where the recruitment of male servants was concerned. The 'luxury' aspect of their employment was emphasised by the fact that until 1937 a small tax of 15s a year had to be paid by employers for each male domestic. Despite the economic depression of the inter-war years, which led landed families to cut back on their male staff, employing perhaps a parlourmaid instead of a footman, a number of wealthy households did keep a retinue of male retainers. At Eaton, the Cheshire seat of the Duke of Westminster, his future wife, Loelia Ponsonby, remembered her first impression of the mansion: 'it was not a house but a town'.[16] The household was run by four senior servants – the housekeeper, the butler, who 'looked like an elder statesman and had the ability of a General', the clerk of works, who looked after the fabric of the building, and the head gardener.[17] Each of them regulated the activities of their subordinates, and in houses of this kind that normally included hiring and firing. For the largest house-parties, such as those for the Grand National, squads of butlers and footmen would be brought in to supplement the regular staff. With visitors' servants further boosting numbers, as many as one hundred people might assemble in the servants' hall.[18]

The lady's maid and a member of the nursery staff with the children of the Earl and Countess of Lichfield and their friends at Shugborough Hall, Staffordshire, in the 1920s. (*Arts and Museum Service, Staffordshire County Council*)

Another large establishment was Cliveden, the Buckinghamshire estate of Lord and Lady Astor. In 1928 there was an indoor domestic staff of nineteen, plus four maids in the laundry, and fifty-two outdoor workers, including gardeners, gamekeepers, labourers and craftsmen and others employed on Lord Astor's stud farm and on the dairy farm.[19] In the 1930s some economies were made, with the closing of the laundry and the pruning of the chef's kitchen staff, while the number of maids in the stillroom fell from two to one. But the household continued to run on lavish lines up to the Second World War.

At Shugborough Hall, Staffordshire, home of the Earl and Countess of Lichfield, there were seventeen female servants and seven men working indoors in the early 1920s, although, again, numbers declined in the 1930s, with the closure of the laundry and the stillroom around the middle of the decade.[20] The Scottish-born housekeeper, who took up her post in 1935, had begun her career with the Lichfields in the late 1920s as head housemaid. She described the estate as 'a world of its own. I never knew about the outside world. . . . I was so interested and I was so happy.'[21]

Although country house entertaining was on a lesser scale than in the Edwardian era, much hospitality was still dispensed. That included Friday to Monday house parties, especially during the shooting season and large gatherings for special celebrations. According to Harold Macmillan, the Duke of Devonshire's Christmas family party at Chatsworth often numbered a hundred and fifty people, including servants. Each of the family of two sons and five daughters brought their children, together with attendant nurses and

Servant ceremonial in a great household. The Marquess of Londonderry's state coach outside Londonderry House, 19 Park Lane, London, on the occasion of the wedding of HRH Princess Mary to Viscount Lascelles in 1922. The two footmen were: standing, Gilbert Mant; on the coach, Albert Hallet; the coachman was Mr Barnes. Gillbert Mant later became the butler at Londonderry house. (*Arthur R. Inch*)

nursemaids, while there were lady's maids and valets, as well as grooms to look after the children's ponies.[22]

Many of the servants, for their part, relished their links with these great households. As Gordon Grimmett, one of the footmen employed by the Astors, later declared:

> It was from the moment that I went into service that my education began. . . . It was impossible to live among beauty without it getting under your skin; you learn to distinguish what is good and what is not, you learn taste and appreciation, you look at books lining shelves and eventually you pick one up and begin to read; overheard conversations spark off a desire to know more. You also learn moral values, not always by example but by observation and comparison. . . . This is real education.[23]

Most servants, whether working as single-handed maids in small households or as part of a ducal retinue, came from five principal backgrounds. First, as in the early years of the century, there were country girls and boys, for whom household work offered almost their only employment, in the case of the girls. Many had to move considerable distances to find a place. A survey of Merseyside in the early 1930s concluded that one reason why families there could afford to keep domestic staff, when those similarly placed elsewhere were unable to do so, was because of the availability of maids from rural Wales and Ireland.[24]

Winifred Foley, who grew up in the Forest of Dean, Gloucestershire, during the 1920s, remembered that once girls in her village reached the age of fourteen they were considered 'old enough to get [their] feet under someone else's table; going into service was our only future. There was no employment for us in the village, and leaving home at fourteen was common to us all. . . . The bony finger of poverty was pushing me out into an alien world.'[25] She decided to go to London rather than take a post locally and answered an advertisement in the *Daily Herald* for a general maid in Stoke Newington. Although her mistress was kind, she was desperately homesick. 'Mam wrote to me every two weeks. Those letters were my lifeline.' After three months her little sister became seriously ill with pleurisy and when her mistress saw how distressed she was, she allowed Winifred to go home. She even made up the girl's fare, since she had not yet saved enough out of her wages.[26]

Soon after her return the sister recovered and Winifred began looking for another place. This time she went to an old lady living in the Cotswolds, where she determined to stay for six months. That, she felt, was the maximum time she could bear to be separated from her family without any visits. 'Though I had some loyalty to my mistress . . . it didn't stop me giving her my month's notice when the six months was up. I should have to wait another six months before I earned the annual two weeks holiday she allowed. But I knew I couldn't bear the separation from my family that long.'[27]

Other country girls, like Winifred Cardew in Cornwall, got a place locally through family contacts. Like many girls from labouring families, Winifred began working in the evening and at weekends in a farmhouse when she was about twelve years old. She looked after the children, did the washing up, helped prepare meals, and carried out general scrubbing and cleaning. For this she received 6d per week. When she was fourteen she moved to a larger farm and began full-time employment, learning to milk cows, separate the cream and make butter, as well as carrying out domestic chores. She also had to feed the cows and take them out to the fields.[28] Small wonder that farmhouse service was regarded as particularly arduous, along with that in lodging houses. A Scottish girl, who became a general maid on a farm outside Stirling, later described it as 'slavery for very little money'.[29]

Sometimes girls moved around to fit in with their father's employment. This was true of Flossie, who started work on a farm in the East Riding of Yorkshire in 1925. She stayed there happily for about three years, despite the fact that she was only paid once a year, in arrears, each November, at Martinmas. But when her father obtained a new job as hand on a nearby farm, the farmer's wife wanted a general maid and, out of a sense of duty, Flossie agreed to take the post. As well as the usual cleaning tasks, she had to help prepare meals for eleven labourers each day, plus six members of the household, including herself. At harvest time the work was still heavier, with extra men employed and twenty-two workers coming in for meals: 'you were filling the great big kettles up on the fire for lunch again, and then there was our teas for harvest, and then the men were coming in at eight.'[30] In such cases it is clear that parents connived at the exploitation of their daughters, either because the girls' earnings were needed to boost family income or because their employment helped to secure a parental position. The fact that most of the girls were used to firm discipline at home and regularly helped with domestic chores there, led them to accept their lot without a fuss. As Pam Taylor has pointed out, this kind of upbringing, which applied also to poorer working-class girls in the towns, led them 'to expect very little for themselves and to comply with parental decisions, which were reinforced, ideologically and economically, by the fact of the family's poverty'.[31]

A second source of domestic labour was provided by the offspring of families who were already in service or had spent much of their life as servants. Cyril Rice, who grew up at Cwmbach in mid-Wales, began his career as a hall boy in 1930 on the large estate where his father was a carpenter. The butler asked his parents whether he would take the post and they agreed, without consulting him: 'It wasn't my type of life at all but you didn't say no.' He disliked the strict rules he had to observe and the deference he had to show. Whenever he met his mistress he had to touch his cap and say '"Good morning, Madam", or "Good afternoon, Madam." No matter how many times you met her.' He had to be up at half-past six each morning to stoke the boilers for the hot water and baths. 'Then when other lads were out enjoying themselves in the evening, . . . there you were, waiting on the table every night. . . . You finished at about eleven o'clock.' After two years he handed in his notice and took up painting and decorating instead.

Cyril's reluctant entry into service was in marked contrast to the attitude of Arthur Inch, who had also grown up on a landed estate, this time in Yorkshire. His father was a butler, and after a brief and unhappy spell as a motor mechanic when he left school, Arthur decided to follow his father into domestic work. Through parental connections he became a house boy at Aldborough Hall, Boroughbridge, but before he took up the post his father made sure he acquired the skills needed for his new career. He learned to press a suit correctly, to clean hunting clothes and to dismantle, clean and reassemble a 12-bore shotgun, in case he was required to act as a loader at a shoot.

> He also taught me how to lay out a gentleman's clothes. . . . He also taught me the rudiments of wine cellar work and the keeping of a cellar book etc. Of course he realised that I wouldn't need to know a lot about the subject until I became a butler myself but he believed in teaching me as much as I was capable of taking in. . . . I was also passed on to the footmen who taught me many of their duties such as how to mix platepowder with ammonia and clean the tarnish off silver. . . . They also showed me how to lay the dining room meals, starting (in that household) with a lovely white damask cloth which had been finished to perfection in our own private laundry.[33]

With these preparations he began a life in service which, with brief interludes, lasted to the end of the twentieth century.[34]

Inevitably, the number of young servants to be recruited from this kind of background was limited. More fruitful, particularly for small households, were the offspring of poor urban families. Among them was Daisy Noakes, of Brighton, who, like Winifred Cardew in Cornwall, began her domestic career while still at school. In her case this meant scrubbing, brass cleaning, washing up and knife cleaning for a

Arthur R. Inch as a footman in the livery of the Marquess of Londonderry, c. 1938. (*Arthur R. Inch*)

scout master's wife. For this she was paid 6*d* a week and she proved so efficient that the woman recommended her to a friend, who also employed her, at 3*d* a week. One of her tasks was to carry a heavy bundle of washing to a hand laundry each week. 'This was a Saturday when I was 12 years of age. I did complain to Mum about it being hard, but she only said, "If you want money, the only way to be sure is work for it".' Two of her older sisters were already in service, the second of them being employed at Ovingdean Hall Boys' Preparatory School. When Daisy was about to leave school at the end of 1922 this sister mentioned there was a vacancy for a dormitory maid at Ovingdean. Accompanied by her mother, she duly went for an interview. She was wearing a second-hand costume, far too big for her, which had been purchased from a neighbour and on her head was a large brimmed black hat, 'with several foldings of newspaper inside to make it fit, and every wisp of hair out of sight'. When they reached the school, her mother told her to add 'Ma'am' to every answer and to stand up when spoken to. 'We went round the back door, as staff were never allowed to use the front door or the front drive.' The butler showed them into a large drawing room, where Daisy was bewildered and overawed by the elaborate surroundings, which were so different from her own poverty-stricken home.

> Madam entered, and asked us to sit. I perched myself on one of the chairs, while Mum was asked if I was honest, hardworking, reliable, an early riser. (I did not know that would be 5.30 a.m.) To all this Mum replied that I was.
>
> I was asked to stand up, and Madam said 'You will look taller when you have a longer skirt and hair done up in a bun'. She asked me how old I was. I replied '14 next month', so she said my wage would start at my age, £14 a year, with 2*s* 6*d* a month rise at the end of a year, and I could start work as soon as I attained my 14th birthday.
>
> Now began the preparation for my leaving home. I would need a servant's uniform and a box to pack it in.[35]

With the help of Daisy's small savings from her part-time work, a second-hand trunk was purchased from the market, and her mother made a uniform: 'two blue dresses for morning wear, half-lined, one black dress for afternoon wear, and four large bibbed white aprons. . . . I had two Dorcas type caps for morning wear, frill caps for afternoons were supplied, one pair of ward shoes for mornings, one pair high-lows for afternoons and three pairs of black stockings. . . . Celluloid collar and cuffs.'[36]

For those seeking cheaper servants, or who had a philanthropic wish to train disadvantaged youngsters for 'gentlemen's service', a fourth possibility was to recruit maids from poor law schools and orphanages, or from industrial schools, reformatories and from 1933, approved schools, these last being all under the aegis of the Home Office. In 1923 an official report on the Home Office schools noted that three-quarters of the girls went into service when they left. This provided employment and a home, as well as 'very often a sympathetic and kind friend in the mistress'. But it recognised that some ex-pupils had little interest in the work and, with appropriate training, would do better in another direction.[37] Fifteen years later, however, domestic work remained the principal outlet for such school leavers, even though there had been some diversification in the direction of factory and shop employment. But places could always be found for girls in service, with the demand exceeding the supply. '"Institution" girls are apparently looked upon by some women as cheap drudges', an official commented tartly, adding that headmistresses were 'fully alive to this and can generally find the right type of place'.[38]

As in Victorian and Edwardian times, these girls were vulnerable to exploitation by employers, not least because they usually had no home or relatives on whom they could rely if they lost their place. One girl who had attended a training home for domestic servants in Liverpool remembering being placed in a 'Home for Wayward Women' because she did not like one of the jobs she had been sent to and decided to run away.[39] In her case, her parents were separated and she and her sister were eventually able to rejoin their mother, who had got employment as a chambermaid in various London hotels.

Mrs Slade moved from an orphanage to the Mid-Kent Training Home for Girls in 1933. There she remained for three or four years before being sent as an 'in-between maid' to a Mrs Luck of West Malling. She was to be paid £18 a year and the Home provided her uniform at a cost of £12. This had to be refunded by Mrs Slade from her wages during the first year. Her fellow servants were a butler, a cook and a housemaid.

> As an 'In-between maid' I was torn between the other three servants, all demanding my assistance at various times of the day. I soon learnt to adjust my times for each job. With the cook from 8.30 a.m. until 9.30 a.m., washing up or preparing vegetables, etc. After this, upstairs with the housemaid, making beds, cleaning rooms. Downstairs in the kitchen again, more washing up as the cook was preparing a four course lunch. Scrubbing out the dairy, servants' hall, store room, pump room, gun room, stone passageways, servants' landing and stairway – the tasks were endless spread over the week. By 1 p.m. I had to be wearing my afternoon uniform ready to transport the various courses of lunch from Kitchen to Dining Room. . . .
>
> Any breakages had to be reported to Mrs Luck when she paid her daily visit to the kitchen to discuss menus with the cook. I was charged 1s out of my wages for every crest plate [i.e. plate with the family crest] broken, and made to feel very guilty about the whole affair. . . . When Colonel and Mrs Luck were entertaining, I had to remain in the dining room to help the butler serve. . . . I always had to stand just behind Mrs Luck's place at the table. . . . I found this performance extremely humiliating because I knew only too well that I was . . . there as a sort of 'status symbol'.[40]

Mrs Slade stayed in the post for eighteen months, but when she asked for a rise in pay from £20 to £22 a year, Mrs Luck refused. 'I got a lecture on the cost of living and land taxes, that the last generation of Lucks had left little money and yet a big house to be kept up.' She decided to leave and handed in her month's notice. However, she had to find another place quickly as she had 'no home to go to'.

The last source of servants in the inter-war period was girls from the depressed industrial and mining areas of England, Wales and Scotland. In the case of youngsters from mining villages, there was no tradition of daughters working outside the home. The heavy labour associated with washing miners' clothes, providing meals and other tasks had given them enough to do at home. But when the men lost their jobs in the pits they could no longer support the household and the girls had to go out. In 1936, Thomas Jones, a former deputy cabinet secretary and close friend of the ex-Prime Minister, David Lloyd George, described the deprived homes from which a number of these girls came:

> what we have found in some of the more remote mining villages is this: Girls of 17-20 who have never slept alone in a room, who have never known what it is to have ordinary bed-clothes, and some who are unfamiliar with knives and forks, all of which seems incredible today. You can imagine the bewilderment of one of these young girls when transferred to a strange house in London.[41]

The problem was addressed in some instances through the introduction of government-backed training programmes. However, many girls made their own way into domestic employment, either by answering advertisements in the newspapers or by relying on information supplied by servant registry offices, or by friends and relatives already at work. Added to the difficulties created by inexperience of household work and homesickness, was the fact that many were physically undersized and weak, as a result of their deprived upbringing. When they arrived at their new employer's house he or she might decide they were too puny to be of use and so dismiss them. This left them stranded in a strange town, with no means of getting home. Their predicament was highlighted by organisations like the National Vigilance Association (NVA), which while being primarily concerned to safeguard the girls' morals, often arranged for them either to return to their families or to get a fresh post. They had representatives at the main London railway stations and coach terminals where these girls arrived, so they could help them to find their way to their new employment in an unfamiliar city. In 1935 the NVA claimed that its workers at the London railway and bus termini had helped almost five thousand girls in a year.[42]

Sometimes NVA visitors called on maids who had newly arrived from Wales and the north-east of England to see them in their employer's house. This was true of Mary Andrews, a fifteen-year-old from Treharris in south Wales. She had obtained a post in Stoke Newington through a newspaper advertisement, but when she arrived her mistress found she was not strong enough for the work and was utterly untrained. According to the NVA representative who saw Mary in February 1933, the mistress 'regretted having paid the girl's fare' from Wales and was determined to get rid of her. Mary herself wanted to stay on, or else move to another situation in London rather than go home, 'as her father would beat her' for losing her place. The NVA representative took the girl to a Church Army hostel for the night and persuaded her to return home. The headmaster of Treharris school, which she had previously attended, agreed to provide Mary's fare and to arrange for her to be met at the railway station on arrival. The NVA report ended sadly: 'This girl was very small for her age and looked anything but strong and seemed to be undernourished.

Three maids evidently enjoying a brief break in the fresh air at Foxley, Herefordshire, 1929. (*Arts and Museum Service, Staffordshire County Council*)

She seemed pleased to be returning home despite the fact that she told me that her father would beat her for not staying in her situation.'[43]

Mary was but one of many girls who found themselves in this kind of situation, as the records of the National Vigilance Association amply demonstrate. Some may have been glad 'to get away from their miserable homes, if there [was] unemployment and no chance of their being helped or kept' and yet if they were puny and without training, they were scarcely able to earn enough money to send home to their family, as many wanted to do.[44] Often they were hardly able to look after themselves in unfamiliar surroundings in a part of the country they had probably never visited before.

In order to obtain a post, servants could follow several different strategies. First, as we have seen, there was information passed on by friends and relatives already in service, or details were obtained from fellow servants with contacts in other households. One girl, who became a between-maid for a titled family at Kelvinside, in Scotland, formed a good relationship with the head housemaid. After she had been there six months, the latter offered to get in touch with a friend who needed a fourth housemaid, and 'that was me started on the ladder up'. She added: 'We were all great letter writers to keep in touch in service', so they could alert one another when suitable vacancies came up.[45] She claimed that when youngsters were seeking promotion it was common for them to add a year or two to their age, in order to qualify for senior posts. In one household, where she was employed as a second housemaid, a footman asked her how old she was. She replied that she was 'eighteen working as twenty'. He, it turned out, was really aged twenty-two but was working as twenty-six. For career servants of this kind, it was important to move every year or two in the early days, in order to gain promotion (since in-house advancements were relatively rare) and to obtain further experience.

For school leavers living on country estates there was always the chance that they might begin domestic life in a junior post at the 'big house'. Or their mother could approach the clergyman's wife or daughter for a recommendation. Charitable registry offices, like those run by the Anglican Girls' Friendly Society and the Metropolitan Association for Befriending Young Servants, might be contacted, too, for 'reputable' vacancies. One woman who obtained posts through membership of the Girls' Friendly Society later claimed that this enabled her to get places quite easily: 'They knew that you were Christian people.' She added appreciatively: 'Whatever jobs they got you', they were 'all with good titled people, you could rest assured'.[46]

When individual contacts failed, they resorted to newspaper advertisements. Although a number of girls would doubtless have agreed with Eileen Balderson that the 'best' positions were rarely advertised, this was nonetheless a course taken by many.[47] On occasion householders from servant 'deficit' areas, like the south of England and London, would advertise vacancies in provincial newspapers in Wales or the mining areas of the north-east. However, as in the case of Mary Andrews, quoted above, there was always the danger of a mis-match between mistress and maid. Another Welsh girl who got a post through the *South Wales Echo* was shocked to discover when she arrived that it was in a public house: 'You never seen women in pubs in Wales . . . the next morning, I put my coat on and went out the back way; I walked out.'[48] She was fortunate in having a friend in service in London whom she contacted and with whom she was allowed to stay. The friend took her to a West End registry office the next day, and there she was interviewed and her name was put down. Soon she was invited to return to see a prospective employer and her daughter. After probing her background they decided to give her a trial. 'I went on Monday, that was at 5 Grosvenor Crescent, Belgrave Square. I was to be the second housemaid at £2 per month.'[49]

This use of registry offices became increasingly common in the inter-war period, with the number of agencies proliferating in the major towns and cities, particularly London. In the capital alone the servants' registry offices and homes listed in the Post Office Trade Directory increased from 88 in 1925 to 109 in 1939 and there were many small offices which did not advertise in the directory at all. The quality of service they offered varied considerably, and many only stayed in business a very short time, or else combined their agency work with some other activity. Despite the fact that London agencies, unlike those in most parts of the country, had to be registered with the local authority, that did not prevent fraudulent proprietors promising to match mistresses and servants for a fee and then failing to deliver. Among the dubious enterprises was Medway's Domestic Agency in Stoke Newington Road North. It specialised in bringing girls by motorcoach from the north-east of England in batches of fifteen or twenty. But some of those it placed proved to be very unsatisfactory. One such was a maid called Florence, who was sent to a post, but was dismissed after three weeks for dishonesty. She was then sent to another employer, who was not told of the previous dismissal. She again lost her job through dishonesty and in a few days was found a third position. In the end she was arrested and convicted of theft. As a result of this and of several other unsatisfactory

SERVANT LIFE BETWEEN THE WARS

appointments, Medway's Agency had its licence revoked by the London County Council.[50] In each of the cases mistresses had been charged a fee of 15s.

Most registries, however, were reputable firms, and by the early 1920s they were becoming one of the commonest ways of matching employers and servants. Some were highly specialised, like 'Piercey's', a small select agency for menservants, where it was possible to get many of the top jobs in private service.[51] It was to this firm that Arthur Inch applied in the 1930s when he obtained the prestigious post of first footman of three to the Marquess of Londonderry at his large town house. Others, such as the Regina and the Mayfair, not only concentrated on high-class service, but had separate entrances for employers and for servants. When Lily Milgate went to the Mayfair Agency in North Audley Street for the first time she was unsure by which of two doors she should enter. In the end she chose the wrong one:

> When I stepped inside the elegance of white and gold paint, velvet curtains and delicate chairs and sofas piled with cushions I just stood on the thick carpet and stared until a very smart woman came sailing towards me. She knew at once . . . 'Please go next door, this is for ladies only'. And she gave me a hard poke in the back towards the door. . . . I went to the next door which said 'Please walk in'. My word what a different scene this was. No thick carpet here, or velvet curtains, no fragile chairs and cushions. The floor was covered with brown linoleum, benches lined each side of the room, one side for maids, the other for menservants; down the length of the room were small desks with chairs each side for interviews. I sat down to await my turn and eyed the young men on the opposite bench.[52]

When it came to her interview, she said she wanted to be a housemaid and was offered an under-housemaid's position at a high-class residence in Bruton Street. There she was seen by a supercilious head housemaid and was appointed. 'She didn't bother to ask me my name, she simply stated "Her Ladyship always likes the under-housemaid to be called Mary" so Mary I became.'[53]

Among the smaller reputable firms was the Fairbairn Agency in Edgware Road, London, which specialised in supplying Scottish maids to families in England. The agency was run by two sisters, one of whom lived in Edinburgh and recruited the maids to be sent south. The London-based sister insisted they would not deal with Glasgow girls 'as they are too rough. She only caters for very good families (mostly titled people). She has nothing to do with Hotels, Boarding Houses or any such places . . . Miss Fairbairn always sends each girl a list of about ten questions to answer, before she entertains the idea of getting them down. She takes no stockingless or made-up girls.'[54]

As well as the commercial registries, employment exchanges helped to fill domestic vacancies, free of charge. Much of their work was undertaken in association with the government-backed training programmes run under the aegis of the Ministry of Labour and it was generally recognised that prestigious vacancies were rarely notified to the exchanges. They did, however, play a role in bringing former factory and shop workers in touch with possible vacancies and filling seasonal posts at seaside resorts and the like, as well as positions for charwomen and day servants. In 1930 a specialist exchange was established in London to recruit staff for hotels and catering establishments. In 1938 alone it filled over 32,000 posts. In the same year the availability of seasonal work at holiday resorts was widely publicised by the exchanges with posters, leaflets and cinema advertisements. Appeals were inserted in the Press and broadcasts were made advising potential recruits of the opportunities which existed. Employees from the north-east of England were encouraged to apply by short films in cinemas. As a result of these various efforts, 200,406 domestic vacancies were filled in hotels, boarding houses and restaurants in that year by employment exchanges, while 47,608 vacancies were filled in private domestic service.[55] But whereas some of the best-known London and provincial hotels and restaurants were prepared to notify vacancies to the exchanges and to recruit staff through them, in the case of private householders it was normally the humbler, less remunerative positions that were reported, or those for domestic staff in hospitals, nursing homes, and other institutions. Some officials at employment exchanges were encouraged to circularise householders in their area in an effort to obtain 'a better class of vacancy'.[56]

Other ways of recruiting servants included application to likely shops, where staff may have heard of suitable candidates through the servant grapevine. One woman who worked in well-to-do households in London as a kitchenmaid recalled that she normally went to Jackson's of Piccadilly or Fortnum and Mason when she wanted to get a new place. She was known to the stores because household groceries were purchased there and chefs, in their turn, made the shop assistants aware when they had a vacancy in their kitchen. The maid would then go to the house and be interviewed by the chef, who would arrange pay and conditions. 'You never saw the lady. She never interviewed you.'[57]

For some farmhouse servants in Cumbria, the East Riding of Yorkshire and parts of Scotland, a further alternative was to attend a hiring fair, although this increasingly lost favour as a way of recruiting female staff because of the slave market atmosphere engendered and the encouragement allegedly given to drunkenness and immorality. Marian Atkinson was one girl who obtained posts in this way. She went to her first hiring fair in 1919 at the age of fourteen, in Ulverston. The fair there was held at Whitsuntide and in November, at Martinmas, and the girls were hired for six months at a time.

> You used to stand on one side of the street. The farmers stood on the other side by the *County Hotel*. They would walk up and down and look you up and down.

They then asked whether the girls could milk and bake and

> a whole list of things. They'd say, 'What are you asking?' I always remember my first hiring when I asked £15 for six months. . . . In the end he beat me down to £12 10s. He'd say, 'Right lass' and he would lift his hand up, spit on it and then pat his hand against mine. Then I got the shilling and was hired. I couldn't back out then.[58]

However, Marian always enjoyed her visits to the fair, not merely because it offered the chance to change employers, but because of the recreations on offer. She and a group of former school friends would meet together. The hiring was usually over by 1 p.m. and they would then go to a fish shop and have a packet of chips. After that came 'ice cream, which we never had at home. Then off we tore down to where the fairground was. There was swing boats, hobby horses, stalls where you could buy ribbons, buttons and knick-knacks. Everything you could want.'[59]

As well as permanent domestic posts to be filled, there were always many part-time or temporary vacancies, with men and women hired to help out on special occasions or to fill gaps between the departure of one servant and the arrival of another. At Cliveden, extra staff were recruited from among the wives of estate workers to help in the kitchens when there were large house parties. Additional chefs and waiters were brought in from London. Gordon Grimmett, who had once been a footman both at Cliveden and at the Astors' town house and had then left for a business career, was employed by Edwin Lee, the butler, to help on these occasions. He also worked in a number of other London households in the evening on this *ad hoc* basis:

> I was occasionally asked to go as an auxiliary matching footman to Arlington House. A matching footman meant that we were selected because we were all of the same height and build. We powdered [our hair] for state occasions, visiting royalty and such like. We were chiefly there as ornaments, for after we had dinner we lined up in the beautifully dim-lit corridor and just stood there for the rest of the evening.

For this he earned £2 5s per night, with an extra 5s if he were required to wear powder. That was good pay, but there was always a small deduction to take into account. 'At the end of the evening when you went to collect and sign for your fee you threw five bob back to the butler and got a "Look forward to seeing you again" for your pains.'[60]

Some men took on these additional posts when they were working full-time as a domestic for another employer. One footman, engaged by Lady Hulton, occasionally agreed to assist at big parties in Mayfair. This meant arranging to have the appropriate evening off and, where possible, taking an inconspicuous role in his temporary post. For 'employers didn't like to hear of their servants working for anyone else. . . . I'd try to act as plate man, receiving and feeding back the dishes, glasses and silver from the other side of the green baize door.'[61] In this way he was able to supplement his wages without offending his employer.

As a general principle, the larger the establishment the easier it was to recruit efficient staff. As E. S. Turner has commented, it was not for nothing that advertisements boasted 'eight footmen kept' or 'large staff of maids'. 'Staff tended to seek staff; even a life of bickering was better than a single-handed situation in suburbia. Besides, in the rich man's house there were valued perquisites and comforts.'[62]

DAILY DUTIES

The daily round of domestic workers varied not only with the size and grandeur of the household in which they worked, but with the age and position of the individual concerned. There was a general trend during these years for staff sizes to be pruned and for the tasks they carried out to be merged. This was particularly true of landed families affected by agricultural and industrial depression and by a rising tax burden. Early in the 1930s the owner of Rise Park, near Hornsea in Yorkshire, cut his indoor staff from sixteen to eleven and closed part of the house. The butler was dismissed and the footman took over his duties, while the housemaids and kitchen staff were reduced to two each, with a between maid recruited to spend part of her time with the remaining housemaids and the rest in the kitchen. The old cook refused to accept what she doubtless saw as a lowering of standards and of her personal status and when she left the former head kitchenmaid became cook-housekeeper.[63]

Similarly, at Plas Newydd, home of the Marquess of Anglesey, staff reductions meant that the former house carpenter became an odd job man, carrying luggage, linen hampers and similar heavy items, as well as moving furniture, carrying all the household coal, cleaning the passages, and performing any other tasks required. His wife, who had originally been employed as laundress to wash the family's personal and 'best' linen, found herself taking on more and more because she was a good deal cheaper than commercial laundry prices. Even so, as she confessed in a letter to Lady Astor, by whom she had once been employed, it was difficult to feel there was much permanency in the current situation: 'one feels it is a question how long the present arrangement may last, but at any rate it is work and for that we are thankful'.[64]

Elsewhere, housekeepers did some of the baking and the making of preserves that had formerly been the lot of stillroom maids, while parlourmaids took over duties which had previously been carried out by footmen. Often these were combined with helping the housemaids, so that their numbers could be reduced as well. The use of commercial services meant that in-house laundries were closed, while labour-saving appliances cut the duties carried out by domestic staff in many households. This meant not only that staff numbers fell, but the hours worked could be shortened, perhaps allowing cheaper day servants to be substituted for resident maids.

Nonetheless, among the very wealthy there were those who still wanted to enjoy the luxury and display of a large retinue of retainers. Ernest King, who joined the household of Mrs de Wichfeld in the 1920s as her husband's valet, was struck immediately by the lavish staffing arrangements. There were six women in more or less constant attendance upon her, including a French and a Belgian lady's maid, a personal laundress and three secretaries. The male staff was headed by a steward, but there were three under-butlers, six footmen, two 'odd men' who carried out miscellaneous duties and a hall boy. When she entertained at Blair Castle, which was leased from the Duke of Atholl, there were, according to King, 'never less than some eighty or ninety servants' to cater for thirty-six guests. Some of those servants were, of course, valets, lady's maids and other domestics brought by the guests.[65] King himself was responsible for Mr de Wichfeld's clothes, but he also looked after some of the guests who were without valets, as well as cleaning Mrs de Wichfeld's shoes and those of other lady guests. 'I seldom finished before midnight', he wrote, but it 'was worth it. My tips never came to less than sixteen pounds a week' – a very large sum indeed for those days.[66] When necessary he was expected to make travel arrangements for his employer and to look after the packing:

> The good valet is not told what is wanted on a journey, he must know. He should be prepared to dress his man for a funeral or a fancy dress ball. He must never be caught napping, he must be able to produce everything, even shoes so well-polished they may be used as a mirror in emergency! At home, he will probably order all suits and shirts, socks and underclothes, in hotels he will be given sufficient to defray any tips.

In short, a valet was 'depended on to do everything and forget nothing', according to King.[67] However, few inter-war employers were able to enjoy the luxury demanded by the de Wichfelds.

In small households, in particular, there was a tendency for job titles to change to incorporate the wider duties expected of staff or to give enhanced status to them. Instead of maids-of-all-work, inter-war householders asked for cook-generals, while the housemaid perhaps became a house-parlourmaid, undertaking both the cleaning duties of the housemaid and the ceremonial role of the parlourmaid, particularly when receiving guests and serving at table. Some mistresses, finding difficulty in recruiting individual servants, began to advertise for married couples, with the wife acting as cook-general and the husband as manservant, gardener and chauffeur. Typical of these was an appeal in *The Times* in May 1939 for an 'experienced Married Couple as Cook-Housekeeper and Handyman-Gardener for two gentlemen away all day; wife must be good cook, capable manager'.

For many girls the position of general servant was the least attractive in the domestic world. 'If you were just a little maid-of-all-work they called you skivvy', declared Mrs Milgate, 'and she probably did have a hard time. . . . Only twice I tried to have a go as a maid-of-all-work; I just flipped out again. One I went out within a few days and the other after two weeks. It wasn't my job. . . . In that sort of job you never finished, you had to scrub floors and all sorts. That didn't suit me . . . I was used to large houses and large staff.'[68] Or as a Welsh general servant recalled bitterly, 'I just worked as long as there was work to be done. . . . It's always been the same drudgery but with different people.'[69]

Yet there were some, like Mrs Lodge of Preston, who went into service in about 1937 when she was fifteen, who enjoyed the independence which working on her own gave. 'I really loved it . . . I love to clean up, I like working on my own. I wasn't over-fond of a lot of people.' Significantly, however, she was a day servant and, therefore, could spend her leisure hours as she wished.

The situation was also affected by the financial resources of the employer. Winifred Foley, at the age of about fifteen, went to work in Cheltenham for a family with two small children and limited means.

Punch mocking the growing trend to employ older servants and 'dailies' to compensate for the general shortage of younger maids. (Punch, *3 December, 1930*)

> They were in need of a strong young fool – one who could be housemaid from six
> till one for cleaning the house, then parlourmaid for waiting at table, then nanny for
> the children's afternoon outings, then washerwoman in the evenings. They needed a
> creature that would run on very little fuel and would not question her lot. . . . I escaped
> to home as soon as I reasonably could, and determined never again to look for a job
> where my employers were trying to keep up an appearance beyond their means.[71]

Her next post was on a farm in Wales, where food was plentiful but monotonous, she was not required to wear the much-hated servant's uniform, and she learnt to use a milk separator and to help with the haymaking, as well as carrying out general household chores. She also did the family's weekly shopping from the village, located two miles away. 'As I shut the farm gate behind me, and set off down the lane . . . my spirits rose. For the next hour or two, unsupervised by my mistress's sharp eye, I could belong to myself'.[72]

Edith Hall, employed by a sub-editor on a leading newspaper and his wife near London, remembered the many duties she had to carry out as a general, beginning at 6.30 a.m. when she cleaned her employers' shoes and got the children's clothes ready for school. Although she was only fifteen she was never treated as an adolescent. She had to wait at table and get her own meals as best she could, there being no time allotted for them in that household.

> I took the food into, the dining-room and was given a plate with mine served ready to eat, which I could take back into the kitchen and eat standing up by the draining board, or at least attempt to, because by the time I had taken the vegetables round to the other diners at the table and returned mine was invariably cold. There was no point in my sitting down because in about ten or twelve minutes the bell would ring for the sweet to be brought in. Before I could start on my sweet, the bell would ring again for me to clear the table. [73]

Edith's memories of this place were that she was 'always tired, always hungry' and had to listen 'to the wrangling of [her] employers'.[74]

In some small households the mistress worked alongside her maid, cooking the meals and perhaps helping to make the beds. In other cases it was all left to the maid. Mrs Goodman became a general servant for a Market Harborough doctor in about 1932 when she was sixteen. At first she worked with a cook, but after eighteen months the cook left and she was given sole responsibility for the household. Carpets were cleaned with a brush and dustpan, as she was only allowed to use the vacuum cleaner about once a fortnight or once a month, because her mistress was concerned about the electricity it used. Washing was done in the kitchen sink and for some time she was not allowed to use an electric iron, even though her mistress had one upstairs, in case she fused it. Instead, the iron had to be heated on the gas. When she first went there she sometimes failed to do the dusting properly and her mistress would rub her fingers over the surface and point this out.

> When I'd been there a little while I knew what wanted doing and I just had to get on with it and pull it in when I could. She might hot the soup up on my day off but she wouldn't do it when I was there . . . in those days you were paid for the job and had to get on with it.[75]

Many girls, faced with the drudgery and the loneliness of these single-handed places, simply moved, leaving the tasks to be carried out by charwomen or by the mistress herself, if full-time help could not be secured.

In larger households the situation differed, even with the reductions in staff, as every servant had his or her particular duties to carry out and was not expected to go outside them. There was a definite hierarchy in larger households where there was a network of largely independent departments, each with its own head. They included the kitchen, the nursery, the butler's pantry, the stillroom, the housekeeper and the housemaids and sometimes a laundry. They were supplemented, by various craftsmen – carpenters, painters, plumbers and the like, who carried out maintenance work on both the house itself and on estate cottages. Cliveden in

Veterinary Surgeon. "Who's that on the phone?"
Maid. "An Alsatian puppy with distemper, Sir."

Efficiency in answering the telephone was regarded as a desirable accomplishment for domestic workers between the wars. (Punch, *23 July, 1930*)

the mid-1930s had six full-time painters, two carpenters, four labourers and two electricians, who were responsible for generating the household's electricity.[76]

Yet this dependence on a large staff had its disadvantages. Servants were likely to notice if there were any untoward happenings, such as clandestine love affairs.

> They guarded the front door, they drove the carriage, they stamped and posted the letters . . . and they were always coming in and out of rooms to make up the fire, to pull the curtains, to announce callers, to bring in the tea or to tidy the cushions. . . . Whispered scandal flourished delightfully, the servants being particularly well up in paternity theories as they were not only in a position to make their own observations but they also heard what was said in the dining-room. '*Pas devant les domestiques*' was often hissed across the table, but generally too late.[77]

The young Lesley Lewis shared this unease, especially when she was staying in other people's houses as a guest. 'However pleasant the servants almost invariably were . . . there was an uncomfortable feeling of having a cloud of witnesses about one.'[78] Another worry was giving an appropriate tip to the housemaid who had looked after her during her stay, especially when, as in Lesley's case, cash was limited. 'Single girls could get away with five shillings', was her recollection, although in the grandest households more might be expected.[79]

The female staff in these large properties was headed by the housekeeper, although increasingly in the inter-war period it was customary to combine this post with that of cook and, often enough, with duties formerly carried out by the stillroom maids. At Shugborough, the housekeeper, Mrs Courtenay, took up office in 1935, after the closure of the stillroom. It was she, therefore, who had to ensure that sets of china for early morning tea for the guests were duly laid out, together with a plate of thin bread and butter for each person. The sets of china matched the decor in each of the guest rooms, so that the housemaid who took in the tea knew which room to enter. But it was a great rush, 'everybody was running, you didn't have time to live'. Then there were stores to distribute, since supplies were purchased in bulk and then given out to the individual departments. Friday was 'store day' and in the morning staff arrived with lists of what was wanted:

> soaps, Brasso for cleaning the brasses, black lead for doing the grates and all the general working stores as well as the food stores . . . you had to give out. . . . And the same with the linen . . . all the beds were changed on a Friday. Lady Lichfield had her bed changed twice a week, Friday and Tuesday. . . . Anyhow you had to have all this ready for the morning. And . . . when I was housekeeper sometimes I was till midnight getting all this out. . . . And then for the kitchen they got round towels, for drying their hands, and . . . tea towels for drying dishes and oven cloths and little fine linen cloths for straining soups and all various little bits of things. . . . And the same with the housemaids. . . . The butler, they had ever so many linen towels, and they had red and white square-checked, thin pure linen towels for drying the silver. . . . Each department had different things for working, both in stores and the working linen.[80]

Spare brushes, dustpans, soaps and general cleaning materials were also kept, so that it was 'like an ironmonger's shop'. The housekeeper had to check the linen too to see what needed mending. This was then carried out by the housemaids in the evening. However, the finer needlework was the responsibility of the housekeeper herself: 'you had an awful lot of sewing and mending to do all the time. You were never idle.'

Housekeepers had to supervise the housemaids and make sure that the public rooms of the house were ready for the family and their guests when they came down for breakfast, usually at 9 a.m. Room allocations for guests would be discussed by mistress and housekeeper and it was the latter who, along with the butler, ensured the smooth running of the household. Where there was much entertaining that was no easy task. At Eaton there were fifty-four bedrooms to be prepared on occasion and it was the housekeeper, Mrs Crocket, who dealt with the intricacies of them.[81] Housekeepers were always known as 'Mrs', whatever their real marital status, as a sign of their superior standing.

The housemaids carried out the cleaning, polishing, bed making, carrying of hot water for washing and taking away of slops. When female visitors arrived without their own lady's maid, a housemaid would be given the task of 'maiding' her, unpacking her clothes, laying out the things she needed for the day, helping her to dress in the evening, preparing her baths and similar duties.

At Shugborough the housemaids in the mid-1920s were expected to be down in the front of the house by 6 a.m., ready to collect their cleaning boxes, which had been put out the night before. They had to pass the housekeeper's room on the way down and 'woe betide anyone that was late'. Firegrates had to be cleaned, hearths whitened, and then the fires were lit and the carpets brushed by hand, all this being done by the light of a candle lamp, pushed along as the maid worked. Often wet tea leaves were put down on the carpet, to keep the dust to a minimum while the sweeping was in progress. The floorboards were polished with beeswax and a 'donkey' or 'jumbo', which was a heavy stone slab with a felt pad on the bottom on a long handle. This had to be pushed backwards and forwards.[82]

In carrying out these tasks a clear division of labour applied. The head housemaid at Shugborough Hall did not clean any grates, while the second housemaid dealt with the two drawing rooms and the third housemaid cleaned the dining room grate and the sitting rooms of Lord and Lady Lichfield. All of the work had to be completed well before 9 a.m. Small wonder that at Cliveden Michael Astor remembered the housemaids moving 'with light nimble footsteps, like mice scuttling from one corner to another', as they hurried to complete their duties. At Cliveden they rose at 5 a.m. to ensure that they were 'invisible' by the time family members appeared for breakfast.[83]

Later on, when the family was at lunch or dinner, the housemaids tidied the public rooms once more. Eileen Balderson, who worked at a large house near Peterborough, remembered that each housemaid had her allotted evening tasks. The head housemaid straightened the newspapers and magazines and stacked them neatly on a table set aside for the purpose; the second maid, Florence, shook the cushions and emptied the ash-trays. 'I, being third, swept the ashes into a pile under the grate, and folded the towels and cleaned the wash basin in the cloakroom':

> We then went back upstairs where we cleaned out any baths which had been used, emptied wash basins and tidied wash stands. The beds were then turned down; Annie [the head housemaid] and Florence doing the 'front' ones and I turned down the cook's bed . . . I also turned down the lady's maid's bed. . . .
>
> Between these evening duties, we had all the household linen to repair; also the gentlemen's socks and underwear. . . . Where a personal maid was kept, the housemaids never touched the lady's dressing table; her personal maid always dusted it and cleaned her toilet articles.[84]

When housemaids moved about the house together, perhaps when they were going to meals or tidying rooms while the family and their guests were lunching and dining, they usually walked in single file, with the head housemaid in the lead and the most junior at the rear. The latter had to walk forward when they neared a door, open it, and stand aside while the others passed through, before closing it behind her.[85]

The transition from dirty work in the morning to lighter duties and needlework in the afternoon and evening was marked by changes in uniform. During the morning housemaids wore striped print dresses with large, white aprons and caps. A blue drill apron was usually worn over the white morning one for the dirtiest tasks, like cleaning grates and scrubbing and then was removed when it was time

Staff at Noseley Hall, Leicestershire, in the mid-1930s during the August house cleaning carried out while the family was in Scotland. On the far left was the schoolroom maid, followed by the third housemaid, a footman, the head housemaid and the second housemaid. At the rear, standing on the bay window, were the odd job man and probably the estate carpenter. (*Leicestershire Museums, Arts and Records Service*)

to take round the early morning tea. In the afternoon black dresses were worn with a smaller apron and a cap.[86]

As well as the daily sweeping, dusting, scrubbing and polishing, there was a weekly rota for turning out rooms, with furniture put out in the passage and woodwork and parquet floors vigorously polished. The annual spring-cleaning, which lasted for several weeks, usually took place when most members of the family were away and the need for coal fires had ended. At Pilgrims' Hall, Essex, Lesley Lewis, a daughter of the household, remembered this yearly upheaval took place each May while her parents were off on a walking holiday. Some of the men from the stable and the garden came to help move the heavy furniture and to take up the carpets, which were beaten. Paint was washed in high and awkward places and a carpenter or plumber might be called in to carry out some small job while all the chimneys were swept. According to Lesley Lewis, there would be 'a lot of cheerful banter between the men and the maids, between those on the top of step-ladders and those holding them steady, and though curtains were sometimes dropped on people's heads and buckets overturned nothing seemed to matter very much'.[87]

Yet, if spring cleaning was a break in the regular routine, it was also exhausting. Margaret Powell, employed as a kitchenmaid in a substantial London household, recalled the spring cleaning there lasted for four weeks. 'During these four weeks I got up at five o'clock every morning and I worked until about eight o'clock at night. . . . I used to crawl up to bed, too weary even to wash.'[88]

The butler headed the male staff unless, in the grandest establishments, a house steward fulfilled that role. The butler oversaw arrangements for major dinner parties, receptions and other entertainments. He was responsible for the wine cellar and for the household plate and he superintended the work of the footmen. The male staff would normally be hired and fired by him and this responsibility was taken very seriously by butlers like the Astors' Edwin Lee. On one occasion in the 1930s, when experienced footmen were already hard to find, Lee interviewed a man whom he thought suitable. Lady Astor also saw him and began asking if he would be prepared to clean windows, bring in coals or do 'anything that needs doing'. The footman, standing on his dignity, refused to do anything not normally expected of a footman and was told by Lady Astor that he was useless to her. When Lee learned of this, he was furious and 'gave her a piece of my mind'. Significantly, he referred to the men as 'my staff', comparing himself to the captain of a ship: 'there was no one to whom I could go with my problems.'[89]

Where no valet was kept the butler generally took over those duties as well. If his employer were a hunting man the task could be onerous. Red coats had to be washed as soon as the employer returned, while the white leather hunting breeches were hard to clean. A Leicestershire butler claimed it took him about twelve months to acquire the necessary expertise.[90]

John Henry Inch, butler at Nidd Hall in Yorkshire during the late 1920s, had to care for about four pairs of these leather breeches during the hunting season and on many nights he stayed up working till midnight. His employer, Lord Mountgarret, also had a pheasant shoot on the estate and Mr Inch was required

John Henry Inch, flanked by two footmen in 1922. They were employed by Mr Latilla at Marland, Itchingfield, Horsham. (*Arthur R. Inch*)

to act as his loader, 'tramping over ploughed fields all day carrying heavy bags of cartridges and a 12-bore shot gun was no light task either'.[91] On his return he had to change into the butler's formal evening attire of tail coat, white starched front dress shirt, starched wing collar and white bow tie, ready to serve a dinner which commenced at 8 p.m. and if there were guests, might last until midnight. According to his son, Mr Inch 'never had a set day off, but was expected to be on duty from early morning till late at night. Neither was he ever able to have a holiday.' His only relaxations were to go out shooting rabbits with the gamekeeper or cycling to the local public house for a drink and a game of dominoes or darts with him.[92]

In many cases, as with Edwin Lee at Cliveden, butlers were peripatetic, accompanying their employer as he moved from house to house. Mr Lee travelled regularly between Cliveden and the Astors' London house.

If an under-butler were employed, he was responsible for the plate and for laying the table for dinner each evening. That included ensuring that the floral decorations were in place and the china, glass and silverware properly arranged. Meticulous under-butlers like Arthur Inch might spend a whole afternoon preparing and laying the table, if there was to be a large dinner party.[93] When his employers were away Inch also organised silver cleaning sessions with the footmen. This involved using a special rouge or very refined rust powder, to which water was added to make a red cream. The silver was then rubbed with the finger tips until all the scratches were removed. As Mr Inch later wrote, the work meant 'sore fingers and hands, but we just had to put up with it and many is the blister I've raised on my hands doing this job'. But to him it was worthwhile to ensure a brilliant display when his employers were entertaining.[94]

As well as cleaning plate and carrying out other pantry work, including looking after the lamps where these were in use, footmen were expected to open doors, take notes and letters and wait at table. On occasion they valeted some of the visitors, as well as the sons of the house, if they had no servant of their own.[95] Arthur Inch, who became first footman to Lord and Lady Londonderry in 1937, remembered that up to the Second World War it was customary for *The Times* to be ironed into four folds before it was sent through to the front of the house. 'Some gentlemen have been known to check to see if their paper was warm when receiving their copy!' A little earlier, when employed at Blenheim Palace by the Duke of Marlborough, he had to carry a red-hot, long-handled iron cup filled with perfume through the public rooms shortly before dinner. The perfume vaporised and clouds of scented air greeted the guests when they came down. At Blenheim the under-butler and three footmen all donned elaborate liveries and white cotton gloves to serve dinner.[96]

Some footmen had to perform car duty, with the man concerned sitting in the front with the chauffeur. When the car halted at its destination, he alighted quickly, opened the doors and helped out the passengers before getting in again smartly and moving off to park somewhere until it was time to collect them once more.[97]

The kitchen formed another separate department within the household. It was presided over by a chef in the grandest establishments, or by a female cook. At Shugborough the French chef was remembered as a man of uncertain temper who expected his female underlings to curtsey to him when he entered the kitchen in the morning. He and the female cook, who worked alongside him, each had a kitchenmaid, who was expected to have the table laid out with the appropriate utensils, ready for work to begin. One Shugborough kitchenmaid recalled that the chef never moved from the table, 'everything had to be within his reach' and she had to fetch anything he needed. However, he would retire to his own pantry to make pastry on the large marble-top table installed there. Perhaps this was to preserve the secrets of his art or just to ensure a cool temperature for his work. A family's reputation for hospitality could rise or fall on the quality of the food presented.[98]

Female cooks, too, could be highly esteemed. Mrs Harris, who worked for Lord and Lady Londonderry in the 1930s, was considered equal to any chef and received many tokens of jewellery and the like from distinguished visitors who appreciated her culinary skills. According to Arthur Inch, she 'ruled her kitchen with a rod of iron and could quell even the bravest footman (who dared to come along to hurry up the courses) with just a word and a look. But this was understandable when she had so much responsibility for the production of a superb meal.'[99]

Menus were drawn up after consultation between mistress and chef or cook, and in most households this took place when the mistress visited the kitchen at about 10 a.m. each day. Visits at other times were not welcome, as the kitchen was considered the cook's exclusive domain. When Margaret Powell worked as kitchenmaid in a large household in Hove she remembered the butcher and the greengrocer would call round for orders when they thought the cook knew the requirements for that day's meals. They returned with the requisite items within half an hour. Although the cook had no 'arrangement' with the shops for the payment of gratuities in return for orders, as some cooks did, when the quarterly bills were settled she often received a small gift. At the year's end, too, 'quite an appreciable discount, as they called it, was paid to her. It was the cook who really chose the shops, so when she went in they laid the red carpet down for her.'[100]

As a result of the stress of working in a hot kitchen and preparing high quality meals three times a day (to say nothing of special food for the nursery), many cooks – like the Shugborough chef – earned a reputation for ill temper. Their kitchenmaids and scullery maids were the main victims of it. Although it was only through being a kitchenmaid that most girls could hope to rise to the position of cook, it was a post of low prestige and one of growing unpopularity during the inter-war years. The kitchen and scullery maids did all the rough work, cleaning, scrubbing, washing saucepans and other utensils, fetching and carrying for the cook and helping with simple tasks like preparing vegetables and dressing poultry and game. Mrs Milgate, who began service life in 1922 at Bradford-on-Avon, in Wiltshire, as a scullery maid, recalled that although the other servants were called by their surname, 'as I was never seen or spoken to by anyone outside the kitchen, I didn't have a name at all'. She scoured copper pans with silver sand and vinegar until her hands were raw and scrubbed tables and floors, as well as carrying out a range of other heavy tasks. One day she was asked to dress a chicken. She had no idea how to do it, and when the cook saw her efforts she slapped the girl's face and pushed her back to the scullery.

There I was initiated in the art of bird dressing. It was greasy, and smelly, and I felt sick but after several painful pokes on my arm I was forced to go on, with the cook saying 'That's nothing my girl, wait till you have to do game birds that's been hanging for a month'. . . . A few days later a hare was slung at me which I was shown this time how to skin and gut but I vowed never again, I would leave this place and my next job would be a housemaid in London near to home.[101]

She left soon after and did, indeed, become a London housemaid. Sculleries were no place for the squeamish.

Sometimes kitchenmaids secured a small extra income by selling feathers and skins to dealers. At Rise Park in Yorkshire, there was a large wooden chest in the larder into which the kitchenmaid plucked all the poultry. Once the shooting season ended the feathers were sold, while a dealer came to purchase the rabbit and hare skins each week throughout the season.[102]

When Margaret Powell was a kitchenmaid in Hove she had another duty to perform. In the passage between the back door and the kitchen there was a long row of bells with indicators above to show where they rang from. Each time a bell sounded she had to rush into the passage to see which one it was. 'If you didn't run like mad . . . the bell would stop ringing before you got there, and you had no idea whether it was from the blue room, the pink room, first bedroom, second bedroom . . . I was always in trouble over these bells at first, but at last I mastered the art, and nobody shot out quicker than I did when they rang.'[103]

Unlike the departments so far considered, which were all integral parts of the everyday life of the household, the nursery was a separate sphere. Most nannies had close personal relations with their employers and with the children for whom they were responsible. A few nurses exerted cruel and tyrannical power over their young charges, but most had good relations with the children.[104] They were also anxious to identify with the social values of the class they served. Nanny Marks, nurse to the children of the future Marquess of Bath and his first wife, impressed upon them that there were children who were 'rough' and were outside their circle. The eldest son could 'never understand how Nanny Marks instantaneously recognised who was rough and who not'.[105]

Nannies were supported by a nursery staff, who would make the beds, sweep the floors, dust and carry out similar chores. There was also washing and ironing to do and the table to be set for meals. A nursery maid at Duntreath Castle near Glasgow remembered going with the children to tea parties and receiving young guests in return. 'In the summertime we used to get a lot of visiting nannies with the children because their parents were up on the grouse [moor] shooting.'[106] Unlike many nannies and nursery maids she was not expected to make clothes or do any sewing. The children's clothing was all purchased and came in boxes to the house.

In the main, nannies trained the new generation of nurses, who worked their way up from nursery maids. However, by the early years of the century a few training establishments had appeared, such as the Norland Nursing School (later College) at Notting Hill Gate, London, and the Princess Christian Nursery Training College in Manchester. Nevertheless, between 1900 and 1939 only about five thousand graduates from these colleges entered the employment market, compared to perhaps one hundred and forty thousand nannies at work in the latter year alone.[107]

The nursery staff were often unpopular with the other servants, partly because of their close links with their employers and the feeling that, as a result, a nanny might tell tales about her fellow domestics, but partly because of their air of social superiority and their demands for special nursery meals. When Margaret Powell became kitchenmaid in a large household in Thurloe Square, London, a nanny and under-nurse were in residence to look after the children of the daughter of the house. 'Later on in life', declared Margaret, 'I never ever took a place where there were nannies and children, and where they had to have separate meals in the nursery. The nanny would come down with all the airs and graces of a miniature employer, saying what the children wanted and what she wanted. . . . The cook, of course, used always to be furious at the nanny coming into the kitchen. . . . Only the mistress of the house was allowed in it and her only once in the morning to give her orders.'[108]

Similar reservations applied to lady's maids, who, like a valet, worked in close contact with the family. One man, who was at Sudeley Castle in the late 1920s, claimed that the lady's maid was 'easily the most hated servant of all. . . . This was so in most big houses. Nothing escaped her eyes and her tongue wagged unceasingly.'[109] Most came from a 'superior' social background and had received training in dressmaking and hairdressing before they took up their post. A lady's maid was very much at her mistress's beck and call. She had to repair, clean and press clothes, select appropriate day and evening attire and might be expected to accompany her employer on shopping expeditions, visits to charitable events and on other outings. She was often responsible for travel arrangements, too and, as Rosina Harrison recalled, if her mistress went away on a visit she went as well:

> Choosing what to take wasn't easy – mistresses before they leave are apt to be a bit hasty and short with you with their 'Oh, the usual things, you know what I like', or 'I'll leave it to you, Rose', but when you get to the other end and you haven't brought what they want it's a very different story, and you are to blame. I soon learnt to be relentless in my questions to them.[110]

Early in the 1920s Rosina went to work for Lady Cranborne and found her long-standing ambition to travel fully realised, as it had been for that reason she had become a lady's maid in the first place. Almost every weekend they were away. 'In the summer it would be for social visits and in the winter for shooting parties.' There were lengthy visits to the continent, too, including the south of France and Italy, while trips to Paris were frequent. She and Lady Cranborne went to the fashion shows to look at the latest styles. Occasional models were purchased, but in the main they made mental notes of what they had seen and then modified versions were produced by Rose when they got home.[111]

Later in the decade Rosina went to work for Lady Astor, with whom she remained for thirty-five years. Although her new mistress was unpredictable, the two got on well together. But it was a demanding position, with very long hours. Rosina claimed later that she never had time for a social life of her own, working as she did eighteen hours a day, seven days a week. After any sporting activity Lady Astor would throw her clothes into a bath, presumably to ensure they were washed each time. 'She generally got through five sets of clothes in a day. This required from me a deal of organising, pressing, cleaning and repairing. Also there were perpetual messages to be run or delivered, shopping to be done . . . and dressmaking or copying.' She was responsible for her mistress's jewellery and for her furs. They also travelled a good deal, accompanied by a multitude of trunks and cases. On the railway she tipped the guard and porter well. 'They got to know me and would look after me. They gave me a lot of useful advice about taking care of luggage and . . . I never lost as much as a piece of ribbon.'[112]

The final department to be considered – the laundry – was only found in the largest households and became less important between the wars, as commercial services were substituted. Even at a humble suburban level, families preferred to use a laundry, rather than have a washerwoman in to do the weekly wash.

At Shugborough Hall during the early 1920s the head laundrymaid spent much time on Sundays sorting the household linen, so she could make a 'good start' on Monday. Lord and Lady Lichfield's linen was dealt with first, followed by other family members, with the servants' laundry at the end. The washing took until Tuesday or Wednesday every week, with each maid having her particular duties. The head laundrymaid, for example, washed and ironed Lord Lichfield's shirts. A heavy box mangle, operated by the odd man, pressed the linen while it was damp dry. Next came the ironing, folding, and airing of the clean clothes on Thursday and Friday, before they were packed into hampers and taken to the house.[113] Then the dirty linen was collected again and the whole process was repeated.

Nesta Jones, who was third laundrymaid at Shugborough in the 1920s, dealt mainly with the other servants' laundry. However, everything had to be washed and ironed properly. Even dusters had to be folded correctly, so that the family monogram was in the left-hand corner and the edges met neatly. According to Nesta, the laundrymaids always considered themselves 'above the other maids, as they had to wash and iron the family clothes and took credit for them looking well turned out'.[114] The Shugborough laundry was finally closed in 1935.

Many country house laundries received dirty washing from the family's London house. This was despatched in large hampers, with the clean clothes returned in a similar fashion. At Powis Castle, where this practice was followed, it even meant dealing with dirty nappies, since the owner, Viscount Clive, had a young family. The hampers went by train to Welshpool, from where they were collected each Friday. A week later the clean laundry made the return journey. From time to time large net curtains from the town house, soiled by London dust and soot, were sent to Powis as well. 'They needed three laundrymaids to each curtain, for each was surrounded by frills which had to be goffered', using a pair of crimping tongs.[115]

The long hours of ironing were made more attractive to the maids because of the opportunities they offered for gossip and singing. 'The Powis laundress loved singing Irish songs and at Shugborough . . . there were frequent complaints about . . . laundry-maids who could be heard singing away at 6 o'clock in the morning'.[116]

Sometimes the resident laundry workers would be supplemented by local women. One villager came regularly from nearby Milford to Shugborough, working from 7 a.m. to 7 p.m., bringing her own food with her. Unlike the resident staff, she did not wear a uniform.[117]

Despite changes in the number and nature of domestic staff employed between the wars, immense differences still remained in the late 1930s between the daily round of a cook-general or maid-of-all-work in a small household and that of specialist servants in a large country or town household. Some highly skilled workers, accustomed to working for 'good families' preferred to search around for mistresses who were 'ladies', even if this meant taking single-handed posts in flats with impoverished members of the aristocracy and gentry. However, this remained a relatively rare practice.

More important was the fact that domestic service offered a place to 'marginal' characters, providing them with a home and a small wage. That was true of youngsters leaving orphanages or other institutions and, especially in the 1930s, of girls fleeing persecution in central Europe, who were able to enter Britain on a domestic permit.

Even workers with mental or psychological problems might get domestic employment when they would have found difficulty in earning a living elsewhere. They would be taken on by hard-pressed employers who could not afford other help. One such case involved a cotton-manufacturing family from Stockport. When the father's business ran into difficulties his son remembered they still kept a maid, despite their straitened finances:

> I think really because no-one else would employ her . . . she'd been into the local lunatic asylum once or twice. She was a big, strong, hefty woman. . . . Not at all intelligent, used to do the most appalling things sometimes . . . very willing and very loyal and she could carry big buckets of coal and keep the kitchen clean, do the washing up and things like that. And we paid her, I suppose, very, very little. . . . I think . . . she was thankful to get a home. She was kept warm and comfortable and mother paid for her uniform . . . I think she realised the rest of the world was a bit harsh.[118]

Servant scarcity or economic necessity might encourage families to experiment in this way. However, most householders sought more traditional domestic helpers.

CHAPTER THREE

THE ROLE OF GOVERNMENT AND THE VOLUNTARY AGENCIES

Efforts were made in the years immediately after the 1914-18 war to coax, even to coerce, women back into 'service' and to find new recruits from the ranks of the unemployed. The Government . . . provided free uniforms for those who were willing to take jobs as living-in domestic servants but had no suitable clothes or the money to buy them.

Frank Dawes, *Not in Front of the Servants* (London, 1973), pp. 142-3

GOVERNMENTAL INITIATIVES

State involvement in the recruitment of domestic servants was motivated by three principal concerns. These were a desire to use training as a way of raising the status and efficiency of entrants to an unpopular occupation, so as to make it more attractive; a wish to cut the levels of female unemployment; and an anxiety to placate middle-class families seeking domestic help by boosting the supply of household workers. Official interest in the training of females for domestic work had been apparent before the First World War, with the inclusion of needlework, cookery and similar subjects in the curriculum for girls in elementary and secondary schools. In addition, specialist domestic service and domestic economy schools had been set up by a few local authorities. In 1914 there were ten domestic service schools in England and Wales, of which four were located in the London area and eighteen domestic economy schools, of which twelve were in the capital. Students were admitted to London's domestic service schools on two-year courses, either by paying an annual fee of £1 10s or by winning a scholarship, which provided free tuition and a small maintenance grant. One third of the time was devoted to general education and two-thirds to instruction in various aspects of household work. During the second year, pupils decided which area they wished to specialise in and could qualify as kitchenmaids, housemaids, under-parlourmaids, or laundrymaids.[1]

In other places, courses were a good deal shorter. At Brighton, for example, a Municipal School for Home Training gave instruction for twenty-one weeks only, at a fee of 6d a week. Girls so trained were 'specially sought after by mistresses'.[2] Liverpool and Glasgow had similar schemes, while a number of county education committees provided, or subsidised, residential centres where students attended for a few weeks to fit them for domestic work either in their own home or in service.[3]

Domestic science instruction in the 1920s at Wingrave School, Buckinghamshire. The girls made the pinafores they wore for their cookery class. (*The late Mrs. Margaret Horn*)

In addition to the domestic service schools there were domestic economy centres, which prepared pupils to be home-makers rather than servants, and the curriculum reflected this. Whatever the aim of the organisations, however, their impact remained small. At a time when there were around 1.3 million female servants in England and Wales, the domestic service schools catered for about 350 girls and the domestic economy centres for around 700. During the First World War even these paltry numbers fell – by about a third in the case of the domestic service schools and by well over half in the domestic economy centres.[4]

Nevertheless, the belief that training would raise the standing of domestic employment continued to be advanced in official reports in the post-war period. Indeed, in 1923, the Ministry of Labour's *Report on the Supply of Female Domestic Servants* seemed to suggest that the solution of the domestic service 'problem' depended almost entirely on the introduction of an effective training programme:

> Although, theoretically, many people consider that all women are potential domestic workers, in practice there is such a strong reluctance to employ untrained women or girls as to render it impossible to place the majority of those willing to undertake the work. All witnesses who had really studied the question agreed that domestic work is a highly skilled occupation, in which training of a practical kind is essential. . . . It is an unfortunate fact that rural areas, which might otherwise be the chief source of supply, are precisely those in which the facilities for training are most deficient and most difficult to organise.[5]

It also argued that the courses should lead to a formal qualification, which would not only be of value to mistresses in assessing the suitability of a potential employee, but would raise the occupation's prestige in the eyes of teachers, pupils and parents.[6]

Yet it was not the example of the early training centres or the arguments of governmental committees which led to state intervention, but rising female unemployment. That applied both to the training programmes which were initiated and to the work of the employment exchanges which sought to encourage unemployed females to enter domestic work through a manipulation of the benefit system. Private domestic service (together with agricultural labouring) was excluded from the provisions of the 1920 Unemployment Insurance legislation. The argument put forward for the omission was that the necessary cash contributions would place an unnecessarily heavy burden upon servants, since there was plenty of work available for them. There was also hostility among employers not merely to paying their share of the insurance contribution, but to the idea of women getting unemployment benefit at all.[7] Only domestic workers in profit-making organisations such as hotels, guest houses and shops were covered by the legislation. In the early 1930s their number was put at about 350,000 workers, or around a quarter of the domestic labour force.[8] Despite pressure from workers' representatives, private indoor service remained outside the protection of unemployment insurance until the 1946 National Insurance Act, although outdoor workers such as gardeners, gamekeepers and general estate workers, together with indoor domestics employed in non-profitmaking institutions such as hospitals, hostels and clubs were included in the scheme in 1937 and 1938. Official statistics of female unemployment during the inter-war years, therefore, underestimate the true position, in that they cover insured workers only and private domestics, the largest single category of female labour, were not included. The policy also made service less attractive to unemployed factory workers and others, who were already in insured occupations but who, if they took up private domestic work permanently, lost that protection.[9]

In the immediate period after the First World War temporary benefits were paid to women made redundant by the switch from wartime to peacetime conditions.[10] Alterations to the benefit system, however, quickly began to put pressure on such women. Thus, from May 1919 those who had worked in industry or in some other occupation during the war, but had been maids prior to 1914, were reclassified as servants when they were assessed for benefit purposes. If they rejected domestic posts offered to them they could be denied their benefit. 'After the war I refused to go back into service', declared Mrs Lily Graham of Alton, Hampshire. The tribunal before which she appeared 'refused to register us for other jobs and tried to keep our money back. I was drawing £1 a week unemployment benefit, for which I had paid in during the war while on factory work. I won in the end, and worked in my uncle's garage until I got married.'[11]

However, others were less fortunate. The 1923 Ministry of Labour Committee on Domestic Service quoted, with approval, one correspondent who had denounced to the employment exchange girls that she knew had been in service before the war and who were drawing benefit. As a result, 'in every case benefit, was stopped immediately'. The committee regretted such actions were 'unfortunately rare . . . if the public do not assist the Exchanges by giving them the information in their possession, it is they, and not the system or the Exchanges, who are to blame if, in such cases, the law is evaded.'[12]

Although an appeals system was set up, it was common for arbitrators to uphold decisions to disallow or suspend benefits to complainants who had refused posts as maids. In 1921 that process was strengthened when further National Insurance legislation included a clause requiring benefit applicants to be 'genuinely seeking wholetime employment but unable to obtain [it]'. This meant that cotton operatives, who had formerly earned 45s a week, lost their benefit when they refused jobs in service at 17s a week. Similarly, a group of unemployed glovemakers was rejected because there was 'a demand for domestic servants in their area'. Celia Briar quotes examples of girls under eighteen who were disqualified from benefit when they declined to work as maids up to 150 miles from their home.[13]

In 1922 new insurance provisions required applicants to accept any job they were capable of performing. There was no longer any possibility of demanding a position with comparable pay and conditions to their previous occupation. This meant unemployed women, particularly during a depression, had little alternative except service. That applied to a 25-year-old shorthand-typist who lost her job in June 1921. After being unemployed for four and a half months she was offered a post as a 'children's attendant' in an institution. When she refused, her benefit was suspended because, it was claimed, there was no prospect of her obtaining clerical work in the district. The decision was upheld on appeal, it being argued that she should have been willing to give the employment offered a trial.[14]

There were numerous cases of this kind and from March 1921 the government even financed the provision of clothing for women prepared to take up domestic work who were precluded from doing so because of lack of an appropriate uniform. The outfit became the recipient's property if she remained in resident service for three months. If she left before that time it had to be returned.[15] Those who benefited included former factory and industrial workers, shop assistants and clerks, as well as women who had previously been in service and were seeking to return to it.[16] The scheme continued throughout the inter-war period and by 1938 more than ten thousand outfits had been issued.

However, at an early stage it was realised that many of those who had previously worked in factories, offices and shops were unsuitable for domestic work without some instruction. At first the re-training of redundant munition and other industrial workers was taken on by the Ministry of Labour's own Training Department. It was decided that the courses should be 'in women's normal trades, such as clothing . . . and domestic service'. They were to be organised in association with local education authorities.[17]

As unemployment became more severe in 1920, a new arm of the Ministry of Labour was called into operation. This was the Central Committee on Women's Training and Employment (CCWTE), which had been formed initially in 1914 as the Central Committee on Women's Employment to cope with female unemployment caused by the onset of war. However, with the rise in demand for labour from 1915 onwards that role proved short-lived. It was only after 1918 that the Central Committee's real importance emerged. In January 1920 it was reappointed and was

Pride in household skills is emphasised in this advertisement for Mansion polish in 1923. (Good Housekeeping, *September 1923*)

given responsibility for drawing up schemes to train those whose earning capacity had been 'injuriously affected as a result of conditions arising out of the war' or whose circumstances had been adversely affected in some other way, perhaps by the death of the family breadwinner.[18] There was a commitment 'not to trespass upon occupations especially suited to disabled men' and initially, it concentrated on setting up professional and semi-professional courses for applicants from a non-manual background. However, in March 1921 that role was transformed when the Ministry of Labour's own industrial training programme came to an end. Most of the women, for whom CCWTE was now responsible, were unable, on educational or other grounds, to take up the professional courses the committee had financed previously. After 'exhaustive consideration', it concluded 'that domestic service was the only occupation under existing conditions for which training would show an immediate return and in which there was a shortage of workers'.[19] Backed by government grants, therefore, it became the Ministry of Labour's agent for providing female training in vocational and domestic work. Courses for the latter were sometimes established in co-operation with local education authorities, but where this proved impossible, the Central Committee set up centres itself. Women were excluded from the public works programmes offered to unemployed men, on the grounds that these were 'pick and shovel' jobs, and thus unsuitable for females.[20]

Initially, the CCWTE programme was designed only in part to boost servant numbers. That was the purpose of the so-called Homecrafts centres, where students were required to promise they would enter service when they had completed the course. A complementary Homemaker scheme, set up a few months later, aimed at reducing the demoralising effect on women of long-term unemployment by giving instruction in domestic skills while they waited to return to their customary occupations. Nevertheless, in several Homemaker centres around a quarter of the trainees took up domestic work at the end of the course.[21] The blurring of the distinction between the two programmes was further encouraged by the fact that at the Homecrafts centres the Superintendents 'never lost sight of the fact that this training, in addition to its primary object, had a second purpose in view, namely, to make the students better wives and mothers'.[22] As such, it was 'a valuable asset to the nation'. From May 1921 to 31 December 1922 around ten thousand women were trained as domestic servants on the Homecrafts courses and there were 1,560 on the Homemaker scheme.[23] In January 1924 the separation of the two programmes came to an end, as did the promise to enter service which had been attached to the Homecrafts courses. Henceforth new Home Training centres, designed to encourage, but not compel, recruitment into domestic service, were set up.

The Homecrafts, Homemaker and Home Training courses were all short-term, lasting around thirteen weeks and catering for women aged sixteen to thirty-five. While in attendance students received a maintenance grant rather than unemployment benefit. The grant amounted to £1 a week for adults and 10s a week for those aged sixteen to eighteen. However, out of these sums, 3s a week was deducted from the adult payment and 2s from the junior towards the cost of materials for the uniform they made in readiness for entry into service. At this stage all trainees were non-resident.[24]

Instruction was for thirty hours a week and covered cookery, laundrywork, housework and needlework, plus lessons in hygiene and general education, including singing. According to Violet Markham, who chaired the Central Committee from 1922, this latter had been incorporated in the syllabus 'for its value from the physical and cultural point of view. . . . Singing is of special value in contributing to the creation of good morale and the maintenance of discipline, and has assisted in stimulating *esprit de corps*, so essential to the success of training of this kind.'[25] She rejected the attacks of critics, who were anxious that the courses should concentrate on a narrow domestic theme, as 'an ebullition of opinion from an uninformed section of the public who are lacking in knowledge of the psychology of the modern working girl'. Furthermore, weight had to be given to the fact that

> in establishing courses of training to prepare factory workers to become domestic servants, they had to face considerable criticism on the part of the girls and their parents, who at that time displayed opposition to the idea of entering domestic employment, and that suspicion was only allayed by the fact that a curriculum was introduced in all the Centres in which appropriate balance was maintained between purely vocational subjects and humane subjects of a general cultural type.[26]

That broader aspect became all the more important in 1926 when severe economic depression made it difficult to find posts for women trained in clerical work. This, coupled with the continuing demands of middle-class householders for maids, led to a suspension of the remaining vocational (non-domestic) courses offered by CCWTE. Only after four years was recruitment resumed, with vocational schemes drawn up for applicants to train in clerical subjects, nursery nursing, cookery, institutional housekeeping and midwifery. Overall, between 1920 and the end of 1938, 1,510 trainees passed through the vocational courses, compared to around 84,000 students successfully instructed in domestic skills in the same period. It was a graphic illustration of the relative importance of the two programmes. Furthermore, when individual vocational training was revived in 1930, it soon acquired a 'domestic' bias. As early as 1931, the Central Committee was warning that with the current serious industrial downturn, applicants should be discouraged from taking clerical courses. As a result

> a considerable number of . . . candidates were induced to abandon clerical work in favour of a course of cookery. Openings were subsequently found for them in this new field. . . . Only young women were accepted for training in clerical machine operating.[27]

Four years later it was reported that for older women, in particular, cookery training 'offered the best opening', since employers were reluctant to recruit them into offices and shops.[28]

By 1938, CCWTE was supporting three special centres for older women in London where the main emphasis was on cookery instruction. According to the Ministry of Labour Report for that year almost three-quarters of the trainees were placed in employment when they had completed the courses.[29] However, Violet Markham took a pessimistic view of their prospects, lamenting their poor state of health: 'bad eyes, bad teeth, rheumatism and general debility . . . the volume of *feeble* folk in mind and body is appalling. I sometimes wonder how the country carries on at all with such a dead load at its base.'[30]

The Central Committee's concentration on domestic instruction was partly due to the fact that during a period of high unemployment it was a way of reinforcing gender divisions in work. Women could not be accused of 'stealing' men's jobs. It was partly a way of meeting middle-class demand for maids at a time when there were allegations that girls preferred to live on benefit rather than become servants[31] and partly it was because domestic training programmes were inexpensive, particularly where they were supported by the local education authority. There were no costly, specially constructed centres provided, as with the men's schemes, but rather a system of short-term hiring of houses and public halls.[32] Even equipment was sometimes rented in the early days.[33] The trend was further encouraged by high unemployment in other women's occupations. When in 1923 Julia Varley and Margaret Bondfield, as trade union representatives, pressed the Minister of Labour for a wider female training programme, he asked them to suggest suitable alternatives where there was not already serious joblessness. They were unable to do so.[34]

However, surrender to the official view did not satisfy Miss Manicom of the Workers' Union. At the 1924 Trades Union Congress she drew attention to the gender discrimination it implied. When women were displaced from their normal trades, she declared angrily, it was suggested they take up domestic work,

> but who would suggest that a house painter or a stonemason should change his trade? Why, then, should biscuit packers be asked to train as lady's maids, or shop assistants as scullery maids? [35]

TABLE 1 *Central Committee on women's Training and Employment:*
Totals of Trainees on Homecrafts, Homemaker and Home Training* Courses 1920-38

Year	Cumulative totals of trainees who had completed courses by 31 December each year	Still in training on the courses on 31 December in each year
1924	23,058	2,012
1925	29,219	1,758
1926	34,182	851
1927	37,263	430
1928	40,769	810
1929	44,873	990
1930	49,051	1,208
1931	54,593	1,060
1932	59,445	990
1933	63,935	953
1934	68,329	869
1935	72,469	977
1936	75,755	1,026
1937	79,162	923
1938	82,937	1,023

*Home Training courses began in 1924
Source: Calculated from the Annual Reports of the Ministry of Labour. N.B. Around 84,000 trainees had either completed their course or were in process of doing so by 31 December 1938. However, if students who had dropped out were taken into account, the total of those entering the courses over the period 1920-38 was probably around 100,000.

Her comments had little effect. Indeed, although Margaret Bondfield and Ellen Wilkinson, two of the small number of women Labour MPs in the 1920s, expressed reservations in parliament about schemes that drove 'unsuitable women into occupations which were distasteful to them', as Bondfield put it, neither questioned seriously the need for this narrow focus, given current economic and social conditions. Margaret Bondfield, indeed, mentioned the improved health, better clothing and greater self-confidence of previously unemployed women once

Advertisement for a non-slip floor polish intended to help the less experienced housemaid. (Good Housekeeping, *September 1923*)

they had completed their training. Although it had been 'a grave mistake, and a disaster' to narrow the courses to this 'particular sphere of training, thanks to the care exercised in relation to the placing of the girls trained in those classes, we have had the most astonishingly favourable results in regard to the greater popularity of the classes'.[36] In the spring of 1927 she quoted instances of centres in South Shields, Gateshead and Hamilton where applicants for courses had exceeded the places available by a ratio of three or four to one.[37] (Interestingly, when the minority Labour government was in office in 1924 it was noted that during the six months ending 2 June in that year more women were placed in domestic service by employment exchanges (at 62,497) than in the corresponding period of 1923 (at 56,993), when the Conservatives were in power.[38])

In July 1927, Ellen Wilkinson, while maintaining that not 'every woman should be pushed into domestic work' as she knew '. . . what an appalling failure . . .' she would be, nonetheless believed there was a 'very large number of women who [preferred] domestic work, and a very large number of women has been trained for domestic service in these centres'. [39]

The ambivalence of Labour MPs towards domestic training was nonetheless obvious. Some objected to unemployed females being turned into low-paid 'flunkeys' for housewives who could well 'look after their own families'. Yet, when Labour was in opposition in 1928, its leaders, with the backing of women MPs of all parties, campaigned successfully for increased funding to be given to the programme. Admittedly it was at a time when female unemployment was rising and, as Celia Briar comments, 'it was politically more feasible to obtain funds for domestic service training than for any other type of project to assist unemployed women'. [40] In June 1930, Margaret Bondfield, as Minister of Labour, expressed tacit approval of CCWTE's willingness 'to establish further training centres to the extent to which circumstances justify it'. [41]

In the factory districts of Lancashire and Cheshire, however, the programme was unpopular. In February 1932 an official report referred to 'a pronounced and active opposition' to the occupation among unemployed women. [42] A year earlier, Violet Markham, after a tour of Lancashire, had formed a similar opinion: 'It is a paradox that we have to scrape and struggle in some areas to keep a group of forty girls going at a Training Centre', at a time when there were thousands of women out of work. [43] Resident service, in particular, was regarded as a last resort by the average female. It was disliked because workers felt that even during leisure hours they were under the employer's direction and control and that they were despised by fellow workers in other occupations.

These reservations were made clear by a Liverpool trainee. She had taken a seasonal job as a kitchenmaid and was gratified that her employer had been so pleased with her work that he had asked her to return the following year. She had also found her duties enjoyable. But what she objected to was having to sleep in.

When pressed, she expressed herself cogently:

> first of all, one is half a slave; the mistress thinks everything about one's life is her concern too, and because she is the mistress, one never has a chance to tell her she should mind her own business. . . . One is never free. Factory girls have certain working hours and then they are free. We have to work all day and there is never an end to it. On our free day the mistress tells us when we have to be back. One can never have fun or a long dancing night because usually 'it does not agree with the moral code of the mistress'. [44]

The Liverpool centre did, nevertheless, operate successfully, despite the fact that most of its students arrived in what was described as a 'defiant and suspicious mood' and were from a 'rough' background. 'They have little or no discipline, and . . . little idea of personal hygiene and sound habits.' [45] Interestingly, once they had completed their training almost all of them wished to work in institutions or on commercial premises rather than in private residences. [46] Although the work was still hard, the hours were more clearly defined than in individual households and there was greater freedom as to how leisure was spent, as well as some companionship in the workplace itself.

From the late 1920s, however, the main focus of the training schemes became the depressed mining areas, where female work outside the home was, by tradition, very limited and yet where the menfolk, through unemployment, could no longer fulfil their role as breadwinners. The problem was highlighted in the 1931 population census which showed that less than 16 per cent of women aged fourteen and over had a job in Glamorgan and under 17 per cent in Durham, compared to more than 34 per cent in paid employment in England and Wales as a whole. Even among eighteen to 20-year-olds, only 43.9 per cent of girls in Glamorgan and 49.3 per cent in Durham were at work compared to 79 per cent in England and Wales. Furthermore, the poverty-stricken home background of girls from these communities made it hard for them to enter service without specialised instruction.[47]

In February 1929 the *Ministry of Labour Gazette* commented on the 'special difficulties' of finding positions for girls from mining communities. 'There are practically no women's industries in these districts, and the women and girls . . . have been little accustomed to seek work outside their own homes. In these circumstances it was decided . . . to concentrate on finding an outlet in domestic employment.'[48] During the half-year ending September 1928, thirty-eight training centres were opened in mining communities, with 1,200 young women and 431 girls between sixteen and eighteen completing training during that period. Of these, 386 women and 96 girls found domestic work in the locality and 642 women and 283 girls were placed away from home.[49] However, that in itself presented problems and in October 1931 a Ministry of Labour minute blamed the 'reluctance of parents to let their daughters go far from home' for 'much of the difficulty experienced in placing juvenile trainees'. There were few local vacancies and the wages offered compared unfavourably with those in London and the south-east of England.[50] Indeed, a survey carried out in Middlesbrough by the local education authority into domestic employment showed that of 808 full-time day girls considered, almost half had wages of only 2s to 5s a week. About nine in every ten earned under 10s a week. However, as the Minister of Labour, Margaret Bondfield, pointed out, the fact that the supply of girls for this kind of work was large and the demand in the Middlesbrough area was limited created the problem. By contrast there was 'a constant unfilled demand' for maids in resident situations 'offering good conditions in various parts of the country'.[51]

It was accepted that, in the long run, domestic recruitment and female unemployment could best be tackled by turning attention to school leavers. In June 1932, the Ministry of Labour wrote to education authorities in the depressed north of England, the Black Country and Wales asking them to alert girls to the courses available.[52] The response was unenthusiastic. The Secretary to the Coseley Education Committee in Staffordshire confirmed that although courses had been brought to the girls' notice, and a few had 'shown some inclination to take up the training', their parents had opposed the move.[53]

However, the campaign had some success, with the CCWTE reporting that the number of trainees under sixteen had almost doubled in 1931.[54] They were catered for either at special centres or, more commonly, alongside girls between sixteen and eighteen years old. At the end of 1933 the proportion of juveniles under the age of eighteen undergoing training had risen to about 70 per cent of the total, compared to around 55 per cent at the beginning of the year, and there were groups of fifteen-year-olds being instructed in four centres.[55] In 1934 the age of trainees was reduced further, to include fourteen-year-olds for the first time. A longer period of training was envisaged for them, of up to nine months if necessary. No girl was to be employed under the age of fifteen. Three centres, all in Wales, were selected for the initiative and by 1935 that had been increased to eight. As a consequence, during the years 1935 to 1937 the number of juveniles in training at the end of each year had climbed to around 80 per cent of the total. Of those who *completed* a domestic course during those three years, about 70 per cent were under eighteen.[56]

In 1935 the change of emphasis by CCWTE was explained. In 1920, the urgent need had been 'to enable young women who had been engaged in war work or whose family income had been reduced by the death or incapacity of the breadwinner to fit themselves for occupations in which they could earn a living'. Fifteen years later that had 'given place to . . . assisting the younger girls, particularly in those areas where, owing to the industrial depression, they have little opportunity of getting work locally and are not in a position to pay for training in order to obtain employment elsewhere'.[57]

One centre which had concentrated on training juveniles from the start was Ystrad in South Wales. It opened in June 1928 and during its first six months fifty-two youngsters were instructed, of whom nine failed to get a place when the course ended and one was too ill to work. Of the remaining forty-two, thirteen went to London, twenty were offered places in Wales and most of the remainder went to jobs as far apart as Eastbourne, Weston-super-Mare, Weymouth and Bath. Four were described as unavailable for work.[58] Thirty-three of the girls were sixteen when they started the course and none was over the age of eighteen. The wages they received when they obtained employment varied from £17 a year paid to a housemaid at a hospital in Barnstaple, Devon, to £26 a year earned by various maids in London. However, the records also show that such youngsters could be exploited once they were away from home. One sixteen-year-old, who had gone as a parlourmaid to London for a promised weekly wage of 10s, in practice received 8s a week, doubtless because of her inexperience and because her employers were well aware of just how difficult it would be for her to return home, at least until she had managed to save enough to cover the fare back.

A second trainee to face problems was Doris Clarke, who had attended a centre in South Shields in the north-east of England. Prior to taking up domestic work she had been a shop assistant. Her first post after completing her course was at the Old Hall, Threshfield, where she remained for just three weeks, before moving on because the duties she had to carry out were too heavy for her. Not only was she expected to work long hours but she was required to cook for a household of eleven people on occasion. This was too much for an inexperienced trainee. She had difficulty, too, in extracting her wages from her employer, as she told a CCWTE official:

> The week I left they owed me three weeks money, and when I asked if I could have my money on Wednesday, before leaving on the Friday, they would only give me 10s and said 'That was all they could afford at the time'. I should have left on the Friday but Mrs. Metcalfe asked me to stay till Saturday as there was a beagle meeting at the Old Hall and Saturday is a very busy day, so I stayed and helped them and even prepared all the washing for them for the Monday, and they then only paid me 2s 6d for 15 days work, but I've found out since leaving that they never pay their employees if they can possibly avoid it.
>
> I am quite happy in my new post, and I have a very good mistress. I have three nights off every week and my mistress often lets me go over to the village to do some shopping for her, and she always tells me to have a little walk before returning . . . I am afraid my mistress is spoiling me completely.[59]

During the inter-war years the number of training centres open at any one time reflected the fluctuations in the levels of unemployment, both nationally and locally, as well as government expenditure priorities. In 1927, 62 Home Training courses were organised by CCWTE; that had risen to 132 courses in forty-one centres two years later.[60] By 1934 this had changed to six residential and twenty-six day centres open throughout Great Britain and to seven residential and thirty-one non-residential centres in 1938, including provision in London for women over thirty-five whose prospects of finding fresh employment were considered particularly difficult. In its report of 1934 the Ministry of Labour mentioned some of the reasons for these fluctuations:

> In districts where centres have been established for a number of years the supply of older applicants available for domestic training has considerably diminished. Moreover the improvement in industry has increased the opportunities of employment in other directions and thus made the older girls less willing to come forward for domestic training.
>
> In the depressed areas the day centres were well filled on the whole but there was less response in the areas of improving trade. It was necessary to close the centre at Preston in August and to reduce the accommodation at Sheffield and Newcastle. . . . The improved economic position has increased the number of vacancies and the demand for trainees from both day and residential centres was greater than the supply.[61]

In other words, in time of necessity women and girls were prepared to take up domestic training, but once other jobs became available numbers fell off and centres had to be closed. Meanwhile, the upturn in trade, which had brought about a reduction in the trainees, also boosted the number of householders able to afford to keep a maid and led to renewed complaints of servant shortages. The

A cookery class at a residential training centre for domestic workers run by the Central
Committee on Women's Training and Employment, c. 1934. (*TUC Library*)

dilemma this created for the Central Committee was made clear by its chairman,
Violet Markham, in October 1937, when she wrote gloomily to her sister that there
seemed 'no prospect' of the servant question becoming less acute 'while the present
trade boom continues and the rearmament programme lasts. There is a tremendous
demand for women's labour and so long as these girls can get factory employment
there is no chance of their undertaking the unpopular job of domestic service. . . . The
Government training centres for which I am responsible are half empty and we are
having great difficulty with them.'[62] A few months later when 30,000 unemployed
women were interviewed about the possibility of taking up domestic training, two-
thirds of them refused even to consider the possibility.[63] Eventually just 812 were
admitted to the government training centres.[64] (see also totals in Table 1)

It was partly to deal with variations in the numbers on non-resident courses
and partly to cater for potential trainees who were unable to attend day centres
because they lived too far away, that from the early 1930s residential training
began to be provided. The initiative was felt to be beneficial in its own right as
well, since it more closely approximated to conditions in a household than non-
residential arrangements. Centres could also be set up in areas where domestic
vacancies were plentiful. The first of the residential courses to cater for domestics
for *British* employment was opened at Leamington Spa in January 1930, although
earlier experiments had been made in providing residential training for servants
wishing to emigrate to Australasia and Canada.

By 1934 five residential centres were open. A Ministry of Labour leaflet
promoting them described domestic work encouragingly as a 'skilled occupation'
with 'steady employment, good wages and living conditions'.[65] The courses were
shorter than those in the non-residential centres, lasting for just eight or ten weeks.
The curriculum broadly followed that in use on the day courses and included
classes in needlework, with students required to make the uniform they would
need in a post. In addition, they gained practical experience by waiting on the staff

and on each other, while the washing was done in the laundry class, including both the household linen and the girls' personal clothing. Recreational periods were arranged each afternoon and during these the girls were free to go out or to occupy themselves as they liked. There were rooms set aside for games and dancing as well as for reading and study. At the end of the course each trainee was helped to find a suitable post. Training was free and in addition to board and lodging each girl received 2s 6d a week pocket money. The fare from her home to the centre was paid and she was given the materials needed for her uniform.[66]

Irene Thompson, who was born in 1918, was one young resident trainee. She came to the centre at Market Harborough from her home in Redcar, when she was fifteen. Prior to moving south she had had a day job at a local boarding-house, for which she was paid 6s a week. Then a next-door neighbour mentioned that her daughter was going to the training centre and asked Irene if she would like to do the same:

> I had to go and pass one or two interviews and exams and things but they got me through and they sent me to Market Harborough. . . . It was a huge house and we done like a domestic science course . . . you was on the whole time, kitchen, bedroom work, cooking, needlework, knitting . . . making our own uniform, blue dresses and starched aprons. They were a good crowd of girls, about 40, they were all about 14 to 17. We used to have a lot of fun. . . . They were very strict but we were happy. On the whole, I think we were glad enough to get away from home and the poverty and everything.
>
> They asked us what branch we wanted to go into. The girl I went with from next door, she went down to London as a companion to an old lady. I said I didn't mind as long as I went where there was no children, because I'd had enough of them, nine of me own brothers and sisters. . . . These people who came, they said they wanted a 'general'. . . . I didn't mind because I'd always done everything; I'd just been more or less polished off at the training centre.[67]

Her new employers were a retired bank manager and his wife, and although her mistress was strict (even trying to eradicate Irene's Yorkshire accent) she settled down and remained with them eighteen months.

Thus, domestic service became the favoured female training option at a time when men were offered a wide range of schemes, because it was relatively cheap to organise and it gave a home as well as employment to those who became resident maids. It also appealed because it prepared girls for their future role as wives and mothers and it could be seen as an 'appropriate' female occupation, given current social attitudes towards women. It conformed, too, to the government's overall strategy of industrial transference, which aimed at moving the unemployed from depressed areas in northern England, South Wales and parts of Scotland to more prosperous localities in the Midlands, the south of England and, in particular, Greater London. It could claim relative success as well, as most trainees took up domestic employment once they had completed their courses, unlike the graduates from many of the men's training programmes.[68] In 1934, a Ministry of Labour survey claimed that at a time when around four thousand women and girls were undergoing training each year, enquiries made one or two months after the completion of the courses suggested that about 80 per cent of them were still in their new occupation.[69] Four years earlier Lady Astor had suggested that 83 per cent of the trainees had found suitable work. 'That is enormous. I do not think you can say that any men's trade can find such a high percentage.'[70] But the final – and perhaps most telling – advantage of domestic training in government eyes was that it helped to satisfy the middle-class demand for maids.

In the immediate post-war period, as we have seen, there were claims that unemployed women preferred to live on benefit rather than work as domestics. That discontent was fuelled by newspapers like the *Daily Mail*, with its 1923 'Scandals of the Dole' campaign. In addition to publishing articles condemning the payment of 'huge sums every year simply to keep women idle for whom there is plenty of remunerative work', it printed a series of readers' letters along similar lines. One such, from a Mrs Hughes of West Kensington, declared that the writer had been unable to obtain a maid from the 'Labour Exchange although I offered £40 a year and treatment like one of the family. . . . There ought not to be a single healthy young woman drawing the dole and living in idleness upon the unfortunate taxpayers.' However, investigation by the 1923 Ministry of Labour Committee on the Supply of Female Servants failed to discover any trace of an application having been received by the local employment exchanges from Mrs Hughes. In another case a Lieutenant-Colonel Robert Stephens of Bournemouth maintained he had spent £9 in advertising for a servant, without success. Again the 1923 Committee investigated and discovered that no one of his name was known at the address given. Two letters written to him by applicants for employment – after his letter had been published – had been returned to sender through the Dead Letter Office marked 'Not known'.[71] Many of the other claims, published in the *Daily Mail* and elsewhere, proved to be similarly exaggerated or untrue.[72]

However, the training programme and the determined policy of disallowing benefit to girls who refused domestic posts without good reason helped to silence the critics and to boost servant numbers. Nevertheless, problems remained for employers, as girls were willing to accept non-resident or institutional posts, but not residential work in private households. By 1937 the Ministry of Labour admitted that a shortage of candidates meant that only about half of the vacancies notified to the employment exchanges for private domestic servants could be filled. This was principally due to applicants' reluctance to take residential positions.[73]

The response to the hotel and catering trade and to vacancies in holiday resorts seeking seasonal labour proved more positive. During the 1930s the government gave grants to private organisations like the Restaurant Public Houses Promotion Company, which trained young women – and some men – in hotel and bar work.[74] In addition, the special hotel and catering employment exchange set up in London in 1930 was filling 33,261 vacancies a year in the capital and elsewhere by 1933. It dealt with applications for high grade staff, such as managers, chefs and head waiters, as well as more humble employees.[75] In 1937 this had increased to 36,509 vacancies filled, with demand stimulated by the Coronation celebrations in London during that year.[76]

Employment exchanges proved especially valuable in meeting the seasonal demands of the holiday trade. As early as 1928 they were reported to be filling over twenty thousand domestic vacancies in holiday resorts.[77] During the 1930s there was still greater activity. In 1935, for example, seasonal vacancies filled by the exchanges included those for 21,208 resident domestic servants, 8,362 non-resident domestics, 19,364 waiters and waitresses and 952 cleaners. In addition, short preparatory training courses for hotel workers were held in five different centres.[78] The initiatives were seen as important because they increased the number of men and women with experience of domestic service and also cut unemployment levels. When the seasonal engagements came to an end workers were encouraged to seek permanent posts elsewhere. Although most returned home, there were reports that as a result of their seasonal experience 'a proportion' of them were taking up 'permanent residential employment'.[79]

Sometimes, however, as in Liverpool and in seaside resorts like Blackpool, reliance on seasonal work had the disadvantage of creating much winter unemployment. In 1938 a report on female joblessness in Liverpool blamed this partly on the large number of women in 'occasional employment'. These included seasonal domestics who were recruited by holiday resorts in north Wales and on the Isle of Man.[80]

Concern was also expressed about the number of girls leaving the industrial towns for seasonal posts who then became stranded in resorts. Sometimes this was because the positions were unsuitable, but in other cases the girls themselves gave up their jobs in order to have a 'good time'.[81] As a consequence, the Ministry of Labour began co-operating with local voluntary organisations to provide for the welfare of migrants. That included the appointment of 'chaperones' in some larger resorts to provide advice and help to the girls. If necessary, this might include advancing their railway fares home.[82]

The government's preoccupation with, and support for, female domestic training continued until the outbreak of war in 1939. At this point all courses not directly related to the war effort were terminated and that included the Home Training scheme and its offshoots. The Central Committee on Women's Training and Employment was itself wound up in the summer of 1940.[83]

OTHER TRAINING AGENCIES

The various reasons which caused the state to intervene in domestic service training applied to other agencies working in the field. On the one hand some were anxious to raise the occupation's status by applying relevant instructional methods. They took as their model nursing, which had risen from humble Victorian origins to become a recognised profession through the judicious application of appropriate training and firm discipline. On the other hand, there were philanthropists who saw domestic work primarily as a way of providing a home and income for the deprived, the unfortunate and the unemployed. This was a view put forward by the leading charity, Dr Barnardo's Homes, in 1933, when it defended its use of domestic service as a major employment outlet for youngsters in its care: 'this is practically the only type of work that offers a girl of sixteen or seventeen years of age full maintenance and a good home, in addition to a small wage'.[84]

Inevitably, such an approach undermined the general standing of domestic servants. Violet Firth, for one, argued that a 'very potent factor in lowering the standard of conditions' in household employment was the practice adopted by orphanages and workhouses of training most of their girls for that occupation. 'The standard of conditions in domestic service was forced down by what was practically a supply of forced labour', declared Firth, 'and also by the fact that it was regarded as an unskilled calling so far as its lower ranks were concerned.'[85]

Among those seeking to raise the standing of domestic service through an effective training programme was the Girls' Friendly Society (GFS). This was established in 1874 as a Church of England voluntary organisation which combined crusading zeal to promote religious faith, domestic duty and moral purity among young females with an interest in the welfare of servants. They formed a substantial proportion of its working members, comprising 49 per cent of membership in 1906.[86] Even twenty years later, when GFS membership had fallen from a peak of 197,493 in England and Wales in 1913 to 141,523 in 1926, nearly 30 per cent of the girls were still in domestic employment.[87]

From an early stage the society set up servant registry offices to bring together employers and maids. It also arranged for the training of workhouse girls as servants and provided homes and lodging houses for those out of a place, until they could obtain fresh employment.[88] However, by 1914 the supply of maids was failing to keep pace with the demand for them even in the GFS's own registries. The greatest need was for girls with basic skills who could fill posts as general servants, cooks, housemaids and parlourmaids. It was in these circumstances that in April 1914 the Society decided to launch a 'standardisation' scheme whereby those working in GFS training homes and lodges could, after six months' experience, enter for a qualifying examination in theoretical and practical housework. A special curriculum was drawn up and a textbook, *Instruction in Housecraft*, was published. The aim was to show that girls who passed the examination were not only showing that housework merited a 'skilled' status, but that they themselves deserved better pay and conditions than unqualified co-workers. In this context the use of the word 'Housecraft' in the textbook title rather than 'Housework' was instructive. However, the scheme was scarcely launched before the First World War broke out. Many thousands of domestics left the industry and those who remained were able to gain enhanced wages, as workers were scarce, without the need for qualifications. By June 1919, therefore, just thirty-six girls had passed the preliminary examination of the standardisation scheme.[89]

Despite this disappointing start, the GFS decided to persevere with its plan. However, it soon became obvious that if domestic work were to be transformed in the way desired, a wider cross-section of the servant population would have to be involved. To that end support was needed from other organisations working with female domestics, such as the Metropolitan Association for Befriending Young Servants (MABYS), which was particularly involved with former workhouse girls, the Young Women's Christian Association (YWCA) and the National Council of

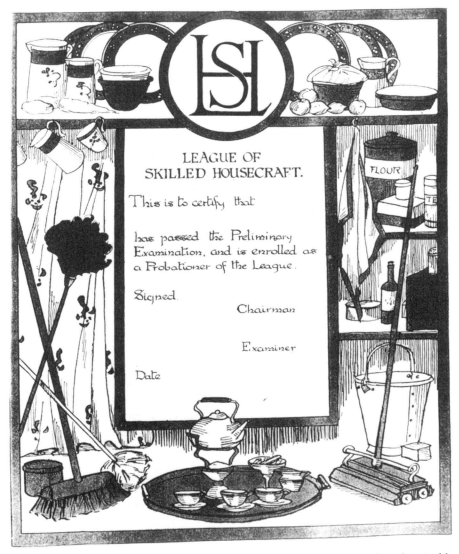

Probationer's certificate of the League of Skilled Housecraft adorned with suitable symbols of domestic work. (*Girls' Friendly Society*)

Girls' Clubs. Representatives from these groups met in December 1921 and formed the League of Skilled Housecraft. It began work early in the following year, under a central board drawn from members of the GFS, YWCA, MABYS and other bodies, plus representatives from the Board of Education, the Ministry of Labour and the London County Council. The curriculum followed that of the earlier standardisation scheme and League examinations were based on the same textbook as the previous arrangement. Candidates had to be over seventeen years of age (although later a special 'junior' category was introduced) and preferably under thirty. They must have worked as servants for at least six months before taking the examination and they must be female. The examination itself was divided into two parts. Success in the preliminary stage led to qualification as a probationer (a term also used for trainees in the nursing profession). Those who wished to become full League members, entitled to wear its badge and distinctive uniform, had to take a second, advanced test. The practical part of the examination was supervised by qualified domestic science teachers, in co-operation with local education authorities. The written test was set by the head of a leading domestic training school.[90]

Despite initial interest – the GFS Annual Report for 1923 suggested 300 or more girls had qualified as probationers – the scheme soon ran into administrative and financial difficulties. After some months of confusion, in 1925 the GFS assumed sole responsibility for the League and new preliminary examinations were arranged in the spring of 1926. Later, representatives of the Girl Guides, MABYS and the National Council of Girls' Clubs again joined the supervisory committee.

By 1927 when the first report of the reformed organisation was issued, 451 girls had become probationers since the scheme's inauguration in 1922 and a number of them were preparing for the more advanced examination or had already become members. Two years later 552 girls had passed the Junior and Preliminary examinations and there were 69 full members of the League.[91]

However, at a time when there were around 1.3 million female servants in England and Wales these figures were derisory. The scheme had failed to meet its objectives, not least because at a time of high female unemployment, girls were able to get jobs as servants with little or no training, except perhaps that given by the government-backed CCWTE. Attempts to present the occupation as a skilled profession must have seemed a mere sham to most maids. In addition, the subordinate social role of female domestics was only too obvious, while the League itself failed to offer coherent training facilities (beyond those provided by its textbook and examination syllabus). Finally, it was always short of funds. This hampered both administration and its ability to publicise its work.

When in 1929 Margaret Bondfield presented certificates to successful candidates, she emphasised the League's importance in raising the reputation of household service:

You are the pioneers in the Crusade to lift domestic work entirely from the unfortunate and bad conditions that have existed in the past; you are helping to bring domestic service up to a high level.[92]

Yet it was already clear that these modest efforts were incapable of improving servant status. The League continued to function and to hold examinations, but the number of candidates coming forward dwindled. In 1936, there were just twenty-five of them, of whom thirteen passed the probationer grade, one the junior qualification and eleven obtained the final certificate.[93] The scheme finally petered out during the Second World War.[94]

Less ambitious efforts at servant reform included the YWCA's Blue Triangle Home Service Corps, which began operation in 1919. It was centred upon a hostel opened by the Association in London for about twenty-eight workers who were trained and tested before becoming Corps members. They went out on a daily basis, earning

Presentation of the League of Skilled Housecraft Certificates by Lady Bertha Dawkins at the Guildhall, Gloucester, on 25 November 1931. (*Girls' Friendly Society*)

10s or 12s 6d a week, according to their skills and experience, plus free board, laundry and uniform and with National Health Insurance contributions paid, for a forty-eight hour working week. Overtime was paid at the full rate received from the employers. A similar organisation was set up by a Mrs G. H. Savournin, again based upon a hostel and with workers going out daily. As with the YWCA scheme, the employer paid the organiser, who then passed on an agreed amount to the workers.[95] Such initiatives were designed to overcome girls' objections to residential service and to ensure that employers obtained efficient staff. However, they proved of little significance in the wider domestic sphere.

The Norland Training Institute (later College) for nursery nurses was, by contrast, far more successful in establishing the superior professional standing of its specialist graduates. Norland was opened in 1892 and by 1903 was charging fees of £66 for a course lasting about nine months.[96] It was targeted at the daughters of professional families and Mrs Ward, the founder, said one of the reasons for setting it up was to offer 'a new career to gentlewomen by birth and education, and to girls of education and refinement'.[97]

Employers who recruited the qualified nurses had to abide by certain conditions. No Norlander was to be asked to eat with the servants, although 'the presence of a nursery-maid at the nursery meals' would not be objected to. She was not to be expected to scrub floors or carry coal; other stipulations covered such matters as salary, holidays, laundry and opportunities for exercise and Sunday worship.[98] When taking up an appointment Mrs Ward advised her students to make sure they had their 'silver-backed hairbrushes with them' and to display these 'so as to impress the servants'.[99]

To confirm the Norlanders' special status they had to wear a distinctive college uniform when on duty. It was similar in many ways to that worn by hospital nurses. Likewise, the informal term 'nanny' was never to be used to describe one of the college graduates, while they themselves must observe strict rules of conduct when at work. These included a prohibition on shopping when out with their charges and on gossiping with groups of fellow nurses or nannies whom they met.

The instruction was Froebel-inspired, but had a major practical input. It included classes in domestic skills, combined with academic lectures, singing, story telling, kindergarten games, walks, needlework and other handicrafts. Much emphasis was placed on the kindergarten aspect and upon instilling moral values, including neatness, tact and punctuality. Most importantly, no child was to be hit. 'The Norland Institute does not recognise the necessity of whipping or slapping and therefore no Norland Nurse is allowed to use corporal punishment in any form.' In the early days three months were also spent in training at a children's hospital.[100]

By 1930 the college's curriculum had been extended to include the principles and practice of education, child psychology, hygiene, nursery management, nature study and children's drawing.[101]

Although not all Norland nurses were able to meet Mrs Ward's exacting standards, there is no doubt that her emphasis on the exclusivity of her students led to an acceptance by employers and fellow servants of their superior standing. They were still seen as 'special' at the end of the twentieth century.[102]

A few other training colleges and schools followed in Norland's wake, such as the Princess Christian Nursery Training College, which opened in Manchester in 1901 and the Welgarth Nursery Training College, which opened in London a decade later. By 1925, when the Association of Nursery Training Colleges was formed, there were eleven constituent members.[103]

Yet, as Jonathan Gathorne-Hardy has pointed out, despite the social and, to some extent, the pedagogical significance of these initiatives, the total of nurses and nannies trained in these pioneering establishments was small. Between 1892 and 1939, 3,832 girls entered the Norland Training Institute, of whom perhaps 200 failed to qualify and a further quarter or third subsequently married. On numerical grounds, therefore, the 'effect of the college-trained Nurse was negligible'.[104] The vast majority of nursemaids continued to be trained by other nannies in private households, as they had always been.

Training organisations concerned to raise the status of domestic workers thus formed only a tiny part of the total servant network. Far more important were such traditional sources of supply as the poor law (or from the 1930s, public assistance) institutions, the orphanages and the Home Office-recognised corrective agencies like reformatories and industrial schools (or approved schools as these two last categories became in 1933). Institutions for unmarried mothers, run on punitive lines, were also involved, with the girls who used their services invited to spend one or two years on unpaid domestic work in recompense for the assistance they had received from the institution at the time of their confinement.[105]

The instruction provided by these organisations differed widely in quality and effectiveness. Often to reduce an enterprise's running costs unpaid trainees were used to cover basic domestic needs.[106] Sometimes cash was earned by having commercial laundries on the premises or by sending inmates out as day servants. In 1919 the chief inspector of reformatory and industrial schools condemned the practice adopted in some places of classifying as 'industrial training' the employment of boys in laundries and 'in domestic work at houses in the neighbourhood of the school'. Henceforth such practices were to cease.[107]

But these methods continued to be applied in institutions elsewhere. Dorothy Hatcher, who was sent by the Tenterden Poor Law Board to a small servant training home in Maidstone, remembered being despatched twice a week to a local household to gain experience. The resident servants there gave her odd jobs to do, such as wood chopping and polishing, but 'I didn't learn much except how to talk about my employer behind her back'.[108] Again, at Dr Barnardo's Village Home at Barkingside in Essex, a laundry was run by around a hundred girls during the 1920s and 1930s. It washed nearly a million articles each year from within the institution itself.[109]

The training regimes in these places were strict and were more concerned to meet the institution's own needs than to equip the inmates for life in private service. Critics pointed out that while poor law girls could scrub floors with commendable zeal they had little idea of how to use ordinary household equipment. This lack of relevant experience, coupled with the uncertain family background of many of the youngsters and their puny physique, made upper middle-class mistresses reluctant to recruit them. Typical of the comments made on girls training for service at the Central London District (Poor Law) School in June 1926 were: 'Neat little maid but small', or 'Pass for Service but very doubtful if she will do well . . . ear trouble; slightly deaf'.[110] In the main such girls went to the households of small tradespeople who wanted cheap labour or to other institutions. Epsom College, for example, recruited two maids in 1927 from the Shirley Poor Law Schools in Bermondsey, London, and a third in 1928. In 1927 out of twenty girls leaving the school, all except one became a servant, although among the boys who left there were varied occupations, including posts in shops, offices, trades and the army.[111] Girls were recruited by employers in Teignmouth, Tonbridge and Bexhill as well as in the London area.

A house-parlourmaid placed in service at the age of fifteen by a charity, after one month's training in a Home (following her father's death), summarised the feelings of many of the girls when she declared bitterly:

> It is usually the retired tradesman and his wife and family . . . a house in some London suburb, who engages these innocent girls and makes them work from morn till night without a break. . . . They are expected to cook, wash, do housework, for the magnificent sum of £8 a year, perhaps.[112]

Their institutional background also made many of the youngsters feel insecure and inferior when they mixed with other people. As a result of their years of obedience and unthinking acceptance of rules and regulations, they were said to lack initiative and they were often emotionally stunted. An experienced social worker claimed she had never heard a former pupil of a poor law school 'speak with anything like gratitude or affection of the school or anyone in it'. They looked back on their training 'not for its teaching of love and other virtues, but only for its punishments'.[113]

A girl sent from a Home in the north of England by her public assistance committee, to be a servant in a middle-class London house during the 1930s, realised how her upbringing had sapped her self-confidence: 'whenever she went into a shop or entered a roomful of people she felt herself to be different'.[114] Many youngsters, too, were unprepared for a life of social isolation in service after being brought up in the gregarious atmosphere of a children's home. Few knew anyone in their new location, except perhaps other inmates from the institution who had been similarly placed.

Mrs Slade of Welling, Kent, experienced these problems of hard work and social alienation when in 1933, at the age of twelve, she entered the Mid-Kent Training Home for Girls, after leaving the orphanage she had known since she was two. There were twenty girls in the training home under the supervision of a matron and her assistant. It was run by a committee of professional men's wives and 'a few other do-gooders', who dealt with the financial side of its work. As Mrs Slade was still of school age when she moved, at first she attended a day school along with some of the other girls. However, that did not exempt them from domestic chores:

we had to help with the cleaning etc. before going off to school. When we returned for lunch, we were usually met at the door by Matron, broom and brush in hand, ready with a list of the faults she had found in our pre-school work. Dutifully we corrected these before getting our meal. After school, in the evenings, we laboured at mending well worn clothes.

At the age of fourteen and a half, I left school to start my real training. This began in the laundry where everything that was washable was put through the rigmarole of soaking, washing, boiling in a copper, rinsing, and finally put through the mangle. Water had to be pumped up by hand. We wore heavy clogs and thick aprons, working over heavy galvanised baths with scrubbing boards and soap. Incidentally, these same baths were used on Friday nights for our own once a week baths. Old blankets were draped over clothes horses to give a little privacy – the only privacy we ever had. Ironing day was Tuesday, and also Wednesday, and it happened to be my particular job to light a closed fire and heat the low flat irons on either side. All this had to be done before breakfast and as I never ever mastered fire-lighting, I never ever made breakfast on these days. Instead I usually received a few thumps on the back! Housework and cooking lessons came next (I think we spent about six months on each job).

As we progressed to becoming seniors in the Home (i.e. the next to be sent into the outside world) the final part of our training was to act as parlourmaid to the Matron's role as lady-of-the-house. Here we would be shown the comings and goings of the

A young trainee learning domestic and childcare skills at Dr. Barnardo's Village Home, Barkingside, Essex. (*Barnardo's Photographic Archive*)

upper classes. We were all anxious to put in our best appearances at all times because we wanted to get away and earn our own living, or we just wanted to get away.[115]

Mrs Slade eventually began work at the age of about sixteen as a between-maid in a small landed household concerned to keep up appearances on a restricted income.

The Church of England Children's Society (originally known as the Waifs and Strays) was another charitable organisation which prepared its girls for domestic service. As a report of 1937 stated, 'The large majority of our girls are trained for ... service, and demand much exceeds supply'.[116] Not all of the youngsters, however, despite their prolonged conditioning to be hardworking and obedient, remained servants for long, if alternative employment became available. One reluctant recruit went to work on a farm for a family comprising father, mother and three grown-up daughters:

> they looked down at me as if I was dirt ... just because I was a servant and came from a Home they put on me. [I]t was one Sunday. I had to clean the breakfast-room, light the fire, cook the breakfast, take it into them, make the beds, wash up and start to get the veg. ready for Dinner, after that I had to scrub the stairs down, there was no lino or carpet, I had to get all that done by ten so as to go to church with them. I have not got a temper but I had one this morning as one of them told me to hurry up, I threw the scrubbing-brush at one of them and threw the water down the stairs and told them to do it theirselves.[117]

It is not clear what happened to this particular rebel, but often 'unsatisfactory' maids were returned forthwith to the institution from which they came so that they could undergo further training and discipline. However, if they failed again, they would probably be left to their own devices. Little effort was made, in most cases, to identify the children's particular talents and to give them the opportunity to prepare for other occupations.[118]

Dr Barnardo's was one of the major charitable suppliers of young domestic servants. Girls were trained both at the Society's main Village Home at Barkingside in Essex and at some of the smaller centres, from where they were usually placed in situations near at hand, so that on their free afternoons and evenings they could visit the Home for tea and a chat with the house-mother. In several, a room was specially set aside for their use. Dormitory facilities were also offered in one of them, so that those convalescing from illness or looking for another place, or perhaps simply having a short holiday, could find a refuge.[119] At the main Village Home a special Service Girls' Home was provided for these purposes and during her first year in employment each former Barkingside resident was invited to spend three weekends and a fortnight's holiday at the Village without charge. In succeeding years any others who came were expected to make a modest contribution towards the cost.[120]

At Barkingside the training began in the communal cottages where the girls lived, under the directions of the 'cottage mother'. Later they passed into one of the staff houses for more specialised instruction in parlour, house or kitchen work, according to their particular interests or aptitude. Almost every week one or two girls would set off on their service career, equipped with an appropriate outfit valued at £8, £2 of which they were expected to refund from their earnings. The clothes were made in the Barkingside sewing rooms by girls who were being trained in dressmaking. According to the charity's annual reports, care was taken in selecting a place for the young trainees and a representative of the Home would accompany each girl on her interview and again when she went to take up her post. She was expected to stay in this first place for two years and would be supplied with the names and addresses of other former Barnardo girls in the area so that she could make contact with them during her spare time.[121]

The success of the scheme, at least from the employers' point of view, is perhaps indicated by the high level of demand for trainees. In most years around 120 to 140 girls left Barkingside, with a few, deemed especially backward or nervous, going for a six months' probationary period as day servants in the locality and residing in two cottages set aside for the purpose. However, the demand for girls outstripped the supply, as about one hundred applications for maids were received a week. In 1938, when 180 trainees were placed in first situations from Barkingside, there were 4,268 applications for maids by letter or telephone, as well as callers applying in person every day.[122]

From the standpoint of the girls, the prospects were less attractive. Although a few opportunities did exist for them to enter a non-domestic career, the vast majority realised that they were destined to be maids. When two new governors of the Barkingside Village Home took up office in the early 1920s they encouraged the youngsters to 'look upon service more as a profession, with future possibilities of obtaining really good posts, such as Head Housemaid in a big house or Head

Instruction in needlework was an integral part of the preparation of future housemaids at Dr. Barnardo's. (*Barnardo's Photographic Archive*)

Parlourmaid or even Housekeeper and, perhaps highest of all, anyhow more exciting, work under a butler'.[123] Under the regime then introduced the most promising girls went to work in the governors' own house, under the supervision of their maids. Places would then be found for them 'with the households where they knew not only family members but also the "tone" of the staff'.[124] Agnes Bowley, who went to Barnardo's in 1934 when she was twelve, was one who followed this domestic path.

> Once you left school you always wore an apron and cap and had training to go into service. You weren't asked what you wanted to do; you were just told. I was the kitchen maid and that was it. There were loads and loads of cockroaches in the kitchen so I had to put down Keating's powder.[125]

After leaving Barkingside, Agnes went into service with the family of the Prime Minister, Stanley Baldwin. He was an enthusiastic supporter of the charity and in 1938 became President of the Homes. But for Agnes the move was not a happy one. 'Workwise it was worse than Barnardo's', she recollected. She 'slept in a cold attic room, crept downstairs at six in the morning to light fires and scrub long stone passages and flights of stone stairs. The cook would come down to inspect [the] work. "My hands were raw with scrubbing all the time. You were the drab, the lowest of the low."'[126]

Until the 1940s, domestic service remained the major employment for Barnardo girls. As late as 1942, 139 girls out of 193 leavers were still going into household work.

During the war some jobs in factories and other occupations were taken up, but even in 1945 around half of the girls leaving the Homes were still becoming maids. However, during the second half of the decade, attitudes underwent a change. Even in charitable institutions the desire to prepare young residents for household duties declined sharply.[127]

As well as the long-term commitment to domestic training displayed by these established organisations, there were various *ad hoc* attempts in the 1920s and 1930s to reduce unemployment levels by setting up servant-training schemes for men and women. There was, for example, a state-aided Roman Catholic training centre which helped to staff servants' halls at Arundel Castle and at the Archbishop's Palace at Westminster, while in 1937 a centre was opened to train Welsh lads as kitchen assistants and houseboys.[128] In December 1935, St Michael's Grange was opened at Tenterden in Kent to accommodate and train men from the depressed areas to become cooks, house-parlourmen, handymen and so on. After two years over three hundred had been trained and placed in posts and the charity was proposing to open a hostel in London so that the men could be sent out on daily work. In a letter to *The Times* appealing for funds to support this venture, the scheme's sponsors suggested that a system of shift working would provide a solution to many of the current difficulties of servant provision and would be a boon to both employer and worker.[129]

A similar *ad hoc* venture was promoted by the Embankment Fellowship Centre in London. This trained destitute, unemployed men over forty-five for domestic work, with a particular need identified to supply cooks and housemen. Even the Boy Scouts Association became involved, opening a new training centre at Newport, Monmouthshire, in the summer of 1936 to recruit boys aged fifteen to seventeen. It was organised in co-operation with the Ministry of Labour and was designed to help unemployed youths to qualify for domestic jobs. The training included cooking, housework and gardening, as well as scouting, with the whole establishment run as a Scout troop under the direction of a warden, who had been a scoutmaster for many years.[130]

But such small-scale initiatives did little to solve the problem of mass male unemployment. And from the point of view of the reformers, anxious to raise the status of domestic work, they merely helped to confirm the view of sceptics that it was, at least in its lower levels, an unskilled and unattractive occupation which most took up only when there was no alternative.

CHAPTER FOUR

OUTDOOR STAFF

As a small boy Shugborough appeared to me to be a labyrinth of mystery and adventure. . . . I was fortunate enough to follow, with wide-eyed fascination and growing respect, the cabinetmaker, plumber, house painter, . . . electrician, head chauffeur and, most important of all, the head forester and head keeper. From the two last, I learned a deep-rooted love of the countryside and, most particularly, of Shugborough Estate and Cannock Chase.

'*Introduction' by the Earl if Lichfield* to John Martin Robinson, Shugborough
(London, 1998 edn), p. 5.

GARDENERS AND CRAFTSMEN

The situation of outdoor servants differed from those employed indoors in several significant ways. That applied both to their recruitment and to their general conditions of service. Whereas indoor workers, especially in larger establishments, frequently came from far away, it was common for outdoor employees to be drawn from the locality. That was equally true of the jobbing gardener recruited by a middle-class suburban family and the man working on a major landed property. On the Flete estate in Devon, for example, village boys joined the garden staff when they were about fourteen, although if 'the head gardener was very keen to get them, he would sneak them away from school before that'[1] Though they were from the village, they had to reside on the estate in a bothy, or hostel, kept clean by a local woman and adjoining the head gardener's own house. Only in the case of senior outdoor staff, like estate agents, head gardeners and head gamekeepers, or those with specialist skills, was it customary to bring workers in from a distance and on some properties, like Chatsworth, even that did not always apply.[2] Again, while indoor servants resided in their employer's home, those engaged out-of-doors usually lived with their families in nearby cottages. Only young, unmarried gardeners and grooms would be lodged communally in a bothy provided by the employer. Wages, too, were paid on a different basis, with outdoor staff normally getting a simple cash sum plus rent-free housing, while their indoor counterparts received part of their earnings in kind, in the form of bed and board and – perhaps free laundry or, for the menfolk, free livery.

The working hours of outdoor staff also tended to be more regular and generally they would stay put on the property for which they had been hired. They were not

Female students at Studley Agricultural and Horticultural College, *c.* 1934. They were pollinating peach trees and marketing lettuces. (*Studley College Trust*)

expected to travel around with their employers, as was the case with a number of indoor servants. Only in the case of chauffeurs was a peripatetic lifestyle the norm.

There were differences in employers' attitudes towards the two groups too. The craft skills possessed by many outdoor servants earned them a respect which was given to few but the most senior indoor workers. In some households the relationship between the head gardener and his employer was more like a partnership and the resultant warm feelings might lead to the gardener receiving a legacy in his master's will.[3] This was true of the strong-minded garden designer, Gertrude Jekyll, and her head gardeners. However, that did not mean the social divisions between employer and servant were obliterated. Of Albert Zumbach, Miss Jekyll's Swiss-born head gardener, who was with her over thirty years, it was said that she demanded 'intelligent obedience untainted by ideas at variance with her own'.[4] Each day he had to present himself at the house at 10 a.m. to receive his instructions.

There was a slow change in the traditional approach to gardening as new horticultural colleges were opened, designed to give theoretical as well as practical instruction to both male and female trainees and with the promotion of examinations by the Royal Horticultural Society (RHS). The cause of women gardeners was temporarily boosted by the First World War, when many male workers joined the armed forces. However, even before 1914 the principal of Studley Agricultural and Horticultural College for Women had reported that some former students had become head gardeners, while others were working in schools.[5]

Preparation for RHS examinations could take place by correspondence course. In January 1938 an advertisement for one of these beguilingly suggested that whereas once 'anything in the nature of theoretical study' had been considered unwise, now men with diplomas and certificates and limited practical experience are preferred to those with fewer academic qualifications, but with a wider practical knowledge. . . . The remedy, of course, is obvious. The purely practical man must add to this store of theoretical knowledge by intensive systematic study. Our unique system of postal tuition enables you to do this without losing a single day of practical work.[6]

Nevertheless, even in the late 1930s most gardeners still would have learnt on the job, and younger qualified men complained that holding a National Diploma of Horticulture was no guarantee of promotion. 'It seems to me that until the various examinations and their resulting diplomas or degrees are better known,' declared one of them bitterly, '. . . a keen young gardener anxious to get on must look to experience, personality and influence rather than diplomas to help him.'[7]

The fact that the outdoor workers' skills often had a market value outside the sphere of personal service boosted the self-confidence of some. Head gardeners, especially those with a high reputation, could easily become tyrannical. According to the Hon. Mrs John Mildmay White, a country house owner 'was never allowed to do any picking of peaches or grapes. I can remember getting the most fearful telling-off from the head gardener, because I had picked my own peach.'[8] Lady Hyde Parker had a similar experience at Melford Hall with her head gardener, Mr Pomfret. Although not of imposing appearance, he had 'quite an air' about him and this was reinforced by the fact that he never smiled. His dress, too,

> gave one the feeling that he was of importance, for he always wore a black bowler hat, a green baize apron covering the front of his black trousers and jacket, and a white shirt. From the large pocket in the front of his green apron hung pieces of raffia, and inside the pocket were his secateurs. . . . If I took a peach from a wall while passing through the garden on a summer's day, Pomfret knew at once, and in spite of informing me most politely that one was missing, he managed to convey that he knew perfectly well who the culprit was and that he disapproved strongly.[9]

Yet even for him there were limits to independence. When he refused Lady Hyde Parker's instructions to move a rose bush because he considered it the wrong time of year, her husband quickly intervened. He called the head gardener to him and said firmly, 'Pomfret, when her ladyship gives you an order, you carry it out at once. If she asks you to plant the roses with their roots in the air, you do it. Is that understood?' 'Very good, Sir William', was Pomfret's laconic reply, and the rose was moved immediately.[10]

Most senior gardeners were anxious to preserve the mystique of their particular skills. Hence the resentment of some over BBC gardening broadcasts in the 1930s which revealed professional secrets. One head gardener even wrote to the *Gardeners' Chronicle*, the leading trade paper, to complain that, 'Professional gardeners who have been through the mill in bothies' disliked 'the attitude of the amateur who listens to the radio and then dictates to the gardener'.[11] By 'amateur' he meant his employer.

George Miller, head gardener at
Shugborough Hall, 1918-21, seen in
the walled garden in 1919, with his
wife and four children. After leaving
Shugborough he became head gardener
to Lady Blythswood, Penrice Castle,
Glamorgan, where he stayed for nine
years. He then moved to Lawrenny Castle
in Pembrokeshire. (*Arts and Museum
Service, Staffordshire County Council*)

Men who wished to earn a living
outside private service could enter the
market garden and nursery sectors,
or they could take posts in municipal
parks and recreation grounds, which
were increasing in number at this
time. Such local authority positions
were usually better paid than private
appointments and they offered the
prospect of an occupational pension
as well.[12]

Skilled gardeners were valued by
employers because of their ability to
create an attractive setting for a house
and perhaps, as with James Comber,
who worked for the Messels at Nymans,
their skill in building up a great
collection of plants.[13] Loelia, Duchess of
Westminster, attributed her own love of
gardening to the influence of Mr Barnes,
the head gardener at Eaton:

Of course I never actually did anything
myself; I never dug a hole with a trowel
or put a bulb in or anything like that,
but ... Barnes ... was marvellous and
creative, and fulfilled my extravagant
plans.[14]

At Eaton thirty-five gardeners worked outside, and a further eighteen were engaged
in the glass houses. All of them were under the direction of Barnes.

Sometimes the sight of a superior floral display in a friend's garden caused
an employer to encourage the head gardener to achieve higher standards. In
September 1928 Lady Astor wrote to Camm, the Cliveden head gardener, to express
dissatisfaction with the tuber roses grown there. She had seen a rose produced
by Sir Philip Sassoon's gardener which was 'much fuller and an altogether better
specimen than those grown at Cliveden'. Camm was instructed to find out where it
had been purchased and how it had been grown. A month or two later, the required
steps had been taken and she expressed her pleasure at the new display. 'Do take
great care of them so that they will last as long as possible.'[15]

A successful head gardener gave added lustre to an estate by making it a
goal for visitors and an attractive setting for garden parties and other outdoor
entertainments. At Overstrand, near Cromer, tributes were paid to Mr Naylor, Lady
Battersea's gardener, for the way in which he had transformed the unpromising

sandy soil into one of the most beautiful gardens in the country, visited by thousands of people when it was opened on summer Sundays for charitable purposes.[16]

Fred Streeter, who became head gardener at Petworth in the late 1920s, had to undertake a multiplicity of tasks. These included preparing accounts, paying the wages of the under-gardeners, looking after insurances and keeping a record of weather readings. He had to organise garden parties and public open days too, and to ensure that on those occasions everything was looking at its very best.[17] Ambitious men like Streeter also added to an estate's reputation, and to the satisfaction of their employer, by exhibiting successfully at horticultural shows. In the early 1930s almost 400 different varieties of vegetable were grown in the Petworth gardens and he asked Lord Leconfield, his employer, to allow him to begin exhibiting in earnest. He was confident he could cover the expenses involved and any cash surplus would be added to the general garden account. Lord Leconfield agreed.

> York was the first objective . . . Streeter won first in all classes in which he competed, besides gaining a large gold medal for a comprehensive collection of vegetables. That was the start. Then came Blackpool, Southport, Shrewsbury, London, Brighton and Wolverhampton. . . . Petworth exhibits varied according to the season, and they gained gold medals for flowers, fruits, vegetables and orchids.[18]

These successes led to Streeter becoming a member of the Fruit and Vegetable Committee of the Royal Horticultural Society and in 1935 he began gardening broadcasts. Like several other head gardeners, he was a regular contributor to the *Gardeners' Chronicle*.

Flowers and plants were displayed in stately homes all the year round and the gardeners had to be able to provide everything from a buttonhole to a bouquet or a wreath for a funeral. In some houses the gentlemen wore a carnation in their buttonhole and this was renewed when they returned for lunch or tea.[19] Each morning the head gardener or a specialist decorator would arrive early to water the plants and to change them and the flowers, as required. In many larger properties there was a special flower room, equipped with a long table and sink, where the floral arrangements were prepared. There were also slippers for the gardener to change into before he went into the house.

At Cliveden, Frank Copcutt came as decorator in 1928, after doing similar work for the Rothschilds at Waddesdon Manor, where his father was a gardener. He also went up each week to the Astors' town house in St James's Square to arrange the flowers there. Although he was nominally under the head gardener, most of his instructions were given by Lady Astor herself. His working day started at 7 a.m.

> If they was in residence, I'd go straight to the house. Well then I would water, and . . . [do] any arranging. . . . The thing that would hold you up would be getting to the ladies' bedrooms. If you had flowers in the ladies' bedrooms you had to wait till they came out before you could get in. Then I went back to the greenhouse. . . . I

went back later on to arrange the lunch flowers. It would all depend how many there were. . . . She might have a lunch party. Well then it was more flowers to do. . . . And then I wouldn't go back till the evening, and then there would be fresh flowers again on the dining room table for the night.[20]

In less extravagant households the flowers were rarely renewed more than once a day. By the 1930s, some country house ladies were beginning to do their own flower arranging, like the Hon. Mrs John Mildmay White at Flete. She took on the task, but later discovered this had not been popular with the two gardeners who had formerly carried it out. They still had to pick the flowers for her and they had enjoyed coming to the house to arrange them.[21]

Gardening was important, however, not only from an aesthetic point of view, in providing an agreeable setting for a house and a supply of flowers and plants to ornament its rooms, but from the culinary angle, too. It was a matter of pride for hosts to serve out-of-season vegetables and fruit when they were entertaining. At Renishaw in Derbyshire, the Sitwells' head gardener boasted that he could produce fresh peas for two hundred days a year.[22] Bob Gregory, who went as a young gardener to Stoke Bruerne Park, Northamptonshire, in 1932, considered the greenhouses to be the most important part of the gardens for this reason. Most large establishments had at least 'four plant houses, a carnation house, orchid house, propagating house, vineries and peach houses, heated frame, potting sheds and a stove house with messroom', where the gardeners could make tea:

> The propagating houses would . . . be used to grow early cucumbers, melons and tomatoes. . . .
>
> To pick tomatoes at Christmas, the seed would be sown in the middle of September and planted in one of the propagating houses in 12" pots filled with a mixture of farmyard manure and new sterilised loam. The house temperature was maintained at 80°F so that just before Christmas the first tomatoes would be ripe ready for the Christmas dinner . . . as well as new carrots, lettuces and radishes . . . . and mushrooms.[23]

The Stoke Bruerne head gardener was a strict disciplinarian and had high standards. Working hours were from 7 a.m. to 5 p.m., but Gregory and the other young, unmarried men who were in the bothy had to undertake a 'duty week' in turn. This meant they remained on the premises the whole time, taking charge of the greenhouse boilers as well as looking after the watering, ventilation and general care of the plants. That included Sunday and for the extra hours required, the duty man received an additional 10s or 15s a week.[24] The duty week was a normal part of the life of most young gardeners on estates where there were hothouses. Not surprisingly it was unpopular. A gardener remembered that when the duty keys were handed over across the 'dinner table on Saturday', a 'few choice adjectives' were uttered, as one man passed responsibility on to his successor.[25]

Garden staff at King's Bromley presided over by the head gardener. (*Arts and Museum Service, Staffordshire County Council*)

Other rules to be observed at Stoke Bruerne included an insistence that each man arrive for work every day with a clean collar and well polished boots. On Saturdays, the potting shed had to be scrubbed out and all the garden tools oiled and hung up ready for inspection by the squire, Captain Meade. The paths had to be kept weed free and that included the kitchen gardens as well as the pleasure grounds.[26]

One of the gardeners was given the task of taking the day's supply of vegetables to the kitchens. This normally followed consultation between the cook and his or her employer, but at Petworth Fred Streeter was given lists of produce to be grown: 'everything was entered and signed, every day.'[27]

When Streeter first arrived at Petworth, he discussed vegetable supplies with the kitchen garden foreman. The latter commented gloomily that he did not know how it was 'possible to grow enough stuff for that lot. There are so many departments – there's the dining room, the steward's room, the housemaids, the pantry and the servants' hall, besides the kitchens. It's like feeding a factory.'[28] Despite his pessimism, however, there was never any danger of supplies running short.

At Stroke Bruerne the daily vegetables were taken to the house on a special two-wheeled handcart at 9 a.m. 'Everything would have to be in perfect condition and, in some cases, washed', wrote Bob Gregory. 'If anything was soiled the head-cook would reject it. In spring and summer, radishes, carrots and beetroots would have to be bunched, washed and tied with raffia.'[29]

The pleasure grounds, with their flower beds, lawns, hedges, rock gardens, lakes, tennis courts and croquet lawns also had to be kept in immaculate condition. According to Gregory, the tennis courts and croquet lawns were swept with a besom each time they were used. Early in July hedge-clipping commenced: 'all done with garden shears, and great care would be taken with the topiary work which had to be perfect when finished as any mistake would show and be seen for a year.'[30] It took at least three years' apprenticeship for a journeyman gardener to become 'fully acquainted with the propagating and growing of all the vast range of plants and the varied work' the pleasure grounds demanded, in Gregory's view. By contrast, the essentials of kitchen garden cultivation could be learnt in about two years.[31]

The superior standing enjoyed by skilled outdoor workers applied not merely on country estates, with their retinues of gardeners, maintenance men, gamekeepers, chauffeurs and grooms, but to those engaged on smaller properties as well. Even employers who had a gardener for a day or two a week or who recruited a single-handed jobbing gardener-cum-handyman shared this feeling. One member of a middle-class family in Gravesend, Kent, contrasted the considerate treatment accorded the gardener with the dismissive attitude adopted towards the two maids: 'we looked upon him as a craftsman ... I worked quite a lot with him. Learnt gardening from him ... I mean one looked up to him and you had to be very careful how you dealt with him.'[32]

Katharine Hopkinson, the daughter of a leading Manchester businessman, remembered the gardener at her Alderley Edge home exercising power over horticultural matters 'like a grand vizier'. He regarded the garden and its contents as his own property, taking the view that 'he who owned the means of production ultimately owned the product' and should decide how and when it was harvested. So diligent was he that 'weeds were rooted out almost before they had a chance to declare themselves. His flower-pots were washed with the same care that Louisa [the parlourmaid] bestowed upon the Rockingham tea service. . . . I dared not pick a flower or eat a strawberry without permission.'[33] Even Katharine's mother had to exercise great tact in persuading him that surplus flowers and vegetables should be donated to Manchester hospitals or that fruit from the glasshouses might be distributed to friends: 'no premature baby could have been snuggled into its cotton-wool jacket more carefully than Grundy wrapped up in cotton-wool his precious peaches and grapes.'[34]

There was, of course, an immense difference between a jobbing gardener of the kind employed by the Hopkinsons, no matter how skilled, and the hierarchy of experts, with their multifarious duties, employed on the larger landed estates. Precise figures of the number of private gardeners employed are difficult to establish, but the 1921 industrial section of the population census suggested 97,979 men and 1,552 women at work in that year in England and Wales. This compared with 118,739 males and a handful of females employed as domestic gardeners in the 1911 occupational census. In 1921 there were also 9,602 male gardeners' labourers and 277 female gardeners' labourers in private service.[35] Changing definitions make accurate comparisons impossible, but there is little doubt that, as with indoor maids, the majority of these gardeners worked single handed, or perhaps aided by a boy.

This trend was encouraged between the two world wars by the sale and subsequent break-up of many landed estates. That led to a narrowing of career opportunities, compared to the situation before 1914. One disillusioned gardener wrote in June 1938 to complain that when a big establishment was broken up, it frequently fell into the hands of builders, who then constructed a number of small dwellings. Their gardens needed 'only one man, on one or two days a week. Many

An elderly gardener at Noseley Hall, Leicestershire, in the mid-1930s. (*Leicestershire Museums, Arts and Records Service*)

people are taking smaller establishments; . . . they make gardening a hobby, and only employ a man to do the rough work.' That meant better times for jobbing gardeners, 'but not every gardener cares to take on jobbing work, especially those who have been used to good service'.[36]

Another man lamented the lack of opportunity for workers to meet together. In the past there had been local gardeners' societies and these had encouraged contacts between those residing in a given area, but in the late 1930s, 'one may live in a district for some considerable time without meeting fellow gardeners in the neighbourhood'.[37]

Contemporary job advertisements confirmed the trend. Even when head gardeners were requested it was often mentioned that they were to be 'working'. That meant they would have a very small staff, rather than exercising a broad supervisory role as men like Fred Streeter at Petworth and Mr Barnes at Eaton were able to do. Jobbing gardeners might be expected to combine their horticultural activities with work as a chauffeur or a groom, or they might be required to run an electric power plant if their employer generated his own electricity. Typical of many was an advertisement in *The Times* of 11 April 1934, for a gardener-chauffeur-handyman, aged twenty-five to thirty-five, 'must be experienced and good mechanic', or an appeal from a Sussex employer in the same newspaper on 17 April, for a 'reliable Chauffeur-Gardener, with knowledge electric plant'.

The high unemployment of these years led a number of men to take such positions when they were unable to find work in their own trade. This applied in 1932 to Mrs Hilda Rickard's husband. Mrs Rickard had been a servant before her marriage and she and her husband decided to take posts with a naval captain's widow as cook-general and chauffeur-gardener, respectively. It was a miserable experience:

> I have never met a woman with such a temper! . . . Heaven help us if our clock didn't show the same time as hers, the car had to be at the front door at 11 o'clock on the dot, not one second before or after! We lived on kedgeree & rice pudding. The store cupboard was kept locked.[38]

They stayed for about two years until Mrs Rickard became pregnant. The mistress 'was furious and we had to go'. Fortunately, her husband got another job and their spell in service came to an end. The fact that they were living in their employer's house and that Mr Rickard was not an expert, but had taken the post as a last resort, doubtless contributed to the autocratic treatment they received.

Most single-handed places were in middle-class households, but with rising taxation, heavy death duties and falling agricultural incomes, a growing number of country house owners had to economise as well. That applied to the Brocklebanks of Bartlow House. They were members of a shipping family and in the mid-1930s their single gardener, Willy Albon, looked after 'the lawns, the bedding on the terrace by the house, and the large walled garden. He mowed until dark on summer evenings with no overtime pay.' For these long hours of devoted service he received just £1 10s a week. And when the family were in London for the Season, he would despatch a hamper of vegetables each week for use in the town house. The contents were listed carefully by his wife.[39]

Elsewhere, as at Pilgrims' Hall in Essex, there might be a good deal of overlap between the garden and the estate home farm. Tom Roscoe, the Lancashire-born head gardener, also ran the farm and the four gardeners shared their time between the two enterprises. 'Haymaking and harvest saw the whole male workforce simultaneously assembled, sustained by tea and beer sent out from the house.'[40] Nevertheless, the head gardener spent much time in the vinery and the other greenhouses which produced peaches, nectarines and pot plants for the conservatory and the porch.[41]

Even major owners were hit by the world recession of the late 1920s and early 1930s. At Petworth in 1931, the garden staff was cut from over thirty to sixteen. To achieve this the number of ornamental beds was reduced and the garden layout simplified.[42] At Shugborough still more extreme measures were taken. The old kitchen garden was let to a market gardener and a new kitchen garden was opened up. The market gardener took on some of the redundant gardeners and the head gardener left. When a new head came in 1938 he was unable to live in the house allocated to the post because this was occupied by the market gardener. Lord Lichfield offered to end the latter's lease, so the new man could assume control of the whole property once more, but he declined. With a staff of only three or four he thought it would be too much to manage.[43]

Advertisements in the *Gardeners' Chronicle* reflected the changing environment. Sometimes former employers or estate agents connected with the sale of a property would give a recommendation to boost an applicant's prospects of getting a new post. Among several such notices in the issue of 23 February 1935 were the following:

> Albany Ward, Esq, highly recommends his late HEAD GARDENER to anyone requiring a thoroughly reliable man. Life experience all branches. Left through sale of estate. Age 34, married, one child.

And

> Mr Jones Lloyd higly recommends W Skipper as GARDENER, HEAD or good SINGLE-HANDED. Life experience Inside and Out; good references. Married, age 37, 1 child. Leaving through reductions. - The Lodge, Newton Cottage, Chester.

Where redundancies occurred, older men (even former head gardeners) and those with large families found difficulty in getting fresh employment. Even at the beginning of the century Joseph Addison, head gardener at Lyme Park, Cheshire, considered himself fortunate that no mention was made of his five children when he was interviewed.[44] But in the 1930s the situation was far worse. In 1935, there was considerable correspondence on the subject of older applicants in the *Gardeners' Chronicle*. One writer complained of men being rejected by people 'often old enough to be our parents and yet at the same time they themselves continue in active business with far less excuse'. Employers were looking for a combination of youth and experience, 'but if it be possible to combine both in other occupations, it is not so in gardening'.[45]

Nonetheless, advertisements continued to impose age limits upon applicants, while, often enough, wives or other family members were expected to work in the house when needed. In February 1938, for example, a Godalming householder appealed for a 'capable Head Gardener' to look after a 2 1/2 acre plot. 'Garden boy. Two cars to clean (no repairs). Wife to work daily in house. Wages 65s per week and cottage.'[46]

The difficulties created by this situation can be appreciated when in one issue of the *Gardeners' Chronicle*, for 22 January 1938, there were twenty-three vacancies advertised (three for head gardeners and the rest for single-handed posts, journeymen and so on). By contrast, sixty-three advertisements were inserted by men offering their services, including thirty-six seeking posts as head gardeners. The following week there were thirty-seven vacant posts advertised and sixty-two insertions by men and boys offering their services.

Furthermore, since most estate gardeners lived in a tied cottage, when they lost their employment they also lost their home. Peter Robinson, who worked for a member of the Sandeman port family in the late 1930s, commented bitterly that once 'you are in a tied cottage you have got no chance. They can play around with you as they want; . . . My job was a good one, . . . but they never paid good money under those conditions.'[47] When the Second World War broke out he hoped that this would enable him to sever the link between employment and housing, but in practice, once the war ended he returned to private gardening and to tied accommodation.

These general anxieties were made worse by the fact that until February 1937 private gardeners (like other private servants) were excluded from the benefits of Unemployment Insurance. If they were unable to find a fresh position they might have to rely on poor relief, or its 1930s successor, public assistance, with what many felt was its associated social stigma. Other private outdoor workers, such as gamekeepers, ghillies, grooms and stable men remained outside the unemployment scheme until 1938. Only if they worked for profit-making concerns were they covered from the beginning of the 1920s, like most other manual workers.[48]

Rising unemployment and cuts in staffing levels also affected the bothy system. Before the 1930s it was common for young, unmarried men wishing to become head gardeners to move from estate to estate to gain experience of different working conditions. According to Frank Copcutt, who rose from a decorator to be head gardener at Cliveden, 'you wasn't a gardener in my day unless you lived in a bothy'. When he came to Cliveden there were two bothies in use for the gardeners, each containing six men, with a further bothy for the unmarried grooms. At that time between twenty and twenty-five men worked in the gardens, twelve of them in the greenhouses, three in the kitchen garden, two in the fruit garden and the rest in the main pleasure grounds or occupied as carters. 'You wouldn't see a dead leaf or a dead twig out in the woods, and in the driveways.' But 'when the depression came along jobs was difficult to get, and there was no dole for agricultural workers which you was classified as, so of course the bothy chaps didn't move quite as much because they didn't know what sort of camp they was going to put their foot in. . . . So . . . that did stop moving around a bit.'[49]

This situation added to the power of head gardeners, who were responsible for the hiring and firing of their subordinates. Albert Butler, who was an under-gardener at Sudeley Castle in the late 1920s, recalled that men like him 'could move on to another job only with the help' of their head gardener. 'The Sudeley gardener kept me waiting a whole year before he helped me to go to Arbury', in Warwickshire. However, that proved a fortunate move because from the outset Albert and the owner, Sir Francis Newdegate, became good friends. It was in Sir Francis's employ that he eventually became a head gardener himself.[50]

On some cash-starved estates surplus produce was sold to local shops or even to Covent Garden. At Nidd Hall in Yorkshire, the butler's son, Arthur Inch, remembered flowers, fruit and vegetables being disposed of to a high-class greengrocer and florist in nearby Harrogate. 'I often used to assist the gardeners . . . to pack carnations, hothouse melons, peaches, nectarines and all kinds of other fruit and vegetables and then go in the lorry to Harrogate for the ride.' Nidd Hall was unusual in that it had two head gardeners, one being responsible for the flowers, lawns and pleasure grounds and the other in charge of the kitchen garden and the growing of fruit and vegetables. They were assisted by twelve under-gardeners, some of whom lived in the bothy or cottage set aside for them. A village woman came daily to cook their main midday meal and keep the premises clean. She also did the washing up and prepared tea for them before going home. The remaining meals the men got for themselves.[51]

The standard of cultivation was affected in many places because things had been allowed to run down during the First World War, when large numbers of gardeners were called up. That applied at Aynho Park in Northamptonshire. When Ted Humphris went there as a garden boy in 1915 there were nine on the staff, including himself. By 1917 that had been reduced to three over-age men, including the head gardener, and one boy – Ted. Early in 1918, temporary help was obtained from a man invalided out of the army. Ted welcomed his advent: 'I soon realised how fortunate I was to be working alongside an expert plantsman.'[52]

The return of peace saw Aynho staff numbers rise once more, only to be cut in the autumn of 1920 for financial reasons. Two men had to leave and the foreman resigned of his own volition when the bothy was closed. At the age of nineteen Ted was put in charge of the greenhouses and decorating the house with flowers and plants. He had a boy to help. 'I was allowed to retain the heat in the four vineries and the two stove houses, but all the others including the peach houses now became unheated.'[53] This regime lasted for two years, until conditions improved. Then in 1928 the squire died and with heavy death duties, economy again became the order of the day. The head gardener retired and Ted took his place, with a smaller staff:

. . . for the first time we were required to sell all surplus produce to supplement the upkeep of the gardens . . . the larger my profits the more funds were available for the upkeep of the greenhouses. With this in mind I quickly cultivated a local market for the surplus produce, fruit, flowers and vegetables. No peaches or nectarines were sold locally however, as they were despatched to Covent Garden Market. . . . Home-grown tomatoes were in great demand and so I decided to grow them in the old vine and peach borders. . . . Early potatoes were another good paying crop.[54]

Students working in the vinery at Studley Agricultural and Horticultural College in 1937. On 27 June 1938, the *London Evening Standard* commented on the rising demand for women gardeners in the outer suburbs, with girls earning around £3 a week. (*Studley College-Trust*)

Apart from casual help hired in the evenings and at weekends, the work force at Aynho consisted of Ted, two other men and 'a high spirited boy who was fond of practical jokes'.[55] Yet, despite all the pressures, the young head gardener found time to develop an interest in the hybridising and raising of new plants and in extending his knowledge of orchid growing, which led, in January 1938, to him being awarded a Certificate of Cultural Commendation for an exhibit entered at the Royal Horticultural Society Hall in London. That proved to be the start of a long period of exhibition gardening and of the awarding of certificates for his plants.[56] In his case, his work became his hobby. Yet at the same time he had to spend long hours labouring to meet his employer's demands for lavish floral displays in the mansion and a wide range of fruit and vegetables for the table, all with minimal outlay.

The growing importation of exotic fruit, such as pineapples, led some employers to cut back on their gardening expenditure. Instead of growing such luxuries in their own hot houses they began purchasing them from a shop. Commercial flower cultivation, too, was expanding and attractive displays could be obtained from florists, especially in the larger towns. 'In this situation', noted Joan Morgan and Alison Richards, 'employers began to reconsider the wisdom of diverting immense resources into maintaining acres of glass and tropical temperatures if items such as winter pineapples and collections of exotic plants had ceased to confer major social advantages.'[57]

All this undermined the head gardener's standing and led to a decline in the importance of his domain. A few men reacted by seeking to defraud their employers. At Erddig, near Wrexham, the gardens became sadly neglected after the First World War and the head gardener, Albert Gillam, concluded there was no future there for him and his badly paid staff. In consequence, he arranged with a local tradesman to sell the wheels from the rarely used family carriages. He told his employers that these were no longer safe and when they were taken out of use he disposed of the wheels.[58] Elsewhere head gardeners asked suppliers for commission before placing an order for seeds, plants or any other items. This provided a useful addition to their income.[59]

A number of gardeners poached game, in order to supplement their diet and also, perhaps, for the excitement. At Brocklesby Park in Lincolnshire, where Bob Gregory went as general foreman in 1937, he soon discovered that many estate workers, including the married gardeners, were expert poachers. Once when he went to see the pleasure-ground workers on a late November afternoon he asked them if they were going with him to collect their belongings, as it was nearly dark. They replied that as they were in view of the mansion's front windows they could not go until the butler had closed the shutters. Gregory waited with them, and once the shutters had been fixed,

> the men went to their workshed and brought two long canes at the end of which was fixed a rabbit snare. They then went to one of the big cedar trees where some pheasants were perched on the lower branches and promptly snared two for their Sunday dinner. This was the silent method of catching pheasants; guns made too much noise! [60]

To attract the birds to particular trees, before the shooting season began they would take some wheat in their pockets when they went to work. Then, during the afternoon, they would scatter this under the trees to feed the pheasants and encourage them to roost there. Once they were fattened up it was time to capture them.

In addition to having large gardens, many country houses had their own dairy. At Shugborough Hall, one man who started as a garden boy in 1931 remembered that his first duty each day was to go with a two-wheeled truck to collect milk from the home farm. On the return journey he stopped at the dairy where he took some of the milk to be separated for cream. He then returned to the Hall, leaving milk in the kitchen and taking cream to the stillroom. There he was usually given a cup of coffee and a piece of cake before returning to the kitchen to collect the chef's order for the day's vegetables.[61]

Cliveden, too, had a dairy farm, with twelve people working on the dairying side and another ten engaged in arable farming under the direction of a farm manager. Lord Astor prided himself on the quality of the tuberculin-tested milk produced and it was supplied to non-estate consumers as well as to Cliveden itself. The Astors even took one of the cows with them when they went on family holidays to their homes at Sandwich, Kent, and Jura in Scotland.[62] Initially, the dairying enterprise was run by the head gardener, Mr Camm and his wife Margaret, but a specialist overseer was later recruited.[63] Mrs Spilman was one of the dairy maids in the early 1920s. She came after undergoing training at Studley Agricultural and Horticultural College, where she was in charge of the dairy for around two years. At Cliveden, the dairy maids began work at 5 a.m. Each girl had about six cows to look after:

you had to wash them, you hosed them down first and then washed them with a scrubbing brush, all their back parts . . . and then you went and changed into your white overalls and little white hat, and milked into these funny little buckets with very small tops . . . and that was quite an art in itself, I mean you hadn't got to spill it about the place.[64]

The four dairymaids lived together in a cottage with a housekeeper to look after them. At weekends Lady Astor often came down with her house party to show off the dairy: 'if there was anybody very important we were sort of warned that they were coming, and everybody had to be looking very nice.'[65] Bonuses were paid to the dairy workers, doubtless to encourage high productivity.

Outside workers such as grooms, coachmen and chauffeurs were often in close daily contact with their employers. Although coachmen dwindled in numbers and importance in the inter-war years as motor transport took over, there were still many grooms employed to look after the horses and ponies used for riding and for drawing small traps around the pleasure grounds and park. At Cliveden, Michael Astor remembered Brooks, the head groom, teaching him to ride. Brooks was a dapper man, with a brisk manner and for riding 'with the young gentlemen he wore breeches, gaiters and a bowler; for driving them in the tub-cart a dark brown suit and a bowler; and for taking them out hunting, top boots and a short felt top hat'. According to Astor, 'Brookie . . . took a pride in his work, in his horses and, I think, in us. His job was simply to take us riding and he made it as interesting as he could.'[66]

But the workers on the estate saw Brooks in a less favourable light, regarding him as a martinet who made the lives of the grooms a misery. Many left after a week or two. As one man put it,

You used to get a medal if you'd been there for about six weeks. The fellow that was in charge there was Brooks . . . and these fellows used to run around. They used to get a drink of tea and I've seen them running back to work . . . and everything was . . . spick and span in there – and every morning, exercising and coming back . . . they used to be swilling down those cobble stones out there . . . and it could be freezing, and they was doing it, and they'd be throwing down sand after them, but it was done – and I've heard fellows say you'd get a long service medal for six weeks there. They were all different every time you'd see them.[67]

There were four grooms employed at any one time and they shared a bothy in the stable yard. They began work each day at 5.30 a.m.

If employers were keen hunting men – or women – there was a good deal of work for the grooms to do, but overall the greater use of motor vehicles inevitably made many coachmen and grooms redundant. Sometimes, as at Lyme Park, Cheshire, or Pilgrims' Hall, Essex, a former coachman learned motoring skills and became a chauffeur. Albert Murrant acquired his new expertise during service in the First World War. When he joined the staff at Pilgrims' Hall he not only looked after

Mr. A. R. Bate, chauffeur to the Meakin family at Creswell Hall, Creswell, in the early twentieth century. (*Arts and Museum Service, Staffordshire County Council*)

the car, but ran the electrical system and, with an undergroom, took care of the remaining horses. He also taught his employers' two children to drive.[68]

Chauffeurs, like footmen, often formed part of a household's public image and, also like footmen, they wore livery. Men seeking posts as drivers often stressed their height, tallness being thought a desirable attribute, as well as their technical skills. 'Exceptionally good Chauffeur-Mechanic, 38 . . . all repairs, own tools, single; tall smart appearance', declared one advertiser in *The Times* during 1934. Many, like Albert Murrant, carried out other duties, such as acting as valet to their employer and perhaps as a loader at a shoot. Thus a 'chauffeur-mechanic of twenty years' experience' offering his services in *The Field*, expressed a willingness to look after 'Lighting plant and would load second gun'.[69] There were many advertisements along these lines in such publications.

The wider use of motor transport from the 1920s meant that staff could be reduced, since one or two chauffeurs would replace a dozen or more grooms and helpers. In 1911 the population census showed 67,228 domestic coachmen and grooms and 25,151 private motor-car drivers in England and Wales. Ten years later the industrial sector of the census recorded 14,512 private coachmen and grooms and 25,857 motor drivers (including 298 women) in domestic employment. Although the figures are not directly comparable because of changes in the census classification, the trend they indicate is clear.[70]

In many ways these were the golden years of the private chauffeur, as Barry Skirrow, the Castle Howard chauffeur, admits. Those who could afford it still chose to be driven by someone else, rather than driving themselves. However, a chauffeur had to be discreet. 'It's part of the job not to hear anything that is going on in the car.'[71]

Wealthy families like the Astors employed several chauffeurs, each with his own particular duties. At Cliveden there were five, including one each for Lord and Lady Astor. According to Noel Wiseman, who became the agent,

> Lady Astor's chauffeur wouldn't drive Lord Astor because Lord Astor had his own chauffeur, and if he wasn't there on the doorstep when he wanted him, if somebody else had taken him . . . there was trouble! . . . Then we had a horse-box driver, carted the horses about; two driver mechanics who also included things like mower repairs when they'd got time. And the young lad he used to run about doing shopping and that kind of thing, as a chauffeur. . . . When the two chief chauffeurs went to London with the lord or the lady, they were fed in the London house kitchen, but when they were here . . . they'd got cottages of their own – their wives were left behind . . . most of the time both of them were travelling.[72]

The day-to-day administration of these large estates was the responsibility of an agent. Often he would be a landed gentleman who had fallen on hard times, but who understood the rudiments of management from personal experience, or like the Flete agent in Devon, he might be waiting to inherit a property of his own. Occasionally, as at Burton Agnes in Yorkshire, one agent would administer two neighbouring estates as an economy measure. Only slowly, as in gardening, did owners begin to demand technical qualifications as well. Noel Wiseman, who went to Cliveden as assistant agent in 1934, had previously spent seven years at the Agricultural Research Institute at Oxford. He later went on to become the agent.[73]

More common, however, was the position of Maj. Basil Kerr, agent for the Eaton estate and according to the Duchess of Westminster, her husband's 'most intimate friend'. He was provided with a large house and domestic staff, as was his colleague, Charles Hunter, who organised the Duke's boar hunting. 'Basil Kerr was the king', but whenever the Duke returned to Eaton, one or other of these men would be invited to dine: the 'wretched wife would be left alone at home'.[74]

The agent had a wide remit. Apart from keeping accounts and records, with the help of an office staff, he supervised forestry work, building and repairs, roadmaking, gardens and, as at Cliveden, had oversight of the home farm and stud farm (although Lord Astor himself took a major interest in the latter).[75] Supervision of the estate maintenance staff was part of the job, aided, perhaps, as at Eaton, Cliveden and Chatsworth by a clerk of works or foreman. For an agent some busy estates, with wagon sheds, a smithy, sawmills and building yard, were more like factories or businesses, rather than private households.[76] Where there was a good deal of hunting, as at Nidd Hall, Yorkshire, or where large numbers of horses were needed for farm work and the woodlands, a blacksmith would be employed. At Killerton, Devon, for example, even in the 1930s there were 150 horses regularly shod at the blacksmith's shop.[77] A smith would also make various iron objects for use on the estate, including hinges and locks, or would repair machinery. At Nidd Hall, Lord Mountgarret, the squire, was Master of the North York and Ainsty

Hunt, so there were hunt kennels on the estate too. The head huntsman lived in a cottage near the kennels and he was assisted by two whips or under-huntsmen.[78]

Many of the craft workers had more than one string to their bow as well. At Kedleston in 1928 Viscount Scarsdale, for example, advertised for a plumber-electrician and a carpenter-painter, while at Dean's Green Hall in Cheshire, the estate carpenter was expected to carry out 'small . . . repairs and outside painting; entire charge of one hunter'.[79] At Eaton, with its lavish staffing arrangements, the clerk of works' department always sent out joiners to all parts of the estate just before the start of the hunting season to ensure the hunting hatches, or gates, were in working order.[80]

At Flete, the house carpenter repaired and wound all the clocks, as well as running the electric power plant. In other households a special 'clock man' came once a week to wind the clocks and effect any necessary repairs.[81]

Maintenance workers were essential to the smooth running of any estate. At Goodwood, Gordon North, the house carpenter, was expected to tackle almost any task. According to the Duke of Richmond and Gordon, 'If one wanted anything, one said, "Where's Gordon?" Gordon *was* Goodwood.'[82]

The largest establishments resembled small villages, both because of the number of people living and working within them and the varied skills they had to offer. Many estates also offered social amenities, such as clubs, societies and seasonal celebrations. But these were always conducted in the shadow of the 'big house', rather than on a spontaneous community basis. Some workers, especially those coming from a distance, disliked the claustrophobic atmosphere this generated. One man who went to Cliveden as a labourer after a period of unemployment in the north-east of England, was wary of the close-knit, deferential world he had entered:

> . . . it was when I'd been there a while I began to see they were all watching one another. . . . In one way, it wasn't a bad job, and on the other hand . . . the more I looked around, I thought estates was . . . queer places . . . people watch each other too much, they're frightened you might get more than he does.[83]

He worked at Cliveden for ten or eleven years, but when war broke out in 1939 he seized the opportunity to escape.

GAMEKEEPING AND FORESTRY

For many owners, the preservation of game, the holding of shooting parties, and the general condition of their woodlands were matters of special interest. At Chatsworth under the 9th Duke of Devonshire it was said that 'sport reigned supreme'.[84]

During the First World War, vast acres of woodland were indiscriminately cut down and both woods and game coverts were badly affected by staff shortages and consequent neglect. Then during the economic depression of the inter-war years numerous estates were so seriously hit that they never recovered. Owners either sold up or ceased to maintain their shooting interests as they were too expensive.

A shooting party in the early twentieth century, including young beaters. (*Museum of English Rural Life, University of Reading*)

(It cost perhaps £1 to raise a pheasant, which when sold as meat might realise as little as 5s.) One estimate suggested that of every one hundred men who, prior to 1914, had run their estates as shoots for themselves and their friends, barely five remained in that position in 1939.[85]

Fifteen years earlier, *Country Life* had lamented the menace posed by 'vermin . . . now that so much land has passed out of preservation. The single-handed keepers who remain are clearly unable to cope with the hordes of furred and feathered varieties which constantly pour in.'[86]

Some estates were hired out to syndicates or to shooting tenants, as at Blair Atholl, where the wealthy American, Mrs de Wichfeld, held a series of shooting parties during the season. According to Ernest King, her husband's valet, there was a constant 'coming and going' when the shooting was under way.[87] In 1928 *The Field* reported disapprovingly that even shipping companies and tour operators had become involved in the business. Early in the year the Cunard Line had made arrangements whereby, in return for a single substantial payment, an American sportsman could be provided with a 'return passage across the Atlantic to the door of the lodge in Scotland, where he would find himself in possession of a grouse moor complete with keepers, ghillies, beaters, ponies and dogs'. The venture proved so successful that other firms, including the White Star Line and Messrs Thomas Cook & Son, entered into competition. They contacted sporting agencies in London with a view to offering American visitors similar facilities to those supplied by Cunard.[88] Such indiscriminate arrangements, in *The Field's* jaundiced opinion, would damage the long-term future of Scottish grouse moors.

Even when owners did not dispose of the whole of their shooting rights, they might rent part to a syndicate, as happened at Elveden, in Suffolk, from the early 1930s. The second Lord Iveagh felt he lacked the time to shoot the whole estate and from 1932 until the outbreak of the Second World War a syndicate of six or seven guns rented about 5,000 acres. The shooting was arranged by the Elveden head keeper, Tom Turner, with the syndicate shooting on thirteen or fourteen days each year. Hand-reared pheasants and partridges were released to make sure that bags were kept at an acceptable level. 'All members of the syndicate were always keen on leaving a good stock of birds each year, and altogether the arrangement was a great success.'[89]

In many places, such as Petworth, owners reduced the number of gamekeepers employed. A Petworth keeper recalled that in his father's day, before 1914, one beat, or territory, had had three men and a boy looking after it. When he took over there were two men and a boy. The size of beats was also increased, which meant that the keepers were responsible for a bigger area.[90]

Game stocks were only kept up if the owner was interested in shooting. At Badminton, the Duke of Beaufort concentrated mainly on hunting, so there were only about five keepers and a head gamekeeper employed. 'We didn't have very many big shoots. . . . It was mainly rabbits in those days', recalled the Duke. 'We did rear a certain number of pheasants, but hunting was the main thing.'[91] At Cliveden, too, Lord Astor had no great interest in game. According to his agent, about a thousand pheasants were raised annually and there were three gamekeepers. But there were only about four shoots a year, 'nothing very big'.[92]

Where economies were unsuccessful, estates might have to be sold. They were then often broken up into smaller lots and disposed of to sitting tenant farmers. As a result game ceased to be preserved or there was at best rough shooting only. In 1923, *Country Life* advised syndicates how they might rent some of this land from the farmers. However, they were warned that if they did so and employed a keeper, he

> should be rather a first-class trapper than an expert in the latest rearing system, for while you can have good shooting without rearing, you get nothing whatsoever without trapping. A second quality of almost equal importance is tactfulness in dealing with every grade of worker on the land. . . . A good keeper, resourceful and all things to all men, is essential to a good shoot.[93]

Game managed under these conditions was very different from the old squire system. A generous distribution of pheasants and rabbits to farmers and villagers was made to compensate them for any damage caused to crops. It was considered particularly important to conciliate farmers, for as one poacher turned gamekeeper commented, a farmer was always about and could 'put his foot on a nest of eggs and no one be the wiser', if he was dissatisfied.[94]

Although more people were shooting at the end of the 1920s than had done so before 1914, the dominance of estate-run sport was in decline.[95] At the same time gamekeepers were fewer in number than before the First World War. That trend was reinforced by the difficulties of the war itself, as even famous shooting estates had to close their Game Department when many of the keepers joined the armed forces. In 1911, there were 17,148 gamekeepers in England and Wales and 5,908 in Scotland. That had fallen to 9,367 in England and Wales and 3,967 in Scotland a decade later. So, while there had been 23,056 gamekeepers and game watchers in Britain in 1911, there were only 13,334 in 1921. Numbers recovered a little over the following years, but even in 1931, England and Wales could muster only 10,706 workers in this category, and Scotland, 4,050, making a total of 14,756 for Britain as a whole.[96]

Advertisements in *The Field* for keepers indicate the problems faced by existing and would-be workers and also that even where gamekeepers were employed they were often expected to operate single-handedly. Great emphasis was placed on their role as a destroyer of rabbits and of a wide range of 'vermin', including rats, stoats, weasels, hawks, jays and magpies. In 1926 and 1927 on the Elveden estate alone over twelve and a half thousand predators were killed annually, including over ten thousand rats and seven or eight hundred stoats each year.[97]

There were more men looking for work as keepers than posts available. In *The Field* on 12 January 1928 there were only thirteen vacancies for keepers of all grades advertised, but there were ninety-two situations wanted. On 16 February, there were just nine vacancies (including one for a river watcher to protect a fishery) and sixty-eight applicants for posts. Many keepers seeking a fresh position gave details of their height and weight, presumably so that potential employers would realise that they were energetic, athletic figures rather than over-weight idlers. Like estate gardeners, those who lost their job lost their home as well, and if they could not get a new post they might have to take up agricultural labouring, with lower pay, probably poorer housing and an inevitable loss of status.[98] It is possible to detect a note of desperation in an appeal in *The Field* on 16 February 1928 from a man seeking a post as a head keeper or a single-handed worker. He declared himself to be

> married, one child; aged 35, height 5 ft. 8 in., weight 11 st. 6 lb.; thoroughly reliable and capable of discharging all duties connected with the work of first-class gamekeeper, including management of large numbers of stock birds of all varieties; duck, quail and partridge rearing, training and working sporting dogs; personally took charge of rearing field, 7,000 to 9,000 pheasants in last two seasons; not afraid to work hard building up run down shoot; three-and-a-half years' service in the late war; rank, sergeant; excellent references past employers; willing for interview anywhere.

In another advertisement, Maj. Wykeham Musgrave strongly recommended the former head keeper at Ashridge Park in Hertfordshire for re-employment, 'owing to estate being sold; life experience pheasant rearing, partridge driving . . . four years present, three previous as Head; married, no family, age 39 years, height 5 ft. 10 in., weight 12 st.'[99]

Some estates, of course, survived virtually unscathed, like Chatsworth or Eaton, where the immensely wealthy Duke of Westminster employed twenty gamekeepers even in the 1930s.[100] Norman Mursell, who came as a young under-keeper in 1929,

Fred, Ted and Will Thurgood, gamekeepers at Terling, Essex, out rabbiting, in the mid-twentieth century. (*Museum of English Rural Life, University of Reading*)

remembered the pride felt by those associated with the lavishly run estate. 'There was a lot of prestige. . . . If anything needed doing it didn't matter what time of the day or night it was, they did do it and wouldn't even think about the extra pay.'[101] This loyalty persisted, despite the duke's apparent lack of consideration for the men. Mursell recounted how on one occasion, he announced that he was going snipe shooting. It was a cold winter's day and he was due to start at 10.30 a.m. The four keepers who were to accompany him were in position by 10.15 a.m., ready to drive the withy beds, where the snipe were found. Time went by but there was no sign of the duke:

> Midday passed and by now we were all frozen to the marrow but dared not move. At 2.45 Sandy Myles [head forester] appeared on the skyline and signalled to us to go to him. . . . It transpired that the duke's instructions had been misunderstood and that he had just left for London in the Rolls.[102]

Other events mentioned in Mursell's autobiography suggest this was no isolated incident.

Gamekeepers, and particularly head keepers, exercised considerable power on an estate, as well as being 'the eyes and ears of the remote places', because they were often about at night.[103] The head keeper's word was law, with regard to his particular responsibility – the raising of game birds for shoots. His status was reinforced by his close relationship with his employer, with whom he consulted before a shooting party was held. Among issues to be decided upon were the direction of drives, the arranging of transport for the guns, the recruitment of beaters, whose task it was to ensure the birds flew over the heads of the guns waiting to shoot them, and the briefing of the under-keepers. Sometimes special consideration was given to important guests, particularly royalty. That applied at Elveden, where King George V shot regularly during the 1920s. According to the head keeper, Tom Turner, this affected the shooting plans for the whole season:

> For instance, the hand-reared birds would be placed on the beats where His Majesty would be asked to shoot. . . . Shoots taking place beforehand would not be allowed to encroach on the area required for the royal party. Thus it was that although earlier parties were held, and considerable bags made on other parts of the Estate, the cream was always left untouched. This required the most careful planning. Once the royal shoot was over the whole territory could be freely shot over a second time.[104]

The objective was to secure the largest bag possible and those estates which offered vast numbers of high-flying birds enjoyed a good reputation in game preserving circles. Repeated failure to achieve satisfactory results could lead to a keeper losing his job; that remained the case even at the end of the twentieth century. [105]

Another responsibility of the head keeper was to arrange for the sale of surplus game, over and above that allowed to members of the shooting party and in so doing to get the best possible price from the dealer. Adequate supplies of cartridges also had to be ordered.

A keeper's knowledge of the countryside and of wild animals often gave him a special rapport with the children of his employer. David Spreckley, who grew up on a Sussex estate, had a close relationship with the gamekeeper, Joe. 'I didn't like my father and Joe really became a substitute father. He took me out, taught me how to shoot and taught me a lot about the land, livestock and the countryside too. I learnt from him and he was a friend.'[106] Mrs John Dower, whose father owned Wallington in Northumberland, remembered George Slade, the keeper, as a 'splendid person', who took the children on the moors, to show them grouse and plovers' nests. He also taught them to shoot and fish. 'We were all taught to shoot at the age of twelve. . . . I cried whenever I hit anything.' George told her father of her dislike and as a result she 'never had to pursue this unwanted sport'.[107]

The head keeper's special position meant that he must be able to converse freely with royalty and other important shooting party guests and yet maintain good relations with his underlings. On shooting days he had to preside with 'quiet authority', while liaising with his employer to ensure the guests were enjoying their sport.[108] John Maclauchlan, head keeper at Chatsworth from 1905 to 1950, also accompanied his employer on private days out on the estate, perhaps shooting rabbits. According to the 9th Duke of Devonshire's granddaughter-in-law, the game books included entries when perhaps a single rabbit was killed next to days when over two thousand pheasants were slaughtered.[109] The close relationship between duke and keeper added to the latter's power on the estate.[110]

To be successful, a head gamekeeper had to bear several major facts in mind. First, he must keep tenant farmers happy by judicious gifts of game and take their agricultural requirements into account, both by timing shoots to avoid damaging the crops and by keeping in check marauding rabbits, hares and game birds.

Second, and most importantly, he must rear and release substantial numbers of game so as to achieve large bags for shooting parties. On most estates that meant pheasants. To this end, eggs were collected from the laying hen pheasants, either from their nests in the wild or from a special laying ground where hundreds of hen birds and a smaller number of cocks congregated. The eggs were hatched by broody hens, purchased from local farmers, rather than by the pheasants themselves. This policy gave the farmers a profitable sideline.

The hatching season began in April or May. The chicks emerged after twenty-four days, and then they were taken with the hens to coops already set out in a large rearing field. There they were fed four times daily by the keepers. The coops also had to be moved to fresh ground each day, to prevent the soil from getting stale. On the Eaton rearing ground there were around eight hundred coops of birds gathered from hatching yards all over the estate. Around twenty thousand birds were reared each year in this way, with about twelve coops to an acre. When the coops were all filled with chicks, each man had more than a hundred to attend to. As the chicks grew they needed extra food, plus fresh water and grit, which involved several journeys round the coops. According to Norman Mursell, that not only meant a great deal of walking, but considerable worry over the welfare of the young birds:

> 'Old' Ted Milton . . . was in charge of boiling the food for the growing chicks. . . . I had to help him with the boiling, a rather tricky job. . . . First, crates of eggs had to be boiled. They were Irish eggs, I remember, 360 to a crate, and to save time and handling the eggs were boiled in the crates! . . . Once the eggs were cooked, the harder grains like buckwheat and hemp were put into the boiler, which held forty gallons. They took longer to become soft than did groats and rice, which were added later. When these were boiled until soft, the fire was withdrawn and maize grit slowly added until the whole mixture was dried off. This brew was added to biscuit meal and egg, which had been rubbed through a sieve, and there you had the feed for the birds. Later, when the chicks had grown, a dried meat called 'greaves' was added and the whole lot mixed into a crumbly consistency by adding barley and bean meal.[111]

Sometimes the diet was varied by the addition of minced rabbit, while herbs might be included for medicinal purposes. Working hours were long, lasting from 6 a.m. until 11 p.m. or even later. On occasion, as on the Benacre estate in Suffolk, a keeper would live on the field in a hut throughout the rearing process: He rose at 4 a.m. to begin preparing the food and when his underlings arrived at 6 a.m. it was in buckets waiting for them.[112]

When the birds, now known as poults, were six weeks old it was time to take them to the woods. At Eaton two or three of the Forestry Department's horse-drawn lorries would arrive on the rearing field at about 3.30 a.m. The keepers, working in pairs, would then drag a sack under each coop and gently load coop, hen and poults on to a lorry. When fully laden it would trundle off to the woods where the coops were unloaded and the sacks withdrawn.[113] After about two hours, the poults were released and were fed in their new surroundings. Initially, they were given food three times a day by the keeper in charge, but as they became firmly settled in their tract of woodland, the feeding programme was cut back. Meanwhile the hens which had hatched them were sold off at about half price, usually to cottagers.

As well as carrying out these tasks a keeper still had to look after his beat. That meant finding wild partridge nests, which would be recorded field by field in his notebook. When the partridges reached the poult stage they formed coveys and the keeper could then estimate how many birds there would be when partridge shooting began in September.[114] Other duties included the destruction of vermin. Vast slaughter campaigns were undertaken. Traps, poison and shooting were used to kill rats, stoats and all the other predators. It was common for the tails and heads of ground 'vermin' like stoats and rats to be nailed to a keeper's gibbet, to indicate his diligence. Rabbits, too, had to be controlled, especially in the early 1920s, when they abounded after the wartime years of neglect. At Elveden from 1920-21 to 1924-25 more than one hundred thousand rabbits were killed each year.[115] Any keeper who failed to curb rabbit numbers risked losing his job, because of the damage they did to crops and young trees. Many were sold to dealers, with rabbits from Eaton ending up in Liverpool and Manchester. Numbers were also given regularly to local cottagers.

The control of poachers was a major concern for most keepers, since the loss of hand-reared pheasants meant the loss of several months' hard work. Norman Mursell described the 'grand feeling when you got a poacher cornered and nabbed him because you had it in your mind, "Well, I beat that devil this time."'[116] Even estate workers poached, despite the risk of losing both home and job if they were caught. For some it was a contest to outwit the keeper, as well as a means of getting food for the pot. For a few it was a way of exacting revenge as well. Cyril Rice, who grew up in a village in mid-Wales and had for a time worked at the 'big house' as a hall boy, claimed to be able to earn £1 a pheasant when he went poaching in the 1930s:

> There were two places I could sell them; one supplied hotels in the area with game. It would be wrong to say that poaching was all poverty-driven. Part of it was the thrill and part of it was that you were giving these old toffs you had to doff off your cap to, their come-uppance.[117]

Cyril's poaching career received a special boost early on when he was given a day's beating at a shoot on the estate and did not receive any of the birds that were handed out to the tenants and other workpeople.

> I think it was because I'd had the audacity to leave them as a hall boy. . . . I was in such a fret that night that I went out and shot six pheasants out of sheer temper and got away with it. From then on . . . I was killing pheasants right, left and centre.[118]

Unlike many men, he was never caught.

The punishment of poachers varied from estate to estate. At Eaton, as at many other places, rabbit poachers were not taken to court. Instead, when keepers caught them they were asked to pay £1 to the local hospital or infirmary and to get a receipt. This was then sent to the estate office.[119] Even in more serious cases the Duke of Westminster was reluctant to prosecute poachers, because he disliked the publicity. Only if they had assaulted the keepers was it likely to happen. In other cases, their names and addresses were taken and their equipment confiscated; they also paid a contribution to a hospital or infirmary.[120]

Nine months of the keeper's year were spent in preparation for the shooting season. This started with grouse on the 'glorious Twelfth' of August. Grouse shooting was the preserve of the rich, because of the high cost of running or renting grouse moors. Many were in Scotland or the north of England, but the Duke of Westminster had a grouse moor in Wales, about 20 miles from Eaton. Norman Mursell took part in a shoot there in 1930, when he accompanied the duke's loader, who was also one of the Eaton keepers. Norman was to act as cartridge carrier and general dogsbody. The two arrived early, ahead of the ducal party, and had an opportunity to meet the moorland keepers before the shoot commenced. All of the loaders, except Norman's companion, were local men, as were the beaters and keepers. Once the duke arrived it was time to start. 'We climbed steeply over fairly rough paths and, being well laden with cartridges, coats and lunch boxes, those of us used to flat country found it rather heavy going.'[121] Eventually, the guns reached the butts and the beaters became visible in the distance, walking through the heather about 40 yards apart, each waving a flag. This helped to put up the grouse and enabled the keeper to see their position. Once the grouse came over in appreciable numbers the guns fired incessantly and the toll of dead birds mounted. They were collected up by men with dogs standing some distance behind each of the butts.

The party then moved off to the next drive. After the second drive there was a halt for lunch. That involved a short walk to a large wooden hut where, to Norman's surprise, two footmen in livery were at the door.

> They had come to attend to the wants of His Grace and his guests, having followed the shooting party up from Chester. . . . His Grace and his guests went inside the hut where a table and chairs could be seen. . . . The keepers, beaters, loaders and dog men, finding what little shade there was, sat down on the heather. . . . The lunch boxes were brought out and the contents polished off. [122]

Two further drives took place during the afternoon before the party descended from the moor to the valley, from where the shooting party drove off to Eaton. Keepers and beaters quenched their thirst at a nearby public house before returning home. Many of the beaters were local hill-farmers who would probably have to carry out almost another day's work when they reached home.[123] Meanwhile, Norman and his companion returned to Eaton by car, taking some of the grouse to be distributed among members of the shooting party. The rest were sold by the Welsh head keeper. At the Hall, the guns were cleaned and the cartridge bags emptied, as was customary at the end of any shoot.

Partridge shooting commenced in September and pheasant shooting in November. Before a shoot began keepers spent several days 'dogging in', that is making sure the birds did not wander from the centre of the estate. Indeed, beat keepers were anxious to ensure their particular territory put on a good display and might stay up the night before a shoot to ensure that rival keepers did not tempt birds away to add to their own stock.[124]

When a shoot was held it was the practice on some estates for beaters and keepers to be dressed in a special livery. At Eaton and Elveden, white smocks were worn by the beaters, and at Elveden they had red collars and a red band on their hats. The smocks were worn over everyday clothes. They not only made the beaters more visible to the guns, but also protected their clothing from thorns and bushes and, to some extent, even from the rain. On Norman Mursell's first pheasant shoot at Eaton in 1929 there were over eighty beaters, mainly recruited from estate staff. Others were paid for their services. The keepers wore a picturesque outfit of a green velvet jacket and waistcoat with white breeches, box-cloth leggings and a hard bowler-type hat with plenty of gold braid, especially for the head keeper.[125]

When the party moved off, each keeper took the beaters allotted to him. A number of them were placed as 'stops', their task being to ensure that once the birds were in the woods they did not escape into the fields and hedgerows again. Meanwhile, the loaders and the lads, like Norman, who were carrying cartridges for them, assembled at the shooting stands. Once the guns reached their respective pegs, the head keeper blew a whistle and the beaters started work. Soon a barrage of pheasants was flying overhead, with the loaders handing over guns and reloading those just fired with great speed, amid deafening bangs. The shooting went on for at least half an hour until the beaters emerged from the bushes and the firing stopped. The 'pickers up' with their dogs then collected the birds, while the guns moved on to the next drive. Meticulous planning ensured that no time was lost between drives. A note of the size of the bag was made before the birds were loaded on to the game cart, to be taken to the Hall larder. At the end of the day the size of the bag was given to the head keeper. The duke's private secretary then typed the relevant figure on to special game cards, which also listed the names of those shooting, the beats shot over and the number each had killed. Every guest had one of the cards placed on the dinner table that night.[126]

On some estates, gratuities were handed to the head keeper by members of the shooting party at the end of the day. At Benacre, the head keeper kept these and shared them out among his staff at Christmas.[127] However, at Eaton tipping was not allowed. Instead, the duke sent the keepers £5 at Christmas.

The forestry department was closely linked to the needs of game preservation on many estates. Small thickets or clumps and larger areas of woodland were planted to cater for the game rather than to produce timber.[128] Equally, the zeal of keepers in curbing rabbit and hare numbers was important in preventing damage to newly planted saplings. At Chatsworth in the 1930s, where the main priority was game, the then Duchess of Devonshire wrote plaintively in a notebook: 'Someone must decide whether rabbits or trees are to be grown on this estate.'[129]

After the First World War there was much replanting of trees, to make good the devastation of the previous four years, when felling had taken place on a massive scale. On some estates, like Cliveden, the main preoccupation of the foresters was to preserve and improve the appearance of the woodlands, rather than to sell timber. Cliveden had three men working in the forestry department during the 1930s.[130]

Eaton, by contrast, had a massive forestry staff of about eighty, under the direction of the head forester, Sandy Myles. Their duties were manifold. Although woodlands had to be preserved, the estate supplied the mills with timber for fencing, gates, and similar items. Myles had to keep a delicate balance between these competing demands. Fencing was supplied free of charge to the estate's tenant farmers, but the work had to be properly executed and Myles himself inspected the finished product. It was not unknown for him to make a tenant dismantle the whole thing and start again because the line of the fence was not straight or its top level.[131]

The trees were felled by hand, with trunks cut down to ground level. Great care had to be exercised during felling, as a false move could lead to disaster. In 1927 a forester on the Duke of Richmond and Gordon's Huntley estate in Scotland died when a section of the trunk fell on him, driving the axe he was holding into his head and fracturing his skull.[132]

Other tasks carried out by foresters at Eaton included planting, thinning and pruning trees, haymaking in the park, hedge-cutting and faggoting, which involved cutting three-foot lengths of thinnish undergrowth and binding them into bundles to be taken to the Hall's 'stick house'. One man worked there full time chopping the faggots into convenient sizes for lighting fires. During the winter months willow wands were harvested from marshy ground for sale to basket-makers and bushes were trimmed and leaves were swept from the drives. Three of the men concentrated on drainage work to ensure a free flow from estate watercourses to the River Dee. The forestry department also directed the maintenance of the nine-hole golf course and provided staff to run the private railway. This was used to haul freight, especially coal, and also had passenger coaches for when there was a shooting party.

However, the main preoccupation of the Eaton foresters, like their counterparts at Chatsworth, was to promote game preservation. That meant keeping large areas of shrubs in a condition to serve as flushing points for pheasants and retaining mature timber, which would otherwise have been felled and replanted, in order to provide roosting places for the birds.[133]

In the deer forests of Scotland, shooting estates provided employment for numerous stalkers, gamekeepers, foresters and ghillies. Just under nine hundred men were permanently employed in this way in the early 1920s. A further 1,178 worked part-time for two or three months a year, attending to the sportsmen when they came north to shoot. It represented a welcome boost to their agricultural earnings.[134]

Many stalkers combined this work with cropping a few acres near their houses and perhaps keeping cattle and sheep. However, it was upon their stalking skills that the success of a shoot depended and, in the long run, the profitability of an estate, in terms of shooting rentals. They had to manoeuvre carefully to guide a would-be marksman over several miles of rough terrain in order to get him in a position to kill his stag. In addition, during the early winter months, the stalkers had to cull surplus hinds. This often meant leaving home at daybreak and returning 'dead tired and chilled to the bone' after dark.[135] 'Because of the very life he leads', concluded *Country Life*, 'the average "stalker" is a man of great reserve', but there was always a 'great satisfaction in seeing a stalk expertly performed'.[136]

CHAPTER FIVE

SOCIAL RELATIONSHIPS

The maidservant's place of business is also her home, and where the employer recognises this and treats her as a member of the household and not as an adjunct, and the maid responds, an atmosphere of mutual affection, loyalty and consideration is engendered that makes happiness inevitable. . . . The domestic worker has unquestionably fewer chances for indulging in or developing artistic, intellectual or athletic interests. . . . Yet the reference by a witness to the domestic worker's lack of opportunity of cultivating a talent for music aroused only ridicule and sarcasm in the daily press.

Report of the Ministry of Labour Committee on the Supply of Female Domestic Servants (London, 1923), pp. 8 and 19

SOCIAL LIFE BELOW STAIRS

The social life of domestic servants was influenced, in large measure, by the kind of household in which they worked, the attitude of their employers and whether or not they were resident. If they lived out, they could keep in close touch with family and friends and choose how they spent their time when they were away from work. In that way they seemed less differentiated from workers in shops, offices and factories and were less likely to be despised by members of their own social class than resident staff. Significantly, a survey based on the 1931 population census for England and Wales suggested that two-fifths of all females in indoor private service and one quarter of the males lived out.[1]

The feelings of many of those living in were expressed in 1923 by a parlourmaid when she complained that invitations out often stated, 'Be sure and do not let it be known you are a domestic. We should not like our friends to mix with servants.'[2] A London cook likewise admitted that when she went on holiday to the seaside she was careful to conceal from the business girls who were her fellow guests how she earned her living. 'I do detest . . . the scornful phrase "only a servant".'[3]

Even relations with the opposite sex might be affected. Margaret Powell, when working as a kitchenmaid in London, remembered a worldly wise fellow servant warning her never to reveal to a potential boyfriend that she was a maid. 'If you do you'll only be called a skivvy and you'll never keep him'. However, as she admitted ruefully, it was impossible for her to pretend she did anything but manual labour, because her hands were so red and raw that they were 'a dead give-away'.[4]

Parents might also influence how leisure time was spent, especially for younger girls. A Scottish maid was forbidden by her mother to go to dances or even to look in the windows of dance halls. On her afternoons off in her first post she had to visit her grandfather in Glasgow each week.[5] Another youngster employed by an invalid lady in Paisley used to walk to a 'Christian meeting in Gaelic' on her free evenings, just for something to do, even though she could not understand it. However, her mother made clear that she disapproved of the girl 'walking the streets at night'. She, too, visited her grandfather on her afternoons off and was cross-questioned about her movements: '"Where have you been? What were you doing?" Oh, heck! And then they chased me away early. . . . Well . . . in service you didn't like going in before ten o'clock.'[6]

Although the amount of free time allowed generally increased between the wars, with employers frequently promising 'liberal outings' when they advertised for staff, by no means all servants obtained these better conditions. That applied even in large households. At Chatsworth, the Duchess of Devonshire admitted that although the housemaids were supposed to have one afternoon a week and every other evening off, in practice there was too much work for this to happen. As a consequence they had 'very little free time' and since wages were also low, the turnover of junior staff was high. That only changed when the housekeeper introduced monthly staff dances to which the maids were able to invite their boyfriends.[7]

At Cliveden, one of the footmen resigned in July 1932 after only two months' service because during that time he had had only one half-day off. On that occasion he went home and his family were so shocked by his 'worn out, thin and ill' appearance that they persuaded him to leave. The problem here was that the servants (and the Astor family) were divided between the London house and Cliveden and he not only had to carry out extra work, but spent much time answering the telephone. Consequently, he had to carry out some of his regular duties, such as cleaning the silver, at night when he should have been at leisure.[8]

In smaller households mistresses might exert a cramping influence by imposing extra chores on servants before they were allowed out on their free afternoon and evening. A Devon maid, who generally enjoyed her work in a doctor's house, was nevertheless angry that on her afternoons off the wife would go into town and would not return until nearly 4 p.m. She could not leave until her mistress came back because there were children to be looked after. 'I don't think she really liked me having time off', she concluded bitterly.[9] Another device was to expect the servant to do cleaning when she returned home. Mrs Winifred Cardew, who worked in a Cornish rectory, remembered that when she returned from a concert in the village hall – and she had to be in by 9.30 p.m. – there would often be cooking utensils, some of cast iron, on the table. With them was a note from the rector's wife saying 'clean these properly'.[10]

For single-handed resident maids like these, and they formed almost 55 per cent of all resident female servants in 1931, there were few leisure activities within the household beyond reading, sewing, knitting and perhaps writing letters to the family. However, lack of cash for stamps and notepaper, as well as limited literacy, often restricted this. Sometimes a radio or gramophone was supplied, but even then restrictions might be imposed on listening time. Irene Thompson was only allowed to

"His Master's Voice"
or why the dinner was late.

Servants listening to the gramophone, early in the twentieth century. An advertisement for 'His Master's Voice'. (*Author's collection*)

tune in at teatime, when she could listen to Henry Hall's dance music. Once when she overslept her mistress confiscated the radio for a month as a punishment.[11] Another maid was told by her employer that if she wanted to listen to the wireless she should stand outside the drawing-room and hear it through the closed door.[12]

Many girls complained that even though they had free time during the afternoon or when they had finished work in the evening, they were rarely allowed out, except on their official half-days. Books, too, might be difficult to obtain, unless there were a lending library close at hand or the mistress provided a kitchen library. However, her choice of literature and that of the maid might not coincide. Small wonder that one girl complained of being 'shut . . . indoors from one week to another. . . . I consider all maids should have two hours each day to call their own, with the option of going out or remaining in the house, but in any case the time to be their own.'[13]

The isolation was felt most keenly by young servants brought up in the gregarious atmosphere of a large family or a children's home. The latter often suffered from a lack of confidence as well, making it difficult for them to make friends when they did go out. For this reason Dr Barnardo's Homes normally supplied each of their girls going as maids with the addresses of others from the charity who were in service in the same locality. The hope was they could exchange visits on their days off. It was also stipulated that every girl must be given the opportunity to attend a place of worship on Sunday and she was encouraged to join the organisation's 'old girls' association', which published a magazine to enable them to keep in touch with one another.[14]

In small households servants rarely had anywhere but the kitchen to sit when they had finished their chores, and their day-to-day social encounters, besides with members of the family, were normally confined to tradesmen who called for orders or came with deliveries to the door. Bedrooms were usually sparsely furnished and as late as the 1940s there were complaints that mistresses felt free to enter servants' rooms at will and 'open their cupboards and drawers; and there are even some who claim the right to censor the clothes in which the girls go off duty'.[15] The wearing of cosmetics was frowned upon by the more strait-laced, as was the purchase of silk underwear, which was presumably felt to indicate that the girls had ideas above their station. A vicar's daughter remembered her mother's annoyance when the maid spent all of an increase in pay 'on silk underwear'. But the daughter regarded the servant as an ally, who smuggled out love letters 'to unwelcome admirers (unwelcome by my father, as he was very severe with his daughters)'.[16]

Meals were eaten alone or perhaps snatched between serving different courses. The position was worse if, as in a lower middle-class household in rural Wales, the employer ate in the kitchen as well. In this case the maid had to wait until the family had finished before she could have her meal and although she was encouraged to go out in the evening when she had finished work, there was nothing to do except to wander the village streets. Like most servants she had to be in promptly at night – by 10 p.m. in her case, 'unless I'd been to an *eisteddfod* or something like that and it had gone a bit later'. On the Sabbath she attended Sunday school and went to chapel in the evening.[17]

The fact that domestic staff had to work most evenings made it difficult for them to attend classes at night, to improve their education. A London cook, who had formerly worked as a collar maker, complained that although she enjoyed her new job, since she had entered service she had had 'to give up all my church work and musical education. A girl in a shop or factory can take up any social work and . . . improve her education.'[18] Another frustrated student wanted to learn shorthand and typewriting, or dressmaking and millinery because she thought these 'would have helped one to pass off the monotony of domestic service'.[19]

An unofficial 'recreation' enjoyed by some maids was to eavesdrop on their employer's private conversations, perhaps through closed doors. In the enforced intimacy of domestic life they learned many family secrets which they might pass on to fellow servants whom they met on their day off or to tradesmen calling at the door. Certainly, the middle-class Monica Dickens, who took several posts as a cook-general in London for the experience, rather than from necessity, unashamedly listened to household gossip. When her employers resorted to speaking in French, or 'Franglais' (a common middle-class practice when discussing private matters before a servant), she was careful not to reveal she could understand what was being said. Monica's well-to-do background and the fact that she lived out meant she had less to fear from an employer's unfavourable reactions than those servants who needed to earn a living. Once, when her employer was away, she invited friends to an impromptu Christmas party in the kitchen.[20]

Mistresses' attitudes towards visits by friends varied widely, although most drew the line at permitting men to call. 'No followers allowed' was the usual cry. Irene Thompson, who met her future husband after a Sunday church service in Leicester, remembered that he had to wait for her at the end of the road. Later she moved to a larger house in the country where a more liberal attitude prevailed and she had her own sitting-room, with a radio. There the boyfriend was allowed into the kitchen when he called.[21]

Those employing younger girls often felt they had a duty to safeguard their morals; this was a view shared by the 1923 edition of *Mrs. Beeton's Household Management*. It advised a mistress to show interest 'in the lives of those about her', although not to appear over-inquisitive. When necessary, she should warn her maids against the evils of bad company:

> An hour should be fixed, usually about 10 p.m., before which every servant is expected to be in. To permit breaches of this rule, without good reason, is far from being a kindness to the servant concerned. The moral responsibility rests largely on the employer who permits late hours. Especial care is needed with young girls. They should be given opportunities of welcoming respectable friends at their employer's house, and not be forced to spend their time out of doors, often in driving rain, possibly in bad company, or at questionable entertainments.[22]

Yet, however well-intentioned such intervention might be, to the girls themselves it often seemed they were being denied a private life and it encouraged subterfuge. One young maid in Stirling remembered going with two friends on Sunday afternoons to listen to the band in the King's Park: 'that's how you met the fellas'. Another favourite rendezvous was a fish and chip shop, where they gathered to eat their chips and gossip about their mistresses. She used to see her future husband in the park, although they had first become acquainted through her sister's boyfriend.[23]

Some employers were anxious that their maid should always go out of the house on her half-day off. This may have been because they thought the girl needed fresh air and company, but it may also have been, as a Scottish maid suspected, because they wished to have the house to themselves, free from the servant's prying eyes.[24] Or perhaps they did not wish her to know they had poor relations. One youngster who visited an aunt in Bromley remembered that the aunt was anxious to ensure no one knew she had relatives in lowly Deptford. As a result, they were only allowed to call if the maid was out 'to keep the class you see.'[25] 'Keeping up appearances' applied not merely to the neighbours, therefore, but to the servant as well.

For domestics in these single-handed places, friendships formed outside the home were particularly important and that often involved having access to a suitable club or society. For those employed in isolated rural communities or quiet suburbs there was usually little alternative but membership of the local church or chapel and any associated organisations. Often maids in such places moved on quickly in a search for locations with more life and companionship. In May 1931, a member of the National Vigilance Association, visiting a potential employer in Highgate, London, noted sympathetically that she, like most of the residents, suffered 'much inconvenience because the girls employed find the neighbourhood too quiet, and too far away from Hyde Park; which is the happy hunting ground for the Welsh & Northern girls'. There they often struck up acquaintanceships with soldiers, as Margaret Powell and her friend used to do on their Sunday afternoon strolls in the Park.[26]

Amateur theatricals at a Girls' Friendly Society club. (*Girls' Friendly Society*)

Some of the most popular clubs were those provided by the Girls' Friendly Society (GFS) and the YWCA. Both were concerned with the moral and religious welfare of members, but they also offered recreations. These included Red Cross classes, study circles, lectures, singing groups, country dancing, concerts, amateur theatricals and sales of work for charity.[27] Some had their own libraries. Another organisation, the Wayfarers' Sunday Association, promoted centres where country girls in London could meet on Sunday.

By 1924 the GFS had more than 350 registered clubs throughout the country and Miss Goff, who worked in Paignton, was one domestic worker who joined in their activities.[28] She went first with a friend from another household and then with her sister, who also came to work in Paignton. Visits to the cinema formed part of the programme on their afternoons off.

> We usually hurried up as quickly as we could in the winter to get lunch cleared away and washed up, dashed up and changed, and rushed madly down the hill to catch a bus to the Palladium cinema to see the 6*d* matinee. I think the latest you could get in was 3 p.m. When my sister came down we usually went to Wellars or Addisons for tea (you could get a good one for ls). At about 7 p.m. we went to the Girls' Friendly Society meeting where we met with our mates and always had a very pleasant evening, singing, folk-dancing, holding little competitions, and sometimes a social, or concert when we would all be expected to contribute an item.

In the summer they donned their prettiest frocks and spent the afternoons on the beach, where they swam, sun-bathed and listened to the band.

We nearly always went to church [on] Sundays. . . . In the winter, someone (I think it was the GFS secretary) had the bright idea of opening the Church Library for girls who had no homes in the town, and for 6d each the caretaker would come in, light us a huge fire, bring us in a pot of tea and we would all have a nice cosy time, we would pool all our food and have a nice tea. My sister was a born clown and always kept us in fits of giggles. . . . We never got a chance to meet any boys, as I at any rate was never allowed to go to a dance or anywhere where I could meet them and who wanted a girl who had to rush in at 10 o'clock? However, a Young People's Fellowship was formed . . . connected with the church. They opened it with a dance, and I was refused permission to go. I gave notice the next morning, to my old lady's amazement.[29]

For the rest, she spent any spare minutes reading, as she was not allowed a wireless. 'I read in bed, I read when I should have been cleaning silver. I read novels, travels, biographies, anything readable.'

In the 1930s, when efforts were made to establish a trade union among servants in London, the holding of tea meetings, amateur dramatics, table-tennis competitions and dances was seen as a way of attracting members. The Domestic Workers' Guild, for example, formed at Hampstead in 1932, listed its objectives as to 'advance and protect the general interests of all employed in Domestic Service' and to 'promote social and recreational activities' for its members. There was an entrance fee of 3d and minimum monthly contributions of 6d. Meetings were held on the premises of the Hampstead Trades Council on five nights a week and by the end of 1933 there were about 250 members. A list of fixtures for January in that year included a New Year's Party, a fancy dress dance, a dance with an orchestra, and a whist drive.[30] When, in June 1938, the National Union of Domestic Workers was inaugurated, with backing from the Trades Union Congress, it too, quickly organised social events in connection with its branches. They included outings, tea meetings and a Sunday Social Club, with the tea meetings arranged to coincide with recruitment campaigns.[31]

For many servants, especially in country areas, bicycles brought a degree of freedom and an opportunity to visit family and friends in the vicinity on afternoons off. Mrs Slade, who worked for a minor landed family in Kent, recalled that her bicycle was her 'only pleasure'. It was acquired on a hire-purchase system and took two years to pay off.[32] Mrs Timms of Oxfordshire also purchased a bicycle in 1920, when she was twenty-two, and rode round the country lanes where she worked. But she spent much free time with a pencil and sketch-book, since she enjoyed drawing and painting. For several years she also cleaned the parish church brasses on her half-day off, apparently of her own volition.[33] However, she also experienced the snobbishness and class distinctions which plagued sports and pastimes at that time. Tennis and music were both regarded as middle-class pursuits and when Mrs Timms expressed a wish to learn to play the piano and to take up tennis, her mistress poured cold water on the idea. 'Whoever heard of a domestic servant wanting to do such things, what would my Father have said', she declared. The father was 'a clergyman in the 1880s', commented Mrs Timms bitterly.

Miss Gerdgoens, who was a parlourmaid in 1926, was made of sterner stuff than Mrs Timms. She joined a church club for girls which booked a tennis court in the local recreation ground during the summer. She recalled the ridicule she had to face each time she went off with her racquet and shoes, because she was felt to be 'aping [her] betters'. 'How could a maid play tennis? Why we were seen as a different species I'll never know.'[34] Despite the difficulties, she persisted.

The most popular leisure activity for many girls, including Margaret Powell, was to visit the cinema. The picture house offered romance and excitement, where girls in shabby clothes with work-worn hands could rest in the comforting darkness and be transported into a world far removed from their mundane daily round.[35] Films offered glamour and a glimpse of a glittering existence very different from their own lives. When they were escorted by a boyfriend, the cinema also gave a chance for some discreet courting.

Households with several servants offered opportunities for friendship, impromptu sing-songs and gossip within the domestic circle. However, there were quarrels too, with kitchen and nursery staff particularly likely to be at odds. Yet despite this, as Margaret Powell recalled, they almost always showed solidarity when dealing with their employers, often referred to simply as 'Them'. '"Them" was the enemy . . . to "Them" servants were a race apart, a necessary evil.'[36]

Servants at Shugborough Hall, c. 1938. From top to bottom: the cook; the first kitchenmaid; the second kitchenmaid; and the scullery maid. They seemed to be enjoying life in service. (Arts and Museum Service, Staffordshire County Council)

There were occasions for fun as well. Mrs O'Donnell, who worked as a between-maid in a manor house in the mid-1920s, remembered that she and the other servants were all 'music mad, for it was the early days of the Charleston. My friend and I mastered it by hanging on to the backs of our chairs, until in would come the mistress saying "Whatever is all this dreadful noise?"'[37] A young Scottish maid living in the country noted that she and her fellow maids would go walking or cycling on their afternoons off, but if it was raining the under-housemaid played the mouth organ, 'and I used to dance away out the room'.[38]

Jean Hunt, visiting her grandmother's home in Wales, remembered standing at the top of the kitchen stairs, listening 'to gales of laughter coming from down in the kitchen'. When the maids wanted fresh air they could stroll round the back garden, 'often with their knitting'. They were not allowed in the front garden, however. They always went home on Mother's Day with cakes presented by the grandmother, frequently supplemented with jam and other things.[39]

Another young between-maid (or 'tweeny') took her free time in the form of a weekend off once a month, when she visited her family. This involved a long bus journey, but when she arrived there was the joy of being reunited with her 'own folks again with the boyfriend there as well'. On Sunday there was a celebratory tea followed by musical entertainment, with her father playing a mandolin, a friend playing the violin and she herself strumming on the piano. The rest of the company joined in the songs. 'This little gay party lasted me until next month, and sometimes out of my meagre pay, I'd be able to afford a new piece of music.'[40]

However, if fellow servants in larger households proved uncongenial that soon made for tension and unhappiness, since unlike staff in other jobs, they could not get away from one another when work was over. Eileen Balderson left one post when the kitchenmaid with whom she shared a bedroom moved and her successor proved to be 'rather rough. I couldn't take to her at all and found sharing a room with her not too comfortable.'[41] Margaret Powell discovered working with two elderly servants a difficult experience in one of her places. 'You just sat in the kitchen surrounded by the "Ideal" boiler, the gas stove, the kitchen table, and the dresser.' There was no laughter or gossip and so once her chores were finished she decided to go out in the evening to visit a friend living nearby. The friend was also in service and Margaret went out at about 8.30 p.m. and returned before 10 p.m. However, the visits were unofficial and the two older servants soon informed the employer of the illicit outings. Margaret was severely reprimanded and gave in her notice to leave soon after.[42] However, even working out her time proved difficult in the face of hostility from both her mistress and her fellow workers.

In the largest households, much of this claustrophobic atmosphere was missing, although younger staff often complained that their seniors were more authoritarian and status conscious than the employer. In these establishments a hierarchical approach permeated all aspects of life, including eating arrangements. Often the senior servants (sometimes known as the 'Upper Ten') ate in the housekeeper's or steward's room (nicknamed the 'Pugs' parlour' by irreverent juniors) and the younger staff in the servants' hall. The seniors might appear in the servants' hall for the main course of the mid-day dinner, but then retired to their own room for pudding. Only when they had left were the juniors allowed to talk. When they dined together at the same table, they sat in order of precedence, with grace said by the most senior. As a young male servant recalled: 'When the butler put his knife and fork down that was the signal for everyone to do the same, so God help you if you were a slow eater.'[43] Eileen Balderson recalled that in her first place in Yorkshire she (as the tweeny) and the second housemaid had to wait for permission from the head housemaid before they could leave the table. They also had to wait for her to lead them to the servants' hall for the commencement of the meal.[44]

Another girl, who worked as a housemaid in Bruton Street, London, during the mid-1920s, described supper as the 'big event of the day, when protocol and snobbery' took over. All the staff assembled for that meal, except for those working in the kitchen. As in many large establishments, the latter kept to themselves and ate in the kitchen – which might mean they had better food than the rest of the servants, including titbits from the dining-room menu. At Bruton Street, due ceremony was observed:

> First came the butler with the housekeeper. He sat at one end of the long refectory table, she sat at the opposite end. The butler was dressed in full evening dress, wing collar, white tie and tails. The housekeeper wore a black silk dress, sometimes relieved with lace and always jewellery, earrings, necklaces, bracelets, rings, brooches and anything else she possessed. Next came the lady's personal maid dressed much the same as the housekeeper, next came the first footman, his uniform was the same as the butler's with one exception. All footmen [had] yellow and black striped waistcoats. They sat one side of the table looking like wasps at a feast, at the end of their row came the odd job man, then the hall boy who waited on us at table under the keen eye of the butler who corrected him if he made a mistake or forgot any small item or spilled water as he filled our glasses. This was . . . to give him his first training to being a footman . . . and last not least at the end of the row was the boot boy.
>
> On the other side of the table sat the maids, the head housemaid with her three inches of lace on top of her head (I always thought this rather ridiculous but it showed rank), then the other maids according to position.[45]

When visiting lady's maids, and valets were present during house parties, they joined the 'Upper Ten' and took precedence in accordance with the rank of their employer.

In large country houses, employers often provided facilities for social activities. Clubs were set up which particularly benefited outdoor staff. Sometimes, as at Cliveden, this might be partly because of an estate's isolated location, which made visits to town difficult, but it was also a means of fostering staff solidarity. At Cliveden the club was used mainly by the gardeners and estate workers and their families, since the indoor servants were usually working in the evenings when it was open. However, Edwin Lee, the butler, did visit it from time to time. There were football and cricket teams, too, while the estate had its own Women's Institute which provided club refreshments. Dances and whist-drives were held fortnightly, and the staff had their own boat on the River Thames. They were allowed to use the tennis courts and the golf course when the family was away.[46] The Astor boys played both football and cricket with the estate teams and these had regular fixtures with clubs in the area. There were annual events, too, such as a staff sports day and summer fête, with running, putting the shot, climbing the greasy pole, and similar events. The Maidenhead town band played all the afternoon. At Christmas there was a big party and a fancy dress dance.[47]

A similar policy applied at Lyme Park in Cheshire, with dancing, table tennis and darts organised in the club room. There was also a cricket team in which members of the family played, alongside estate workers, particularly the gardeners. So enthusiastic was the squire, Lord Newton, about the game that when advertisements for a new gardener appeared 'they used to put Cricketer Preferred'. The squire himself captained the team when he was available. If he was away, the head gardener took over. Team meetings were held in the gardeners' mess room, with the butler in the chair.[48]

Staff from Shugborough Hall picnicking on Cannock Chase in 1926. They went blackberrying on the Chase for large-scale preserving in the stillroom. (*Arts and Museum Service, Staffordshire County Council*)

The staff Christmas dinner was a major event at Lyme Park, with all the unmarried staff, both indoor and outdoor, present in the servants' hall. Eva Walton, who worked as a laundrymaid in the 1930s, remembered the impressive array of food and wine laid out on the table, which was about six yards in length.

> Mr Sherwood [the Lyme butler] was at the head of the table, and the London butler was at the bottom. . . . The Christmas pudding used to come in all lit up. . . . All the kitchen staff, every servant sat down. . . . All the lady's maids. . . . Everyone sat down.[49]

Such events promoted staff unity and gave them a sense of belonging to a superior establishment which mirrored the employer's elevated social status. Nevertheless, they were pleasures organised at the behest of the employer and conducted on his or her terms. That applied even to the running of the clubs. As Mr Henderson, an odd job man at Cliveden, observed drily: 'there was a committee . . . and Lord Astor put so many men on the committee . . . most of the men was Lord Astor's . . . that's how it worked'.[50]

For servants elsewhere the main event of the year might be the staff ball. At Chatsworth there was dancing in the Great Dining-Room to a band which played in the vestibule. The buffet was set up on a table which ran the length of the Orangery. Two hairdressers arrived with curling tongs and spend the day 'coiffing the maids. Dancing went on till four-thirty in the morning, and no one bothered to go to bed.'[51]

Arthur Inch, first footman to the Marquess of Londonderry in the late 1930s, described the annual ball held at Mountstewart, the Londonderrys' home in Northern Ireland. It took place when the Marquess and Marchioness were there for the summer. The thirty-six servants were supplemented by guests, including the staff of Clandeboys, a large house nearby. They in turn invited the Londonderry servants to their own ball. In all about a hundred people attended and the largest room in the house was used as the ballroom. A dance band was hired from Belfast and the kitchen and stillroom staff produced a sumptuous cold buffet. The Marquess and Marchioness opened proceedings, with the Marchioness dancing the first waltz with the butler and the Marquess doing the same with the housekeeper. After that they retired discreetly and left the staff to enjoy themselves.

> Eventually we would reluctantly call a halt at about three in the morning and after speeding the guests on their way we would all set to and clear up the . . . rooms. The kitchen staff would deal with the food, the menservants all the glass, china and silver and put the dining room straight again and the housemaids would tidy up the ballroom and other rooms used; in fact the housemaids who usually started work at about 5.30 a.m. didn't used to go to bed at all but just carried on with their work to get the house ready for later.[52]

There was a good deal of entertaining at Mountstewart while the Londonderrys were in residence, but there were also opportunities for recreation which were absent when family and servants were in London. Staff tennis courts were available and during the afternoons many younger servants were able to play. They also swam in the nearby loch or, if the family and guests were out yachting, they were allowed to use the indoor pool. There were walks in the surrounding countryside and if they were not too busy they might be allowed to take the afternoon and evening off and go into Belfast to the cinema or a dance.[53]

In the more remote country houses employers might ease transport problems by making their own special provision. Eileen Balderson, who went as third housemaid to Burwarton House in Shropshire, discovered there was no bus or train service. Instead, the staff would be taken into Bridgnorth, with half going each Saturday afternoon, along with any estate workers who wanted a trip out. They were taken in the shooting brake by the under-chauffeur. However, this had its disadvantages. 'We left the house at 2 p.m. and returned at 4 p.m., so we went to town for two hours per fortnight!!' The sense of isolation was increased by the fact that the twenty-two indoor servants ate in their separate sitting-rooms, except for the main midday meal, when the senior servants joined the rest of the staff for the meat course in the servants' hall. However, it was the silence which most oppressed Eileen. 'You could hear a pin drop. The deadly atmosphere was enlivened only by birdsong. As in other establishments, most mealtimes passed in purgatorial silence. We longed to talk or laugh, but had to remain silent.' Only at suppertime were the prohibitions relaxed and then 'we had a fine time gossiping with visiting maids and chauffeurs'.[54] It was mainly on account of the isolation that she left after a few months.

In many large households there were occasional staff romances. However, they had to be handled with great discretion, since if they became known one, if not both, parties would be dismissed. In a later post Eileen Balderson herself discovered the difficulties of this. When she was working at Grove Lodge, Windsor, for Sir Colin and Lady Keppel, she and the butler, George Higgs, started going out together.

THE SERVANTS' BALL.

First Footman. " 'ERE COMES 'ER LADYSHIP." I 'OPE I GET A DANCE WITH 'ER."
Butler. " YOU FORGET YOURSELF, 'ENERY; DANCING WITH 'ER LADYSHIP IS THE *BUTLER'S* PERQUISITE."

The due formalities had to be observed at a servants' ball, with the maids dressed in their finery and the master and mistress attending to open the proceedings. (Punch, *31 December 1930*)

> We used to meet away from the house and on our return I usually went in first while he had a drink in the village, returning later. Our half-day during the week was usually spent in Windsor, walking in the Great Park . . . then to the cinema in the evening. Sundays were spent either at Virginia Water [where her married sister lived] or visiting his widowed mother and younger sister at Yateley, near Camberley.

When the Keppels' moved to London for the Season George and Eileen made excursions around the capital, touring places of interest, visiting the cinema and theatres and taking tea at a large Lyons restaurant in Piccadilly where there was an afternoon cabaret. However, when they returned to Windsor, George decided that keeping the relationship a secret was too stressful and he moved to another post in London. For a time he and Eileen kept in touch, but when he went north with his employers for the shooting season the relationship was broken off, to Eileen's great sadness.[55]

Others were more fortunate. Many marriages took place between servants in these large households, and between maids and gardeners or other estate workers. 'You mostly married domestics; they were the only ones you ever met', declared a Leicestershire butler. 'Butlers always married a housemaid or a kitchen maid, or a lady's maid sometimes.' He himself had married a lady's maid.[56]

Eric Horne, too, described how 'a lot of canoodling' went on between young footmen and the housemaids. However, he warned susceptible young males against ruining their future 'for the sake of five minutes excitement'.[57] The same warning might have been addressed to the maids, since if they became pregnant they would

Perhaps a little gentle flirting below stairs. Servants at Shugborough Hall in 1937. Left to right: Maisie (housemaid); Molly (first kitchenmaid); the pantry boy; and Janet (second kitchenmaid). Janet is dressed for her half-day off. (*Arts and Museum Service, Staffordshire County Council*)

be dismissed. Margaret Powell described the desperate efforts of a young under-parlourmaid in one of the houses where she worked to procure a miscarriage. However, it was in vain; when her condition became obvious she had to leave. However, in her case the father was not a fellow servant, but probably a nephew of the employer, although the girl herself refused to reveal who it was.[58]

Unwise sexual encounters were not the only hazards. Excessive drinking was another problem, especially in households where there were plentiful supplies of wines and spirits. Butlers were felt to be particularly susceptible to this. Indeed, Daisy Noakes, who worked at a boys' preparatory school near Brighton, remembered that when the butler there decanted the wine he 'always had a bit over for himself'.[59]

Gambling, particularly betting on horses, proved attractive to servants whose employers were racehorse owners. Even female servants became involved when sweepstakes were organised among the staff for the major racing events.[60] Albert Thomas took time out of private service to become a club steward. At one club in Yorkshire he ran an account with three bookmakers and took bets from the members, at a time when off-course betting was illegal. 'I was more or less their agent, and the bookmakers used to allow me 1s 6d in the pound for all moneys "taken". . . . I usually took between thirty and forty pounds a week there for bets, so that my commission was a useful addition to my salary.'[61] He retained his gambling habits when he went back into service.

Even blameless characters like Arthur Inch indulged in a flutter from time to time, to while away the tedium when they had to stay on duty in the evening until family and guests had all gone to bed. Often those not on late duty 'would stay up with the duty ones and have a card session in the pantry and [lose our] hard-earned money on some card game or another. Of course some of [them] won so I suppose that's why [they] persisted.'[62]

More surprising was Mrs Woodman, the cook at Flete, in Devon. She and Mr Brown, the valet, were enthusiastic followers of greyhound racing, and Mrs Woodman owned several racing greyhounds. They ran at the White City in London and at the City Stadium in Plymouth. When the daughter of the house and her brother were taken along by the cook to one of the evening races they were 'treated like princes, entirely because Mrs Woodman was such a successful owner. Her dog won the West of England Cup – a sort of greyhound Derby.'[63]

Finally, there remained the question of holidays. Many employers allowed their servants a week or a fortnight's vacation a year, perhaps when they themselves were away, but that was not universal practice. 'We never used to get regular holidays in service', declared Arthur Inch. When he worked at West Wycombe Park as a single-handed footman in the 1930s he did not even have a weekend off until he had been there for fifteen months. After about two years he felt the need for a holiday in order to visit his family in Yorkshire, and he decided to resign.[64] Many other servants adopted a similar strategy, fitting in a holiday between jobs.

In some cases, as with a young Welsh housemaid, lack of cash, rather than the mistress's attitude, might delay a visit home. Most youngsters wanted to be smartly dressed in a new outfit when they returned and they also needed money for the train or coach journey and perhaps presents for those at home, or to give to their mother. This particular girl did not go home for two years. 'You didn't have money to buy a lot; I bought a nice coat and a nice dress once and lent them to my friend and she went home, in my coat!' Eventually she scraped enough together to make the trip back to south Wales. After that, 'I went home . . . every year. Mother used to like to hear everything; dinner parties, "Oh fancy all that food", she used to say.'[65]

For many maids, household service represented a phase in their life, between leaving school and getting married. But for career servants, both male and female, the benefits of domestic life had to be weighed against the disadvantages. Rosina Harrison, Lady Astor's lady's maid, saw it as a means to enable her to travel. With the Astors that ambition was more than fulfilled in the grandest manner. 'I've stayed in the best hotels in the world, and in many of the greatest houses', she, wrote in her autobiography. Yet she admitted that her duties with a demanding, if well loved, mistress left her little opportunity to pursue an outside social life. 'We had a deal of fun', she noted of herself and her fellow servants, 'heightened possibly by the hard work that surrounded it. My life was made more enjoyable by the travelling I did and even at home it was never boring; my lady's unpredictability saw to that.'[66]

Others regarded domestic work in a hotel, restaurant or public institution as more attractive than private service, because the hours were usually more clearly defined and the off duty times more firmly fixed. One girl who worked as a waitress at a good class restaurant in Folkestone, after a not very happy spell in a Margate guest house, enthused over her tips and the limited shifts she worked in the new post:

The enjoyment was there. And you had your food at the restaurant. That's the first place I had a peach melba. . . . Then they used to have a lovely German band. It was beautiful.[67]

The fact that the customers were holidaymakers and were presumably in a cheerful mood and that she was not working under the close personal control of an employer, as would have applied in most private households, doubtless contributed to her general sense of satisfaction.

EMPLOYER AND SERVANT RELATIONSHIPS

The period between the two world wars was, in many respects, a transitional one in domestic labour relations, bridging the years before 1914, when almost every householder of means expected to recruit some help, and after 1945 when mistresses reluctantly came to accept that labour-saving appliances and 'dailies' represented the future for most of them. Books of advice, including the 1923 edition of *Mrs Beeton's Household Management*, suggested ways in which the new situation could be met. They including drawing up a list of duties for any servants recruited. 'The most successful mistresses are those who . . . make themselves felt rather than seen or heard', declared Mrs Beeton. 'Constant nagging never yet made a good servant; on the other hand, a too-easy rule and undue familiarity are bad alike for mistress and for maid.'[68]

Other writers advised employers to avoid arrogant hectoring in their dealings with the lower orders and instead adopt what could only be called kindly condescension. *The Woman's Book* of 1931 implicitly recommended this approach when it declared:

As we expect civility and courtesy from our maids it is only fair that we should render them the same. A fear of familiarity should never be the excuse for a curt answer nor justify the omission of please, nor a word of thanks for service rendered. Neither should we be reluctant to wish them the common salutations and good morning and good night.[69]

Similarly, Irene Davison, in advising on 'Little Courtesies that Count', recommended that one should never 'omit to thank a servant for any special little service rendered, and to say "Please" and "Thank you" as conscientiously as you would to anyone else'.[70] Many domestics doubtless accepted these acknowledgements at their face value, but others saw them as enhancing social distance rather than narrowing it, which they resented.

In essence, the relationship between employer and servant revolved around the issues of earnings, status and personal attitudes. Loyalty was stressed as an important virtue by employers and personal liberty became a core concern for domestics. Many resident servants, as we have seen, disliked not being able to invite friends to visit them and that they were not only restricted in the amount of leisure time, but in the way it was spent. These tensions were heightened because the servant's place of work was also his or her home and because the control exercised by the mistress covered almost all aspects of daily life. As Violet Firth commented in the mid-1920s:

> A mistress does not demand of her servant work only, she also demands a certain manner, a manner which shall clearly indicate her superiority and the inferiority of the woman who takes her wages; there is nothing derogatory in performing the work but there is something very derogatory . . . in assuming the required attitude.[71]

It was partly in response to this situation that non-resident domestics increased over the period. This trend also suited some employers who were moving into smaller, more modern, houses. It likewise minimised the danger of sexual contact with the men of the household who might be tempted by the presence of attractive young girls in the house all the time. It was a solution which commended itself to Mrs Alfred Sidgwick. 'The truth is that we want work done in our houses, but we do not want companions', she wrote. 'We greatly value the privacy of family life.' In her view, the main objection to domestic service was the 'loss of social prestige attached to it, and that would be done away with if a better class took it up and if it became an ambitious, graded calling like that of soldier, sailor, or civil servant'.[72] Unfortunately for her, and for others taking a similar line, potential servants were not persuaded by such high-flown notions. They took up day work to suit their own convenience, rather than from any belief that it meant entry into 'an ambitious, graded calling'.

A similar approach lay behind the Domestic Services Exhibition which was held in London in January 1938. Its motto was: 'Good Domestic Service is the foundation of National Health and Happiness'. Demonstrations of new equipment and competitions for valets, laundrymaids and kitchenmaids formed part of the programme. The intention, according to the catalogue, was to 'imbue the minds of our visitors with our own aspirations, give them a vision of that higher and finer standard of Domestic Calling'.[73] There is little evidence that it stimulated servant recruitment, although, as we shall see, it may have boosted efforts to form a domestic workers' trade union.

Perhaps the most significant of the 'day servant' initiatives was the establishment of the home help service. This was set up in 1918 to allow local authorities to provide aid to expectant and nursing mothers with children under five. The home helps carried out domestic work in households where mothers were confined at home, for a minimum of fourteen days after the child's birth. They could also give aid when a mother, during the ante-natal period, was ordered to rest by the doctor or to go to hospital.[74] The helps were paid by the local authority and mothers' contributions to their costs were recovered subsequently either in whole or in part, according to local policy. In this way domestic work became linked to social service provision and the helps benefited by becoming employees of the councils, rather than of individual householders. The weakness of the scheme was that it was optional and some authorities failed to adopt it. Nor did it allow support to be given to other groups in need of assistance, such as the aged or the chronically sick. That aspect of home help provision was only to be expanded during the 1940s.

Such schemes apart, most servants, both day and resident, were recruited by individuals employers, using personal contacts, advertisements, domestic agencies and employment exchanges. High male unemployment in the inter-war years may have encouraged some wives to take up domestic work in order to maintain family income. It is noticeable that by 1931 over 8 per cent of all female domestic servants were married, compared to under 6 per cent in 1921.[75] Around a third of maids were aged thirty-five or over in 1931. This trend towards older workers may have been encouraged by the provisions of the Widows, Orphans and Old Age Contributory Pensions Act of 1925. Under the Act, women became eligible for a pension (subject to certain conditions) at the age of sixty-five instead of seventy, from January 1928, so long as they and their employers contributed to the National Health Insurance scheme. The initiative not only benefited older servants, but encouraged mistresses to engage and retain elderly maids now that they were relieved from the potential burden of having to give support to them in old age or sickness.[76]

Day service was one way of countering the unpopularity of domestic work. Another was the attempt made in some places by mistresses and servants to negotiate agreed working conditions. This was a course commended by the Ministry of Labour's 1923 *Report on the Supply of Female Domestic Servants* when it recommended the setting up of voluntary Women's Sub-Committees, established in conjunction with Local Employment Committees, including representatives of employers and workers, as well as some independent members.[77] According to the Report, schemes laying down employment conditions had already been accepted by mistresses who were not party to the original discussions. However, in the long run, these arrangements had little effect. The working conditions of most servants were influenced by market forces rather than by collective action. Only in a few special cases, as with Norland College nurses, might pressures be successfully exerted on mistresses to provide minimum standards.

By the late 1930s, it was also clear that servant supply was being affected by developments outside the control of employers. These included demographic trends, with fewer young people between fourteen and eighteen available to enter the labour market. In a gloomy assessment in April 1937, *The Times* suggested that unless female employment ratios increased among this age group, by 1940 there would be around one hundred thousand fewer girls seeking work than were doing so in 1937, when servant shortages were already manifest.[78] *The Times* also highlighted the growth in female industrial and commercial occupations over much of the country and that conditions in these were improving and were therefore attracting young workers. It concluded that 'the competition of industry and commerce with domestic service' was 'likely . . . to become more and not less acute'.[79] In these circumstances, even if mistresses made concessions over the hours and working conditions of their staff, they would still face formidable competition from other employers, given the dwindling supply of young people entering the market.

It was against this background, therefore, that employer and servant relations evolved between the wars. Implicit in that process was the question of double standards, as domestic workers observed the luxury of the mistress's own apartments and contrasted

"And now they want another place at table for Henry, Earl of Bolcester, whoever he is!"

Footman, with a fashionable striped waistcoat, displaying a less than servile attitude in the seclusion of the kitchen. (Punch, *27 September 1939*)

this with their own often comfortless quarters. Likewise they were expected to prepare food for the dining room which they were not allowed to eat. Their social subordination was symbolised by the rituals they had to observe, including the wearing of a distinctive uniform, the use of bells to summon them, even in quite small, modern houses, and the segregation of their living space from that of the family.[80] Servants were expected to run up and down uncarpeted back stairs as they went about their duties. In country houses, this sometimes meant the construction of small 'hidden' staircases fitted into dressing rooms 'to preserve the invisibility of housemaids'. By contrast, privacy among servants was regarded as an undesirable 'attack on social barriers', at least until staff became sufficiently senior to warrant a move from 'dormitory to private bedroom'.[81] In this way, argues Pamela Sambrook, 'the denial of privacy and comfort inflicted on junior menservants in their basements and teenage housemaids in their attics' became 'an expression of social differentiation'.

Similar discriminatory policies applied in single-servant households, and here, because relations between mistress and maid were more intimate, they led to a deeper sense of grievance. Years later Mrs Cardew remembered the way in which the cake and buns intended for her consumption were made specially and were kept in a tin box for the remainder of the week. 'If an odd job man came in during the week, I would have to share it with him. The 1920s and early 30s were very hard times for domestics', she added bitterly, 'but if they complained they might get the sack and would not get a reference for any job. No reference no job.'[82]

These class attitudes pervaded Daphne Robinson's account of life in her Bangor home; the maid was not allowed to wash in the family bathroom. Instead, she had to make do with a 'toilet set' in her attic bedroom. 'She did not, of course, use the family lavatory, hers was outside, by the coal cellar, and nobody used it but her. She also . . . always had a cake of pink soap', bought specially.[83]

Mrs Rothwell of Morebath Manor, Devon, took so little interest in her young maid, Doris Southwood, who had worked for her for two years, that when she wrote out a reference for her she called her Doris Southcomb. She had found Doris 'honest, sober, quite a good worker, if she likes, and as a general rule she did do her work really very well'. Doris was leaving because she could not get on with the head housemaid, who was really too young to supervise and train a new girl effectively. This had been the girl's first post.[84]

The social distinctions which demonstrated the unequal relationship between mistress and servant were compounded by the fact that it was 'normally a relation between an older woman of one class and a younger woman of another'.[85] A young maid must modify her behaviour to meet her mistress's expectations once she entered a new household and she could expect to be reprimanded when she made mistakes. Margaret Powell felt deeply humiliated when on one occasion she handed newspapers to her employer, Mrs Clydesdale, without using a salver. The mistress did not speak, but just looked at Margaret 'as though she could hardly believe that someone like me could be walking and breathing'. Eventually she spoke and warned the young maid, never again to hand anything to her 'in your bare hands, always use a silver salver. Surely you know better than that.' Margaret felt terrible. 'Tears started to trickle down my cheeks; that someone could think that you were so low that you couldn't even hand them anything out of your hands without it first being placed on a silver salver.'[86]

Occasionally a mistress's power over her maid degenerated into outright cruelty, as in the case of a seventeen-year-old servant from Sunderland who entered the household of a Mrs Malet-Warden in Rochester in November 1927. Not only did the mistress withhold the 5s a week wages due to the girl, but she systematically beat and kicked her and encouraged her children to do the same. She also cut off the maid's hair. After six months neighbours alerted the National Society for the Prevention of Cruelty to Children of the girl's plight and they successfully prosecuted Mrs Malet-Warden. Medical evidence showed that the girl had injuries all over her body. In this case the mistress was sentenced to a month's imprisonment and had to pay a guinea to cover the doctor's expenses.[87] However, in another case, heard at Chertsey in Surrey, a seventeen-year-old maid was unsuccessful in her attempt to have her former mistress convicted of assault for having forcibly cut off her hair. The mistress claimed that the maid had consented to have her hair bobbed and this was accepted. Elsewhere servants had their possessions confiscated or their wages withheld if they attempted to leave an unsatisfactory situation without giving due notice, or if their mistress wanted to prevent them from leaving. In some cases legal advice and help were given to maids who found themselves in these situations by the YWCA's Law Bureau.[88]

A maid was always expected to maintain a clear separation between her own family and that of the employer. Minnie Cowley, who entered her first post as a thirteen-year-old general servant in 1923, was dismissed when she took her mistress's small son to her home during their daily walk. 'She could be admitted to the employer's home to care for children there; that children should visit the servant's own home was unthinkable.'[89]

This petty discrimination was underlined by the fact that when carrying out their duties, domestics were expected to remain oblivious to the conversations and the actions of those around them. As Violet Firth noted, there was something innately offensive to individual self-respect in the way in which a servant was treated as an automaton, with 'people laughing and talking and being agreeable to one another all round one, and at the same time ignoring one's existence'.[90] Such conduct added to the servant's sense of isolation and contributed to her feelings of indifference towards the employer's best interests.

The way in which names might be changed to suit a mistress or the manner in which controls were exercised could cause further resentment. Mrs Martin, who worked for a Sheffield doctor's family, remembered that the wife helped her to make the beds, but she 'always inspected my fingernails at this time to make sure they were clean. . . . I also had to clean the windows of course. One day, I didn't have time to clean the window, and Madam put a big cross on it with her finger which remained until I cleaned the window'.[91]

In another case Daisy White, who worked in a vicarage, remembered her mistress complaining about her hairstyle. She was told it must be arranged so that no hair showed under the cap at the front:

> that made me feel fed up, so I said to Mrs L. my hair is my own and I shall do it how I like, and walked away from her. I was given one more chance, no more rudeness.[92]

Daisy also disliked her employer's meanness. At Christmas she was presented with a pencil and the food was kept so short that she had to supplement her rations out of her pay. Then she began using the store keys to increase supplies until her mother warned her 'it wasn't the proper thing to do. . . . Mother said if I was seen . . . I would lose my reference.' That would have been a fatal blow to future job prospects. After a few months Daisy took another post.

The ease with which servants could move to other jobs was a feature of the inter-war servant scarcity and it helped to encourage mistresses to improve working conditions, so as to retain staff. As the 1923 edition of *Mrs Beeton* warned, a wife should never lose 'for the sake of a trifling saving in wages, the services of a trusted and efficient servant. . . . A really good one can save her employers far more than her wages and keep; a bad one would be a poor bargain if she gave her services for nothing.'[93]

Attempts were made in the press and elsewhere to encourage servant loyalty by accounts of faithful service and the way in which this had been rewarded by legacies when employers died. In one case, in 1927 the Rector of Longford, Warwickshire, left his entire estate, valued at over £25,000, so that the income could be divided equally between his housekeeper, his gardener and his secretary, for life.[94] In another, the 'remarkable bequest' by a gentleman of £300,000 to his housekeeper for 'kindly services rendered in the course of a number of years' was mentioned in the catalogue of the 1938 domestic services exhibition.[95] In that year

"WAS YOUR LAST MISTRESS SURPRISED WHEN YOU LEFT?"
"SHE 'AD A BIT OF A SHOCK. WE 'APPENED TO 'AVE WORDS WHEN I WAS USIN' THE ELECTRIC IRON."

A maid showing an independent attitude towards her mistress at a time of servant shortage. (Punch, *10 September 1930*)

the London Evening Standard published a series of letters form satisfied employers describing their happy relations with long-serving domestics. They included Mrs Frank Easton of London SW3, who noted that her cook had been with her for over thirty years and the cook's sister had served as a parlourmaid for almost as long: 'Between mistress and maid there has never, in all these years been disagreement or ill feeling. Meals are always a pleasure to eat and to look at'.[96]

In large households, it was the senior servants who hired and fired junior staff; the juniors might have little or no personal contact with their employers. Eileen Balderson worked at one country house where she never spoke to the male head of the house or saw him except at a distance; 'we were . . . in awe of the unknown, since the master was a remote figure'.[97]

Yet, while junior servants in these households were made aware of their subordinate status, they rarely experienced the feelings of inferiority which applied in small establishments, where a mistress's petty discriminations were personally applied and underlined. In the case of major land families, workers also enjoyed the prestige of being associated with an important property and helping to look after its contents. 'I learned a lot in my days of domestic service about dress sense and good manners', wrote Eileen Balderson, 'and I acquired an appreciation of quality furniture, china and pictures'.[98]

Others enjoyed their part in the ceremonial life of such households. Arthur Inch considered 'the highlight' of his career to be the occasion when he wore the Marquess of Londonderry's state livery on the occasion of the coronation of King George VI in 1937. When the day arrived he, a fellow footman and the coachman rose early to dress themselves in the elaborate livery, which they wore with silk stockings, patent shoes, 'the final touch was to powder our hair'. Both footmen also wore a bicorn hat, while the coachman had a tricorn. This was the 'one and only time I wore full state livery and rode the box on a state carriage'.[99]

However, there could also be resentment at the dictatorial attitude of some senior servants. Mr Inch resigned from his post as first footman at Blenhim Palace after about nine months because of disagreements with the butler there. He was 'quite a martinet to work under . . . we all had to suffer from his jibes and sarcastic remarks and not all justified'. He finally left after an incident in which he felt he had been treated unfairly.[100]

From the employer's point of view, efficient servants ensured the smooth running of the household, with minimal effort on their part. One young wife even wrote to the *Western Mail* to complain about the domestic shortage and to announce that women like her were 'not going to undertake the responsibilities of Motherhood when they cannot get servants on reasonable terms and conditions . . . no maid, no motherhood.'[101]

In large establishments, responsibility for day-to-day organisation lay with the senior staff. Patricia, Viscountess Hambleden, recalled nostalgically the butler at Wilton during her youth:

> Everything was done impeccably. If he felt somebody was really unsatisfactory he would come and say 'I'm afraid George is no good. I think you should get rid of him', and he would find somebody else. And the same for the housekeeper and cook . . . my Mother had two maids the whole of her life. They always stayed till they retired or died.[102]

Mary, Duchess of Buccleuch, likewise confessed to relying 'enormously' on her staff: 'I left the menus and the ordering of the food entirely to the cook . . . one footman always came in every hour or so to make up the fires. One would never put a log on oneself.'[103]

Older employers were particularly dependent on the ministrations of a trusted servant. In 1906 Florence Hayter, Gertrude Jekyll's last housekeeper-cum-personal maid, arrived. She remained in the household until her mistress's death in 1932. Florence's vigilant care ensured the mistress's well-being into her late eighties and she eventually died in her maid's arms. In her Will Miss Jekyll left Florence £100 and her bedroom furniture. A similar bequest was made to the cook.[104]

Younger mistresses and their maids might also enjoy gossiping together. The Hon. Mrs John Mildmay White used to take her lady's maid with her when she went to stay in other country houses and she considered that great fun: 'you found out what was going on. She told you everything she'd heard.' [105]

Senior staff were responsible for disciplining the juniors and making sure that they came in at the proper hour when they had time off. A housemaid who worked at Thornby Hall, Leicestershire, in the 1920s remembered that she had to be in by 10 p.m. 'or else the old cook-housekeeper came out of her sitting room. . . . There was a manhole coming along the passage and I bet a shilling if you were a bit late you'd step on one end' and thus alert the housekeeper.[106]

The drawing up of formal staff rules helped in the disciplinary process. At Standen near East Grinstead, the Beale family's lists of 'do's and don'ts' included a prohibition on the servants meeting in cottages, presumably to prevent gossiping

Servant ceremonial. Arthur R. Inch dressed in the full state livery of the Marquess of Londonderry on the occasion of the Coronation of King George VI in 1937. (*Arthur R. Inch*)

with the villagers or the growth of unwelcome liaisons between male and female staff. They were also forbidden to go into the stable yard, where they would be likely to encounter the grooms, and were to attend 'Evening church on Sundays'.[107]

At Chatsworth housemaids and kitchenmaids were not allowed to speak to one another. But that only applied at Chatsworth itself, so when the household travelled to Lismore and Bolton Abbey, two other estates belonging to the Duke of Devonshire, they were able to make friends without hindrance.[108]

Employers were expected to conform to certain standards too. That applied to punctuality at meals. According to Eileen Balderson, if the family were occasionally a little late for a meal and it had to be delayed for a few minutes, nothing would be said. However, if that happened many times, 'the mistress would soon be told about it. Likewise, if she wanted to take the children out, she always asked Nanny if it would be convenient, and she usually went with them, so the children were still in her charge, and mother wouldn't think of going against Nanny's word.'[109]

Servants in most major households were normally recruited from outside the local area. That even applied at Chatsworth and when the present dowager Duchess of Devonshire asked a former housemaid why this was, she responded quickly: 'Oh, talk . . . tittle tattle. They never had local people in the front of the house.'[110]

Occasionally, as at Cliveden, religious restrictions were introduced. The Astors, as Christian Scientists, did not attempt to impose their beliefs on their servants, but they did refuse to employ Roman Catholics.[111] Advertisements in the press confirm that others shared their anti-Catholic sentiments and as late as June 1937 at least one householder in West Kensington placed an embargo on the recruitment of Welsh and Irish house-parlourmaids.[112]

As well as ensuring the smooth running of a household, senior domestics could shield their employers from uncomfortable problems or serve as a 'buffer zone' to protect them from confrontations with unwanted visitors or junior servants.[113] Daisy Noakes remembered that when she, as a dormitory maid, wanted to see her mistress at the Preparatory School where she worked she had to ask the butler to arrange an appointrnent.[114]

Servants also served to demonstrate the importance of a family to neighbours, visitors and casual callers. An employer's superior status was confirmed by the special livery worn by the footmen and the studied formality with which their duties were carried out. The number and kind of servants employed were important as well. Lady Burrell remembered that in her family home, Balcombe Place, there were only nine indoor servants: 'you didn't have a lady's maid, nor a second footman, so you were rather looked down on.'[115]

However, that did not mean that mistresses were able to avoid all unpleasantness. When Patricia, Viscountess Hambleden, first became châtelaine of her husband's family home, Greenlands, the housekeeper resented her arrival to such a degree that she sought to humiliate her in the eyes of guests, perhaps by giving the grandest of them cotton sheets instead of the expected linen ones. 'I'm glad to say she left after a bit and we didn't replace her. I got on very much better without her – with a charming old still-room maid and five housemaids.'[116] Lady Mander, too, experienced difficulties with the housekeeper at Wightwick: 'her resentment at my arrival was not improved by my failure to impress her.'[117]

Sometimes this uneasy relationship spilled over into more damaging actions. Maids might unofficially wear some of their mistress's underwear on their days off, while one servant who had got into debt buying expensive clothes on hire purchase then stole jewellery from her employer in an effort to pay off the debt.[118] A prison visitor claimed that in her work she constantly came across young girls who had been in domestic service and had found the monotony and loneliness of the life too much for them. They had 'sought relief in anti-social ways. . . . Theft of jewellery or clothes is the usual crime with these domestic servants.'[119] Perhaps, too, such girls were jealous of the mistress's expensive possessions, compared to their own meagre belongings, and used this as a way of paying her back.

Youngsters prevented by poverty from taking up scholarships to secondary or higher education were particularly likely to resent an employer's patronising approach. Jean Rennie, who had qualified for a university place which she was unable to accept, considered the reason she found it difficult to get a second post was because she was dismissed from the first for 'questioning the Divine Right of the Gentry'.[120]

Finally, there remained the matter of earnings. If bed and board were taken into account, the pay of domestic servants in many households was not inferior to that of workers in a number of other occupations. Interestingly, too, when a survey of domestic workers was undertaken by the *Wayfarers' Sunday Association* in 1937 it revealed that pay was not a major grievance, when compared to the issues of working hours and leisure opportunities.[121]

However, if pay was not a prime issue, there remained problems at a local level arising from the wide variations between the income of senior and junior staff, the differing size of households and the maid's age and experience. Pay increases were difficult to obtain in post, unless promotions were secured and the in-house advancement of servants was not common. At the beginning of the Second World War a general servant from Welford in Leicestershire remembered asking her mistress for a rise from 16s a week to £1: 'She went all sort of huffy and went into the dining room and came back and said, "We really don't know how we're going to manage it with all our taxes and things we've got to pay but we will give you a pound".'[122]

In large households it was usually necessary to move in order to gain higher pay. Arthur Inch, who began his working career as a house boy in January 1931 at £26 a year, eventually became first footman for the Marquess and Marchioness of Londonderry in December 1936 at £60 per annum, plus livery and a dark suit of morning clothes.[123] His salary rose to £80 a year when he was promoted to under-butler.

Rosina Harrison, as a lady's maid, complained of employers' reluctance to increase pay. After five years with Lady Cranborne in the 1920s she was still only earning £24 a year: 'Any request I made for an increase was flatly, almost rudely, refused. I don't know whether there was a conspiracy among the upper classes to keep servants' wages down, but everyone I knew in service at that time met with the same brick-wall attitude.'[124] As a consequence, Rosina decided to move, but was told curtly by Lady Cranborne that it was not convenient for her to leave. This meant she would not provide a reference. Fortunately, Rose had a reference from a previous employer and using this she was able to get a post as maid to the Hon. Phyllis Astor, Lady Astor's daughter, at £60 a year.[125] That was in 1928 and within months she had been promoted to be Lady Astor's own maid. She then earned £76 a year, but when after six years she asked for a rise she was granted a meagre £5 a year. 'I was disappointed and disgusted. I said nothing. . . . I'd learnt my lesson. I never asked for another rise, and I never got one. At that time goodness was supposed to be its own reward.'[126]

In other households payments were made at irregular intervals. Jean Rennie worked in a large house in Yorkshire where the monthly payments were often a fortnight late. 'I did hear tell of a kitchenmaid who went on strike till she got her pay on the sixteenth. She got her pay, and her month's notice.' But the effect of this uncertainty was that 'between not knowing when we'd be paid and not knowing when we could get off to go even up to the village to send some home, even if it was only a pound out of my two pounds a month, it always seemed as though we were working for nothing'.[127]

At Chatsworth there was an even more controversial employer innovation. At an earlier period when tea was substituted for beer, cash was paid in lieu, hence 'beer money' was given as an addition to the wages. In the late 1920s that amounted to £6 10s a year. However, in 1931 when income tax rose to 5s in the pound, the then Duchess of Devonshire decided on 'stringent economies and stopped the beer money'. This was a considerable part of the wages, especially for junior staff, and was included in the contract of employment. Not surprisingly, the decision rankled greatly.[128]

In small households, wages varied according to the employer's assessment of a worker's ability and what he or she felt able to afford. The general trend was for pay rates to rise, but the situation was affected locally by the laws of supply and demand. Hence, in depressed areas, where alternative employment was in short supply and in many provincial towns, families were able to recruit maids for a very low wage. At Bangor, where most of the girls came from rural Anglesey, Daphne Robinson's mother paid as little as 5s a week (or £13 a year) for an inexperienced maid, on the grounds that she was being trained. This was in the 1920s. Later the wage rose to 7s 6d a week (or £19 10s a year) and finally to 10s a week (or £26 a year).[129] In Middlesbrough as late as 1929 an adult resident general servant could be hired to do all the housework and washing and most of the cooking for 10s a week, plus free uniform and the payment of the National Health Insurance stamp.[130]

These rates may be compared to those offered to young girls leaving the Ystrad government training centre in South Wales in September 1928. Their pay varied from £20 a year to £26, which was paid to a sixteen-year-old housemaid going to London. Similar sums were received by trainees leaving the course in November of that same year.[131] The relatively low levels of pay reflected their youth and inexperience.

Finally, there were clear differences between the earnings of senior staff and their juniors in the same household. The seniors were also more likely to receive tips to boost their income further. In the 1920s the staff wages of a shipping magnate in Cheshire ranged from £60 a year paid to the housekeeper and £50 to the cook down to £15 to £20 a year paid to the 'tweeny'. As a butler at Nidd Hall, in Yorkshire, between 1923 and 1934, John Henry Inch earned £120 a year, plus a free house,

Butlers had an important role to play in ensuring the household ran smoothly. John Henry Inch in the dining room at Nidd Hall. (*Arthur R. Inch*)

with electricity provided from the estate generator and free wood for his fires.[132] This was far more than the pay secured by his subordinates.

In 1934 a social survey of domestic employment in Merseyside drew attention to the importance of regional pay differences, with the lack of alternative female jobs in Liverpool, creating a pool of lower-paid general servants. For higher-grade workers the regional difference was less noticeable, even when London was compared with Liverpool. (This is shown in Table 2.)[133]

Such figures were, of course, only averages and a cursory examination of advertisements for domestic staff in *The Times* confirms the wide range of pay available at any one time. On 7 July 1925, for example, vacancies included a post of cook-housekeeper at Sevenoaks for £80 to £85 per annum, 'could bring own kitchenmaid', while £90 was offered for a cook at Maidstone, with 'three in the kitchen' and £30 per annum for a cook-general at Kingsbridge in Devon. Similarly, an upper-parlourmaid near Birmingham could obtain £55 a year, while a parlourmaid in St James's Park, in

TABLE 2 *Average Annual Wage Rates for Different Types of Servant as Shown by Housewives' Returns*

	Liverpool (1932)	London (1929-30)
Senior staff		
Cook	£52 10s	£56 0s
Parlourmaid	£48 0s	£50 0s
Housemaid	£44 0s	£45 0s
Lower-grade staff		
Cook-general	£45 10s	£52 0s
General maid	£39 0s	£45 0s

London, 'able [to] carve and valet' might obtain an annual £45 to £48; but a parlourmaid who was expected to work in both London and Sussex was offered only £43 per annum. Even wider discrepancies occurred in respect of housemaids, with £26 to £28 a year offered at the bottom of the pay scale and £40 or more at the upper end. Among the men, a butler-valet for Victoria in London could secure £52 a year, plus an outfit of clothes, while one prepared to work in town and in Scotland might obtain £80 to £100, 'would [suit] first footman taking first place', it was suggested.

Such differences reflected the varying wealth of employers and their expectations of the skills to be offered by their domestics. Yet, while upper limits of pay and conditions ranged widely, at the bottom of the scale, domestic service reformers were concerned to establish minimum standards for hours, pay rates, accommodation, food and holiday entitlement. These were objectives which had been included in 'A Charter of Emancipation' published in *The Labour Woman* in February 1919. They were reiterated throughout the inter-war period and included in a Labour Party Domestic Workers' Charter, published in 1931.[134] In June 1938 these demands were to lead to the inauguration of a new trade union to cater for servants, the National Union of Domestic Workers (NUDW).

DOMESTIC WORKERS' TRADE UNIONISM

Attempts to form trade unions among domestic workers had been made before the First World War. In 1910, for example, at a time of general labour unrest, the Domestic Workers' Union of Great Britain was formed in London with a young servant named Grace Neal as secretary.[135] It optimistically chose as the colours for its banner 'Red for progress, Green for hope and Gold for dawn'.[136] A year or so later a similar organisation was set up in Glasgow under the leadership of Jessie Stephen, the daughter of a Socialist tailor and cutter. Jessie was employed as a cook, but for some time she had been trying to establish a union, going round to houses when she knew employers were likely to be out, in order to contact the staff. As a result of these efforts the Scottish Domestic Workers' Federation was formed and soon achieved a membership of around six hundred in the Glasgow area.[137] However, its demands for higher wages, two hours' free time each day and regular rest days every month aroused employer hostility. Membership was further hampered by the fact that the majority of maids in the district were drawn 'from the Highlands of Scotland or Southern Ireland and it would have been a great risk for a lonely servant to become militant by joining a trade union'.[138]

Miss Stephen's own experience certainly confirmed the dangers of victimisation. She lost her post and was blacklisted by mistresses and by servant registry offices in Glasgow. After fruitless efforts to get work she came to London and joined the Domestic Workers' Union. This had its own registry office and through that she obtained a fresh position with employers who did not object to engaging a trade unionist. She continued her propaganda work, but in the meantime the Glasgow union, deprived of her energetic leadership, faded away.[139] The same fate was to attend the Domestic Workers' Union. In 1912 membership had still only reached about 245 and it was slightly lower in 1913. When war broke out, the union's attempts to carry on were further undermined as domestic workers left to go into munitions factories and other war-related occupations; it was wound up in 1918.[140]

Both of these early unions suffered from problems which were to hamper their post-war successors. They included the limited spare time and general political apathy of most domestic servants, coupled with their reluctance to pay even a small weekly subscription from their often meagre earnings and their general isolation, working in units of one or two people only. This made them difficult to contact and vulnerable to intimidation by employers, since dismissal without a good reference at short notice meant not only the loss of a job and a home, but difficulty in obtaining a fresh place. For girls who had come from a distance that presented an especial problem, particularly if they lacked the funds to get back to their family. Servants in larger households, with paternalistic employers, often shared the snobbishness and the anti-trade union views of their employers and so took no part in the movement.

In the immediate aftermath of the First World War there was renewed militancy among many groups of workers and efforts were again made to form domestic workers' trade unions. They included an organisation set up in Birmingham by the Workers' Union. This negotiated with local employers to establish an agreed working day of from 6.30 a.m. to 10 p.m., with 4 1/2 hours off daily, including two hours for meals, plus free time during the week and a minimum wage of £34 16s a year for servants aged twenty-four and over. A social club was opened and weekly dancing lessons were offered by one of the mistresses.[141] A meeting to establish a similar body in London was held at around the same time, while in Edinburgh a National Domestic Union (NDU) was formed in 1919.[142] The NDU survived to the end of the 1930s, but the others died out, hit by similar difficulties to those which had undermined their predecessors before 1914.

Sporadic attempts to form unions were attempted elsewhere, but it was not until the franchise was extended to women of twenty-one and over in 1928 that the Labour Party, encouraged by its Women's Section, took an interest in the question. In a pamphlet to promote the cause, issued in 1930, the party pointed out that private resident servants accounted for between a quarter and a third of all the women voters in wealthy constituencies like Westminster and Kensington. That potential electoral influence could be used to bring about better working conditions. It was proposed to draw up a Domestic Workers' Charter which would be put before a National Conference of Labour Women to be held in the spring of 1931.[143]

When the conference was held the proposed charter covered such issues as the need for better training of workers, help in finding new jobs and the necessity for references to be provided, as well as the more familiar demands for annual holidays and minimum standards for wages, working hours and bedroom accommodation. If employers wanted a special uniform to be worn, they should provide it rather than expect the servant to purchase it, and in any case it 'should not consist of any badge of servility, such as a cap which serves no purpose of utility'.[144] The Transport and General Workers Union (T&GWU) and the National Union of General and

Municipal Workers (NUGMW) were invited to consult with the Trades Union Congress's (TUC) Advisory Council on Women's Organisations in order to plan a recruitment campaign. In the event, both unions, aware of the pitfalls involved in organising this predominantly female and politically apathetic sector of the labour force, refused to take part. The only progress made was that Dorothy M. Elliott, Chief Woman Officer of the NUGMW, devoted much of her spare time to co-operating with the Hampstead Trades Council in order to form a Domestic Workers' Guild, in an area where many servants were employed. It was inaugurated in May 1932 and by the year's end claimed a membership of 118. However, its prime interests proved to be recreational rather than politics and unionism. In a letter to Nancy Adam, Chief Woman Officer of the TUC, Miss Elliott expressed a hope that early in 1933 a discussion group could be started to develop the guild's educational

Retired Admiral (being shown the fragments of a statuette). "MY GOOD WOMAN, I BELIEVE THAT IF YOU HAD TO DUST A BATTLESHIP YOU'D BREAK IT."

The continuing low status of daily cleaners is made clear in this *Punch* cartoon showing an elderly, incompetent charwoman. (Punch, *6 August, 1930*)

programme. Out of that she hoped would emerge 'a desire for more active work . . . which should lead to some form of trade union organisation'.[145]

Once again these hopes were to be dashed. Although the guild carried on with its social activities until at least 1936, the efforts to promote trade unionism were unsuccessful. In 1937 one of the leaders of the Hampstead Trades Council wrote to the TUC pressing for the formation of a union and apparently expressing a willingness to take a lead in the matter. The secretary of the TUC's Organisation Department responded unenthusiastically:

> This has been attempted on more than one occasion in the past without success. Several devoted TU officials put themselves and their families into debt in an attempt to form a Union of domestic workers.
>
> As these workers are usually employed singly and difficult to reach, it would be almost impossible to form a really active union of this description. In fact after years of experience several unions have decided they will waste no more time and money on the effort.[146]

Yet within weeks there had been an unexpected change of heart by the TUC leaders. Perhaps they feared that members of the Hampstead Trades Council would take action on their own and set up yet another ineffective body. In any event, at a meeting in December 1937 the TUC's General Council proposed the formation of a union. On 4 December its officials wrote to several voluntary organisations, including the Metropolitan Association for Befriending Young Servants and the Wayfarers' Guild, whose members included servants, asking for support and the opportunity to contact their domestic members. In addition, it was decided to take a stall at the 1938 Domestic Services Exhibition. Special leaflets were prepared asking visiting maids to state whether they would be in favour of a union being formed.[147]

Over a thousand domestic workers indicated they would support combined action and in April 1938 the General Council finally decided to break with tradition and set up an organisation of its own. Hitherto the TUC had merely accepted into affiliation unions which the workers in an occupation had themselves formed. In announcing the decision the General Council appealed to the wider union movement to help ensure that through this initiative 'domestic workers will find their "Prince Charming".'[148]

A month later the post of organiser for the National Union of Domestic Workers was advertised. Out of over three hundred applicants Beatrice Bezzant was chosen. She was thirty-nine years old, one of eight children of a Wiltshire farm labourer and had entered domestic service in 1914. After five years she left to care for an elderly relative and also to take up teaching and free-lance journalism. She then won a scholarship to Hillcroft College, a working women's college in Surbiton. After completing a course there she returned to Wiltshire as an assistant teacher, but her thirst for education was such that she decided to return to Hillcroft in 1931 as a maid. There she remained for two years, studying in her spare time. She joined the NUGMW in 1932 and a year later won the first of three scholarships which enabled her to study at Ruskin College, Oxford, for three years. She left to become an assistant poor law relieving officer in Rotherham. When not studying in Oxford she took temporary domestic posts and this combination of servant experience and educational achievement made her an attractive candidate. When interviewed for the organiser's post she confessed that it was the job she had always longed to do.[149]

Around the time of the NUDW's official launch on 29 June 1938, E. P. Harries of the TUC's Organisation Department told the TUC general secretary that he saw the union's main task as raising 'the status of the industry by securing increased leisure, freedom for social contacts, formation of social clubs, legal assistance and probably the development of a Friendly Benefit side, particularly in the direction of pensions'. Higher wages were not regarded as an immediate priority.[150]

At the time of its inauguration the NUDW had a membership of 250 and, as a result of press publicity and the recruitment efforts of Miss Bezzant and other supporters that had increased to 525 at the end of July. Among those trying to win new members was Mrs Savilla Connolly. Years later she recalled how she and some friends had worked hard to get the union going. 'We canvassed houses in the Primrose Hill and St John's Wood areas (they nearly all had servants then). We had just ... got official recognition when the Second World War broke out and we all drifted apart.'[151]

In the autumn of 1938 the NUDW issued a Domestic Workers' Charter entitled *Steps*. This demanded a maximum working period of eighty-eight hours a fortnight for servants under eighteen years and ninety-six hours a fortnight for those over eighteen, with the precise breakdown of these left to the contracting parties. A scale of minimum wages for all categories of workers was proposed, while the same quality of food was to be served throughout the household, rather than inferior ingredients being offered to domestics. Other provisions covered holidays, uniform, the receiving of visitors, the mode of addressing a worker (such as Christian name, surname or title) to be decided by the two parties and finally the need to have a written contract. 'No worker should accept employment without the conditions of employment being stated in writing.'[152]

By March 1939 NUDW membership had risen to 1,052, with recruitment extending beyond Greater London to include some provincial centres such as Derby, Chesterfield and Sheffield. Success in the first two towns was attributed to the efforts of one enthusiastic member, a Miss Davies.[153] The largest branch was at Knightsbridge in London, with 229 members, of whom thirty had been secured by a single activist. Membership meetings were organised at which refreshments were served and discussions were held on conditions in domestic employment and the merits of unionisation.

But when the TUC's annual congress was held in the autumn of 1939 the NUDW's problems were already apparent. Total membership now stood at 805, of whom 599 were in local branches and 206 were scattered in various parts of England, plus a few in Scotland and Wales. The London membership accounted for 549 of the total, being mostly organised in fourteen branches, while the four provincial branches in Bristol, Chesterfield, Derby and Sheffield had just sixty-two members between them. Several hundred other members had been recruited during the year, but they had lapsed or resigned. This was attributed partly to the mobility of the workers; when they changed jobs they often proved impossible to trace.[154] Problems of victimisation and employer hostility also occurred. As early as July 1939 a letter was read to a NUDW Committee meeting in which a member tendered her resignation 'as her employer wished her to do so'. A note was received from another member in which a prospective employer had stated 'that as she was a member of the Union her application would not be considered'.[155] A month earlier Miss Bezzant and Mr Harries of the TUC had gloomily referred to 'the difficulty of making contact' with workers and had stressed that progress

The way to a better future in domestic service. This illustration appeared on the front cover of Steps, a charter for domestic workers issued by the NUDW in 1938. (*TUC Library*)

depended on members bringing along non-member friends to meetings, so numbers could be boosted.[156]

Alongside its general efforts to promote working conditions, as laid down in its charter, the union offered other advantages. These included an accident benefit of 7s 6d per week for four weeks in any one year, and the offering of a free holiday at a TUC holiday home for selected candidates. Legal help was given to members whose wages had been wrongfully withheld or who had been dismissed without proper notice, and various sums of compensation were obtained. A Sunday Social Club was opened in London and a newsletter was sent to each member every month. On a broader front, concern was voiced about the influx of foreign domestic workers, with fears expressed that some of them (especially the refugees fleeing persecution in Europe) would accept work for lower pay and poorer conditions than British servants and would thereby undermine the latter's position. In another aspect of this unfortunate 'anti-foreigner' sentiment, the union refused to accept foreign domestics as members, despite its evident recruitment difficulties.[157] The fact that membership was confined to domestics in private employment proved an additional limiting factor. Although unions like the T&GWU had attempted to recruit workers in the hotel and catering trades, their efforts had not been successful. As in private service, long hours, the ease with which junior staff could be hired and fired and low pay, all proved inhibiting factors.[158] Yet by not recruiting from this labour force (by not poaching the preserves of other unions) the NUDW further restricted its sphere of action.

With the onset of war in September 1939, union membership plummeted to 476 in 1940 and 294 by 1945.[159] With the drop in numbers Miss Bezzant ceased to be organiser and moved to a position at the Ministry of Labour, never returning to her old post.[160]

When the war ended in 1945 the NUDW carried on with a few faithful members. Attempts were made to revive it in the late 1940s, but they proved fruitless. In the post-war world private domestic service itself was shrinking and yet TUC leaders were reluctant to admit that their experiment, like those that had preceded it, was a failure.[161]

Eventually, after pressure from the Ministry of Labour for the submission of membership returns, the union was officially reported as having ceased operation. Miss D. Hunwicks of the ministry minuted on 30 August 1955 that she had been told by a TUC official 'in strict confidence that the union isn't functioning – and really does not exist, no contributions are collected and the members have been advised to join either the T&GWU or the NUG&MW, but Sir Vincent Tewson [the then General Secretary of the TUC] will not admit that this trade union does not exist'. At that point the ministry decided to allow it to slide into oblivion.[162]

Unique among major occupations in the first half of the twentieth century, therefore, domestic service never achieved an effective trade union. Workers were too scattered, they had difficulty in obtaining time off to attend meetings and, above all, they were too vulnerable to possible victimisation from 'upstairs'. Some undoubtedly shared their employers' suspicions about labour organisations anyway and they were reluctant to invest hard-earned cash in subscribing to a body in which they had little faith. Most dissatisfied domestics preferred to move on to a new post, rather than engage in a lengthy struggle for better conditions in their existing one.

CHAPTER SIX

THE OVERSEAS DIMENSION

The need of women for women's work in the household and as wives of the present and mothers of the future generations is urgent throughout the Dominions.
Imperial Economic Conference: Record of Proceedings and Documents,
Parliamentary Papers, 1924, Vol. X, p. 144.

GERMAN-JEWISH Couple, 45, 42, seek post as Servants; able and willing to do any work; wife experience in all household duties, good cook, baking. – Write W Baer, Hamburg 13, Hansastr. 71.

GERMAN Housemaid (24) seeks position in English family; understands cookery, housework, and sewing. – Write Frau Irene Kadisch, Berlin W50, Spiechernstr. 19.
Advertisements in *The Times,* 11 March 1939

BRITISH MIGRANTS

Female domestic servants played a significant role in the rise in emigration from Britain to parts of the Empire that occurred immediately before the First World War. During the years from 1904 to 1907 16,124 maids went to Canada alone from the British Isles.[1] Canada was especially attractive as a destination because it was the nearest of the major dominions and so the cheapest to reach. Australia and New Zealand, as the most distant, were the costliest, although from time to time free and assisted passages were offered to female domestics.[2]

British migration in these pre-war years was encouraged for a number of reasons. From the point of view of the maids and of the emigration organisations which assisted them, it provided an opportunity to settle in a new country where wages were higher and their social status as household workers was more assured than in the home country.[3] Indeed, at the beginning of 1920 one English promoter of domestic workers' trade unionism told her audience that she wanted the occupation in Britain to be 'like what it is in Canada'. She described three English girls who after three years as servants had amassed sufficient savings to take a six months' holiday in Britain. 'In Canada they had their own flat where they could spend their week-ends, and they told their friends in England that the girl who was earning her living in domestic service was more respected there than the business girl.'[4]

Other commentators painted a less favourable picture, although they agreed that female servants would be 'welcomed everywhere'. In the case of New Zealand, for example, domestic work was described as 'one of the most profitable of women's occupations', but also 'the least popular work open to women'.[5]

Also significant was the growth in imperial sentiment which emphasised the importance of strengthening the British presence in the white dominions. The migrating maids were seen not merely as workers, but as future wives and mothers in countries where male settlers far outnumbered females.[6] For religious organisations like the Girls' Friendly Society (GFS) there was a wider role to play, as well. It was not merely taking British moral values to the new lands, but it was exporting a whole way of life.[7] Mrs Joyce, a GFS activist, founded the British Women's Emigration Association in 1884. Almost thirty years later, she described the migration of society members as 'the most practical bit of religious work that anyone can take up. Its missionary influence is the largest: it is missionary work done by hundreds.'[8]

Farmers' wives in the dominions were in particular need of domestic help. Stanley Johnson, writing in 1913, suggested that so great was the demand for maids in Canada that householders frequently forwarded 'sufficient money for a girl's passage to one of the better known emigrant societies in England, with the request that a suitable servant be sent out to them'. In other cases, passage money was entrusted to 'lady organisers', who came to England and personally chose as many domestics as they required. One such organiser, connected with the Girls' Home of Welcome at Winnipeg, claimed that she had been given a thousand pounds in a single year for advance passages.[9] In 1913, the Employment and Emigration Department of the YWCA in Britain also became a migration agency, though this time for the government of South Australia. It worked in conjunction with the British Women's Emigration Association and was paid a bonus for any domestic migrants it secured.[10]

General servants were those most in demand, since few colonial households had more than one maid. She was expected to clean, do the washing and some cooking. Equipment was often primitive, but in recompense, in country areas at least, such girls were treated as members of the family, sitting at the same table for meals as their employers and joining in their social activities.[11]

Dr Barnardo's Homes and other children's charities became involved, too, seeing in the predominantly rural society of the dominions an opportunity for their young charges to grow up in a less corrupt environment than the cities in Britain where many of them had originated. 'Snatched from the slime and vice of the slums and transported to the healthy fresh air and wholesome hard work of a new country', writes June Rose, Barnardo's believed the children 'would surely flourish'.[12] The policy had the further merit of allowing new children to be brought into the charity's British orphanages as former residents went overseas. Girls were hired out as servants to Canadian farmers from thirteen years of age. However, many of them were deeply unhappy, living on isolated farmsteads among strangers in a country with a harsh winter climate. They also faced the possible threat of physical and sexual abuse and enjoyed few leisure pursuits.[13] Around one in seven of the girls were so badly treated by employers that they had to be removed or their employers were reprimanded. Even then, on average, the girls moved about four times in their first five years.[14] Not until 1925 did the Canadian Government ban the entry of child migrants under fourteen who came without their parents. At first the ban was temporary, but in 1928 it became permanent.[15]

Mass migration to parts of the Empire was not the only kind of emigration to affect British servants. Some chose to move to the United States and, at the upper end of the scale, there was a demand in Europe and the USA for specialist workers such as butlers, valets and nannies. The records of Norland College show that its nurses were recruited by European aristocrats and royalty. Lilian Eadie was working for a cousin of the Tsar when the Russian Revolution broke out in 1917. She escaped on the last train to depart, but had to abandon her belongings. Marian Burgess, employed by the Grand Duchess Kirill of Russia, was another Norlander caught up in the revolution. She died in 1920 and her mistress paid tribute to her loyal service. 'Weeks of sleepless nights – surrounded as we were by bloodshed, murder and terror – her courage never gave way. Living for nearly a year on starvation rations she managed by her untiring devotion to keep our three children in good health.' After the murder of the Russian royal family, the Grand Duchess Kirill and her household were banished to Poland, where they contracted typhoid. Marian Burgess nursed her young charges through this before succumbing to influenza.[16]

With the outbreak of the First World War emigration virtually ceased, which included the movement of domestic servants. Instead, many left their occupation to take up war work in Britain. When migration was resumed during the 1920s it was in a very different world. Although the spirit of imperialism was still strong, the unthinking optimism about the Empire which had existed earlier in the century had diminished, as had the number of those wishing to settle abroad.[17] Yet among the governments of Britain, Canada, Australia and New Zealand many of the motives which had encouraged migration before 1914 still existed, some in an even stronger form. Thus, as a result of the male death toll during the war there was increased concern about the 'surplus' female population in Britain and the possible effects of unemployment when they lost their wartime jobs once the peace was signed. As Celia Briar writes drily, 'Whereas employed spinsters were at best tolerated, unemployed spinsters were described as "surplus" to the requirements of the nation; and the objective . . . was to channel them into the least desired jobs in another country'.[18]

At the same time, within the dominions there was pressure to provide domestic assistance so as to ease the burden on wives and mothers. It was thought that the servant shortage would keep down the birth rate. It was this which led the Oversea Settlement Committee of the Colonial Office in London to conclude that there was in these countries 'an urgent and unlimited demand for women, especially as household helpers'. It admitted that problems had arisen from the servant shortage in Britain itself, but the scarcity 'of such women overseas has been incomparably greater and more serious . . . the birth-rate overseas has been prejudicially affected'.[19] It was accepted that females were, in general, less inclined to migrate than men, but poor employment prospects in Britain might change that, especially since there were 'immediate chances of employment' and 'prospects of happy married life' overseas which were unavailable in this country.[20] The arguments had strong gender overtones, in that it was clearly believed that women's proper role in the world was as homemakers, either in their own house or in that of someone else.

These views were made clear by the Oversea Settlement Department in special reports on Canada, Australia and New Zealand, published in 1919 and 1920. Without exception they agreed that domestic work was the most appropriate occupation for female migrants. They also stressed the need for migrating maids to be equipped with appropriate skills, since training facilities overseas were almost non-existent. It was essential, too, that they should be flexible about the jobs they were prepared to carry out. As the report on Canada pointed out:

> settlers intended to enter domestic service should be experienced not only in one particular branch of work, but have knowledge of all the various duties connected with house service, and be prepared to undertake every kind of domestic labour, including cooking, laundry and mending. . . . Canadian homes . . . are organised on lines different from those in the United Kingdom. The vast majority of mistresses keep one maid and supervise all the work themselves.[21]

It was important, too, that the problems of isolation should be made clear to those planning to settle in country districts. In Victoria, Australia, for example, those employed on farmsteads would work alongside the farmer's wife and daughters and would be expected to carry out light outdoor tasks, such as milking cows or feeding poultry, as well as their domestic chores. In such homes the maid would usually share in 'whatever amusements may be provided'. However, those 'whose only recreation or pleasure can be found in picture-halls or crowded streets should not go to country homes'.[22]

To facilitate the migration programme the three main pre-war women's emigration societies merged in 1919 to form the Society for the Overseas Settlement of British Women (SOSBW), which was itself associated with the Colonial Office's Oversea Settlement Department. Mrs Joyce of the Girls' Friendly Society, who had formed, the British Women's Emigration Association over thirty years before, welcomed this new body as they shared the same aims. These were the careful selection of candidates, 'watchful protection' of them on the journey to their new home (including the provision of female superintendents on board ship), and their 'judicious distribution' in the country of destination.[23] In 1920 the GFS entrusted all its migration arrangements to the new organisation.

A further boost to the movement came with the passage of the Empire Settlement Act of 1922. This authorised the British government, in association with organisations in the dominions, to provide aid to subsidise the passage costs and the training of 'suitable persons' from the United Kingdom who were seeking to settle in one of these countries. The British contribution was restricted to a maximum of one half of the cost of any scheme.[24]

As a result of these initiatives, New Zealand began offering free passage to domestic servants from 1919, while in the early 1920s the government of the

Province of Ontario, Canada, offered assisted passages to two thousand single women prepared to come as maids. The aid took the form of a loan to cover the cost of the voyage, but those who remained in service on a farm for a year would be entitled to a refund on the amount to be repaid.[25] Soon Australia, other provinces in Canada and southern Africa began offering free or assisted passages.

As well as relying on the efforts of SOSBW and organisations such as the GFS and the Church of England Council of Empire Settlement to secure migrant maids, would-be employers advertised vacancies in the press, often through London-based servant agencies. Thus, in November 1927 there was an appeal for a single-handed cook for a post in Canada. Wages were a substantial £90 a year, three maids were kept and a good home was promised. Similarly a cook-general and a house-parlourmaid were

MIGRATION NOTICES.

If you { are desirous of settling overseas, } there may { are free to do so, and } { have your parents' consent, } be something to interest you in the following list of vacancies of posts overseas. Application should be made to The Secretary, G.F.S. Central Office, Townsend House, Greycoat Place, London, S.W. 1—and please be *sure* to put the name of your Home Branch at the foot of your letter !

Nurses.—Fully-trained, with C.M.B., under forty, for Orange Free State. Salary £120 resident. Similar posts in Kenya and Cape Province.

Children's Nurses. — Required in March for a few months in England, then Canada with the family, for children aged eight and five and baby from birth. Not college or hospital trained. Age twenty-five to thirty. Salary £55-60 per annum.

Experienced Children's Nurses for Cape Province, S. Rhodesia, Kenya, are required. Salaries from £50-100 according to training and experience.

Governesses and Nursery Governesses.—S. Rhodesia ; to teach four children usual subjects, music and one foreign language. Salary £84, assisted passage. Kenya : Froebel-trained, to teach three boys, seven, five, and four. Salary £120 per annum, passage paid. Nursery Governesses under thirty-five can be placed in Melbourne, also in Canada.

Teachers.—Classics Mistress, with Honours degree, and a Science Mistress for Toronto and British Columbia respectively. A music Mistress for New Zealand. Full particulars on application.

Domestic Workers.—A Cook required as soon as possible for small family in New Zealand, 30s. a week, free passage. Cook-Housekeeper for Bulawayo in March, £8 per month, free passage. Home Help for Bulawayo, £5 per month.

Women with references for Domestic Employment can apply for assisted passages to Canada and for free passages to New Zealand. Training Centres in different parts of England have been opened for suitable applicants to be trained in household work for six to eight weeks before going overseas.

Vacancies for domestic staff overseas advertised in *GFS Magazine*, February 1930. (*Girls' Friendly Society*)

wanted for New Zealand, at wages of 30s and 25s per week, respectively. A free passage was offered and the two were to leave together in December. Both of these advertisements were inserted in *The Times* by the British Empire Bureau, located in Edgware Road, London.[26] From 1928 the *GFS Magazine* provided lists of overseas vacancies, including a few for children's nurses in southern Africa as well as more general posts in Australia, New Zealand and Canada. In Africa, black servants carried out the domestic chores and South African mothers played an active role in the bringing up of their children. As a contemporary pointed out, 'many a job in Africa is waiting for a well-trained girl as under-nurse under the mother but at head nurse's wages'.[27]

Dr Barnardo's also embarked on a new migration programme, this time exploring the possibility of moving youngsters to Australia as well as Canada. In Australia it found a favourable response in the early 1920s from those supporting the then government's 'White Australia' policy.[28] The first party of Barnardo girls arrived in 1923, with considerable care taken over their placement. No youngsters were to be sent to isolated locations, but were to be settled in groups. A minimum wage of 14s a week was fixed for those aged fourteen and a ladies' committee was formed to keep in touch with them in their new homes. They were to be visited once a month by a specially appointed 'lady visitor'.[29] Marjorie Bicker migrated in November 1937, when she was about fourteen. She had some reservations about moving to Australia and on arrival spent time at Barnardo's Mowbray Park Farm School. In all she worked as a servant for two years, receiving help during that time from a 'very approachable' official employed by the charity. But when she was eighteen she asked permission to join the Armed Services and spent almost four years in the Forces. Then, at the age of twenty-one, she returned to Britain.[30]

Marjorie's doubts about emigrating were shared by other girls, and it was recognised by the mid-1920s that the number of those prepared to move was limited. The Girls' Friendly Society attributed this to the unpopularity of domestic service in Britain itself and to ignorance about the Empire. To meet this last point the society instituted Empire Study Circles, in conjunction with the London and Southwark dioceses. Essay competitions with an imperial theme were arranged and at Sunday tea parties at GFS Lodges girls were encouraged to bring letters they had received from fellow members who had settled overseas and to read them aloud. This was seen as an 'excellent means of spreading knowledge among the Members'.[31] Later an Empire Scrapbook competition was organised and publicity material concerning the dominions was distributed to branches throughout the various dioceses.[32]

Success stories were also publicised in GFS literature from time to time, as in 1922, when it was reported that a member who had migrated from Norwich to become a servant in the rectory at Barberton, Transvaal, had organised a Bible Class for fifteen Indian girls. As a result the girls had become regular church attenders. In addition, 'happy accounts' had been received concerning the parties who had gone to Canada.[33]

On a broader front, however, it was realised that many potential female migrants were unable to take advantage of domestic vacancies overseas because they lacked appropriate training. In 1926 discussions were held between the Australian and British governments over the establishment of a joint training centre to provide about two months' instruction to single girls and childless widows aged eighteen to thirty-five from a non-servant background. They were to be carefully selected, unlike some earlier migrants to Australia and New Zealand who had allegedly 'got thoroughly demoralised on the journey and had refused to do a hand's turn of work when they arrived'. Such a development would immediately 'destroy the success of the Centre'. Assurances were to be obtained as to wage rates in Australia, and there should be 'adequate oversight as to the terms and conditions of employment'.[34]

Agreement was finally reached in the spring of 1927, with part of the cost of the scheme borne by the Oversea Settlement Committee in Britain and part by the Australian government.[35] The running of the course was under the direction of the Central Committee on Women's Training and Employment (CCWTE), which was already responsible for the non-resident training centres provided for women and girls taking up domestic work in Britain. Publicity was given about conditions in Australia by the showing of films in more than three hundred cinemas during 1927, under the auspices of the Ministry of Labour. It was estimated that around two hundred women had emigrated as household workers as a result of these alone. A smaller number had also emigrated to Canada and New Zealand as a result of this initiative.[36]

The first CCWTE course began in September 1927 at a residential hostel in Market Harborough, where forty girls could be accommodated at any one time. Selection was undertaken by a representative of the Australian government and candidates had to be physically fit. They had also to sign an undertaking they would leave for the dominion on a free passage as soon as they had successfully completed the course. Instruction was free and covered cooking, laundry work, the general care of a house and needlework. To ensure it had a practical bent the women undertook all the domestic chores of the hostel and made dresses, aprons and other garments in readiness for their new occupation. Pocket money of 2s 6d a week was paid and they were given free travel from home to the hostel. One of the skills to be taught was the use of wood-burning stoves of a type common in Australia.[37]

The first trainees completed the course and left in November for their new employment, which was found for them by the dominion government.[38] Soon others were following in their wake. Before their departure, the female emigrants were entertained to tea at Australia House. Early in February 1928, the Labour MP Margaret Bondfield, addressed one group and, as in her efforts to promote female domestic training in Britain itself, she emphasised the importance of women's role within the household.

> The proper keeping of the home, and the proper feeding of the inmates, was the most important work that fell to women to do. The conditions under which domestic servants had to work in this country might well be objected to, but to look down on domestic service, as unfortunately was often done in this country, was one of the worst survivals of a bad tradition of social status. The women would not find that feeling in Australia. All that would be expected of them was to do their job well, and doing that they would be afforded many opportunities of pleasant social life.[39]

This optimistic view of the absence of class distinctions in Australia was confirmed by the dominion's director of migration, who also attended the tea party. The tenor of the speeches underlined the general domestic bias of female training programmes at this time. It was a return to the Victorian view of a society of 'separate spheres', with women's role seen very much as in the home.

But whatever hidden agenda was attached to the Market Harborough experiment, it proved to be successful and popular. Recruits were described as an 'unusually high class of girl', although their previous occupational background differed little from that of recruits to the existing British training centres, including as it did clerks, shop assistants, factory workers and dressmakers in the main.[40] Between September 1927 and December 1928, 286 trainees completed the course and sailed to Australia.[41]

In these circumstances the Oversea Settlement Department contacted the Scottish Committee of CCWTE to suggest the establishment of a similar centre in Scotland, with part of the cost to be borne by the British Government and the rest to be raised locally from voluntary sources. Trainees would also be free to travel to other dominions as well as Australia. The Scottish hostel opened at Lenzie, near Glasgow, in May 1929 and by the end of the year ninety-seven trainees had left for domestic employment overseas, eighty-six going to Canada and eleven to Australia.[42] Voluntary centres were also opened with British Government backing at Newcastle upon Tyne and Cardiff, where the Church Army took the initiative, and at St Mary's Training Hostel, Portobello Road, London, where thirty-six places were provided under the aegis of the Association of Ladies of Charity of St Vincent de Paul.[43] A further centre at St Albans was in the course of being opened at the end of 1929.[44]

But by the late 1920s economic conditions in the dominions were becoming bleak, as agricultural depression and world recession caused financial difficulties and unemployment. Late in 1929 a new Australian government took office and suspended the offer of free passages. In the spring of 1930 it withdrew altogether from the Market Harborough scheme.[45] The hostel remained open for a few months longer, with the backing of SOSBW and with trainees now free to settle in Canada and New Zealand as well as Australia. However, by July 1930, the number in residence had shrunk to sixteen.[46] During the almost three years the centre had been in full operation, 558 women had completed training and had sailed to, or at the date of closure in 1930, were about to sail to, Australia.[47]

The problems affecting Australia caused similar hardships in Canada and New Zealand and by the summer of 1930 the emigration of domestic servants to the dominions was virtually at an end.[48] Early in 1931 the CCWTE agreed with the Oversea Settlement Department to take over three of the centres previously used for instructing the prospective migrants. These were at Market Harborough, Newcastle upon Tyne and Lenzie. They were to be used to provide residential training for domestic workers seeking employment in Britain. At the time of transfer the hope was expressed that the change of use would be only temporary and that they would return to their original purpose.[49] However, they never did.

With the ending of government-sponsored emigration and assisted passages, the number of female servants moving overrseas fell sharply. The *GFS Magazine* advertised a few vacancies in southern Africa early in 1930, while the Annual Report for that year noted there were vacancies for English nannies, mother's helps and nursery governesses in northern and central Europe.[50] In 1932, vacancies for servants in Western Australia were also reported: 'In nearly every case, where a girl can cook and do housework, she will have a position.' But without financial aid to cover the passage money, it was accepted that few British maids would be able to save up the requisite sum.[51] In total, eighteen GFS members migrated in 1932 (not necessarily all to domestic posts); in 1920, it had been 280.[52] In 1934 the Migration Department ceased to exist as a separate entity within the society's administrative structure.[53]

Dr Barnardo's Homes also cut back on its emigration programme, with the 1933 Annual Report referring to the 'complete suspension of migration . . . (save for a limited number sent to Australia)' and seeing that as throwing 'increased responsibility on those who place out our young folk in England'.[54]

As before 1914, there continued to be vacancies for a few 'superior' British servants overseas. In December 1927, for example, a vacancy for a head parlourmaid of three in Biarritz was advertised, 'equal to butler', with the substantial salary of £100 offered, together with the inducement of working in a household of seven servants.[55] Sometimes, as with Charles Dean, formerly an under-butler at Cliveden, posts were obtained in the United States; for others, like Ernest King, opportunities to work on the continent came when an employer in Britain also had an establishment in Europe.[56] Later, at the end of the 1930s, King worked for a short time for the Duke and Duchess of Windsor on the French Riviera. The staff of French and English servants combined well and just after the outbreak of the Second World War, King became the Duke's valet. However, by refusing to rejoin the Army as his employer's soldier servant, he 'sawed clean through the branch on which [he] was sitting'.[57] After losing his position he returned to England, where he was employed by Mr Philip Hill, a wealthy financier and businessman.

Norland nurses, too, continued to be in demand among the well-to-do overseas. In 1921 Kathleen Wanstall joined the royal Monegasque household where she eventually raised two generations of princes and princesses. Four years later, another Norlander was recruited by the Archduke Charles of Austria, although she earned the disapproval of the Norland College committee of management by asking for an exceptionally high salary, which she obtained.[58]

By the 1930s, however, emigration had ceased to play any significant role in the lives of British domestic servants. On the other hand, a very different story applied to foreign workers coming to the United Kingdom. Their numbers peaked in the 1930s rather than fell away. They came overwhelmingly from mainland Europe.

FOREIGN DOMESTIC WORKERS

At the beginning of the twentieth century foreign servants formed a small specialist sector of the domestic labour force. French and Swiss lady's maids were much in demand among fashionable ladies because of their dressmaking and millinery skills and their greater vivacity, compared to their British counterparts. Many well-to-do mothers similarly employed French, Swiss or German nannies and nursery governesses in order to provide their offspring with a grounding in a foreign language from an early age. Sometimes, too, as with the Marchioness of Bristol, they disliked the strict discipline imposed by English nurses. According to her daughter, Lady Bristol refused to employ nannies and instead hired Swiss girls as mother's helps so that she herself could keep a controlling hand on the way the nursery was run.[59] Years later her daughter followed this example and recruited Swiss-born nursemaids. 'I cannot remember a time when I learnt French', she later wrote, 'I can never ever remember not knowing it; sometimes now a French word comes to me when I am looking for the English one.'

Most popular was the recruitment of foreign (usually French) chefs by affluent households. At Cliveden the Astors employed M. Papillion from 1909 until shortly before his death in September 1914. According to Edwin Lee, then a footman, he was the best of the many chefs employed by the Astors and this was doubtless why his salary was a substantial £150 a year, plus 7s a week to cover beer money and washing and £1 a week board wages for food when the family was away. The

Cliveden butler at that time earned £120 a year only.[60] M. Papillion's successor, another Frenchman, was paid £125 a year. Later there was M. Gilbert, who, like most chefs, had a volatile temperament. 'I think of the kitchens even now with trepidation', wrote Rosina Harrison, Lady Astor's lady's maid, decades later. 'On big party days or even the day before, they were places to keep out of.'[61]

However, some critics condemned the extravagance and the pretensions of the chefs. Lady Violet Greville wrote scathingly of the 'man-cook' who practised 'his extortions and raises his demands daily. Year by year Italians and Frenchmen invade our shores, and take possession of our kitchens ... ruling obsequious kitchenmaids and scullions with a rod of iron. After a few years they wax fat and retire ... to an old age of comfortable competency in their native land.'[62]

Lower down the social scale the servant scarcity around 1900 led to efforts to recruit other staff from overseas. There were reports of Scandinavian girls coming to South Shields, Sunderland, and other Tyne ports to fill local vacancies. 'Their employers state that they are attentive and industrious, and without any of the foibles of English domestics', declared one optimistic report.[63] They came over partly to improve their English and partly because the pay and prospects in Britain were better than at home.

Nevertheless, foreign servants remained a very small part of the total domestic labour force. In 1911, when there were about 1.3 million female servants in England and Wales, just 10,827 of them had been born overseas and around a third of these came from Germany. Thus they comprised less than 1 per cent of all female indoor servants; their male counterparts, numbering 1,750 in 1911, formed under 4 per cent of the indoor menservants.[64]

Foreign chefs were widely recruited by the most important hotels before 1914, with the Savoy in London establishing its reputation in the late nineteenth century under the famous French chef, Auguste Escoffier, and the Swiss hotelier, Cesar Ritz. When they left they were replaced by two Frenchmen, with another famous chef, Thoraud, taking over from Escoffier. The skills of such men could make or break the reputation of a hotel. At the Savoy, one guest who examined his bill for a 'princely dinner' commented drily: 'Everything at the Savoy is French except the prices; they are tropical and grow to a great height.'[65]

Foreign waiters were employed by leading hotels and restaurants as well, especially in the West End of London. The training they received on the continent was superior to that in Britain and a knowledge of one or more foreign languages was essential in some of the most prestigious London venues. At the 1911 population census, of 23,054 waiters employed in hotels in England and Wales, no less than 7,888 were foreign – 3,263 coming from Germany and 1,591 from Italy.[66] During the First World War, large numbers of these workers lost their jobs and many returned to their homeland. Some, as 'enemy aliens' were interviewed by the police and a few were interned.

In the inter-war world a more restrictive policy towards foreign workers prevailed in Britain. Concern about high unemployment levels and a desire to encourage the training of local workers meant that few foreign waiters were allowed in. Under the terms of the 1920 Aliens Order all overseas workers had to have a Ministry of Labour permit before they could be employed and these were firmly limited for

Xavier Marcel Boulestin (1878-1943) was a highly successful French chef and restaurant owner. He is shown here giving a cookery demonstration on BBC television in 1937. He was praised for 'his simple bonhomie, his lack of ostentation, and the engaging friendliness of his delivery'. (*BBC Photograph Library*)

male staff. In consequence, leading hoteliers began training British youths, aided by the London County Council School for Waiters in Westminster. However, it was recognised that experience in other countries was essential if the young waiters were to achieve the highest standards. As a result, an exchange system was set up to enable trainees from Britain to gain experience in France, Switzerland and certain other European countries, while waiters from those countries were admitted on a pro-rata basis to gain experience in the UK and to improve their knowledge of the English language.[67] A small number of specialist hotel staff also received permits, with men like W. A. Hofflin coming to the Savoy in 1928, after attending the famous hotel school in Lausanne. In 1941 he became the Savoy's general manager.[68]

French chefs, too, continued to work in the most famous hotels and restaurants. Xavier Marcel Boulestin became London's first twentieth-century celebrity chef when in 1925 he opened his Restaurant Français in Leicester Square. Two years later he moved to Covent Garden where he established the Restaurant Boulestin. He was largely self-taught and only turned to cooking for cash in 1921 when his interior decorating business went into liquidation. Boulestin's restaurants were famous for their high quality French cuisine and fashionable decor. He wrote a series of cookery books, beginning with *Simple French Cooking for English Homes* in 1923. This was an immediate success and he later contributed cookery columns to *Vogue*, the *Daily Express*, the *Daily Telegraph*, the London *Evening Standard* and a number of other newspapers and journals. He even ran a cookery course at Fortnum and Mason's and in 1937 appeared in British Movietone News demonstrating how to make his famous Omelette Boulestin. In the same year he gave some very successful cookery demonstrations on BBC television.[69]

Disgruntled British waiters claimed that Italians were able to evade the regulations, sometimes by using illicit British passports. They then stayed with Italian friends living in Britain while they sought employment in London cafes and hotels. In February 1939, *The Times* reported the successful prosecution of one British family of Italian origin who had harboured an 'illegal alien' in this way.[70]

Despite such problems, the number of foreign staff employed in hotels and restaurants was much smaller than before 1914. The 1931 census reported that there were only 2,699 foreign waiters in England and Wales (or around a third of the 1911 total). Of these 1,038 came from Italy, 511 were Swiss and 244 were French. There were just 271 foreign waitresses (137 of them Italian).[71] At a time when, as we shall see, maids were permitted to enter the country for private domestic employment on a fairly liberal basis, the restrictions on their recruitment by commercial enterprises caused resentment. In November 1938 a meeting of the Residential Hotels Association appealed to the Ministry of Labour to relax its prohibitions on the use of foreign maids in hotels on the grounds that English workers were unavailable. 'In the past it had been accepted that foreigners should be employed in hotels since . . . Englishmen were unwilling to work in hotels . . . the importation of aliens would not throw one honest and competent British worker out of employment, nor would it lower the conditions of work.'[72] However, the Ministry was unmoved. It was anxious not to provoke worker hostility by a step which might be interpreted as taking jobs away from British men and woman, or of undermining further the already poor working conditions of the nation's catering staff.[73]

Nevertheless, a very different philosophy prevailed for the recruitment of foreign women and girls for resident, private domestic work. Under the terms of the 1920 Aliens Order, restrictions were imposed on the recruitment of male workers, but the situation was comparatively relaxed for maids. Work permits were granted by the Ministry of Labour to employers, authorising them to bring in female servants, providing they could show that they had made efforts to find staff in this country and that the wages offered were similar to those paid to British servants in the area.[74] Immediately after the First World War visas had to be obtained by foreign maids in some cases before they could enter the country, but that was phased out during the 1920s. In 1927 it was ended for Austria and Germany, the former 'enemy' countries.[75]

As a result of these developments, British employers unable to obtain servants began to advertise for foreign staff and, as before 1914, there was a special demand for lady's maids and nannies. In November 1927, for example, *The Times* included an appeal for a 'Young Lady's Maid, German or Swiss, age about 30-35, good appearance; entire charge of girl, aged nine; maiding young lady'. This was inserted by an employer in Gloucester Place, Portman Square, London. In addition a French or Swiss Lady's Maid was sought by two ladies, for an annual salary of £60: 'winter on the Riviera'.[76]

Agencies were set up to provide foreign staff, such as the Anglo-French Bureau of Regent Street, the Anglo-German Agency in the Haymarket, the Marika Agency in Notting Hill Gate and the Continental Domestic Agency in Regent Street.[77] A number of them embarked on recruitment campaigns in Europe itself or contacted foreign agencies in order to bring in the girls. Sometimes, as with a Mrs Kenning of Golders

Green, they advertised in German periodicals like *Daheim* appealing for domestic staff, ostensibly for friends, but in reality as a commercial venture. Fees had to be paid by both mistress and maid, with the former expected to cover the administrative cost of obtaining the Ministry of Labour permit as well. In one case Mrs Kenning asked for a £3 fee for acting as an intermediary. The girls were expected to refund their share of the charges out of their wages when they reached Britain.[78]

In some instances the National Vigilance Association was approached by female protection agencies in mainland Europe anxious to ensure that the girls were not being recruited for immoral purposes. Thus a Dutch Bureau wrote to enquire about a Mrs Bockling from Pinner in Middlesex who was visiting Utrecht on a recruitment campaign. 'Foreign girls must pay Mrs Bockling 1 shilling per Pound sterling of their yearly wage, for intermediation, payable within 3 months. There must be a garanty (*sic*) that the family can employ the girl for the time of a year. . . . Could you tell us if this is a *reliable* Employment Office, which we can safely recommend to girls that ask us for posts in England. Will you please make a *thorough investigation*?' The National Vigilance Association's secretary quickly assured his Dutch correspondent that Mrs Bockling was 'a perfectly respectable person so far as we can gather' and that she was about to be licensed by Middlesex County Council to run a registry office. However, he pointed out that in Britain such agencies were private, commercial undertakings and were not 'precisely the equivalent of Government [recruitment] offices which exist in many countries of Europe'.[79] A few months later a similar inquiry was made by a Dutch clergyman when Mrs Bockling inserted advertisements in a Dutch newspaper appealing for applicants 'for first class posts London & suburbs kitchenmaids, Parlour maids, and helps. . . . Start at once.' Again the NVA sent a cautiously reassuring reply.[80]

Apart from possible moral dangers faced by foreign maids coming to Britain in this way, there were other potential hazards, such as employer exploitation and problems arising from the girls' inadequate knowledge of English. The YWCA established social clubs where foreign servants could meet together, particularly in London, and offered legal advice and hostel accommodation when necessary. One case considered by the YWCA's Social and Legislation Committee in July 1920 involved a French maid. She appeared in great distress, having been told by her mistress in Berkeley Square that she must leave immediately, and without any wages. The mistress accused her of stealing silver spoons and declared she would only be paid when these were returned. The girl denied the theft and told the YWCA that her mistress drank 'and she was the only remaining maid of a staff of servants, others having been sent away, some on the pretext that they had stolen goods'. She was told to return to the mistress and again ask for her wages, also stating that she knew of a hostel to which she could go. 'She was to report to us if her wages were not paid or if her trunk were retained. She came next day and said that her wages had been paid and she had been allowed to take her trunk with her. She said she would have appealed to the police but could not speak English.'[81]

In another case two Swiss girls obtained posts as cook and house-parlourmaid through a Geneva agency. The cook was paid £60 a year and £6 was advanced for her fare. If she stayed less than a year this had to be repaid. Both girls were promised free time each week, but when they arrived they found that their mistress, who lived in the country, was highly eccentric and refused to allow any time off other than two hours per week for English lessons. At Christmas the mistress went away for a week and shut up the house, leaving the two maids to fend for themselves. They were not paid board wages, but fortunately managed to get rooms at the YWCA's International Hostel in London, at a cost of £2 9s. Immediately after Christmas the cook gave in her notice, as she had got another post, but the mistress refused to pay her anything for the month in which she was working out her notice, on the pretext that she owed this sum to cover the cost of her fare from Switzerland. Her new employer brought her to the YWCA for advice, and after a lengthy correspondence between the organisation's solicitors, acting on behalf of the girl, and the mistress's legal advisers, the latter eventually agreed to send a cheque for £6, £5 of this being wages due and £1 compensation for expenses incurred at Christmas. This the cook was advised to accept. Her new mistress was so grateful to the YWCA for the trouble taken that she donated £1 to the funds of the Industrial Law Bureau as a 'token of her appreciation of what the Society stands for'.[82] YWCA records include a number of similar cases involving non-payment of wages, the physical or sexual exploitation of young workers and other matters, which underline the potential difficulties of this kind of long-distance migration.

At the beginning of the 1920s the total of domestic permits issued to foreign maids remained relatively low. Each permit was for an initial period of twelve months, although extensions were possible and the maid had to report to the police in her new home area on arrival. There was nothing to prevent her from moving to a fresh post, providing she continued in private residential service and that she informed the police of her change of address. This led to concern that employers who would not have qualified for a foreign servant were subsequently able to offer higher wages and better conditions in order to entice a girl away from her first mistress. In a few cases, too, there were accusations that employment agencies, anxious to boost the turnover of their business, encouraged domestics to move in order to get more engagement fees from employers.[83]

In 1923, 1,025 domestic permits were issued and by 1925 this had increased to 1,540. In that year, 21 per cent of applications from employers were rejected by the Ministry of Labour, presumably on the grounds that local labour was available, or the wages offered were inadequate, or the proposed servant was in some way unsuitable. But during the 1920s, as demand in Britain for domestic staff rose and particularly following the abolition of visas for German and Austrian maids in 1927, the total rose rapidly, to reach 4,275 permits granted in 1929 and 5,581 in 1930. In both of those years, a mere 5.8 per cent of applications were turned down.[84] At a time of high unemployment among British women, this trend caused alarm in official circles, anxious to avoid accusations that jobs were being 'exported' to foreigners or that the immigrants were undermining the already unsatisfactory working conditions of many domestics in Britain by accepting lower pay and poorer standards. The dire economic plight in Central Europe at this time meant that girls were prepared to take up domestic employment not merely to widen their experience or improve their language skills, but to make a living. As a result, in 1931 the Ministry tightened up its authorisation procedures. Henceforth, permits were to be granted to employers only if they could demonstrate that they had made 'every possible effort' to find suitable labour from among permanent residents in this country, that the wages paid were at least £36 a year (or 15s a week) and that no local workers would be displaced if the permit were granted.[85] No householder could employ more than two foreign servants, since it was argued that larger households found it easier than smaller ones to recruit British staff. Employers particularly resented the strict enforcement of the 'every possible effort' clause, since it meant they had to advertise in the newspapers and enter their name at one or more domestic agency (paying a booking fee) even when the large number of vacancies in their area, particularly in and around London, made it unlikely that these efforts would be successful.[86] Yet failure to follow this procedure led to a rejection of the permit application.

As a result of the changes, the number of servants coming in fell sharply, from 6,172 in 1931, before the restrictions had taken full effect, to 2,923 in 1932 and 2,814 in 1933. In both 1932 and 1933 around 22 per cent of all applications were refused.[87] Economic depression in Britain, which made it more difficult for families to afford resident domestic staff and the greater availability of unemployed British women willing to take up household duties, reduced migrant numbers. However, by 1935, numbers started to increase, with 4,651 permits issued in that year and with less than 20 per cent rejected. These rose to 8,449 permits authorised in 1936, with 13.1 per cent rejections. Of the 1936 entrants, 4,155 were Austrians and 1,393 were Germans, while the Swiss provided 1,164 of the total.[88] Those proportions were in marked contrast to the 1931 population census figures, which had shown a total of 9,284 foreign maids employed in private residential service. Of these, 2,235 came from Switzerland and 1,628 from Germany.[89] The number of foreign domestic permits issued continued to rise, reaching 13,792 in 1938 – the last full year before the Second World War broke out.[90]

Numbers rose from the mid-1930s not only because of a renewed demand from British housewives seeking domestic help, but also because there was a serious economic situation in Austria, which caused even middle-class girls to seek domestic posts abroad in order to support themselves. The activities of a large servant recruitment agency operating in Vienna also helped the process along. However, from 1933, when the Nazis came to power in Germany, many Jews and left-wing activists fled persecution in search of a better life elsewhere. Some came to Britain as domestic servants. The relentless 'aryanisation' in Germany spread to Austria in March 1938, when the country was absorbed into a greater Germany with the *Anschluss*. This was quickly followed by a programme of Jewish persecution as families were deprived of their political and economic rights and, as in Germany itself, subjected to physical attacks and imprisonment as well. Bronka Schneider, who came from Vienna with her husband on a British domestic permit in the spring of 1939, remembered the atmosphere of terror that prevailed:

concentration camps, people picked up off the street never to see their families again. Women were taken from their homes to wash the sidewalks. . . . I myself

Refugee Advertisements

AUSTRIAN Refugee (42), still in Vienna, seeks position as Mother's Help: very fond of children, sewing, dressmaking for babies, experienced all house-work. Write to Mrs. A. Sternlieb, Swingonola, Aberdorn Road, London, N.W. 7.

DOMESTIC Work required by Berliner and Viennese: homes asked for girl (12), Vienna, boy (14). England. Write Unitarian Minister, Hinckley, Leics.

MARRIED Couple, Austrian refugees, seek Positions in the country; ages 33 and 37; Wife excellent cook, experienced all housework, knowledge butter-making, husband used to most household duties, gardening, joiner. Mrs. Alice Sternlieb, Swingonole, Aberoorn Road, London, N.W. 7.

MARRIED Couple (39 and 35) urgently seek Post: wife, experienced in cooking and all household duties, now working in England: husband, trained as butler and valet, must leave Vienna immediately. Address D 70. " M/c Guardian " 2.

MIDDLE-AGED Couple, Austrian refugees, seek Positions in the country; wife excellent cook, husband used to most household duties, nursing, masseur, chiropodist. Mrs. O. Robitschek, 31, Wyndham Street, London, W. 1.

Urgent pleas for employment inserted by Austrian refugees in the *Manchester Guardian*, 15 February 1939. (*Guardian and Observer Syndication*)

was hit by a woman, spat on by a man for no reason whatever, and no one could do anything about it. We were without rights, without any kind of protection; no court or judge would have taken our case.[91]

Bronka lost her job as an accountant in a major firm and her husband was forced out of business. It was around this time that she heard from a friend that it was possible to come to England as a domestic servant if the people who were providing the job were prepared to apply for a permit. Like others in this position, she and her husband decided to advertise their services in British newspapers, but without success. Then another friend gave her the address of someone in Scotland who was in contact with an agency for domestic help in Edinburgh. On the basis of this somewhat vague information they wrote to the woman and, after weeks of anxious waiting and repeated appeals, they eventually heard that a post had been found for them. In the interim they took a course at a special school for domestic servants in Vienna promoted by a Jewish welfare agency: 'My husband learned how to become a butler, and I tried to improve my cooking.'[92]

Many other desperate people sought to get out of Germany and Austria by following a similar path. Gerta Jassem, also from Vienna, remembered her sister, Lily, advertising for a job in *The Times*. Unlike Bronka, she was successful and got a post as a housemaid. She went off with a friend, who had obtained a position as a cook. Yet, as Gerta drily commented, neither had boiled an egg or made a bed in their lives prior to their departure. Their only preparation for their new lives was to take a few English lessons. Nevertheless, once in England, Lily sought to arrange the escape of young Gerta by advertising for foster-parents for her. Again, she was successful. An elderly couple whose own children had left home agreed to take the girl. Another child migrant, Inge Engelhard from Munich, left Germany only two months before the outbreak of war. Her sister, who had obtained a post as a housemaid in the Midlands, persuaded the family for whom she worked to take Inge as well. However, the two girls were forbidden to speak German together and as it was a non-Jewish household they had many adjustments to make.[93]

Older women, like Dora Frischmann, also came. Dora was born in Vienna and was almost fifty-six when she arrived in Britain in September 1938 and took up her first servant post in Hove. In June 1940 she moved to London as a cook-general. There she had two positions in quick succession, before going to Llangollen, in Wales, in October. In 1943 she moved to Hoole, in Cheshire, and remained in the county until she acquired British nationality in December 1947.[94]

Dora Frischmann's registration certificate, issued on 13 September 1938 at Hove. (*Manchester Jewish Museum*)

Following the *Anschluss* a special category of refugee domestic workers was allowed into Britain under permits issued by the Home Office, rather than the Ministry of Labour, from April 1938, and following investigation by the Central Committee for Refugees, set up by various refugee agencies. They included the Society of Friends, the Catholic Committee for German Refugees, the Jewish Aid Committee and the International Solidarity Fund.[95]

In November 1938 the procedure was formalised with the setting up of the Domestic Bureau of the Central Committee for Refugees, which was given sole responsibility for investigating applications for refugee domestics and securing Home Office permits for them. In January 1939 the process was speeded up by issuing blocks of around 400 permits a week, so that in the first three weeks alone 1,400 permits were issued.[96] Other concessions to the refugees included an agreement, from September 1938, to grant permits to a few married couples between eighteen and forty-five, with the husband expected to work as a butler and his wife as a cook for a minimum joint annual salary of about £100. The men were not supposed to become gardeners (though a number of them did), because this might impinge on the work of British men, thereby arousing anti-refugee feeling.[97] They were also to work outside the London area. A further relaxation in the spring of 1939 meant that instead of the usual eighteen to forty-five age limit for awarding domestic permits, the lower figure was reduced to sixteen for females, thereby enabling some younger girls to escape through the domestic route.[98]

Ministry of Labour permits were also issued to a few *au pairs* and these too might include refugees. But entrants were restricted to 'the interchange of languages' rather than domestic work. Inquiries were made by the ministry to ensure that this scheme was not used as a means of obtaining domestic labour, though doubtless some slipped through the net.[99] In 1938 alone 267 *au pair* permits were issued, with a further 212 admissions authorised for girls who had come into the country for another purpose – perhaps as a visitor – and had then applied to stay on.[100]

Thus, there were two methods for foreign workers to get domestic employment in Britain. The first was the normal Ministry of Labour work permit scheme, which had operated since 1920 and applied to foreign domestics generally. The second was the special refugee category, under the aegis of the Domestic Bureau and working in conjunction with the Home Office. It allowed married couples and younger servants to come into the country, as well as the usual female entrants. Many refugees, of course, came in under the Ministry of Labour's work permit arrangements, as well as through their own special route. Precise numbers are difficult to establish, but one estimate suggests that 14,000 women, about one thousand girls and several hundred married couples were rescued by domestic permits issued under the auspices of the Home Office. In addition around seven thousand Jewish women managed to escape from Germany and Austria with Ministry of Labour permits, without resort to the Domestic Bureau.[101]

Meanwhile, the British Government was wrestling with three different strands of the foreign servant question. On the one hand, there was pressure from middle-class housewives for more servants and for these to come from abroad, if necessary. In October 1937, the Annual Meeting of the National Council of Women of Great Britain (representing about two million women) passed a resolution claiming that 'the difficulty of obtaining domestic help' was contributing to the low birth rate and thereby restricting 'families to an extent dangerous to the state'. It urged the Ministry of Labour to 'grant permits freely to approved young women of other nationalities, who desire to come to this country to enter domestic service; such permits to be renewed automatically upon satisfactory evidence that these foreign women continue to be engaged in domestic service'.[102]

Yet, there was an equal awareness in official circles that a too liberal admissions policy would arouse opposition among the unions, which would see the foreign domestics as threatening the position of British workers, and from middle-class critics who argued that at a time of high female unemployment in Britain it was wrong there should be a reliance on foreign assistance. Some, like Lady Longmore, suggested that if the dole were stopped to female industrial workers they 'would perforce go into domestic service, and there is no reason why they should not become as efficient at that trade as at any other'.[103] Another critic, James Thursby-Pelham from London, claimed that when he applied at employment exchanges and servant registry offices for a maid he was told that his 'only hope is to get a Swiss or Austrian girl. This I am exceedingly loth to do while I am helping to support the English unemployed women and girls.'[104] For these reasons, therefore, and to avoid encouraging anti-Semitic feeling, figures for Jewish refugees admitted were, in large measure, kept out of the public domain.[105]

Hostility towards foreign domestics was also apparent among British maids, as became clear when the National Union of Domestic Workers was set up in June 1938. Despite its low membership it resolutely refused to accept foreign entrants and in this it had the overwhelming backing of its supporters.[106] E. P. Harries, Organising Secretary for the TUC, even claimed in August 1938 that there were instances where 'in large houses, with a staff of four or five, the English workers had threatened to throw up the situation if a foreign maid was engaged'.[107] Likewise, Nelly Marsh, a union activist from Chelsea, complained in November of that year that there were

> many more foreign domestic workers . . . than there was in May last when I canvassed this district and where there are British domestics as well in the houses the majority tell me the foreign workers are making it hard for them by getting up at 6 o'clock in the mornings and not taking any off duty time and accepting a very small wage, sometimes 5s or 7s 6d a week.[108]

Such low pay was, of course, illegal since the minimum supposed to be paid to foreigners was 15s a week. Significantly, despite repeated union efforts to obtain evidence that entry restrictions were being flouted, little was found to back up the claims.[109]

Nevertheless, opposition to the influx of foreign staff continued and as late as July 1941 an application from fifteen Czech domestic workers from Llangollen for membership of the NUDW was rejected. Not until the following December was a change of policy apparent, with seventeen Austrian maids admitted to what was, by then, almost a moribund organisation.[110]

Some English servants carried their anti-foreigner sentiment into membership of Sir Oswald Mosley's British Union of Fascists, with accusations made that the advent of Jewish immigrants had reduced the wages and conditions of British workers.[111] Margot Pottlitzer, who came to England in February 1939, encountered this ill-feeling at first hand from the old nanny in one of the houses where she worked. She accused 'me of being [either] German or Jewish'. Margot 'just . . . tried to keep out of the way of those people'.[112] Another girl, employed as a parlourmaid, sensed the hostility of her fellow worker, a cook, who had been employed in the family for five years. She determined to win her round and when the Hampstead Club of the Austrian Domestic Workers was opened in November 1938 she took the cook along to show her how some of the foreign domestics spent their free time. Special evenings were arranged to which English servants were invited, with dancing and singing. As a result of all this, 'good relations have become a real friendship'.[113]

The British government faced another problem. It realised that as conditions in Germany became more desperate, so large numbers of those seeking to enter the country as domestic workers were from middle-class families, with little practical experience of household chores. Many had themselves employed maids in happier times: 'it wasn't so easy, suddenly to become maids ourselves', declared a woman who took up domestic work in Scotland, but employers 'made no allowance for this'.[114]

The desire to escape intensified for Jews after *Kristallnacht* on the night of 9-10 November 1938, when Jewish property was attacked, synagogues were ransacked and large numbers of Jewish people were rounded up and imprisoned. Margareta Burkill, a Cambridge don's wife, who was involved in the city's Refugee Committee, discovered that of around 500 women who came with domestic permits under its auspices, only two had ever been servants: 'all the others were middle-class women, or professional women who had kept their own servants'. This meant that not only

Refugee Advertisements

A Good Home sought, free of charge, for Refugee brother and sister, aged 11 and 7: together if possible: well brought up, lovable children: Please address M. 16. "M/c Guardian " 2.

AUSTRIAN Boy, 14, excellent family, well educated, with affidavit for America, seeks Home for few months in England. Schick, 6, Buckland Crescent, London, N.W. 3.

AU PAIR.—First-class Austrian Cook, cold and hot dishes, diet cooking, knowledge sewing, 55 years old, doctor's widow, seeks Post: references in London. O 212 to R. Mosse, Prague 1., Czecho-Slovakia.

FASHION DESIGNER.—Textile Pattern | Designer, Silk Dyer, Colour Printer, Wax Printer (Batik) seeks Position in England or Dominions: late manager textile printers (silk and flags): many years' experience. Address Willman, Hotel Raglan, Russell Sq., London, W.C. 1.

GERMAN Jewess, 34, well-educ't, speaks English, seeks post as Mother's Help or Housekeeper: two yrs.' exp. domes. service, gd. cook & needlewmn.: excel. refs. Goldstein, Berlin-Schoneberg, Landshuterstr, 23.

GERMAN Woman Refugee (35) Wants position, as Domestic Servant, Housekeeper, or Guardian for children: well trained, intelligent, and reliable: speaks fluent English. Address K 92. " M/c Guardian " 2.

LADY offers good Home and small flat to refined young Refugee in return for light domestic duties. Address K 75. "M/c Guardian " 2.

MARRIED Couple, 28 and 40, have to leave Germany, pay own fare, seek Position: experienced Cook General, children's care: both do any work. Address D 93. "M/c Guardian " 2.

MARRIED Couple, still in Vienna, Want position as Cook (domestic) and Butler. Address K 86. " M/c Guardian " 2.

TWO Young Viennese, 20 and 25, very diligent, experienced in cooking and housework, fond of children, seek post, eventually together in one house: both excellent testimonials. Flora and Martha Bisler, Vienna 4, Goldegasse 30/4.

VIENNESE Lawyer and Wife seek generous person willing to give them guarantee to be able to wait in England until their quota for America is due. Dr. Hochsinger, Vienna IX, Porzellangasse 37/12.

VIENNESE, first-class Cook, anxious to leave Germany, urgently seeks situation Cook-Housekeeper. Apply Daughter, Rabl, 1, Shakespeare Road, Harpenden, Herts.

Desperate appeals for domestic employment from refugees in the *Manchester Guardian*, 25 February 1939. They included middle-class people who had probably employed their own servants in better times. (*Guardian and Observer Syndication*)

were many of them traumatised by events in their own country and deeply worried about relatives left behind, but they experienced feelings of humiliation and social dislocation at being reduced to what they saw as the inferior status of domestics. Most mistresses, for their part, were determined to maintain the traditional distance between employer and servant, no matter what the servant's background might be. Mrs Burkill found it 'just completely fantastic that dons' wives could treat somebody who was in every way as good as them in an absolutely terrible manner'. In one case when the mistress and her children went out walking with their refugee maid, she had to keep three paces behind them to indicate that she was not part of the family group:

They overworked them terribly. And of course you had the . . . little irritations. . . . In Germany you lay a table differently than in England and there were permanent rows about that. Instead of saying in a friendly way 'Look we do it that way, would you like to . . . do it our way', there used to be terrible rows about such simple little things. . . . It was really quite heartbreaking. [115]

Mrs Gordon, who came to England on a domestic permit when she was eighteen years of age, was another victim of what Tony Kushner has labelled 'the interplay of class, gender and ethnicity in Britain' during these years. She was a German doctor's daughter and was recruited as a cook-general by a well-to-do doctor's family in England. Her parents were delighted that she was going to a medical man's household, thinking that she would be treated as a member of the family:

Alas, I soon learned that my job was in the kitchen, rising at 5.30 a.m. to tend the boiler so that the bathwater [was] hot in time. Then the reception rooms had to be cleaned, the fires laid and lit and breakfast prepared and served. This consisted of several courses, laid in the dining room with the dishes over hot flames. . . . Cooking, cleaning, preparing for Tennis and Music Parties was the daily routine. This was a big house and a large family, and I rarely had time to have my meals, there was just too much work to be done. . . . After my experience in domestic service, the . . . years as a student nurse appeared like a holiday to me. [116]

Even Bronka Schneider and her husband, although they got on quite well with their employers in a Scottish castle, nevertheless resented the petty discriminations they experienced.

> We had our own milk and butter that came from a nearby farm while the milk and butter that Mrs Harrington was using came in sealed bottles by train from some town. We also had our own bread, cake and jam . . . .
>
> Next I had to go to Mrs Harrington's bedroom and help her make the bed. It was the first time she called me by my first name. We only called our best friends and our servants by their first names. And as I wasn't Mrs Harrington's best friend, I was her servant. And it was then that I felt a little pang in the vicinity of my stomach and, though I knew we were hired as domestic servants, I couldn't help feeling a slight resentment at being on the other side of the fence. We also noticed that my husband was not Mr Schneider any more, but just Schneider.
>
> I had to get over that feeling. It was a job like any other. There was nothing degrading about it. . . . And, as the time went on, we accepted being called by our first names and even found it amusing.[117]

Apart from their inexperience of household duties and, often enough, their limited knowledge of English, the foreign domestics found difficulty in coping with British housekeeping methods. They were unused to open fires that scattered ash everywhere and required constant attention, and to scrubbing stone or tiled floors. Many shivered at the draughts from doors and windows which their English employers regarded as 'healthy' fresh air.[118] A girl who went to work in a large Scottish farmhouse remembered beating carpets with a beater – 'something you don't even know of. Things like that, and huge amounts of washing, and everything, no machines, nothing.'[119]

In a pamphlet entitled *Mistress and Maid*, issued by the Domestic Bureau in April 1940, servants were warned not to grumble because English household customs differed from those on the continent. 'Adapt yourself as quickly as possible to your new surroundings. English houses are often colder than continental ones, and you must expect to guard against the cold by wearing thick underclothes and woollen indoor coats. . . . Do your best to improve your knowledge of English and always speak English in the streets and public places.'[120]

Yet, if the maids had difficulty in coming to terms with their new situation, there were problems for employers, too. Ilse Lewen from Wuppertal had been training as a dress designer when her married sister, who was already settled in Birmingham, found her a post as a cook:

> I hadn't been with my employers long when the lady of the house said to me, 'Ilse, I want you to tell me the truth. You have never been a cook in your life, have you?' On the first day I was there she asked me to make toast. I looked for the electric toaster, but she gave me a fork and the bread fell into the fire. Another day, I burned the potatoes. I also had to light the kitchen range, and once in desperation threw petrol

on it . . . it was a wonder I didn't blow the house up . . . I had to wait on them. . . .
They ate in the dining room, while I had my meals in the kitchen.[121]

Even maids like Hildegarde Schantin of Vienna, who came over not as refugees but
in order to learn English, could be less than satisfactory. Hildegarde was employed
by the Town Clerk of Rugby and his wife and had taken a domestic science course
in Austria. However, according to a son of the household, what his mother 'really
wanted was a cook-general, who would scrub the doorstep etc., as well as doing
the cooking. Hildegarde however liked fancy cooking and probably was not very
keen on scrubbing doorsteps. I remember once my mother remarking on how long
Hildegarde had spent on making a lattice jam tart . . . my mother would have
preferred her to do something more straightforward, to allow . . . time for other
duties.' The employment was terminated after a few months, 'with the maid moving
to another post in the Rugby area. She eventually married a local man.'[122]

One incensed employer even wrote to the government in August 1939 to
complain of the inefficiency of two Viennese Jewish couples that he had recruited.

> The first pair were very worthy persons, but they had never done domestic work
> and were incapable of ever doing any. The second pair, Joseph Langsam and wife,
> arrived in England last February. They are idle, ignorant and impudent. In spite
> of their testimonials they had obviously no experience of domestic service. Such
> people will eventually be a burden on the rates and, I suggest, should be returned
> to their country of origin.[123]

There is no indication that notice was taken of his remarks. A return to Austria at
that date would have meant almost certain imprisonment and probably death for
the couple concerned.

In a few cases, rudimentary training was given to the refugees when they reached
Britain. The YWCA, for example, opened month-long courses for Czech refugees
early in 1939, following the partial German dismemberment of Czechoslovakia in
the autumn of 1938. Daily lessons in English were provided, as well as instruction
in the duties of housemaid, parlourmaid and cook. The trainees carried out the
domestic chores in the hostel where they lived and were expected to be 'punctual
at meals, clean and tidy in appearance, polite and obliging'.[124] After completing
the course they were placed with employers who had been vetted by the YWCA
and contacts were maintained with them for some time afterwards. Many of the
placements were very successful, as with Anna Deisingerova, a 28-year-old political
refugee. Within weeks, her mistress was praising her as a 'willing . . . hard worker,
strong & very intelligent. . . . She has come in the nick of time as I have been
ordered a month's complete rest owing to high blood pressure & she is so kind
& anxious to be of use. She sings all day long!'[125] In May 1940, Anna was still in
her post and was described as 'an absolute treasure . . . could be recommended
without reservation as housekeeper, or to any post of responsibility'.[126] Other girls,
like eighteen-year-old Helena Voglova, who had been brought up in a prosperous

home with three maids, found adjustment more difficult. She eventually took up nursing.[127]

The British Government were aware that many of those entering the country on domestic permits were coming because this was their only means of escape. In July 1938 Sir E. W. E. Holderness of the Home Office conceded that a large number of the women were

> not of the domestic class and we anticipate that they will not be content to remain in domestic service and will probably wish to take up some other occupation. . . . We intend so far as it is possible and in this we have the support of the refugee organisations to keep them to domestic service for at any rate two or three years, though I have no doubt that we shall be asked to make concessions on individual cases for special reasons.[128]

However, other government officials were less sympathetic. In June 1939, Captain Jeffes of the Foreign Office's Passport Control Department criticised the 'bad type of refugee presenting . . . authorisation cards and Ministry of Labour permits to enter the United Kingdom' at the passport control office in Vienna. Some of the women 'were so filthily dirty both in their person and their clothing, that they were utterly unfit to go inside a decent British home. I think it is imperative that something be done to prevent this indiscriminate distribution of permits.'[129] Such comments took no account of the desperate plight of many of the applicants, deprived of the means of earning a livelihood and compelled to sell many of their remaining possessions in order to survive. Even Bronka and Joseph Schneider were forced to send their books, a few at a time, to relatives living in Switzerland, so that they could be sold and the cash remitted, for by the time they left Austria they had 'lost all ability to make a living'.[130]

Most migrant maids found their spell of domestic service in Britain an unhappy one. A few enjoyed good relations with their employers, but many felt humiliated and resentful at being treated as mere domestics by mistresses who were seemingly oblivious of their middle and upper-middle class upbringing.[131] Some, like Lore Segal's mother, were snubbed when they attempted to talk to their mistress on terms of equality. When Lore's mother was taken on a tour of the house by her new employer, Mrs Willoughby, she immediately noticed the Bechstein piano in the drawing room. She told her mistress that she herself had had a Blüthner, which the Nazis had taken, and that she had once studied music at the Vienna Academy.

'Oh, really?' responded Mrs Willoughby coolly. 'In that case you must come and play sometime when everyone is out.' She then 'gave my mother a paper she had written out to hang on the back of the kitchen door, showing a list of the rooms and on which day each must be turned out, to help my mother organise her work. My mother thanked her earnestly. She had no system of her own, she said, but she would do her very best for Mrs Willoughby.'[132] Lore's father, who was also employed by the Willoughbys, proved of little use as a butler, something for which his past career as a chief accountant in a bank had been little preparation. He was then set to work in the garden, about which he knew even less, pottering about the vegetable beds with little idea what to do. Lore's mother watched sadly as he received orders from Mr Willoughby, dressed in his tweed knickerbockers and green gardener's apron.[133]

Some women responded by moving from job to job, in a search for congenial employers or because they had been dismissed. Many tried to get posts in the larger cities where they had an opportunity to meet fellow refugees in their spare time or spend their leisure in some constructive fashion. Ira Rischowski, a German-born female engineer, who came to Britain in June 1936, had three different jobs in just over a year. The third was with a well-to-do German woman who was studying at the London School of Economics and who rented a luxurious house in Chelsea. However, that luxury was not extended to the maid: 'I slept on a camp bed and instead of sheets I had tablecloths. . . . I was supposed to do the whole household, [but] I never had enough money for it.' Ira's main consolation was that on her afternoons off she was able to attend meetings of the Women's Engineering Society, where she was accepted as a fellow professional rather than as a domestic: 'that was like a poor soul in hell who is allowed an afternoon in heaven. It was absolutely wonderful to be there amongst women engineers and to be lectured on some engineering topic.'[134] During the war she was able to resume her engineering career, but in the meantime she performed her household duties with as good a grace as she could muster.

When the Second World War broke out in September 1939 the tensions between mistress and maid were intensified. German and Austrian servants were classed as 'enemy aliens' and less than a fortnight after hostilities commenced some eight thousand of them were dismissed on various pretexts, but probably because of 'the unwillingness of British employers to continue to employ Germans'.[135] Hungarian servants suffered a similar fate. In September 1939, Ethel Snowden wrote to *The Times* to complain that at the outbreak of war many British employers 'summarily dismissed their Hungarian maids without even paying them the week's wages legally due to them'.[136] This created immense problems for the refugee organisations, which found themselves having to support large numbers of former domestics on inadequate funding and with insufficient accommodation. This applied not merely to the Jewish refugee agencies, but to the YWCA as well. The situation was made worse when 'protected areas' were established from which refugees were to be excluded. This meant more had to leave their posts. By the summer of 1940 the YWCA was complaining that its London hostels were 'full of these women and girls', since London remained an 'open area for aliens'. Most of the former maids could pay little or nothing towards their keep.

One London hostel has lost £500 in the first six months of the year because it has taken in so many women in distress. This hostel . . . usually is an income producing place for the London YWCA.

A rough estimate of the amount expended (or lost) in refugee service – clubs and hostels throughout the country, must be at least £5,000 to date.[137]

Only when, towards the end of the year, the demands of the war effort led to a relaxation of restrictions on refugee employment, were they able to enter a wider range of occupations, easing the crisis.

In the meantime, not only were many servants dismissed, after the outbreak of war, but all enemy aliens had to appear before tribunals to decide on their degree of loyalty to Britain. Three categories were established, with those considered to be in 'Class A' interned at once. Class B refugees were subject to certain restrictions, mostly relating to their place of work, and Class C men and women (the vast majority) were free to go wherever there was employment. However, they could not change their address without prior permission and even short absences had to be reported. 'Maps, cameras, radio sets had to be surrendered, and the possession of cycles and motor cars was forbidden.'[138]

Bronka and Joseph Schneider were greatly relieved when the Glasgow tribunal that they had appeared at in November 1939 gave them a C classification after several anxious weeks of waiting. However, they had already noticed a coolness in their employers' attitude towards them, caused perhaps in part by the fact that soon after the outbreak of war the police had come to inspect the Schneiders' belongings. 'While they looked through the suitcases and drawers, they talked to us about Vienna and about our people, how awful it must be to be cut off from everything and everybody that meant so much to us. It didn't take them long to see that we had nothing which we were not supposed to have.'[139] When they were awarded their C classification, Bronka and Joseph hoped that Mr and Mrs Harrington's attitude towards them would change. However, that proved not to be the case. When they went on a short trip to London early in 1940, unlike previous occasions they had locks fitted to all the doors: 'only the back door and that that led to our rooms was left open. At first we were terribly hurt. If Mrs Harrington would have just explained. . . . Or did she still resent us because of the war? Whatever it was made me really mad now.'[140] Soon afterwards they wrote to a friend in London and she told them that posts were available there. They then gave the Harringtons a month's notice. When Mrs Harrington received the news she smiled and Bronka 'couldn't help but notice that her smile had an expression of relief'. They left in February 1940, but within months Joseph Schneider had been interned on the Isle of Man, along with many thousands of other enemy aliens, despite his C classification.[141]

The public mood was largely responsible for the distrust between employers and foreign domestics. Suspicion fell on refugees as potential 'Fifth Columnists' during the invasion scare of the spring and summer of 1940, particularly following the German occupation of the Netherlands. This was despite the fact that they had fled to Britain as victims of Nazi persecution. As early as March 1940, one MP drew attention to the fact that there were 'about 250 German servant girls employed in and around Aldershot' and asked whether they were 'a danger to the country'. He appealed to the Home Secretary to make 'a radius around all military and air stations within which enemy aliens shall not be allowed to enter'. The Home Secretary, Sir John Anderson, responded in temporising fashion, declaring it was 'a mistake to assume that every German domestic servant' was 'a menace to the security of this country; . . . in my view, there would be no justification for a policy under which all aliens of German and Austrian nationality were treated alike, without regard to the fact that the majority of them are refugees from Nazi oppression and are bitterly opposed to the present regime in Germany. Each case must be considered on its merits.' Nevertheless, he agreed to institute 'further special inquiries . . . about the position of Germans and Austrians employed in or around Aldershot'.[142]

Increasingly, however, there were demands for the mass internment of enemy aliens. The campaign was fuelled by the popular press. In April 1940, the *Daily Mail* demanded the police round up every 'doubtful alien' in the country. A month later, Mr Ward Price suggested 'every German is an agent'.[143] *The Daily Herald* also took up the cry, 'Don't trust a German', while Beverley Nichols in the *Sunday Chronicle* of 26 May 1940 wrote about 'the Fifth Column' and complained that we had 'not interned anything like the lot'.[144]

Perhaps most disturbing of all was a broadcast by Sir Neville Bland, British Minister in Holland. It was made at the end of May 1940 and spoke of the role of the 'Fifth Column' in the fall of the Netherlands. He warned his listeners to be careful 'at this moment how you put complete trust in any person of German or Austrian connections'.[145] About a fortnight earlier he had written to the government to express his fears concerning the role of domestics in any possible betrayal:

> the paltriest kitchen maid . . . not only can be, but generally is, a menace to the safety of the country. . . . Every German or Austrian servant, however superficially charming and devoted, is a real and grave menace. . . . All Germans and Austrians, at least, ought to be interned at once.[146]

In these circumstances, and alarmed by reverses in the war itself, the government changed tack. Early in May 1940, internment was introduced for all male enemy aliens over the age of sixteen and under the age of sixty (excluding invalids and the infirm) who lived in certain eastern counties of England and Scotland. This was followed by the internment of all male Germans and Austrians in the relevant age group who were in the B classification. However, that did not satisfy the critics. Viscount Elibank, for example, asked why only male aliens were being interned: 'Is it not . . . well known that very often one female spy is better than ten men, or at least equal to ten men? . . . Today this country is ridden by domestic servants of alien origin; they are serving in houses all over the country, and many of them are not trustworthy.'[147] In the weeks that followed, the internment procedure was extended to include women in Class B and some even in Class C, as well as most males. Sir John Anderson admitted the decision had been taken because of military pressure (and doubtless because of public opinion), but he conceded such a blanket policy would 'necessarily [involve] the internment of many who, as far as I know, are anxious to assist this country'.[148] It was in this atmosphere that Joseph Schneider was interned, although Bronka herself escaped.

But many women, even those like Margot Pottlitzer, who had a qualified C category, were interned. In Margot's case she was taken first to Holloway prison and then to the Isle of Man. Biaria Heller, a former dressmaker from Vienna, who had begun her servant life as a lady's maid and ended as a parlourmaid for a banking family in Chelsea, was another internee. She had been given a B classification and was interned early in 1940. She travelled to the Isle of Man via Liverpool, and remembered the crowd that gathered to see the 'enemy aliens' walk to the boat. They were under police escort and some of the onlookers spat at them. When she reached the Isle of Man she was sent to a hotel in Port St Mary. There the internees seem to have enjoyed a considerable amount of freedom, although a 9 p.m. curfew had to be observed. Biaria spent a good deal of time sewing for her landlady. After nine months she was allowed to return to the mainland.[149]

By the autumn of 1940 a general release programme was getting under way, but it was often implemented in a random and haphazard fashion. Furthermore, not all of those who were released could find work. In November 1940, 3,000 refugees were registered as unemployed with the Domestic Bureau. However, by then the demands of the war economy were expanding and at the beginning of 1941 only 500 domestics remained out of work. Jobs were found in nursing, offices, factories and engineering works. Margot Pottlitzer found a post in the sales office of a meat producing company and worked there for a year.[150] As these new employment opportunities became available, the Domestic Bureau was no longer needed and in September 1941 its offices were closed.[151]

As Tony Kushner points out, most of the refugee women left domestic work as soon as they could. Of 134 female refugees surveyed by the Manchester Jewish Refugee Committee in May 1943, for example, just fourteen remained in service. The rest had become nurses or were working for industrial and commercial firms. [152]

In considering how far domestic permits helped to rescue the victims of Nazi oppression in Central Europe, Kushner's reservations about the scheme are salutary. He admits that in the months before the outbreak of the Second World War, in the 'period of greatest need', thousands of women and girls, as well as some married couples, were able to get out, but he points also to the self-interest which underlay the government's policy,

> concerned as it was to help meet the servant shortages of the middle classes. One needs to question whether it was really necessary for academics, lawyers, doctors and other professionals in the 1930s . . . to become menial servants in Britain before they could gain their freedom. . . . The domestic service scheme thus illustrates both the strengths and weaknesses, the generosity and callousness of British refugee policy.
>
> The same can be said of British popular responses to the refugees. . . . Some servants were treated with understanding by their British employers. . . . Yet . . . it was more common to treat the refugee domestics as ordinary servants and to make no allowances for their peculiar circumstances. . . . Moreover, the refugees found it hard to explain why they had been forced to escape. This suspicion against them was reflected in the mass sacking and policy of internment that took

place in the war. There was thus some warmth in the British popular response, but also a major failure of comprehension and elements of xenophobia and anti-Semitism.[153]

As British domestics had long ago discovered, those maids employed by 'marginal' families barely able to afford a servant were the ones most likely to experience exploitation. According to the refugee organisations there were even some unscrupulous employers prepared to put pressure on 'these terrified girls' by threatening deportation. However, more typical was the situation of a refugee who worked for a married couple in Manchester. They themselves had had to leave Germany because of their political beliefs but, as she commented drily, 'they certainly did not practise their socialism on me'.[154]

Part three

1939-2000

CHAPTER SEVEN

THE SECOND WORLD WAR
AND BEYOND

The proportion of households that employed paid domestic help has never been large. . . . But among those who were accustomed to employ such help, the shortage and increasing cost of domestic labour have been keenly felt, particularly as conditions during and since the war have aggravated the difficulties of housekeeping. . . . The burden is felt in the actual domestic work, in the tie which children involve and in the physical and nervous strain of continuous care of children.

Report of the Royal Commission on Population, Cmd. 7695 (London, 1949), pp. 148-9.

THE PRESSURE OF WAR

Between 1939 and 1960 domestic service in Britain underwent a profound change both in its scale and its nature. In 1931 almost 5 per cent of households in England and Wales still employed a resident domestic; by 1951 that had fallen to about 1 per cent and in 1961 the figure was put at just 0.6 per cent.[1] Even if non-resident maids and those engaged in commercial establishments were included, the decline was sharp, with 1.3 million female servants recorded in England and Wales in 1931 and 0.72 million in 1951 – a fall of 46 per cent. Among the men, there was a reduction from just over 78,000 in 1931 to a little over 66,000 two decades later. Almost 41,000 of the latter were chefs, cooks and kitchen hands.[2] In Scotland, a similar picture emerged for women, with numbers falling from 138,679 in 1931 to 73,278 two decades later. For men, the situation differed slightly, as the 1931 figure of 4,543 had risen to 4,961 in 1951, but almost 4,000 of these were cooks, chefs and kitchen workers, mainly employed in commercial premises like hotels and restaurants. According to the census there were fewer than 1,000 'other' male domestic servants in Scotland in 1951.[3]

The Second World War played a major part in bringing about these developments, both psychologically and through its demands upon the nation's labour force. A contemporary report claimed that it had 'not so much solved as dissolved the whole structure of domestic service'.[4] Already before 1939 there had been a marked reluctance among women to take up paid domestic work and some of those who became servants were of indifferent quality. However, once female recruitment for industry and for the services got under way, the drift away from the occupation

"Another word of complaint, M'm, and I quits civilian life."

Punch was drawing attention to the difficult mistress-servant relations which manifested themselves in some households at the beginning of the Second World War. (Punch, *13 December 1939*)

accelerated. A new spirit of egalitarianism made the thought of performing menial duties in private households unacceptable to many. Even those who continued with the work were often unenthusiastic. Thus a Kettering 'daily' confessed that while she was not ashamed of her employment, she much disliked continually meeting 'people who think of one as only the "char"; it doesn't add to one's self-respect by any means, particularly when some of those one works for, and is paid by, have less intelligence and consideration than oneself'.[5] Margaret Powell, who took up daily domestic work during the war to make ends meet, also resented the autocratic attitude of certain mistresses. One complained because Margaret failed to address her as 'Madam'.[6]

It was in these circumstances that the *Ministry of Labour Gazette* concluded that if household employment were 'to make its essential contribution to the health and welfare of the nation on the return of peace, a concerted and sustained effort would have to be made to eradicate the causes of its unpopularity'.[7] The effort was made, but the unpopularity persisted.

At the beginning of the war there was a general slowness to mobilise women, whereas for men conscription began immediately for those aged eighteen to forty-one (raised in December 1941 to an upper limit of fifty-one).[8] This affected traditional areas of male service, with gardeners (unless they could claim exemption as agricultural workers), gamekeepers and indoor domestics being called up or doing other war work.

The trend was reinforced by the widespread requisitioning of large country houses for military and other purposes. Chatsworth was taken over by a girls' school and Woburn Abbey was used by the Imperial Intelligence Committee. Thousands of properties were commandeered, with the armed services requisitioning the majority of them for anything from barracks, billets, supply bases and officers' messes to strategic planning headquarters, or signals and training bases. The Air Ministry alone occupied twenty thousand properties and the Ministry of Health almost nineteen thousand.[9] This led to a reduced demand for domestic staff. In some cases, evacuees from the major industrial towns were dispersed to country houses and there they often encountered the hostility of the servants who looked after them. In September 1939 Violet Markham complained of 'snobbish and difficult' maids who 'when hostile to the incursion of strange children may create a very difficult problem for the mistress'.[10]

Evelyn Waugh's novel, *Put Out More Flags*, described the effect of evacuees on one fictional country house early in the war. On the morning after their arrival at Malfrey the head housemaid resigned, saying that with her bad legs she could not cope 'with children all over the place'. An hour later the three housemaids declared they were going to work in a factory. The butler and cook remained loyal, but the footman was due to leave for the army in a few weeks and the valet had already joined the yeomanry with his master. Out of doors the situation was little better. 'The leaves fell in the avenue at Malfrey, and this year, where once there had been a dozen men to sweep them, there were only four and two boys.'[11]

Many evacuees returned home after a few months, while in other cases cooks and housemaids came to accept the additional work the children created. *The Lady* praised the way most had considered it 'a patriotic service', to which they had risen 'nobly'.[12] In the summer of 1942, however, it became official policy to return as many evacuees as possible to their families so that the country houses they had occupied could be used by American troops preparing for D-Day.[13]

Much of the requisitioning proved long lasting and as a result buildings became dilapidated and even damaged, especially when used as barracks, while gardens were overgrown or were turned over to vegetable production. At Aynho, the army commandeered part of the mansion as well as large areas of the pleasure grounds and adjacent park. These became pockmarked with concrete emplacements, Nissen huts and petrol stores, while trees were felled and lawns neglected. In 1940 Ted Humphris, the head gardener, found himself tending the gardens virtually single-handed. In the summer of that year, at his employer's suggestion, he started running the greenhouses and the vegetable plot on his own account as a market garden and continued the arrangement for the duration of the war. This meant concentrating on food production, with house plants giving way to tomatoes in the greenhouses and luxuries like asparagus and strawberries being replaced by potatoes and other essential vegetables. Much produce was sold to villagers, although some customers came several miles from the market town of Banbury. The military also purchased produce. Initially, Ted's only help came from his wife and school-age son, plus a little casual assistance from neighbours on summer evenings. Not until the spring of 1941 did he secure the aid of a girl in her late teens with an interest in gardening. She provided much-needed energy and enthusiasm.[14]

Female participation in the war effort was part of a campaign promoted by the Women's Farm and Gardens Association whereby women aged between sixteen and forty were to be apprenticed to head gardeners for six months before taking on the duties of an under-gardener. The scheme was backed by the Ministry of Agriculture and the trainees had to demonstrate they were suitable for garden work and were unable to afford the fees of a horticultural college.[15] Within weeks the owners of forty large gardens had agreed to participate in the scheme, but the prediction that it would lead to a greater role for women gardeners after the war proved over-optimistic. In 1951 there were just 2,160 'other' female gardeners, that is not engaged in market gardening, in England and Wales, compared to 125,724 males so occupied. In Scotland, there were 206 women to 12,650 men.[16]

Feed restrictions leading to a prohibition on the artificial rearing of game birds and the shortage of gamekeepers and powder for cartridges brought a virtual end to game preservation, although, as at Elveden, periodic shoots continued to be held on some estates. In other places, there was a general emphasis on shooting for the pot.[17] At Eaton, the change was dramatic. When Norman Mursell returned after the war in February 1946, he found only four keepers, compared to twenty before the war.[18] Efforts were made to revive game preservation after 1945, but it was never on the pre-war scale.

Pheasant rearing was re-established in a major way in the early 1950s, when animal feed supplies improved, but the number of keepers remained low. In England and Wales, in 1951, there were 3,776 gamekeepers and game watchers whereas in 1931 there had been 10,706, a fall of almost two-thirds. In Scotland, the decline was rather less severe, with the 4,050 recorded in 1931 dropping to 2,126 twenty years later.[19] In the post-war world many estates still preserving game sought to exploit the financial possibilities by letting shoots to syndicates, as they had done before 1939, and also by arranging commercial shooting parties. That affected the kind of sport offered, since syndicates expected large bags. It meant a greater concentration on pheasants at the expense of partridges, whose yields were more variable. As one keeper, Angus Nudds, commented: 'You cannot expect a syndicate member to pay for a season's shooting only to be told he cannot shoot that year because the partridges have not been able to rear any young due to the wet summer.'[20]

Male indoor servants who enlisted often found military life easier than their civilian occupation. Arthur Inch, who joined the RAF in June 1940, considered it 'no hardship' after the long spells on duty to which he had been accustomed in service: 'In fact the comparatively shorter hours in the forces was a revelation to me, I'd never had so much free time plus all the free passes when going on leave.'[21] When the war ended, having enjoyed this greater liberty, he did not look for domestic employment, but became a silver cleaner for a firm of Edinburgh jewellers. Only in 1956, when he heard of an attractive vacancy for a butler through his brother, who had remained in service as a chauffeur, did he decide to return to domestic work.

Another former male servant, who had spent the first fourteen years of his working life as a footman, went into a factory during the war. He stayed there until he became redundant in the late 1960s. The employment exchange, 'learning of my previous experience in private service offered me a job in Buckingham Palace', but he turned it down. 'I had tasted freedom I had never known and all overtime paid.' He added: 'I have never regretted leaving private service.'[22]

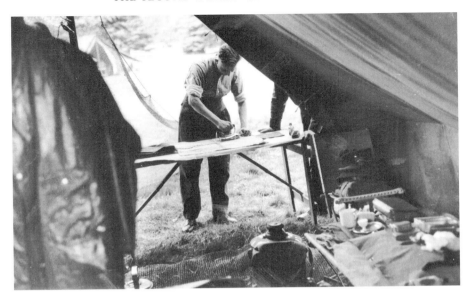

Aircraftsman J. Dowling, an RAF batman, doing some ironing in the open air at a tactical air force station in Britain. (*Imperial War Museum Photograph Archives*)

During the war male staffs were much depleted as only older men or those who could gain exemption in some other way remained in domestic employment. At Cliveden, Edwin Lee and the housekeeper ran the household with a small core of co-workers, including a chef and some older married women who came in daily. To Rosina Harrison, Lady Astor's maid, however, the greatest change for long-established workers like herself was in their relationship with their employers. Under war pressures the distinctions between master and servant were blurred. 'We were family.' Rosina and Lord Astor's valet, Arthur, accompanied their employers on their travels, including to Plymouth, where Lady Astor was an MP and Lord Astor was Lord Mayor, and they experienced the severe bombing raids the city suffered at the time.[23]

Many junior female servants abandoned domestic work at an early stage. Among them was Phyllis Elms, who had reluctantly entered the kitchens of a large house in Wiltshire because her family considered it an appropriate occupation. Of her life in service, she declared bitterly: 'I loathed it. . . . Mostly because I think I had a lot of pride and . . . you have to bow and scrape to people, that's not on with me.'[24] When an ECKO factory was opened at Malmesbury, it took her two months to win her father's consent for her to work there, but eventually he relented. Her new job involved winding electrical coils for use in aeroplanes and in radar and wireless equipment. Not only did she earn more than in service (£1 2s 6d a week instead of £1 a month, plus board and lodging), but the hours were shorter and more regular and she had far more free time. She called the factory 'a gift from the gods'.[25]

Other women wanted to 'do their bit' because their menfolk were at the front or because they themselves wished to play an active role in the struggle. Frances

A batwoman in the WAAF in 1943, relieving the officers in her charge of the 'spit and polish' considered necessary for smartness and efficiency. (*Imperial War Museum Photograph Archives*)

Partridge's maid, Joan, announced she was taking up war work when her fiance was sent abroad. She got a job in an aeroplane factory[26] in the spring of 1941. However, in the early months of the war female participation was more limited. In official circles a view prevailed of what was appropriate for women, and only when serious labour shortages emerged did a different policy apply. Even then restrictions remained. Amy O'Connor, who left domestic service to become a signals operator in the ATS, felt she 'was helping England', but she would have liked to have used weapons – something from which women were barred. Years later, when expressing strong anti-Nazi sentiments, she added: 'They could have given me a gun and I would have gone. . . . There were quite a few of us asked, could we go out with the men? Could we take guns? They wouldn't let us.'[27]

All too often, indeed, as another female auxiliary drily observed, whatever women applied for, 'they . . . try to get one committed to working in a canteen'.[28] Eileen Balderson, who had wanted to take up transport duties, was rejected because she was too short, but when she told the WAAF authorities that she had been a domestic servant in civilian life, she was promptly made a batwoman.[29] Another former maid, Mary Mackenzie, became a WAAF waitress in a sergeants' mess and was plagued with sexual propositions from many of the groundcrew.[30]

Compulsory registration of both occupied and unoccupied females began for those aged nineteen to forty in March 1941 at local employment exchanges and by 1943 had been extended to those aged nineteen to fifty.[31] Women selected from the register were allocated jobs to which, if they refused to go, they could be 'directed' by law. Conscription of single women aged twenty to twenty-one began in January 1942 and mainly involved entry into the ATS or into munitions production, where labour shortages were greatest. By 1943 conscription had been extended to all single women aged nineteen to twenty-four. From February 1942, under the Employment of Women (Control of Engagement) Order females aged twenty to thirty (with certain exemptions) could be recruited only through employment exchanges, the aim being to ensure that they took work regarded as essential to the war effort. In January 1943 the Order was extended to those up to forty and at that time females could be directed into part-time as well as full-time posts. Throughout the war only single women were regarded as fully mobile and from September 1941 any unmarried female wishing to avoid conscription had to prove she had 'domestic responsibilities'.[32]

Servants were affected by this, particularly those in the age group covered by conscription. The historian of one Coventry firm mentioned a draft of girls from Brighton who had formerly worked in hotels, finding difficulty in adjusting to conditions in a drop-forging shop. They had never before heard any noise like the 'thunder of the great hammers'.[33]

Employers, meanwhile, were anxious to keep their maids and the issue was raised in parliament. In response to this pressure and to claims of personal hardship for the sick, the elderly and mothers with young children, the government accepted that 'essential domestic help' could be allowed.[34] There were demands, too, that 'hardship' households be supplied with servants by employment exchanges or through the home help service. By 1942 it had been agreed that in homes where there were expectant mothers, mothers with young children, sick and aged people or where the wife was engaged in war work as well as having domestic duties, the last remaining servant would not be called up.[35]

That did not solve the problem when maids left of their own accord and no replacement could be found. Farmers' wives, too, complained of the added pressure of catering for extra workers at harvest and at other busy seasons along with their normal agricultural and domestic responsibilities. In February 1943 a Wiltshire farmer's wife described how she was being asked to provide either food and lodgings for additional members of the Women's Land Army or accommodation for Italian prisoners-of-war, as well as cooking for her own household of five, plus four Oxford undergraduates, who were helping and three single farm men who had to live in because of the shortage of cottages. She asked for a 'corps of women volunteers' to be raised to give 'even part-time help to farmhouses' during the 1943 harvest. 'The increasing load that is breaking down the farmers' wives will disrupt the organisation of the farms.'[36]

Many women, like Frances Partridge, reluctantly knuckled down to household chores, perhaps aided by a daily. In February 1944, Frances had Lawrence and Julia Gowing staying with her and noted that they were 'both heroic in the help they gave with bed-making and washing-up, and in Julia's case she hates it so much that it is heroism. When I said I didn't want any help with the cooking . . . she said "Ah yes, I understand and respect that", in a tone of great relief.'[37]

Such attitudes underlined the class differences identified in the Wartime Social Survey, with working-class contributors commenting sourly, 'people with money can do their bit towards the war by doing their own work and releasing maids'. Others did not see why 'women should go about with nothing to do, having a cook and a nannie. If a working man's wife can do work, they can!'[38]

A further cause of dissension was wealthy employers who continued to keep large staffs, thus evading the spirit of the regulations by recruiting servants above and below the registration ages, or else they employed married women, like

Margaret Powell, with children under fourteen years, since they were exempt from regulation. In February 1941, *The Lady* condemned as a 'scandal' servant advertisements which included phrases like 'eight kept, two in family':

> These advertisements could be useful evidence in the Nazi case that we are a decadent people, and they must foster discontent and suspicion among the poor at home. There is nothing necessarily unpatriotic in a large household staff. Some houses require many workers if they are not to fall in ruins. . . . The wrong is in the suggestion of easy lives offered by the advertised number of family to servants. This is not a time to be offering comfortable corners to trained and efficient workers of any kind.[39]

Other critics, like the MP, Eleanor Rathbone, saw the hogging of servants by selfish mistresses as damaging to the war effort, since wives who had been doing essential work were compelled to abandon it when they had to do all their own household chores. 'Is it fair that selfish women should be allowed, as at present, to have so many manual workers on the excuse that they are below or above the registration age?'[40] Affluent householders even forced up the hourly rates of unskilled dailies to such an extent that they priced out modestly placed but more deserving neighbours.[41]

The government, however, declined to be drawn into the issue of labour 'rationing' beyond the limits envisaged by the compulsory registration schemes. This was made clear in January 1942 when an MP asked about the setting of an official minimum and maximum amount of domestic labour in relation to a 'reasonable standard of household requirements'. In reply the Joint Parliamentary Secretary to the Ministry of Labour and National Service declared that after careful consideration, it had been found impossible 'to lay down hard and fast rules' as to the amount of domestic service to be allowed to households of varying size or composition.[42]

Staff advertisements at this time stressed the advantages an individual employer could offer, such as the location of a post in a 'safe' area away from enemy bombs, or the provision of good accommodation, plentiful outings, convenient access to towns or railway stations and a relatively light work load. There was a tendency to avoid the use of the words 'servant' and 'maid'. Instead there were appeals for 'assistants' or 'helps' – lady helps, mother's helps and useful helps. Typical was an appeal in *The Lady* of 13 February 1941, for a

> Domestic help; plain cooking; all duties; help given; comfortable home; family 2-3; country house; safe area; between Bath-Bristol.

The expansion of the home help service in the early 1940s made an attempt to solve the problem of 'hardship' cases by covering, from 1944, the sick, infirm and aged, as well as the nursing and pregnant mothers provided for under the original scheme.[43] By February 1943 home helps were already employed in 150 local authority areas as part of their maternity and child welfare programmes.[44] Employment exchanges began providing both recruits for home help services and domestics for 'hardship'

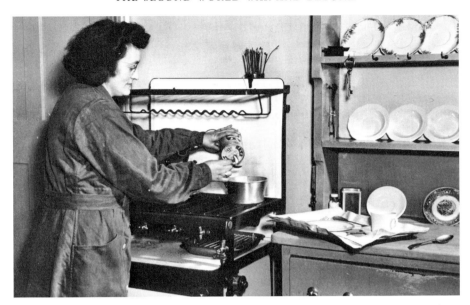

A London home help cooking in a client's home in March 1953. (*London Metropolitan Photographic Archives*)

households during 1944. In the first eight months of the year, 11,967 workers were supplied to these groups.[45] Following the creation of the National Health Service in 1948 responsibility for home helps passed to local authority health departments. However, the weaknesses in the recruitment and training of suitable women remained. Another problem was the reluctance of poorer housewives to let outsiders enter their shabby and badly equipped homes, a difficulty that could only be removed by a general improvement in housing conditions.[46]

When the National Health Service was launched in 1948 there were around 11,000 full-time and part-time home helps at work. Twelve years later, some 50,000 women were helping in 300,000 homes and this had increased to 62,097 at work in 1967 – of whom 41,147 worked for county councils, 16,387 for county boroughs and 9,191 for the London boroughs.[47] For the workers themselves, the scheme meant employment under agreed conditions by local authorities, rather than by individual householders. The issue of extracting payment for their services was left to the authority, rather than being a matter of negotiation between the householder and the home help.

During the war some large houses contrived to keep extra staff by offering accommodation to military personnel. Mary Cocking started work at Standen, near East Grinstead, in 1941, when she was fourteen. There were still seven on the staff and she worked mainly in the kitchens. However, as the war progressed and staff numbers dwindled to four, she was 'promoted' to duties in the 'front' of the house, such as looking after the drawing room fire. When the parlourmaid had time off, Mary took over her duties, answering the door and the telephone, as well as the household bells, taking tea into the drawing room and serving dinner at night. For this she wore a smart green dress, and muslin apron and cap supplied by her employer, Miss Beale. Her morning clothes she had to buy herself: 'I remember I made my aprons out of sheets my family gave me as clothes were on "coupons".' She was 'let off doing any war work as we had officers in the medical corps staying at Standen; they went to the Queen Victoria Hospital during the day and back for the evening meal. They came on Monday evening and left Friday morning. We then had to get the rooms ready for the next lot.'[48]

Despite the wartime pressures, discipline at Standen remained strict: 'We had to ask Mrs Last [the housekeeper] for permission to put the radio on. I was never allowed to read a book. I always had to do something that occupied my hands like sewing or knitting.' Occasionally, the cook would take her round the garden when the Beales were away, while at the appropriate season she and some of the other servants went into the kitchen garden to pick soft fruit: 'at that time we had double summer time so at 10 p.m. it was only 8 p.m. by the sun and still light.'[49] Mary remained at Standen until 1951 when she lost a leg in a motor-cycle accident and had to learn to walk again with the aid of crutches and, later, an artificial leg.

She remembered, too, that during the war, rations for the dining room and the servants' hall were supplemented by milk, eggs, rabbits and pheasants from the estate farm and by fresh vegetables from the garden. These benefits were shared by many other country house domestics at that time.

Sheila Chugg was another young, wartime maid, this time in a small Gloucestershire town. Although she had won a scholarship to the grammar school, her parents could not afford to let her go and at fourteen, in 1941, she began work at the home of an elderly solicitor. Her fellow servants were a staid housekeeper in her thirties and an elderly gardener-cum-handyman. Despite the servant shortage, her conditions were little better than those experienced by maids ten or twenty years earlier. She slept in a sparsely furnished, unheated attic room and was paid 10s a month, plus her keep. She was also limited to one weekly bath and had one half-day a week off, from which she had to return by 8 p.m.

Our sitting room was the kitchen, sitting by the old range in winter to keep warm and [we] went to bed at 9 p.m. with a cup of cocoa. My mother told me I would probably be tested for honesty and one morning [I] found a sixpence in the fireplace; which I handed in, but the look on the faces was enough for me to think mother had been right.

During the winter with the blackout in operation all the windows, eleven in all, had to be blacked out. I was a nervous fourteen-year-old . . . and with the housekeeper on her half-day I decided to fix the blackouts early while it was still reasonably light. I did not relish going around the large old house with just a small glimmer from a partially lit torch. That evening Mr H. left his office early and he came into the house and roared out, 'Who has done this? Remove them at once.' This I did and then had to go around later in the dark fixing them all again. It was not easy either, especially on the stairs when I had to reach a high window. I really thought one day I would fall to the bottom of the stairs.[50]

This treatment reinforced Sheila's general dislike of service and after a year she left to become a railway booking clerk. There she stayed for eight years and 'enjoyed every minute of it'. When she gave in her notice, her solicitor employer declared dismissively: 'Oh! I suppose you're going there just to stick stamps on envelopes.' A replacement maid was found almost at once. Like Sheila, she was a fourteen-year-old school leaver, but she seemed to find domestic work more congenial than her predecessor had done.[51]

By 1943, the unpopularity of domestic service applied not merely to private households, but, more seriously, to hospitals and other public institutions. Concern over the shortage of hospital domestics became so acute that in the spring of 1943 Violet Markham was invited to draw up a remedial scheme. She suggested the formation of a domestic service corps, which would function

Hanging up the blackout curtains in September 1939. (Punch, 27 September 1939)

rather like a military or Land Army unit and would offer prospects of promotion and improved status to members. Even so, Miss Markham doubted whether it would revive what she described as this 'often despised form of employment'. An essential part of the status-building process was the provision of a suitable uniform:

> In a world of great and tragic events the call of duty should, you may think, suffice without any adventitious appeal for clothes. One has, however, to take facts and people as they are. . . . A uniform is a factor of great psychological importance if the Corps is to achieve one of its objects – that of raising the status of domestic workers. In a uniform a ward maid will carry her head as high as her friend in the Forces; an arm band or a badge will have no such effect.[52]

If the Corps were successful it could be extended to other labour-starved public institutions which satisfied its basic requirements concerning 'work and wages as well as supervision, training and a field of promotion'.[53]

In the end, the formation of a Domestic Service Corps proved impractical, partly because of the government's inability to provide suitable uniforms at a time of shortages.[54] It was impossible to 'direct' women into hospital domestic work, because there was still no basic framework of conditions of service covering wages, hours and similar matters. That was remedied by the appointment of the

Hetherington Committee in 1943 to draw up a temporary scheme covering pay and employment conditions. It was to be replaced by a formal National Joint Council, such as already existed in some other industries, as soon as possible. Violet Markham was sceptical about its prospects: 'I am afraid the "welfare" carrot has been dangled before the nose of too many donkeys to produce any sort of a thrill!' Nevertheless, as a result of the Hetherington Report women were directed into hospital domestic service from 1944 to the end of 1945, with 34,211 women placed in this sector by the Ministry of Labour during the first eight months of 1944; 2,287 men were also directed to domestic work in these institutions. However, the problem of staff wastage persisted and during the first six months of 1944 the net increase in full-time domestic staff in hospitals and similar institutions was only about 5,500.[55]

After the war the promised National Joint Council agreement was drawn up, offering, for the first time, national minimum rates of pay and conditions of service for domestic staff in hospitals. By now domestics were accepted as an essential part of the patient care team and in 1946 a book published by the King Edward's Hospital Fund for London placed much emphasis on the importance of good amenities for them, to ensure they were aware that their contribution to the patients' well-being was 'valued at its true worth'.[56]

In the meantime, broader governmental anxieties over the future of private domestic service led to the appointment in March 1944 of Violet Markham and Florence Hancock to report on the sector for the Minister of Labour. Miss Hancock, the national organiser for women in the Transport and General Workers' Union, had helped to prepare a Memorandum on the Post-War Position of the Domestic Worker in the spring of 1943. This drew attention to the way in which former servants were helping the war effort in the armed forces, munition factories, civil defence, transport and other important spheres. 'These workers who are now serving their country so well, are deserving of better conditions in their old employment, when the war ends.'[57] The task of the Markham-Hancock team was to evaluate reform proposals and to draw up a plan for future action.

The report was completed in July 1944, but was only published, after some prodding from Miss Markham, in the summer of 1945. It pinpointed current weaknesses in the occupation, but stressed her conviction that with proper organisation, domestic work could become 'entirely honourable and self-respecting . . . for any woman', as well as performing an essential community service and providing 'excellent training for the girl who subsequently marries and has a home of her own'. The problems of employers were recognised too, particularly those of working-class women with large families, for whom home helps could provide assistance, and of middle-class wives looking after 'an old-fashioned house with stone passages, coal fires and an antiquated range'. Without domestic aid not only were such women overworked, but they were prevented from taking any constructive part in central or local government, or from following a professional career. Instead they had to concentrate on home duties. Finally, there was the demographic effect:

it is idle to preach the need for a higher birth rate if home life is to spell undiluted drudgery for the wife and mother. The demand of the girl who has had a modern education, for personal liberty and self expression is much too strong for any acceptance of an existence wholly circumscribed by home work.[58]

In the report's view, the need to solve the domestic service problem was inextricably linked to the 'future of the home, that cornerstone of the national life'.

It was essentially a class and gender-based analysis of the situation. Housework was seen as women's work and working-class women were to be persuaded to come forward as servants in order that, in the main, middle-class wives could pursue professional careers or take part in political life. This was a theme to which Violet Markham was to return over the years.[59] The working-class wife and mother was merely to have access to home helps, on a short-term basis, to enable her to cope with emergencies.

If the necessary servants were to be recruited, training standards had to be improved, in order to raise the occupation's status. In many ways this was a reiteration of views put forward after the First World War to popularise domestic work, but unlike the earlier initiatives, Markham-Hancock suggested formal machinery to achieve the desired end. The National Institute of Houseworkers (NIH) was set up to provide training, certification and agreed conditions of employment at wages that would apply, initially, to its own graduates, but which would, it was hoped, also influence other domestic employment.[60]

Another possibility to cover the shortfall, although one not mentioned by Markham-Hancock, was the recruitment of foreign servants and *au pairs*. This began in 1945, with the securing of a few hundred Belgian women for domestic work in hospitals, but became of major importance after 1946.

The Ministry of Labour also put pressure on women to enter private service in 1945, in some cases by threatening to withdraw unemployment benefit. As a result, around 25,000 women were placed in 'hardship households'. But despite these campaigns, the post-war servant deficit persisted. The opportunities for females to work in better-paid, higher status and more varied occupations elsewhere hampered those anxious to persuade them to take up household employment. This even applied to children's homes, which at first were attacked for failing to develop the talents of female residents by continuing to prepare them for domestic work.[61] At Dr Barnardo's in 1946, 86 of the 176 girls leaving the homes went as 'general house assistants', with a further 9 going as domestic hospital staff, 10 as cooks and 12 as nursemaids.[62] However, the girls were increasingly reluctant to take up these careers and by 1952 Barnardo's had ceased to train youngsters for paid household employment.[63]

This did not stop some of the charity's supporters from demanding they supply servants. In October 1947, Lady Blackford, who was a regular subscriber, called the shortage of maids 'the most crying need of the day and one of the most desirable in the interest of girl children . . . yet because of idle nonsense . . . not half of your girls are thus prepared. I have of late tried to get a young girl from the Homes without the slightest success.'[64] A Barnardo official responded soothingly by stating that although 'most girls would be much better off in domestic service', they themselves preferred to train for other employment. He added that in 1946 Barnardo's had received 250 applications for every female servant placed.

At a time when great stress was placed on the need to boost population growth, concerns about birth rates continued to be voiced. In February 1946 a young mother wrote angrily to *The Times*, pointing out she had a child of two, a husband overseas and no domestic help of any kind:

> In common with most of our friends we are quite prepared to have a family of at least four children, provided we have adequate help at reasonable wages. . . . The local Labour Exchange and servants' agency have yielded no one after weeks of dogged inquiry; my advertisements brought forth one reply from a cook who asked £3 10s a week and a private sitting-room.
>
> Either we young mothers must have home helps at a sensible wage . . . or else the government must accept the fact that we will simply have to forgo all hopes of a family exceeding, at the very outside, three children. There is a limit after all to what the human frame can tackle.[65]

Other critics, like Angus Maude and Roy Lewis, pointed to the many people who felt life was 'scarcely worth living unless it is civilized (as distinct from mechanised).' To them, this meant having 'a modest amount of domestic service. . . . [I]f good furniture, good silver and good pictures (all of which need careful maintenance) are to be banished . . . to museums; and if entertaining is to be permanently restricted . . . then emigration to Eire or South Africa seems the only hope'.[66] Presumably in those two destinations it was felt plenty of domestic help could be found. It was an exaggerated example of a fairly common upper middle-class view that home life without servants was intolerable.

For some, the remedy lay in the employment of 'dailies' for a few hours a day or a week. Significantly, the number of charwomen and office cleaners in England and Wales jumped from 140,146 in 1931 to 215,336 twenty years later; by 1961 it had reached around 317,400.[67] As Margaret Powell recalled, during these years women 'didn't have to worry about references on a daily job. You just said you'd never been out before, or, that the people you last worked for had died.'[68] But even at this time the increased use of contract cleaning for offices and institutions attracted many 'dailies' who wished to avoid the fraught personal relationships that often went with private service.

More optimistically, there was a wider acceptance of the benefits of labour-saving appliances. In 1949 a new edition of *Mrs Beeton's Household Management* noted that the shortage of domestic staff and the high wages they demanded had forced many wives to take on more housework themselves. In that context, labour-saving devices were of major importance, even if some of them, at first sight, seemed expensive: 'the labour they save will soon make the housewife appreciate how economical they really are. And it must be remembered that they are saving servants' wages as well.'[69] In the long run a wider use of domestic appliances would overcome many household difficulties and some former servant-keepers came to welcome their new independence. An Elstree householder wrote in August 1974:

I am a good butler, my wife is the best cook I've ever met. We both of us drive a car very much better than my grandmother's old chauffeur. . . . Now that we do all these things for ourselves we do them much better.[70]

Similarly, Lady Mander admitted she did not regret the loss of staff as a result of the war: 'It is a relief now not to have to try to keep up appearances or to guard one's speech at meals or to catch hostile glances from the gardener for picking a flower instead of waiting for him to bring plants in from the hothouse.'[71]

Where full-time domestics were employed, their long-term commitment to a single family was no longer expected. Even prestigious Norland nurses rarely stayed on once the children were nearing school age. High taxation, which reduced parental incomes and the larger salaries expected by staff meant that 'the very best nurse' was 'regarded as a luxury'.[72]

Staff also had to demonstrate versatility in their domestic skills rather than pursue the specialist approach which had applied, particularly in large households, in the 1930s. A butler, writing in 1950, described how he and the cook-housekeeper looked after their employer's country house:

sometimes I go to London to do some cleaning and polishing in the flat and offices of my employer. . . . Besides the work of the house, I can find time to mow the lawns, look after the hens . . . and drive the small car. . . . Since I have been single handed, we have sent all the ornamental silver . . . rose bowls, loving cups, etc, to the jewellers to be lacquered. This has been a great success . . . and the silver looks as if it were cleaned by a butler every day. . . . Lacquering . . . saves hours in cleaning copper coal scuttles, antique brass fenders, and all the hundred and one things that had formerly to be cleaned each week.[73]

Arthur Inch, when he returned to service in the mid-1950s, found himself 'covering the jobs of ten men in the pantry. . . . As well as being butler/valet I also did a few chauffeuring jobs such as taking the children to school. . . . For a while we had a temporary daily cook in and then a couple were engaged as cook and gardener. . . . My wife did lady's maid duty and any visiting ladies. A local girl on the estate also came in to do housework. After a couple of years the married couple departed . . . and we then had a cook who came in for week-ends only.' Soon after he decided to take a post as single-handed butler to a titled family, but on discovering that his employers were heavy drinkers, he quickly moved, to become a butler/valet/chauffeur: 'but chauffeuring children to school and washing cars, etc. was interfering too much with my indoor work so after a year I left there.' The other staff comprised a chef and his wife and a couple of dailies for the housework. Then in 1960 he saw an advertisement for a butler/valet's job in Sussex, for the Kleinwort family. He applied and was appointed. He remained there as single-handed butler-valet for the next twenty years, with his wife doing a few hours weekly as a housemaid and looking after and mending the household linen. There was a full-time cook and two charwomen from the estate to do the cleaning.[74]

Staff in other large country houses had similar experiences after 1945. A long-serving butler at a substantial property in south Leicestershire claimed in the mid-1980s that he could not name a place in the whole county with two full-time resident servants, while another Leicestershire butler, who began as a footman at Quenby Hall in 1949, declared: 'Footmen almost died out with me. In later years they wanted a butler-valet or a chauffeur-valet, we started merging jobs.'[75] As the columns of *The Lady* showed, by the late 1950s advertisements for domestic help had increased sharply compared to the low point reached immediately after the Second World War. However, the emphasis was on cooks, nannies and mother's helps, rather than on the wide range of staff that had been at work before 1939.[76]

Inevitably, these changes and the need for economy to meet a growing tax burden, led to modifications in the lifestyles of stately home owners. Some, like the aged Lady Airlie, left their residence and moved to a hotel.[77] Others, like the Earl and Countess of Crawford and Balcarres, concluded they could not maintain more than one property. Immediately after the war they disposed of their English estate and settled at Balcarres in Scotland.

> Our household varied in numbers over the years – sometimes we had foreign couples, mad cooks and bad cooks, an ex-housemaid married to an ex-footman who remained with us as a couple till they retired. The head gardener's wife, who came as cook, was with us for eleven years and though a good cook was a woman of uncertain temper and very jealous. When she departed in a huff and took her reluctant husband with her, the relief was enormous. Two dailies then came to our rescue with the housework, and I took on the cooking, and, if the house was full, got outside help. . . . Hoovers took the place of brooms and mops in the housemaids' cupboards on every floor and wash basins in bedrooms meant no more carrying of hot water cans. . . . There was always a lot to do, but I for one never regretted that I was not a 'châtelaine' of a large household.[78]

Increasingly, as with Chatsworth and Woburn Abbey, houses were opened to the public, partly for tax purposes and partly to boost income. At Chatsworth, once the girls' public school that had occupied it during the war had moved out in 1946, the house was left empty except for two housemaids who 'perched in a distant room at the north end'. The sheer number of girls had made everything look shabby and the lack of domestic staff meant it was impossible to keep clean. Eventually, in 1948 the then Duke and Duchess of Devonshire decided to reopen the house. They engaged two redoubtable Hungarian sisters, Ilona and Elisabeth Solymossy, as cook and housemaid and asked them 'to gather up a team of their acquaintances who were sturdy enough to face the enormous task of cleaning and making ready the house for the opening'. In all, eleven Hungarians arrived and worked through the winter of 1948-9, so that the house was ready to receive the public at Easter 1949. Despite petrol rationing '75,000 people came to see it at half a crown each and a shilling for the garden'.[79] In November 1950, however, the 10th Duke died and there were heavy death duties to pay. Not until the mid-1950s did the eleventh Duke and

Duchess decide to move to Chatsworth themselves. There then followed a major refurbishment, presided over by the Solymossy sisters with as much energy as they had displayed in setting the public part of the house in order a decade earlier.[80] The Duke and Duchess finally returned in 1959. As the Duchess recalled, during the 1950s the Hungarians continued to clean, mend, scrub, polish and tidy. 'Sometimes they brought forth wonders that had lain beneath other wonders in hopeless heaps of *things* in attic room after attic room. They made order out of disorder.'[81]

At Woburn Abbey, the 13th Duke of Bedford found an almost derelict property when he inherited the estate at the beginning of the 1950s. After much hard work it too was opened to the public in 1955. However, it was very different from his grandfather's day in 1940, when there were still fifty or sixty indoor servants employed. Soon after the public opening, the Duke described the way he and the Duchess ran their own wing at Woburn:

> Where my grandfather had scores of servants in Belgrave Square and at the Abbey, we made do with seven, to cover both houses, with all the public engagements that the stately-home business entails. We do have fourteen dailies and six night-watchmen who come in on a part-time basis from Woburn village, but their job is to clean and look after the whole vast complex of the house, including the public rooms and the tea-room and restaurant in the stables.[82]

Outside similar modifications of pre-war practice were apparent. At Aynho the army finally left in 1947 and the task of renovation began. Badly damaged box hedges that surrounded the flower beds near the mansion were rooted out and a simple design of eight beds, each surrounded with new box hedges, was substituted. Many pre-war methods of cultivation for the kitchen garden were abandoned because of labour shortages. As Ted Humphris noted, a motor plough and cultivators were used instead of spades and rakes. 'The war years had certainly hastened the end of the old methods of cultivating and running a garden.' By the early 1950s Aynho Park House and its pleasure grounds were open to the public and once again Humphris provided flowers to decorate the house.[83] However, it was very different from the spacious hospitality that had prevailed in 1939.

Even wealthy landowners like the Wernhers at Luton Hoo and Lord Leconfield at Petworth became more economical in the post-war years. At Luton Hoo, the garden labour force was financed by selling some of the produce at Covent Garden market each week. That meant one of the gardeners going up to London with vegetables and plants, the latter being sold to leading florists in South Audley Street. Bob Gregory had this task, but he came to dislike the new spirit of commercialism. After two years he moved as head gardener to Bitham Hall, Avon Dassett, in Warwickshire, where there were two small kitchen gardens, a greenhouse block and a large plant house. The property had been neglected during the war, but after twelve months' energetic effort it began to take shape once more. Bob remained about three years before he moved to a higher paid job. There followed a brief and unhappy spell as head gardener at the Kesteven Farm Institute in Lincolnshire, before he became head gardener at Maidwell Hall, Northamptonshire, then a preparatory school. With four under-gardeners, he had to grow enough vegetables and fruit to supply the staff, pupils and domestic helpers – a total of about 110 people. Flowers, too, were, raised, while the pleasure grounds, lake, rock gardens and playing fields had to be kept in good order. Nevertheless, Gregory adapted to the new situation and remained at Maidwell until the mid-1970s.[84]

At Petworth, too, there were great changes. Whereas thirty-six men had once worked in the gardens, by the end of the war that had dropped to just three, including the head gardener, Fred Streeter. In 1950 staff numbers recovered to nine, but despite a sharp reduction in the acreage of the private gardens, this was still inadequate. One of the stud grooms mowed the lawns and any surplus produce was sold. Where once the cultivated area and grounds had covered 300 acres, in 1950 that had shrunk to fifteen.[85]

In the 1944-5 *Report on the Post-War Organisation of Private Domestic Employment*, Violet Markham and Florence Hancock had concluded optimistically that 'I serve' was a 'princely motto'. However, in the post-war world, with a changed economic and social climate, it became increasingly difficult to persuade people to accept that concept. One means proposed in the report, at least with regards to the women, was the setting up of the National Institute of Houseworkers. The aim was to train efficient domestic staff and at the same time, by the award of diplomas and the drawing up of a code of working conditions, to raise the status of the occupation. In future, declared contemporary newspapers, there would be 'no more servants in Britain, only house workers'.[86]

THE ROLE OF THE NATIONAL INSTITUTE OF HOUSEWORKERS

The Markham-Hancock report was published in the summer of 1945, but it was February of the following year before the Minister of Labour and National Service announced that the government had decided to set up the National Institute of Houseworkers (NIH) along lines recommended in the report. The Institute was formally incorporated as a non-profit-making company in June 1946 and in the following month a board of directors was appointed to manage its affairs. As Dorothy Elliott, who chaired the board in its early days, put it, the scheme had 'two main aims: to turn out a domestic worker skilled in her craft; and to give to that worker a sense of confidence in herself as a member of the community, breaking down the idea that domestic workers are a race apart.'[87] To that end, a broad training programme was drawn up, combining general and health education with practical domestic instruction, so that students would not only become skilled houseworkers but 'good citizens' who knew 'how to make good use of their leisure'.[88]

The institute began work early in 1947 with three principal tasks. These were the establishment of a diploma examination which could be taken by experienced workers, as well as by the newly trained; the creation of an instruction programme at NIH residential centres, where students would be taught free of charge and would also receive a small maintenance grant; and the provision of employment for successful candidates at the end of their course under terms set out by the institute and agreed with employers. These covered wages, working hours, leisure time and other general issues. It was realised that a statutory code of conditions for private domestic employment was impracticable, since that would have involved inspection of homes to ensure that the conditions were being observed, but it was hoped NIH standards would influence employers generally.[89] The

Housework training at the Nottingham centre of the National Institute of Houseworkers in 1949. (*TUC Library*)

main concern, however, was to ensure the training was of a sufficiently high quality to raise the standing of the occupation and thereby attract more workers to it.[90]

The NIH also undertook to recruit day helpers, who would be employed directly by local committees. They would work for individual householders on an hourly basis and could be full or part time. They were to be paid by the local committees, which would then recoup their expenses by charging householders the relatively high sum of 2s 6d an hour. That covered the worker's pay, her national insurance contribution and the administrative costs of the scheme. In many respects these women fulfilled a similar role to that of the local authority home helps, but under the aegis of the NIH rather than of a public body.[91]

The standards set by the NIH for resident domestics included agreed pay rates; a working timetable of ninety-six hours per fortnight, beyond which overtime became payable; the provision of a bed-sitting room or a separate bedroom and sitting room with heating; the granting of three half-days a week free time; a fortnight's paid annual holiday for the first five years of service, with three weeks thereafter; and opportunities for the servant to entertain her friends out of working hours.[92] In many respects this reflected the programme put forward by the National Union of Domestic Workers in its *Steps* document during the autumn of 1938.

The NIH was financed by government grants and loans. Thus, in the year ended 31 March 1949, grants of £75,637 were made, plus loans of around £77,000 to cover the acquisition and equipment of the training centres and other projects. The following year, ending 31 March 1950, Ministry of Labour grants totalled £113,935, with a further £22,000 by way of loans.[93] Yet, despite this expenditure, the training programme was slow to develop and some early centres were very small. That opened at Oxford in the autumn of 1947, for example, was set up in a Victorian villa and by September 1948 had just fourteen students, six of whom resided on the premises.

Chilton Cantelo House, the first training centre to be opened by the National Institute of Houseworkers. (*Mrs. S. Whiting*)

They attended a local technical school for lessons in English and for extra tuition in cookery, laundry work and sewing. First aid and general health instruction was given at a nearby Red Cross station.[94] Perhaps not surprisingly, the Oxford centre closed in August 1950, with its students transferred to new, larger premises at Harrow.[95]

The first centre, opened at Chilton Cantelo House, near Yeovil, was more ambitious. In January 1948 it had thirty students, aged from fifteen to fifty-one. Domestic training took place at the centre itself, with the students performing all the chores as well as learning household skills. Leisure activities included community singing and play-reading and there was a weekly class in Civics at the Yeovil Technical School.[96] This accorded with the NIH's avowed aim of providing trainees with a 'full and interesting life'.[97]

By late 1949 a total of nine centres were in operation, with places for 365 students; 327 students had completed courses, of whom 173 were adults and 154 juveniles.[98] But juveniles (those under seventeen) soon outstripped adult entrants, comprising about 70 per cent of those entering between September 1947 and 31 October 1950.[99] They were recruited with the help of the Youth Employment Service. This preponderance of young people doubtless encouraged the NIH to be more authoritarian in its approach than might otherwise have been the case. Around two-thirds of the trainees' time was devoted to practical instruction, with a further one-fifth taken up with general education. The rest of the course involved practical work in selected private households. For those aged seventeen and above the course lasted six months and at the end they took the qualifying examination which gave associate membership of the institute. For juveniles a nine-month course was arranged. After this they went out as pre-diploma students to spend a year working in a household chosen by the NIH, before returning to sit their examination.[100]

In order to develop the wider interests of the younger students, each was supplied with a special notebook when she left the centre for her pre-diploma year. In it she was to enter points of interest in her job, comments on any further education course she took, a list of books she had read and information about the area where she was working.[101]

Sheila Chapman went to Chilton Cantelo when she left school, aged fifteen, in 1949. The trainees were housed in dormitories and despite the reluctance of many pre-war maids to wear caps, their uniform consisted of a cap and overall. Most girls were homesick at first, 'but the teachers were very good. . . . They were very strict on keeping our rooms tidy and clean, and we had inspection of lockers regularly.'[102] Sheila's first residential placement was in the household of a local vicar, where she spent about a month. Her friend went to a nearby doctor: 'It was quite lonely there, looking back I think it could have been cheap labour.' At the end of the nine-month course she went on a one-year placement to the home of a store manager in Plymouth, where she carried out housework, baby sitting and laundry: 'we were supposed to have gone to college for half a day, I'm afraid I didn't attend.'

Sheila Chapman in her National Institute of Houseworkers uniform, in training at Chilton Cantelo, August 1949. (*Mrs. S. Whiting*)

She had limited time off – just Tuesday and Saturday afternoons each week. This was below the standard stipulated by the NIH. Yet, despite the hard work, she was happy. Unlike many servants, especially those before 1939, she was treated as part of the family and had her meals with the rest of the household, rather than in the kitchen. When the year was up, she returned to Chilton Cantelo to take her examination and on completing this successfully, returned to the placement family. There she remained until her marriage in September 1954.[103] NIH reports suggest that a high proportion of trainees stayed with their first employer. The institute considered this confirmed the care with which mistress and maid were matched by its training officers.[104]

Most successful candidates, however, took the examination as 'experienced' workers rather than as trainees like Sheila Chapman. Even in December 1960, when the NIH had been running for over a decade, only 1,537 of the 5,287 holders of the diploma had followed a training course. When compared with the census returns it also indicated the limited success of a scheme intended to boost the domestic labour force. In 1951, there were 724,000 domestic workers recorded, of whom 178,000 were resident servants in private homes. In 1931 there had been an estimated 707,000 servants resident in private homes out of a domestic labour force of about 1.3 million.[105]

It may be asked why experienced workers took the diploma examination, especially as they had to pay an entrance fee. For this there seem to be two explanations. First, some maids were anxious to have the status of certificated workers – something which NIH propaganda stressed. In the May 1948 issue of *The Houseworker*, the institute's journal, several successful candidates gave their reasons for seeking qualifications. One, who had been a domestic for seven years, thought 'it established a guarantee of my experience and also that it would be a very nice thing to have. The Diploma and Badge are two of my proudest possessions and I am now not ashamed to say I am a domestic worker.' Another woman, employed as a cook-housekeeper for a semi-invalid, felt she had 'a trump card to use', should she need to find fresh employment.

The diploma was also an advantage for those recruited as local authority home helps or as day workers for NIH local committees. Indeed, for day workers it was a necessity. From an early stage, the London County Council encouraged its home helps to become qualified and the age range of candidates examined was from twenty-three to sixty-two years. A number of other authorities followed suit, including Oxford, Newcastle upon Tyne, Preston and Essex County Council.[106] Even when there was no formal policy of encouraging staff to take the examination (and unfortunately for the long-term success of the NIH, that was true of the majority of authorities) additional payments might be made to qualified staff. This was Sheila Chapman's experience when, a few years after marriage, she began working for the Cornish Home Help Service, in the early 1960s.[107]

But while girls like Sheila found the NIH and its courses attractive, outsiders pinpointed its deficiencies. A visitor to Chilton Cantelo in 1948-9 compared its spartan atmosphere to that of an 'old-fashioned "reformatory school"'. The principal was described as 'an ideal matron of a "toughs school"'. Apart from that 'the rooms were . . . very cold where the girls were sewing etc.'[108] Still more damaging were accusations of extravagance in the running of the training programmes. These were taken up in the press and by MPs like Angus Maude. He noted that during the year 1949-50 about 290 students had been trained at a total cost of almost £114,000, plus £22,000 in loans:

> I find it difficult . . . to believe that the primary aim of the Institute, which is to raise the status of domestic service, can be achieved by turning out some 300 trained students a year, not by any means all of whom will be going into private domestic service, when the majority of people have probably never heard of the Institute, and when the attractions of domestic service as a trade are not being widely disseminated through the good offices of the Institute.[109]

In December 1952, another MP questioned the Minister of Labour on the cost of publishing *The Houseworker* and upon the size of its circulation. He was told that in the year ending 31 March 1952, there had been a loss of £600 on its publication. Of 4,000 copies of each issue printed around half were sold and from the rest 'a free distribution is made to representative bodies interested in women's employment'.[110]

Underlying the debates was the dismissive approach of the *Manchester Guardian*, which in September 1951 found it was hardly necessary 'to maintain residential training colleges for housework', especially as up to July of that year only 834 girls had completed courses at the centres. About a fifth of them had subsequently married or given up paid domestic work:

Training is expensive and seems to be becoming more so. The Committee of Public Accounts was told last year that it cost about £130 a girl; the Ministry of Labour's latest figure is 'approximately £160' for girls over seventeen and 'about £200' for younger girls, who do a longer course. . . . Could not more training be arranged in hospitals and other institutions, where the work even of beginners could be of immediate value? Whether it is worth maintaining the institute on its present scale is a question that merits careful study.[111]

NIH Diploma awarded to Sheila Chapman in 1951. (*Mrs. S. Whiting*)

To such critics the NIH replied that in the long term it was important to develop the general knowledge and self-confidence of the trainees, and it was working towards making domestic work 'as natural, dignified and honourable as . . . teaching, nursing, administration, agriculture or industry'.[112] The *Manchester Guardian* argued that such improvement in the 'status' of servants as had occurred was more the result of post-war full employment and the consequent competition for domestic help than the influence of the NIH. The institute itself ruefully admitted the attack had been harmful.

Against this background and following the election of a cost-cutting Conservative government in 1951, the NIH's grant was reduced by almost two-thirds in 1952.[113] This meant only one of the nine training centres, that at Harrow, could be retained. However, the Bridge of Allan Centre in Scotland survived as a result of a grant from the Scottish Association for Homecraft Training, a voluntary body grant-aided by the Scottish Education Department, and the Swansea centre reopened after a brief gap, as a result of financial support from local education authorities in Wales and England.[114]

The NIH also had difficulties with its Daily Houseworker Service, which had opened in Portsmouth in 1948 and was eventually to be taken up in seventeen other towns throughout Great Britain. Part of the problem lay in the hourly payment of 2s 6d required for the workers. That was higher than the amount normally paid to charwomen. As a result, householders were reluctant to recruit them or if they were engaged, they were often expected to do a good deal of heavy work during their spell on duty. Staff turnover was rapid and some workers entered into private arrangements with families whom they had first contacted under the NIH. Any local service which failed to pay for itself was closed down.[115] In 1954 a peak of over 500 employees were servicing some 2,000 households each week, but that had fallen to 329 workers by 1960-1. They were helping 1,055 households a week.[116] Four years later the totals had dropped to 266 workers assisting 870 householders. By then the scheme was largely irrelevant at a time when local authority home helps in

Students making pickles and chutney at the Bridge of Allan training centre in Scotland in 1948. (*TUC Library*)

England and Wales numbered around 62,000. In 1966 the service was closed down. Significantly, too, of home helps surveyed a year later, only one in five had received training of any kind and nearly one-third of the courses they had taken had lasted for just half a day.[117] Despite the institute's repeated efforts to offer special courses to home helps, in this sphere, too, it had failed to make an impact.

Disagreements arose over NIH requirements that a full-time residential maid in private service should work a basic ninety-six hours per fortnight and should be free from domestic duties at other times, unless she agreed to put in extra hours, when overtime would be payable. Some mistresses felt that while a girl was on the premises, perhaps reading or sewing in her room, she should be available for work.[118] But the NIH maintained that although give and take between the parties was desirable, it was important to establish that when the worker was 'off duty', she should be 'free to stay in the house, which is her home, as well as her place of employment, without having duties . . . imposed upon her'.[119] It was, of course, this problem of off duty hours within the home that had irked so many resident maids before 1939. The institute argued that as other occupations had 'limited and regular hours and time off', so should domestic employment.[120] The difficulty lay in persuading mistresses that such 'trade union' attitudes were as appropriate within the house as they were outside it.

A final obstacle to the NIH's success was the disintegration of the domestic world for which it had been created. Not only did the new spirit of female independence and egalitarianism make the employment of domestic help less attractive to many wives, but the advent of modern, labour-saving houses and new electrical appliances made their recruitment less necessary. In the 'swinging sixties' traditional bourgeois values were rejected and less store was placed on having immaculately maintained rooms. Instead, families preferred to spend their spare cash on cars, entertainment, holidays and various new consumer durables.

Potential servants, for their part, were sceptical of institute claims that they were entering a skilled occupation which was of vital importance to the well-being of the community. Private service was especially unpopular and those who trained as domestics preferred to take institutional posts in hospitals, schools and similar establishments or to work in hotels. In 1964-5, the NIH's annual report pointed out that the trend towards institutional work was increasing and that 54 per cent of first placements were in this type of employment.[121] By September 1970 that had risen to 80 per cent of placements; only 20 per cent were now in private households.[122] Figures produced by the institute in June 1972 suggested not more than about eighty of its associate members were still in private service.[123]

From the early 1950s, the government seemed to lose interest in the scheme. Following the economy drive of 1952, there was a threat four years later to withdraw the grant altogether. Only after vigorous protests and lengthy negotiations was that changed to an annual sum of £15,000 to be devoted to organising the diploma examinations only. All other work, including the running of the Harrow training centre, was to be financed from outside sources.[124]

Over the years the grant slowly increased, to reach £37,000 by 1970-1, but throughout the period the NIH was starved of cash.[125] Its role diminished further and it was forced to diversify, offering training packages to various organisations, often on a short-term basis only. In 1963, it changed its name to the National Institute for Housecraft, but even in the late 1950s it was already offering brief specialist programmes. These included residential courses at Harrow for the Industrial Welfare Society, the National Society for the Prevention of Cruelty to Children, and the Women's Royal Army Corps. Non-residential training was given to hospital domestic workers.[126] By the mid-1960s these additional activities included a course for Hospital Domestic Forewomen, with over 300 hospital domestic supervisors trained and examined in the period to the end of December 1970.[127] Supervisory courses were organised for hotel staff and were eligible for grants from the Hotel and Catering Industrial Training Board.[128]

The desperate efforts by the NIH to remain afloat were an admission that its original aim of reforming and reviving private domestic service did not match the realities of home life for most British people. Even the diploma lost its modest appeal, with just 186 candidates examined between April 1964 and March 1965. Of these 125 had received residential training. Two years later, the number of candidates examined had fallen to 137; 111 had received training at one of the three surviving centres, while 3 were local authority candidates from Further Education courses and 17 were hospital forewomen.[129]

For its part, the NIH blamed the parsimony of successive governments for its plight. Early in 1971 it complained that since 1956 'the training aspect of the Institute charged as a standard-setting body for domestic employment was not grant-aided although an integral part of standard-setting and examinations. . . . [The] Government's bargain with the Institute has been unusually hard over the last few years. All the modest profits the Institute has made from running outside

Learning to cook at the Oxford centre of the NIH in 1949. (*TUC Library*)

courses are set against the grant rather than put to use to build up the . . . small reserves.'[130] It pointed out, too, that in 1969 of 4,443 girls aged fifteen to seventeen who had entered catering, hotels and similar services, a mere 746 had taken jobs which provided planned training. This, it argued, highlighted the inadequacy of job training for women and girls in that particular sphere and the need for its own particular expertise.

The comments were provoked by the fact that soon after taking office in 1970 the new Conservative Government began a critical appraisal of NIH activities and funding. After more than a year of deliberation, in December 1971 it announced that the Institute would have to close. It was noted that local education authorities and the major employers of domestic workers, such as hospitals and hotels, had developed training programmes which largely replaced those offered by the NIH. 'Last year some 203 people took the housecraft diploma whereas 6,250 candidates took courses of similar type in other institutions, so the size of the task has got out of all proportion.'[131]

After further negotiations it was agreed in the autumn of 1972 that the Swansea training centre would be taken over by the local authority and incorporated into the Swansea College of Further Education. Students at the Swansea centre would be awarded a certificate issued by the Welsh Joint Education Committee.[132] The rest of the NIH's activities were closed down and the organisation went into voluntary liquidation. Despite all efforts, its aim of ensuring that domestic employment was recognised as 'a worthwhile job and career . . . requiring proper training skills and adequate rewards' remained unfulfilled.[133] Domestic service was still the Cinderella occupation it had always been.

THE FOREIGN CONTRIBUTION

Even before the end of the Second World War, government concern over the inadequate domestic staffing of hospitals had led to attempts to recruit workers from elsewhere in Europe. In March 1945 a Ministry of Labour minute noted there were five thousand domestic vacancies in hospitals. A month later 'useful' contacts had been established with Belgian officials to consider the feasibility of recruiting girls from Belgium for employment in London hospitals. Further meetings followed in London in June and at these a spokesman for the Belgian delegation declared their willingness 'to do all they could to help London in her difficulties realising as they did that Belgium owed its freedom to the stand made by Britain in 1940'.[134]

Agreement was eventually reached to allow Belgian volunteers, mainly between twenty-one and forty-five, to work in London hospitals for periods of at least six months, under clearly established terms regarding pay and working conditions. The first party arrived in July 1945, with the Ministry of Labour, through its Welfare Department, making arrangements to ensure the well-being of the volunteers. The amount of work this involved was later described by a Ministry of Labour official as 'amazing'.[135] In all, 880 women and girls came to Britain under this arrangement, with the last party arriving early in 1946.

Despite its limitations, the scheme was successful. But efforts to extend it to other allied and neutral countries in Europe, including France, Switzerland and Scandinavia, proved fruitless, either because of their own shortage of domestic staff or because of an unwillingness among the women themselves to work in hospitals.[136] As a result, the Ministry of Labour turned its attention to the possible recruitment of volunteers from among the refugees in Displaced Persons Camps in the British zones in Germany and Austria. Already in May 1946 the merits of this option were being discussed. It was pointed out that these were being maintained at British taxpayers' expense and yet they had 'little or no future prospects', at least in the short run, of getting a secure home and employment. In consequence it was likely they would be 'only too glad to accept employment of any kind' in Britain. They were to be recruited for particularly unattractive domestic work in sanatoria and tuberculosis hospitals, with plans drawn up to despatch the first one thousand volunteers as soon as possible.[137] Initially they were to come from the Baltic states of Latvia, Estonia and Lithuania, under an arrangement poetically labelled the 'Balt Cygnet' scheme.[138] They were to be granted entry for one year only, but it was accepted that, given their situation, their permits would probably have to be extended indefinitely, so that they eventually became permanent residents in Britain. Only if they broke the terms of their contract or misbehaved in some other way would they be returned to the Displaced Persons Camps from which they had come.[139]

Despite its opportunistic nature, which took advantage of the plight of the refugees, the venture was successful. In all 2,575 Baltic women had come to Britain in this way by the early months of 1947. This success and the continuing need for domestic workers led the government to extend its recruitment campaign to cover a wider range of Displaced Persons from camps in Germany and Austria, including those outside the British zones. From the spring of 1947 a new European Volunteer Workers scheme called 'Westward Ho' came into operation, which was merged with the earlier Balt Cygnet initiative.[140] In total, 8,170 Displaced Persons were brought over to Britain in 1947 to work in hospitals and similar public institutions or in 'hardship' households. A further 2,250 men and 3,430 women came in as European volunteers in 1948. By the end of 1949 it was announced that 5,200 men and 12,400 females had come to work in hospitals, hostels and other public institutions and in 'hardship' households since the inception of the Balt Cygnet scheme in 1946. A further 870 volunteers came in during 1950, before the 'Westward Ho' arrangement was wound up in that year.[141] There was also a small-scale recruitment of Italian women for domestic employment, mainly in mental and tuberculosis hospitals and sanatoria in 1950. However, by then the most acute phase of the hospital staffing crisis was over.

If the government's immediate post-war preoccupation had been to meet the needs of hospitals, sanatoria, public institutions and 'hardship' cases, pressure was also mounting from private householders anxious to recruit foreign staff. As early as August 1945 MPs began to demand that 'suitable women from Germany and the European liberated countries' be allowed 'to come under proper supervision to this country', to work as mother's helps.[142] Soon private representations were being made, with influential people contacting the Ministry of Labour to request permission to bring in staff for their own households. In November 1945, for example, Sir Alexander Maxwell, Permanent Under Secretary of State at the Home Office, contacted Sir Godfrey Ince, Permanent Secretary at the Ministry of Labour, to point out that a number of applications had been received by his department asking 'for the admission . . . of aliens to take up domestic employment in private households':

> It is represented that the prospective employer is in real need of such help; that domestics are almost impossible to obtain among British subjects, or aliens already here; and that the absence of such help entails real hardship, especially where the prospective employer is elderly or infirm, or has public duties which make it difficult to carry the added burden of domestic work. As instances, I may mention Lady Mary Herbert, one of the Queen's Ladies-in-Waiting, who wishes to obtain a French maid as a personal attendant and to help look after her small girl; and Mr Justice Romer, who asked me the other day if his mother, who is elderly and a cripple, could bring over a Belgian woman to replace her present maid who will shortly be going to Canada with her husband.
>
> We have been obliged to refuse all applications of this kind in order to support the policy of your department where, I understand, the view is taken that if aliens were allowed to come here for domestic employment in private households, the recruitment of foreign women to meet the urgent needs of hospitals and similar institutions would be seriously prejudiced; and that it would be difficult to prevent those already here from drifting into more remunerative and attractive private service.
>
> I find it difficult, however, to give a convincing answer to the applicant who says (as Romer said) - 'Yes, I appreciate that the needs of hospitals must come first; but the woman whom I want to engage has no intention of working in a hospital, and if she can't come to me she won't come at all.'[143]

Violet Markham also joined in the campaign to relax the restrictions, writing to the Ministry of Labour in March 1946: 'I know the difficulties about ministering to the idle rich, but honestly I do not think that a handful of drones ought to stand in the way of alleviating the sufferings and trials of people in a far more modest state of life.[144]

The government, meanwhile, was concerned not only about its hospital recruitment drives, but with the logistics of bringing over large numbers of people from countries whose own transport infrastructure had been shattered and where there was an acute shortage of shipping. However, in April 1946 it agreed that householders who were able to make arrangements with potential foreign domestics could apply to the Ministry of Labour for individual work permits, under terms similar to those which had applied before the war. Initially, preference was to be given to 'hardship' cases, but within months all restrictions had been cast aside.[145]

Immediately there was a great increase in demand, as would-be employers made use of any contacts they had with members of the British Control Commission in Germany, or used the services of private recruitment agencies, or even advertised in the foreign press. During 1946 alone 8,041 domestic permits were issued, 7,622 of them in respect of private residential servants. To get a permit, employers had to satisfy the ministry that the vacancy was 'reasonable and necessary', that they had attempted to get a British worker without success, and that the wages and conditions of employment on offer were, as good as those available to similar British workers in the area. If either party terminated the employment, the foreign domestic must obtain permission from her local employment exchange before taking another post with a different mistress.[146] The work permits were issued for a year initially, but could be extended. They were not granted to women over fifty-five on the grounds that 'the period of full and useful service' they could render was limited and when they reached pensionable age they would 'become chargeable to public funds' if they were unable to work.[147]

Initially, the scheme applied to all nationalities except German women whose presence, so soon after the end of the war, was felt likely to cause discontent among British co-workers.[148] In 1948, however, that changed, partly because of the need to boost the government's recruitment campaign for staff for public institutions and hardship households. From August 1948 an initial group of around two thousand women came in under what was called the North Sea scheme, to cover these official vacancies. At the same time individual German women could be employed by private householders. Soon the burgeoning commercial employment agencies were taking advantage of this new possibility.[149] The Ministry of Labour itself remained studiously aloof from these developments, as an official wrote in December 1948: 'If an employer elects to get in touch with a foreign woman through an employment agency that is his own affair; but the Department does not recognise the agency as having any status in the matter.'[150]

One such agency, Isobel Jay Ltd of Hove, was stressing the benefits of continental recruitment as early as 1949, seeing it as the

> most effective answer to the extreme shortage of domestic labour in this country. . . . In recognition of this need, our OVERSEAS DEPARTMENT has been formed. . . . *More than 2,000 women and girls* from various European countries . . . have already been placed, and new arrivals are now landing *almost every day* . . . we have been able to build up such *a well assorted stock if applications*, which we are keeping at such a level as should enable us to nominate potential candidates *for any type of domestic vacancy within a matter of a few days*.[151]

German women and girls were major users of these agencies, with many anxious to escape from the chaos and unemployment in their homeland and also, perhaps, aware that with the enormous loss of men in the Second World War marriage prospects in their own country were relatively slim.[152] As with the refugees who came to Britain before 1939, many of the new, foreign servants had little experience of domestic work and there were complaints in the press and elsewhere that they were taking advantage of the British housewife's need of servants in order to come to Britain for a year to learn the language and to travel around. Agencies were accused of cynically recruiting women with few relevant skills, in order to boost their earnings from booking fees. Some of the girls were of a higher social background than was usual among maids and in the early 1950s Lady Robertson, wife of the British High Commissioner in Germany, commented on this when she met a party of them at a transit camp. 'These fine-looking young ladies do not look like skivvies at all!' she declared in a tactless comment that can have won her few female friends in Britain itself.[153] The *Daily Mail*, in a story headed 'Wunderbar – but can she cook?' was a good deal more critical, observing sourly: 'And when you think of what it cost you to bring her over, and the £3 or so a week you pay her to arrange the flowers and talk broken English, you could kick yourself' for making the appointment.[154]

In some cases the problems were far greater. At Erddig near Wrexham, the eccentric owner, Simon Yorke, engaged three German girls as cheap domestic labour. The house was in an appalling state of repair, with water pouring through the roof into the state rooms when it rained and wet rot rampant. The girls must have been shocked when they arrived, but they clearly resolved to make the best of their situation. Soon they made plans to set up a boarding house in Llandudno, which they partly stocked with items from Erddig. 'Shortly before they left, a procession of carpets and packing cases left the house through the outer stable yard. Subsequently, the shelves for sheets and blankets in the housekeeper's room, neatly labelled in German, were found to be empty.'[155] They had clearly decided to get their own back on their employer.

There were occasional sexual lapses, too, as with a maid from Kassel, recruited by a British doctor and his wife at the end of 1955. She arrived early in February of the following year and three months later gave birth to a child. The employer claimed to have been unaware of the pregnancy because the girl had warned him that she was very stout, nor had it been detected during the medical examination she had undergone before leaving home. She and the baby were returned to Germany a few weeks after the birth.[156]

Overall, during 1949, 8,314 permits were issued to individual German girls to work in Britain. This was more than one in three of all the domestic permits issued in that year (see Table 3). The new Federal German Government, meanwhile, was concerned about the role of the many commercial agencies operating in this field and in late December 1949 an agreement was reached between the British and German authorities designed to bypass them. Under the scheme, British employers could apply for domestic staff to their local employment exchange and, after filling in the relevant forms, these would be sent to a Central Placing Office in Germany. Its task was to match the employer's requirement from its list of German volunteers anxious to take up household work in the United Kingdom. Mistress and maid would then be put in touch with one another and if a satisfactory arrangement were made, the employer would apply for a work permit in the normal way. Once the scheme began in 1950 it was soon followed by an ending of the North Sea recruitment campaign to secure staff for public institutions and hardship households. That was now merged into the new arrangement.[157] From 1950 foreign domestics coming to Britain normally entered either by making individual arrangements with employers or, in the case of German girls, by participation in the Federal Republic's Central Placing organisation. In 1951, a similar central placing plan was applied to Austria.

However, any expectation that these official placements would supersede the role of the commercial agencies was speedily dashed. Even in 1950, under a fifth of the 8,290 German women granted domestic permits came under the Central Placement Scheme. By 1954, when the number of German domestic entrants had fallen to 4,854, under a tenth came under that scheme.[158] The Ministry of Labour in Britain blamed its German counterpart for failing to advertise the plan properly and for creating a situation whereby only about half of British employers applying for staff by this means obtained maids.[159] Yet, it was reluctant to end the arrangement, which limped on into the 1960s.

Already, however, improved conditions in Germany and other European countries meant that by the late 1950s fewer recruits were coming forward. New candidates had to be found, with Spanish and Italian workers becoming more important. By the early 1970s, for example, the then Marquess of Bath depended on a Spanish husband and wife, Michael and Josephine de Soto, to serve as butler-valet and cook. At the beginning of the twentieth century there had been forty-three indoor servants at the marquess's family home at Longleat. Michael, like most butlers at that time, carried out a wide range of duties, including cleaning and doing odd jobs about the house. He also looked after his employer's wardrobe: 'I know when I go to London', declared Lord Bath, 'my clothes are going to be exactly as I want them.'[160]

Not all of the new servants were so successful. Frank Dawes described recently arrived butlers from Spain who turned out to be inexperienced peasants 'dignified with a white jacket'. Already, too, the servant-gathering net had extended into Asia, with 'a vogue for Philippine servants' apparent in the early 1970s.[161] As Table 3 shows, the total of domestic permits granted by the Ministry of Labour remained at a high level to the end of the 1950s, albeit with some increase in the number of workers recruited for schools and other public institutions rather than for private households. It was part of the slow acceptance by some British families that the pre-war world of full-time domestics had gone for ever.

Some wives turned to *au pairs*, a cheaper alternative, whereby in return for a home and pocket money, girls from, in the main, other European countries came to Britain to learn the language and, in return, to take on light household chores and childcare duties. Many of the arrangements worked well. Dr Joyce Chalmers, who was then living in Manchester, remembered that she and her clergyman husband had three *au pairs* from Germany during the mid-to late 1950s. The first was obtained with the help of her mother-in-law, who had earlier been involved in the

Control Commission in Germany and who contacted a likely candidate. Ingrid had already spent a year as an *au pair* in Geneva, where she had not been very happy, but she soon settled down in Manchester and remained for over a year. She then recommended the second girl, Edda, who in turn put the family in touch with their third *au pair*, Renate. As Dr Chalmers recalled, the contacts were made purely between the respective families and no official supervision of the girls took place, despite the fact that they were all aged between seventeen and nineteen:

TABLE 3 *Admission of Individual Foreign Workers under Ministry of Labour Permits: 1946-60*

(a) Year	Total Permits granted (all occupations)	Total Domestic Permits	Total Domestic Permits for Private Service	Percentage of Total Permits Allocated to Domestic work %
1946	10,744	8,041	7,622	75
1947	27,002	18,952	17,707	70
1948	28,460	19,395	18,371	68
1949	35,226	23,892	22,556	68
1950	35,035	22,434	20,714	64
1951	36,570	20,474	18,421	56
1952	32,632	18,960	17,014	58
1953	33,832	18,563	16,529	55
1954	36,473	19,043	16,764	52
1955	41,898	21,728	18,614	52
1956	46,117	22,823	n\a	49
1958	42,992	21,138	n\a	49
1958	42,840	20,863	n\a	49
1959	43,371	20,842	n\a	48
1960	50,355	20,969	n\a	42

(b)   Private Srevice as % of Total Domestic Permits

1947	93.4
1948	94.7
1949	94.4
1950	92.3
1951	90.0
1952	89.7
1953	89.0
1954	88.0
1955	85.6

Source: Annual Reports of the Ministry of Labour.

N.B. The workers recruited under this arrangement were additional to those recruited under the official 'Balt Cygnet' and 'Westward Ho' and similar schemes.

As for duties we shared the daily routine. Two of the girls enjoyed cooking and quite often produced an excellent meal for us all. We, the *au pair* and myself, shared washing nappies . . . shared washing up . . . and fetching and carrying children and shopping as we had no car. They all went to Manchester 'night school' classes to learn English – and we did our best to ensure that they spoke good English before they left. . . . When, on occasion, I knew I would be unable to share the workload, e.g. when I did a locum for a week or so . . . I employed extra help. . . . I certainly could not have afforded a full-time Nannie, and would have had to depend far more on the good will and kindness of parishioners.[162]

Mrs Helen Hall, another clergy wife in the Manchester area and a friend of Dr Chalmers, recruited two *au pairs* during the 1950s. One was French and the second was German and a cousin of one of her friend's *au pairs*. They, too, attended classes in Manchester and met other class members at the vicarage when they had time off. 'Both came on holiday with us and for them, too, it was a holiday.'[163]

But there was a darker side to the *au pair* picture, with newspapers in France running headlines like: 'In Britain 2,000 French girls live like slaves.' Even the British press condemned families who exploited their *au pairs* by treating them as cut-price drudges. As E. S. Turner wrote in 1962:

An *au pair* was supposed to be treated as a member of the family, to accompany them on their social calls, to be given every opportunity to learn the language, and to receive pocket money of between 30s and £2 in return for 'light work'. There were tales of girls forced to do housework or act as nursemaids for twelve hours a day, and to wait at table, or to eat their meals in cafes; there were tales of girls drifting home in a state of dudgeon and, sometimes, in a state of pregnancy; there were also tales of girls who considered themselves above housework of any kind and who arrived with trunks of evening clothes.[164]

There were complaints, too, about the insecurity of the arrangement, with girls sometimes given only a few days notice to leave. They were, therefore, placed in considerable difficulty, unless they had relatives to whom they could turn or were able to get a fresh *au pair* position.[165] The British Government, for its part, refused to take any action to regulate the arrangement by treating the girls as 'employed'. The most it would do was to issue booklets to *au pairs* and their hosts, giving guidance on how to avoid 'misunderstandings and abuse'.[166] It refused all legal responsibility.

In 1964 there were, Celia Briar suggests, around twenty thousand girls coming to work in Britain as *au pairs* through private agencies or informal personal contacts, but in the course of that decade and beyond numbers rose, with many coming to Britain to seek a placement on their own initiative.[167] One estimate in 1993 suggested there were about 170,000 *au pairs* in Britain at that time.[168]

In December 1963, Ministry of Labour figures also suggested around twenty thousand domestic permits were still being issued to foreign servants each year. Around two-thirds of them remained for more than twelve months and most came from western European countries, with Spain, Germany, Italy and Switzerland supplying about two-thirds of the total.[169]

However, not all immigrants wished to take up private, domestic service when they reached the United Kingdom. West Indian women were notable examples of this, although they were prepared to accept cleaning work in hospitals. This they associated with nursing, which they regarded as one of the most desirable professions. When offered private household work, some took the view that this was 'a white woman's job', while most considered they had come to Britain to 'improve' themselves and not to perform menial domestic chores. 'I didn't borrow and save and come all this way just to scrub and clean. I can do that back at home', declared a Jamaican woman on National Assistance, who had refused to take a cleaning job in a café.[170] That was a typical reaction. On the part of employers, too, there is some evidence that racial prejudice played a part in their reluctance to accept West Indian staff and that applied to hospital recruitment in the early 1950s.[171] (See Table 3)

CHAPTER EIGHT

THE FINAL DECADES

Domestic help is now as large an industry in the UK as it was just before the Second World War. . . . Many people with a career and a fair amount of disposable income require, and possess the means to buy in, assistance with cleaning, laundry and even cooking, when necessary. Large numbers of working couples and single parents have to have someone to look after their children on a regular basis. Elderly people are also employing more domestic help, either because they need support in the home or simply to free up more leisure time.

Lynn Brittney, *The Which? Guide to Domestic Help* (London, 1998), p. 9.

THE DOMESTIC SCENE

During the final decades of the twentieth century there was a noticeable revival in paid domestic work, after the years of decline followed by modest resurgence, which had characterised the period from 1939 to the early 1960s. In 1996 the *Economist* announced that 'Britain [had] rediscovered servants'. In evidence it pointed out that whereas in 1985 the nation had spent the equivalent of £1.45 billion on all kinds of home help, by 1995 that had more than doubled to £3.89 billion. As a share of total household expenditure, domestic service had risen from 0.4 per cent at the earlier date to 0.9 per cent.[1] Later research suggests that this upward trend continued.[2] Hence the *Economist's* assertion that between the mid-1980s and the mid-1990s domestic service was the most rapidly expanding area of consumer spending. A contributor to *The Times* in September 1998 agreed, calling it 'Britain's biggest growth industry'.[3]

Yet that did not mean a return to the starchy Edwardian world of upstairs-downstairs, with retinues of uniformed housemaids, parlourmaids, cooks, general servants, butlers and footmen conferring status on the households they served as well as carrying out domestic duties. As in the post-war period, there was a careful avoidance of the words 'maid' or 'servant' in advertisements for staff. Instead of general servants, mother's helps or housekeepers were sought, while nursemaids were transformed into 'nannies'. The new labour force was expected to be more flexible and, in the main, less formal than its pre-1939 predecessor. Its role was generally functional rather than ceremonial. Although multi-staff households survived and still employed a few thousand workers, only a wealthy minority recruited the full

The role of professional cleaning firms is exemplified in this photograph of a *myhome* van delivering clean laundry in 2000. (*myhome*)

panoply of butler, cook, housekeeper, full-time gardener and chauffeur. Even these households were likely to rely on married couples to supply their resident domestic help, with the man taking on the duties of butler or gardener-cum-chauffeur and his wife those of cook-housekeeper. Additional assistance was provided by 'dailies' or by contract workers hired for special occasions. New categories of free-lance service providers emerged to meet the needs of the burgeoning 'cash rich, time poor' dual income households of the professional middle classes. Among these were dog walkers and flower arrangers, as well as outside caterers brought in to prepare special dinner parties or buffet suppers and suppliers of laundry services whose professionalism contrasted markedly with the old-style weekly washerwoman.[4]

In this new world, efforts were made to create a spirit of egalitarianism between employer and worker, but these attempts to reduce class barriers did not prevent cleaning, in particular, from being regarded as a low status occupation. Interestingly, domestic work in private households was explicitly excluded from the protection of the 1974 Health and Safety at Work Act because of the practical problems of enforcement and the invasion of privacy which would have occurred if inspectors had been empowered to enter such households.

One girl, who had formerly been a student, expressed resentment that as a cleaner she was 'looked down upon. People . . . ask me when I am going to do something "proper". I feel quite incensed because somebody has to do cleaning. Why have the attitude that only lesser people can do it?'[5] Another woman, who had set up her own cleaning business when she found office work too monotonous, agreed. 'The people who look down on you tend to be the ones who don't have a lot of money. They are never satisfied and expect you to spring-clean the whole house in just a few hours.'[6]

Even in July 2000, the historian and media personality, David Starkey, could equate domestic service with 'relatively low-level employment', adding: 'It's ridiculous that people at the top are killing themselves in demanding jobs and then coming home to mow their own lawns.'[7]

Although it was widely agreed that a strong revival in paid household work had occurred, the precise numbers of those involved proved difficult to estimate. This was partly because recent population censuses and government employment statistics had stopped covering these sectors of the labour force in detail and partly because it could be attributed to the large amount of 'informal' work that took place. This affected cleaners, in particular and they comprised the largest single category in the new labour force. Many, as part-timers, did not declare an income. Some wanted to be paid 'cash-in-hand' because they were supplementing a state benefit received by themselves or their partner; others might be seeking extra income to boost earnings from another job. That applied to Sharon, who had three children and was married to a milkman. She got into private domestic cleaning initially because she was approached by a potential employer while she was working in a school canteen. After the birth of her third child she gave up the school job and continued with her private work. At that stage domestic cleaning afforded her an opportunity to supplement household income while continuing to be a full-time mother, since she was able to take her youngest child with her when she went to work.[9]

In some cases, especially around London, these 'informal' cleaners included foreigners whose lack of a work permit and uncertain residential status precluded recruitment into the formal labour market.[10] Such women were vulnerable to exploitation by householders – and agencies – who might take advantage of their illegal status. However, after the passage of the 1996 Asylum and Immigration Act, employers could face prosecution and a fine of up to £5,000 per worker if they knowingly took on, or offered work to, a person who did not have a right to work in the United Kingdom.[11] Yet that did not prevent the less scrupulous from hiring this cheap, compliant labour. Even the introduction in April 1999 of the National Minimum Wage of £3.60 an hour for adults and £3 for those aged eighteen to twenty-one is unlikely to benefit such people, because of their lack of legal standing and consequent bargaining power.[12]

The rise in demand for domestic staff, particularly in the 1980s and 1990s, was attributable to four main factors. The first was the growing polarity of incomes between rich and poor which manifested itself especially in London and the south-east of England, the areas where the pressure for domestic recruitment was greatest. In Britain the real disposable incomes of the wealthiest 10 per cent of the population rose by an estimated 62 per cent between 1979 and 1991, while those of the poorest 10 per cent fell by 17 per cent over the same period. In London that polarisation was most obvious with one commentator claiming that during the 1980s the difference between the earnings of those on the highest and the lowest incomes was twice as large in the capital as in the rest of the country.[13] Part of the increasing disparity could be linked to the high salaries that the top earners could command, particularly in the City of London, but it was affected, too, by the reduced tax burden on the wealthy and by the growing benefit dependency of the poorest families as a result of unemployment, single parenthood or invalidity. High unemployment meant that even some of those who stayed in work had to 'trade down' and take less skilled and less remunerative posts when they were made redundant. The outcome was that not only could wealthier householders afford domestic help, but some of the worst off (especially women) wanted to earn cash 'on the side' to supplement their incomes. Casual cleaning was particularly useful in this regard. It was easy to take up, since most employers believed that all women were capable of carrying it out and so they had no need to test competency, and it was inconspicuous. For householders the main concern was that new recruits should be honest, reliable and punctual.

A second factor encouraging the rise in domestic staff and one associated with the first point was the increase in the number of two-income families. Women became an increasingly important part of the labour force, with almost three-quarters of those of working age in paid work in 1997, compared to under three-fifths in 1971.[14] Many at the upper end of the salary scale were holding demanding professional and managerial postions which required long working hours and a good deal of personal commitment. Despite feminist pressure for greater equality between male and female partners in carrying out household chores and despite the proliferation of labour-saving appliances designed to cut down manual tasks, much time-consuming domestic work remained the responsibility of women, ranging from ironing clothes to dusting and polishing the furniture. Hiring a cleaner, while reinforcing the gender divisions within the home was one way in which a woman could avoid the stress of juggling the demands of household and workplace. At the same time she was 'buying' leisure, in that her weekends and other free time no longer had to be devoted to household chores.

In a survey of high-earning working couples in London and in the south-east and the north-east of England, Nicky Gregson and Michelle Lowe discovered during the 1980s that over a third employed domestic waged labour irrespective of geography.[15] That meant, of course, that around two-thirds did not. In those cases, Gregson and Lowe concluded, there was either a greater willingness by the male partner to share the chores, or the female partner was anxious to demonstrate that she was a 'proper' wife by taking on traditional household tasks in the way her mother had perhaps done.[16] This was true of the Collins family. Pauline Collins was a medical researcher and her husband was an investment banker. Until their first child was born they employed no domestic labour. Neither Pauline's mother nor her mother-in-law had been in paid employment and they had always done their own housework, as had Pauline herself prior to her marriage at the age of thirty-two. When she married she had been 'very keen to be a proper wife'. She had wanted to show her husband, her family, her in-laws and herself that she was able to combine a successful career with the duties of a housewife. Only when children arrived was that no longer feasible and she then recruited a nanny and a cleaner.[17]

Pauline Collins's dilemma was shared by other highly paid women who continued to work after having a baby. Kay, a psychologist and mother of four, who had been brought up with the egalitarian ideals of the 1950s and 1960s, felt uncomfortable about taking on domestic help when her first baby arrived. 'I had decided I could not cope with employing another woman because of the status thing, but I found two salt-of-the-earth types who seemed to get real pleasure out of cleaning. But I was always very apologetic and used to give them extra money from time to time because I felt guilty.'[18]

Significantly, in 1998 it was estimated that half of all women with children under ten years were in paid employment.[19] That inevitably meant a high demand for childcare facilities. While some mothers found these in the form of childminders, nursery schools and through the help of family and friends, for a substantial minority, nannies were the solution. They were, in some respects, a product of the post-war view in Britain that motherhood was not only a full-time occupation, but it was home-based. Parents who were anxious that their child should spend his or her earliest pre-school years in the security of the home, or those who had several young children to be cared for, were particularly likely to find nannies attractive. In such situations, a nanny was far more flexible and probably cheaper than the alternative forms of childcare. Another possibility was to share the nanny's services with a neighbour, thereby dividing the cost as well. As a result, nannies became second only to cleaners as a rapidly expanding sector of the 'new' domestic economy. They might be resident or non-resident, but were often in sole charge of the household during the day. When employers' marriages broke up or there were serious family difficulties, the nanny might be the only stable influence in the children's lives. The number of nannies employed is hard to quantify. Estimates made in 1996-7 ranged between 100,000 and 200,000. Again, the fact that some women were employed under casual 'cash-in-hand' conditions meant that they were not entered in any official records.[20]

A fourth cause of the increased demand for help (and one largely ignored by writers like Gregson and Lowe) arose from the greater number of old people in the population. In the mid-1980s this contributed to an increase in the number of local authority home helps, but in the 1990s budgetary pressures and changes in government policy meant a reduction in the supply of such helpers (who, in any case, were now expected to take on more nursing duties and less domestic work). The charges levied for their services also increased in many areas. Nevertheless, in the mid-1990s around 8 per cent of people over the age of sixty-five were being assisted by local authority home helps, and a further 7 per cent were using the services of private helpers. This latter proportion had increased from 4 per cent reporting the use of private helps in 1991-2. Among those aged seventy-five or above, 15 per cent had local authority help and 11 per cent relied on private provision in the mid-1990s. In other words, among the oldest group of pensioners more than a quarter depended

A London home help arranging flowers for an elderly client in 1963. Such helpers provided social contact as well as domestic assistance for invalids and those unable to get about easily. (*London Metropolitan Photographic Archives*)

on some form of home help.[21] In addition, the increased number of nursing homes and residential care facilities catering for the elderly had their own domestic help requirements, which added to the general level of demand from this sector.

Some domestic cleaning businesses, like Gene Riley's Help Unlimited, set up in Loughborough in the mid-1980s, concentrated on providing for the elderly or for invalids. Gene set up her firm when serious illness forced her to stop teaching and, for a time, she had to rely on the aid of friends and neighbours: 'It occurred to me that there must be a hell of a lot of people who can't. . . . There is a thin line between caring and cleaning that's to do with well-being.' It was that need her business was designed to satisfy.[22]

For older people who were housebound or who had few relatives living locally, these services were often an important source of companionship as well as domestic assistance. Mrs Sheila Whiting, who became a home help in Cornwall in the early 1960s and continued in the post for over twenty-six years, welcomed the work, not only because it fitted in with her own domestic responsibilities, but because it enabled her to meet a variety of people. Among many elderly clients she discovered that a well-scrubbed front doorstep 'was their pride and joy'. Other tasks she carried out included blackleading grates, washing and lighting fires: 'one dear old soul never had any sticks so we would make newspaper curls . . . many confided in you with family problems, close secrets, but it must have been very hard for them to lose their independence and rely on others to do their work. . . . I have always enjoyed cleaning, cooking; it gives great satisfaction to the mind.'[23]

Other home helps found the tight schedule they had to maintain in visiting clients and the hardships they witnessed among poorer pensioners too stressful and gave up the work. That applied to Annie Spike, who was employed in Hackney.

> Home-help work is a very depressing job . . . I was getting too involved in it. . . . I went to . . . people who used to count the pieces of coal they put on the fire, because they were frightened they wouldn't have enough later . . . I used to visit about five old people a day, from 10 till 2 – and I was timed on each person. They expected a terrible lot from you . . . I had to walk from one to the other.[24]

After a few months she left and took a job in a shop. Later she became an office cleaner, working two hours each evening. 'Some women go into office cleaning to get away from the house', she declared, 'for a change of atmosphere from their worries and problems, not so much for the money.'[25]

If householders wished to recruit their staff independently, rather than relying on local authority home helps, they had four main options open to them. The first and the best was to utilise personal contacts and individual recommendations. In London, where there were numerous immigrant workers, ethnic networks might provide a candidate. 'Employers find a cleaner by asking neighbours, who will then talk to their cleaners and cleaners will pass employers on to relatives or friends who need work. In this way jobs tend to stay concentrated within a particular ethnic community.'[26] In the capital women from Portugal, Spain and the Philippines were widely thought to be better workers than their British counterparts and to display a more suitably subservient attitude.

When these methods failed, the second choice was to advertise, perhaps locally in a newspaper or even in a shop window, when a cleaner was required. For specialist staff like nannies, butlers and cooks, prestigious national newspapers and magazines like *The Lady* would be selected. *The Lady*, which has been dubbed the *Exchange and Mart* of domestic help in modern Britain, normally included around 300 advertisements each week. From 1997 it also ran a 'Nanny of the Year' award offering £1,000 and other benefits to the successful candidate and encouraging satisfied employers to nominate their own nanny for consideration.[27]

The advertisements revealed employers' priorities and expectations as well as the vacancies available. Among those seeking nannies, it was more common to mention that applicants must be non-smokers or able to drive a car than that they should possess formal qualifications – although that might be raised at an interview. (The first official qualification for nannies had been established in 1945 with the formation of the National Nursery Board or NNEB.) In some cases, multiple duties might be proposed. Thus of seventy-six advertisements for nannies in *The Lady* during the week 20-26 June 2000, eighteen required cleaning or other household tasks as well. Thirty specified the nanny must be a non-smoker; and twenty-six that she be able to drive a car; just five stated that she must be qualified. Typical of many was an appeal for a resident

Nanny/Housekeeper, Clapham. Mid-July or September. Informal professional family. Sole charge charming schoolboy (6) Monday-Friday plus some housework, laundry and cooking. Experienced non-smoker with excellent references. Must be well organised, reliable, cheerful and flexible.

Then there was an advertisement for a Mother's Help/Nanny/Housekeeper inserted by a 'family with 2 boys, 3 and 5 and a dog in Regent's Park. Live-in, non-smoking person to do housework, childcare and cooking.'

A third possibility, and one particularly useful when there was an urgent vacancy to fill, was to apply to an agency. Many had grown up in the final quarter of the century to match the rise in demand for household help. Their main merits were that they were likely to have people on their books who were available immediately and whom they could send for interview. They could be valuable, too, in supplying temporary staff. William Weber, partner in the long-established Mrs Hunt's Agency in London, noted that June and July were particularly busy for his firm because the season was 'in full swing and customers all require extra staff for their parties and the school holidays'.[28] When engaging permanent workers, his clients demanded someone with diverse skills. 'Someone who can cook, book an airline ticket, dash down to Ludgrove to pick up little Johnny, take the dog to the vet – they want someone just like them.' Yet that did not mean that staff of roughly the same social status as their employers were treated as equals. One helper long remembered the snub administered by a woman whose house she was cleaning. The mistress walked up to her and wiped the lipstick from her face, saying cuttingly at the same time: 'Did you think you had come for a cocktail party?' At the end of the century the bulk of the firm's work was 'in placing dailies (or twice weeklies) who will clean and iron'. They, and the mother's helps, were normally paid £7 per hour, plus their bus fares. Most applicants came from overseas, particularly from Spain, Portugal, Poland and the Philippines.[29]

Agencies, especially in London, could be expensive for employers. In addition to initial registration charges of £15 to £30, several hundred pounds might be required for the successful placing of senior staff in prestigious locations. Even temporary placements might cost between £55 and £500.[30] Employers anxious to ensure they were using reputable firms could obtain a list of approved businesses from the Federation of Employment and Recruitment Agencies, which could be supplemented by information in the Department of Education and Employment's booklet, Need a Nanny? published in 1999 and by its Childcare Link, which could be contacted by telephone.[31]

Another option was to apply to a training school, especially when specialist staff like nannies, chefs or butlers were required. However, apart from the fact that new graduates were likely to be inexperienced, in the case of prestigious establishments like Norland College, they could prove expensive and highly competitive as well, with several families trying to recruit the same candidate. In other cases, as with Ivor Spencer's International School for Butler Administrators, Personal Assistants and Estate Managers (established in 1981) there might be strong foreign competition.[32] A well-trained, unflappable English butler or a British nanny could be a status symbol for employers overseas as well as in the United Kingdom. As Rosie Cox points out, the 'largest training centre in London' had its own placement agency in the United States.[33] As before the Second World War, there was a steady trickle of senior British-born servants who wished to work abroad.

All this forced up staff salaries and the best qualified workers expected good living accommodation, the use of a car and liberal holidays as well. On the other hand, for those lower down the scale or working outside London, the position was very different, with long hours and relatively poor pay the order of the day. The position of nannies might be affected, too, by the fact that when warm relations developed between them and their charges (what Gregson and Lowe label feelings of 'false kinship'), they might be reluctant to pressurise employers over pay. One girl realised after she had been in her post for about six months

MRS. HUNT'S AGENCY
ESTABLISHED 1890
TELEPHONE: 020 7229 3506   9.30 TO 5.30 Mon – Fri.
NO ENGAGEMENT, NO FEE

PERMANENT STAFF

Living-out Staff:
FIRST-CLASS CLEANERS WHO ALSO IRON, COMPANIONS, HOUSEKEEPERS, COOKS etc.

We charge a one-off agency introduction fee of:
Four times the weekly wage for Cleaners, Mothers' Helps, Housekeepers, Cooks etc.
The employee is paid and employed by the Client.

TRIAL PERIOD for all categories of living-out staff:
If the employee leaves within eight weeks of the engagement or if the employee proves to be unsuitable during this trial period, we will make a discretionary replacement on condition that our invoice has been paid by the settlement date as stated on the invoice.

Living-in Staff:
Carers, Companions, Mothers' Helps, Housekeepers, Cooks and all staff who live-in:

We charge the Client a fee of eight times the net weekly wage for jobs within the UK.

We have supplied the best staff for over 100 years.
All staff are interviewed & have excellent suitable references which we verify.

Please read all four sides of the terms and conditions, which are contractually binding.

Domestic agencies, like the long-established Mrs. Hunt's Agency, played an important role in providing household staff, especially in the larger towns and cities. Mrs. Hunt's took great care to ensure that all their foreign domestics had the appropriate legal status, to protect their many 'high profile' customers. (*William Weber, Mrs. Hunt's Agency*)

that the family for whom she was working was in financial difficulties. She knew that her salary was due to be reviewed shortly but 'I thought, I can't say anything . . . I'm so happy that I would rather not mention it and stay. . . .' She kept silent and was eventually given a £20-a-week rise by the employers. However, months later she was still uncertain about what would happen when the next pay review became due. 'I'm not going to say anything. I'm just going to wait for them to say it'[34]

Gregson and Lowe's researches revealed that of twenty-five nannies that they interviewed in the north-east of England during the 1980s, none had take-home pay above £120 a week and over half received between £65 and £80 a week net. By contrast, of twenty-five girls interviewed in the south-east, the highest paid received more than £160 a week and under a quarter obtained less than £100 a week.[35] A fully trained Norland nurse at the end of the 1990s could cost as much as £400 a week, with national insurance contributions to be added on top.[36]

For those seeking cleaners, one possibility was to avoid personal recruitment altogether by going to one of the home cleaning firms which had sprung up in the 1980s and 1990s. These ranged from small enterprises set up by a single person working with a small staff on a very local basis to major businesses like Molly Maids UK, one of Britain's biggest domestic cleaning companies. Their chief executive noted that the kind of client the firm was getting had changed considerably in

Professional cleaning services provided by *myhome* in 2000. Staff were carefully vetted and fully experienced. To achieve maximum efficiency cleaners worked in teams of two, with the back-up of a supervisor. (*myhome*)

the late 1990s. 'More than half are young professionals, couples or just flatmates who don't want to spend the whole weekend arguing about whose turn it is to clean the bathroom. . . . We are talking about people who have never had a cleaning lady in their family before.'[37]

Another of these large-scale enterprises, set up early in 2000, was *myhome*, a subsidiary of Unilever. It offered a high-quality laundry service, home cleaning and the hire of linen. Initially its operations were concentrated in south west London, but there were plans for it to expand across the country.[38]

These home cleaning businesses were normally more expensive than a personally recruited 'daily', but for those able to afford it, the service had several advantages. They included a greater opportunity to arrange times and work schedules which suited the householder, the carrying out of work to a high standard by vetted staff and anonymity. With this method, employers might never meet their cleaners. That appealed to those anxious to avoid the intimacy of face-to-face contacts with a regular cleaner, or who felt guilty because they were not carrying out their own chores. Such commercial alternatives resembled the purchase of other household services, like painting and decorating or dry cleaning.

Anne-Marie Daly, a trainee solicitor in her early thirties, was one young professional who chose to employ a daily cleaner, but in her case it was a local pensioner rather than an agency that performed the service. Despite its greater cheapness, it had its downside. 'She talks constantly and occasionally breaks things, but I don't like to mention it in case she leaves. . . . There's a fine line between being friendly and too friendly. I've found the best way of doing things is to go out and leave her a note . . . she knows she can always help herself to drink.'[39] In the late 1990s, Daly, who lived in Cheshire, paid her cleaner £4.50 an hour and admitted that she had poached her from a neighbour. 'I heard on the grapevine that she was being paid £3 an hour and had to work hard for that, so I rang her up and offered more. Her old boss was furious but I didn't feel guilty about it.' In London and Bath, however, some cleaners charged as much as £9 an hour.

From the worker's point of view, being recruited by a home cleaning firm had the advantage of agreed working conditions and wages, without the need to negotiate with individual employers. Relations with householders could be businesslike,

An old-style 'daily' cleaning the steps at a London public house in 1962. Her shoulders had become hunched by long years of hard work. (*London Metropolitan Photographic Archives*)

without the need for subservience. There was also less opportunity for employers to show arrogance or unreasonable behaviour. Even a householder like Jane Shilling, who referred to the supervisor of the team of young women who had taken over her domestic chores as the Obergruppenführer, kept in the background if she was at home when they arrived.[40]

However, experienced cleaners, working on a free-lance basis in areas where the demand for staff was high, were also able to lay down their conditions. Yvonne, who was in her mid-thirties and had been cleaning for twelve years, had ten different employers in the late 1990s, going to two each weekday. She had a waiting list for her services as well:

> I don't do ironing because I hate it and I won't clean ovens, it would take too much time out of my three-hour stretch and the house wouldn't be done properly. All my ladies are very nice and don't treat me like a servant – I wouldn't stay if they did. I worked for a woman once who used to sprinkle peanuts in corners to make sure I was using the vacuum properly. She also insisted I call her Mrs Bennett, which I don't mind if ladies are elderly but she was only a few years older than me. I only stayed a month. So many women work these days that they need me more than I need them.[41]

While warm feelings could exist between nannies and their employers, there was always the potential for tension and disagreements. Sue Richney, in her early twenties, had been a nanny since the age of sixteen. She had been in her current post eighteen months when she was interviewed early in 2000. As a resident worker she experienced

enforced intimacy with her employers, since unlike the situation before 1939, there
were no longer strict social demarcations between employer and employee, with
each 'knowing her place'. This made for difficulties. 'You are with them every day',
declared Sue. 'You witness their personal lives at first hand. . . . If there's a family feud
going on for example, you just get out of the room and find yourself something to do.
You know it's none of your business. . . . It's a very personal, close relationship. . . .
But at the same time you have to keep a professional distance.'[42]

Kay Crosse, the principal of Norland College, agreed, emphasising the need
for staff to maintain confidentiality and discretion. 'A nanny not only has to be
equipped to look after the children, she also needs . . . social skills to negotiate
the tensions and complexities of family life. . . . It's hard to maintain the purely
employer-employee relationship when you're sharing the intimacy of a family
home.' For this reason many nannies preferred to live out, since this gave them
freedom to develop their own interests and friendships outside working hours.

Further problems arose when working mothers felt guilty because they were not
looking after their child themselves in a way that conformed to social expectations,
even at the end of the twentieth century. One woman, whose two-year-old son
was cared for by a nanny on three days a week, called it a 'doomed relationship',
leading to inner turmoil and even competition for the child's love and attention:

> I think my nanny's really good . . . and I'd recommend her to anyone, but I hate
> her. Everything about her irritates me. . . . You desperately want your nanny to
> love your child because you want her to protect the child as if it was her own.
> You want your child to feel completely secure within a relationship of intimacy
> and love, but at the same time that excludes you. . . . They know if you sack them
> you endanger your child's emotional health, plus you have the whole rigmarole of
> going to an agency, paying out lots of money to find a new nanny who probably
> won't please you any more than the last.[43]

Other mothers told of 'worrying incidents', like the Swedish nanny who ran a
flourishing drugs business from her bedroom and the disgruntled girl who put
a brick through her employers' window.[44] These anxieties became more acute
when occasional tragic incidents of serious child abuse occurred, as in the case of
a young Australian nanny who was found guilty early in 1999 of killing the baby
in her care by violent shaking.[45] There were sensational reports in the press which
gave the impression that such misconduct was commonplace rather than a rarity.
Journalists hastened to describe their own experience in highly coloured language.
One contributor to the *Guardian*, in an article headed, 'We must do better than
this. Another nanny scandal, another child dead', complained of the lack of formal
standards against which parents could measure the nannies who came for interview:

> The reason I've become quite good at making accurate character assessments
> over a cup of coffee, is that in the past I have made so many inaccurate ones. I
> once hired a nanny who fed my toddler Aspirins by the bottle. I hired another

who dropped him on his head *while I was sitting in the next room*. Another had a violent boyfriend. A few others were pathological liars. And even the very best were sometimes really too young to cope with the pressures that came with being 'part of the family', in a job that wasn't really a job.[46]

Her solution was for families who hired nannies to be given tax breaks to enable them to pay higher salaries and for there to be better training. This would mean that 'people would go into childcare work because they were good at it, and not as a last resort'.

It was partly in response to the moral panic aroused by the sad case of the Australian nanny that the government issued its *Need a Nanny?* guide in 1999. A year later it required all agencies dealing with nannies to check the background and qualifications of applicants before passing them on to potential employers.[47] But since under a third of nannies were hired through agencies, with the rest being recruited by advertisements or personal contacts, this still left loopholes which let cruel or inadequate workers slip through the net. Hence the emphasis in the *Need a Nanny?* booklet that it was the parents' responsibility to make sure that they obtained the right person. 'There are no legal requirements on a person applying to work as a nanny. . . . *Remember, it is your responsibility as the employer to ensure that you are completely satisfied with the person that you employ*.'[48]

As in earlier years, many less affluent employers turned to the cheaper alternatives of mother's helps or *au pairs* for their childcare needs. Few of these were likely to have qualifications, although mother's helps might be experienced. *Au pairs* were unlikely to have much knowledge of how to look after children and were considered unsuitable to care for pre-school youngsters whose parents were at work. However, some parents did take that risk. Their conditions were regulated by the Home Office and until May 1998 they had to register with the police. After that date only the nationals of a very few countries were still required to register; of these, Turkey was the most important.[49] They had to be single, aged between seventeen and twenty-seven when first entering the country and were to remain for a maximum of two years. No girl (or from the mid-1990s, boy) was allowed to take employment in the United Kingdom, the light household duties which were part of the *au pair* arrangement being deemed merely recompense for the hospitality afforded by the hostess. He or she was limited to five hours' household duties a day and was to have two free days each week. The intention was that *au pairs* should learn something of the language and culture of Britain while they lived in the country, rather than just be cheap servants. In return for their duties, they were to receive pocket money of around £35 to £40 a week. After the UK's entry into the European Union in the early 1970s, in strictly legal terms they were to come only from a short list of non-EU countries, since citizens of the EU were free to live and work anywhere within its borders. At the end of the 1990s *au pairs* were defined as nationals of certain eastern European countries, such as Croatia, the Czech Republic, Hungary, the Slovak Republic and Slovenia, as well as a limited number of other places, including Cyprus, Malta, Switzerland and Turkey.[50] Total numbers allowed in varied from month to month. In July 1998,

1,680 entered the United Kingdom, of whom 680 came from Slovakia and 610 from the Czech Republic; in November 1998, there were 870 entrants, with the Czech Republic providing 360 and Slovakia 190. Turkey came third, with 120 *au pairs*.[51]

In 1999, there were estimated to be around 25,000 *au pairs* in the country under these arrangements, but in reality that was a gross under-estimate. As in earlier years, the vast majority of *au pair* positions were filled by youngsters coming from such European Union countries as France, Spain, Italy and Germany.[52] There were also illegal entrants from other countries such as Poland.[53] One estimate in 1993 put the true total of *au pairs* in Britain as close to 170,000.[54]

Many *au pairs* also operated outside the regulations. Some because they worked longer hours than laid down, in a capacity described as '*au pair* plus'; others because they were not studying English; and others again because, like the Polish girls, they came from non-participating countries. They might also perform tasks that were outside the 'light housework' category. Adele, a young German girl who came to Britain in April 1969, obtained her first placement in Feltham after scanning a wide range of advertisements in the London *Evening Standard*. Her duties involved dressing and taking a six-year-old boy to school, collecting him in the late afternoon and in the evening bathing and feeding him and putting him to bed. She also carried out various household chores, but normally had the evenings free after about 7 p.m. She had a day off on Sunday. In addition, however, she did a good deal of driving around in the family car. That included taking a piece of machinery from her host's ice cream business to be repaired in Colchester. Relations between family and *au pair* remained good until she had two accidents with the car within a few days of one another. After the second she virtually gave up driving and her weekly pocket money was docked by her hosts to help cover the cost of repairs. She now had to take the little boy to school by train and the underground, rather than by car, and that added to strained feelings within the household. Eventually, in July, the hostess said that Adele was not carrying out her domestic tasks properly. She suggested that the girl should leave within a few days. The charge was later withdrawn, but Adele, resenting the reproofs and feeling that it was the family who had made the rooms untidy, decided to go anyway. She went to stay with her married sister, who lived in Surbiton, for a short time.

Soon other *au pair* placements followed, including one lasting about two or three weeks when she became a receptionist at a hotel in South Kensington, with the hotel manager acting as her 'host'. She was provided with a small room on the premises, but had the galling experience of having her slender cash reserves stolen. Not until January 1970 did she finally obtain a settled position as an *au pair* with an American free-lance photographer and her daughter. As Adele confided to her friend in Germany, she had at last found a pleasant family where she was well treated. Although she did not enjoy housework, overall the placement was first rate (*ganz prima*). Throughout this whole unsettled period she attended her English classes conscientiously and succeeded in passing her examinations. She also enjoyed a hectic social life in her free time.[55]

Rather like mistresses discussing incompetent maids in Victorian times, many hosts and hostesses of *au pairs* had their 'horror' stories. Maureen Lipman described how one girl 'borrowed' her best silk suit and returned with it 'scrunched up in a bag between mud-covered boots and a Braun Ladyshave. . . . There comes a time in every *au pair* employer's life when another three weeks of saying "Zis is ze washing machine" . . . is anathema. At such moments, the urge to buy British is very strong.'[56] Similarly, Martin Plimmer in *The Times* compared his cheerful Spanish *au pair* to a 'euphoric Great Dane. . . . Everything makes her laugh: children, pets, the washing machine. . . . I can't shout at her though: this is a girl who, in her spare time, helps out at a centre for Guatemalan orphans. . . . Other *au pairs* I have disliked with a free conscience. Not Belen. Even as I list these resentments, I picture her playing her trumpet to Guatemalan urchins and I feel ashamed. I cannot sack her.'[57]

However, for many families the attraction of *au pairs* was not their character but their cheapness. When in 1999 it was proposed to bring them within the provisions of the National Minimum Wage there was an immediate outcry from parents, as well as in the Press and in Parliament. In January of that year a contributor to *The Times* predicted such a move would herald the end of the *au pair* system, since working families of modest means would not be able to afford them. A couple who employed a Turkish girl admitted that they could easily pay higher wages, but argued that this 'would break the bond of trust that [existed] between them and their *au pair*'. The husband claimed that as employers they would 'probably be much more demanding, making sure that things like the ironing [were] properly done'.[58] In the end the protests succeeded. The new regulations exempted people working and living as part of a family in the way that *au pairs* did. They were to continue to receive their £40 or so per week pocket money, plus free board and lodging.[59]

A variation on the theme was the 'Working Holidaymakers' arrangement, whereby girls aged from seventeen to twenty-seven who came from Commonwealth countries could enter Britain to work either part-time for two years (that is, up to twenty-five hours per week), or full-time for one year. Many women from Australia, New Zealand and Canada took domestic posts in this way, since these usually provided them with a home as well as a small income. One such girl was Joanne, who came to Britain from Australia. She was a fully trained nanny and decided to become a 'holiday nanny', looking after the families of British expatriates who had returned to Britain for a short time. She worked for up to a month at a stretch, until her employers either returned to their posting or took up a fresh position and all of her jobs were residential.[60]

Immigrant domestics, too, played a significant role in many households and, in general, they worked on a longer-term basis than *au pairs* and 'working holidaymakers'. That was true in the 1970s when, despite a general tightening of the work permit scheme, the need for domestic staff in homes, hospitals and hotels led to the provision of special quotas for foreign servants, of whom an increasing number came from the Philippines, Spain and Portugal. Later, when Spain and Portugal joined the European Union in 1986, their citizens were free to travel without permits. They came because pay and conditions were better than they could secure in their homeland. As Rosie Cox points out, British householders welcomed them, often in preference to local employees. Portuguese women were particularly sought after as housekeepers, while

Filipinos knew 'how to clean everything properly.... And you should see their ironing!
... English women just can't do that, they don't do it right.'[61]

Between 1973 and 1976, 7,278 permits were issued to entrants from the Philippines
alone, mainly for domestic purposes. Indeed, in 1975, two-thirds of permits issued
to resident domestics were allocated to Filipinos.[62] However, over the course of the
1970s the quotas were progressively reduced and from August 1977 only European
women were allowed to enter Britain as domestic workers. At the end of 1979, the
quota system was ended altogether. From 1980, as a special concession, foreigners
visiting or settling in Britain were allowed to bring their domestic servants with
them, as were returning British expatriates. Permits were awarded in respect of the
servants for a year at a time and during the first four years of their stay workers were
not allowed to leave their posts. Indeed, their passports were stamped 'employment
prohibited' and a note was added that they were accompanying a particular employer.
Only after four years could they apply to settle in Britain long term and, if permission
were granted, they might then change their employer as well. During those first
four years they endured what has been described as virtual slavery. Many suffered
physical or sexual ill-treatment, while others lived in poor accommodation or were
unable to obtain their wages and had their passports withheld. One victim was Sally,
a Filipina, who worked for a family from Dubai. Once they reached London, Sally's
already miserable existence worsened. 'They hold my passport and they lock me in
all the time.... And here I have to sleep on the floor of the toilet where the children
trample over me.' Her work was harder, too. 'They say everything in London very
expensive so I must wash the sheets, clean the windows three floors up.' She received
no wages and was told she would only be paid when the family returned to Abu
Dhabi. After enduring this mistreatment for four months, she decided to escape. She
crawled out of a third floor window, but in the process fell to the ground, breaking
her pelvis and arm. She was in hospital for two months and during that time was
visited by the Philippine Consul, who promised to help her. Eventually, she found a
temporary home with a Filipino family who had settled in Britain.[63]

The number of those involved in these arrangements was uncertain. In 1998
there were said to be up to twenty thousand domestic workers in Britain who
had entered the country in this way, most of them women from the Philippines,
Bangladesh, India and Africa; at the beginning of the decade the figure was put at
between two and three thousand. In 1996 a survey by Kalayaan, an organisation set
up to campaign for justice for overseas domestic workers, reported that about half
of them had to sleep on the floor, while four-fifths were either not paid regularly
or received less than the agreed amount and some were locked in the house when
the employer went out, to prevent them from running away. In a debate in the
House of Lords in November 1990, Lord Hylton claimed that many saw only 'the
airport, the employer's house and the road between the two'.[64] Several did escape,
however, and unlike Sally, changed their identity and took other work illegally.
Only those who stayed with their employer for four years had the opportunity to
apply to remain in Britain indefinitely. Campaigners pressed for an alteration in the
law to permit these vulnerable women to change employers during their first years

of entry to the country, providing they agreed to remain in domestic employment and could produce evidence of ill-treatment. That was finally allowed in July 1998, but at the same time the rules were tightened. Henceforward, those whose duties were only cleaning, washing and cooking would not be eligible for admission with an employer. But any workers who did come in, for example to carry out childcare duties, would be free to change to another employer if they suffered abuse from their original master or mistress.[65] From the mid-1990s the minimum age of these workers was also raised from seventeen to eighteen.[66]

A number of women (and some men), who had entered the country in the normal way, also took cleaning jobs in public institutions and in offices and factories. Some did so because they had a poor command of English and so lacked the confidence, and perhaps the ability, to take up private domestic posts. However, for such workers, as for their British counterparts, the 1980s and early 1990s often witnessed a deterioration in employment conditions as a policy of privatising the cleaning of schools, hospitals and government buildings was pursued. The numbers involved were large, with an estimated 134,000 school cleaners and 36,000 cleaners employed in local government offices alone in 1982.[67] Where private contractors took over they often imposed more stringent working conditions than had applied under the previous direct labour arrangements. In Cambridgeshire, where over 1,200 school cleaners were made redundant in 1983 when the work was contracted out, workers' hours were cut from thirty-four to twenty per week and the time allocated to clean each classroom was halved. The poor standard of work and the rapid staff turnover that resulted led the county council to revert to direct labour when the two-year contract ended in 1985.[68] But many other local authorities persisted, because of the apparent cash savings offered by the process, even when levels of performance declined.

One woman who worked for many years as an office cleaner employed directly by the civil service compared the new contract arrangements unfavourably. As she declared bitterly: 'nobody checks to see what's going on. And there's no doubt that cleaning standards go down with contract labour. You can't do the job properly when staff are always changing. There's got to be a lot of money being made by contractors, but it's not going to the cleaners.' Problems were particularly acute in places like airports, where twenty-four hour service had to be provided. In 1984 a report claimed that Asian workers at Heathrow Airport had to work rotating and irregular shifts without weekends off, sometimes having to cover a thirteen-and-a-half hour day at short notice, just to keep their jobs.[69] Eleven years later, a report by the European Commission declared that unlike virtually all the other countries in the European Union, the United Kingdom had no national collective working time or wage agreements for the cleaning sector. 'In effect, only a very small proportion of the estimated 200,000 contract-cleaning workforce is covered by any form of regulation related to these aspects of employment.'[70]

Not until the very end of the century did this situation begin to change, notably with the introduction of the National Minimum Wage in 1999. Research conducted by the Low Pay Commission concluded that this sector had been a particular beneficiary from that initiative, with companies encouraged 'to tender for contracts' on the basis of 'the service they can provide rather than how little they pay their staff'.[71] However, there were also those who sought to flout the spirit of the legislation. One cleaner who received the minimum wage was told by her employer that he expected her to work a great deal harder to earn it. He threatened to 'make something for you to do every minute of the day from now on'. The woman left because she found his attitude so aggressive.[72]

Finally, the increase in the number of rich people in the 1980s and 1990s also revived the demand for multi-staff households. Only in the economic recession of the early 1990s did this process slow down for a time. Lynn Brittney quotes households which had formerly hired a cook-housekeeper, a nanny, a chauffeur and a gardener now recruiting a separate cook as well as the housekeeper. In other cases, there was a demand for butlers or stewards who would also take over administrative responsibility for the running of the household. An advertisement in *The Lady* in January 2000 gives an indication of what was expected:

HOUSE STEWARD AND HOUSEKEEPER – Married couple required for a privately owned stately home in Cheshire. The House Steward will be responsible for the cleaning, care and preservation of this historic house and its contents. A major part of the job will concern the opening of the house both to the public and for corporate events. Further duties will include general maintenance and security. The Housekeeper will be jointly responsible for hall tours, including cooking and baking, and would also be required to carry out domestic cleaning for the owner on a regular basis. During term time may be expected to drive the owner's 8 year old son to school. In addition weekly babysitting will be required. This is a demanding position for a couple who have a flexible approach to their work and significant previous experience of working to the highest possible standard unsupervised. Own car and clean driving licences are essential. This is a live-in post with attractive spacious accommodation within the main building: The applicants will be non-smokers, physically fit and have no dependent children or dogs, although a love of dogs is a must. Salary to be negotiated. Must have impeccable references.[73]

Since few butlers or stewards were now being trained in households, other than those attached to the royal palaces, a number of 'schools' appeared designed to meet this need. Among the best known was Ivor Spencer's, which started in 1981 and at the end of the century was advertising its services on the internet.[74] In 2000 fees of £4,500 were charged for a six week course, which did not include food and accommodation. The aim was

to teach students to become first-class Butler Administrators/Personal Assistants, with the object of taking control of a household or households, and . . . be responsible for the purchasing of food and wines including Champagne, cigars and clothes, booking travel for employers, and hiring of all staff. The School also teaches students how to organise large and small parties. . . . The salary Butlers usually receive when they commence a position is £25,000 Sterling per year in the UK. In the United States the starting salary per year is usually US $45,000, and elsewhere a similar wage structure, plus usually good accommodation, food, medical care, and a car for shopping.[75]

Students came from a varied background. In the late 1980s a survey of sixteen trainees then completing a course revealed that one was a former senior civil servant from Northern Ireland, another was a former member of the Household Cavalry and a third was an ex-cattle feed merchant from Leicester who had taken early retirement. He was the son of a butler and a cook and had been born on a landed estate in Sussex. With these antecedents he proved an apt learner and when the course ended he obtained a lucrative post in the United States.[76] In addition, in order to cater for *nouveaux riches* employers who had no experience of managing a domestic staff, Ivor Spencer ran short courses to guide them on how to handle servants. Without this, relations between the two parties could easily deteriorate, as staff resented what they regarded as their employer's unreasonable demands and the employer complained of uncooperative and sullen domestics.[77]

Early in 1998 the Lady Apsley School for Butlers was opened in a manor house near Cirencester, with five men in mid-to late middle age joining the first course. Each had paid £3,000 to be there and instruction was provided by a former under-butler at Buckingham Palace, who had spent the preceding two years as a gentleman's gentleman to a continental employer and had also run an English family's London home. The course lasted eight weeks, with the prospective butlers being schooled in everything from flower arranging to organising a cocktail party, polishing silver and ordering travel tickets and wine on the internet. At the end of the course there was to be an examination with a practical test at a real dinner party. The School was the brainchild of Sara Apsley, the daughter-in-law of the 8th Earl Bathurst and it was run in her home. 'Houses like this no longer have the full complement of staff', she declared, 'but sometimes we really do need properly trained staff, particularly butlers. After the sloppy eighties, people are starting to regain their sense of tradition and style.'[78] Interestingly, one estimate suggested in that year that there were only about 400 professional butlers in the whole country.[79]

Many men, though, took up these posts with little or no formal training. The philosophy of 'anyone will have to do' became the order of the day.[80] When Arthur Inch retired from the Kleinwort family's service in 1980, he and his wife were followed by a married couple who came as butler and cook and had previously run a public house. They remained for ten years before they, too, retired.

Often, however, the well-to-do opted for just one resident domestic, recruiting extra staff when necessary for special occasions. Ater Mr Inch retired, he began to go out on a free-lance basis to arrange luncheons, dinners and drinks parties in this way: 'My wife came out with me for many years ... now my daughter often helps me', he wrote in 1999.[81] But he was saddened by the fact that once he and the few other remaining pre-war trained butlers had died out, there would be no one 'to take over and carry on the traditions of three to four hundred years of the science of domestic service which helped greatly the art of gracious living'.[82] These skills, he clearly felt, could not be

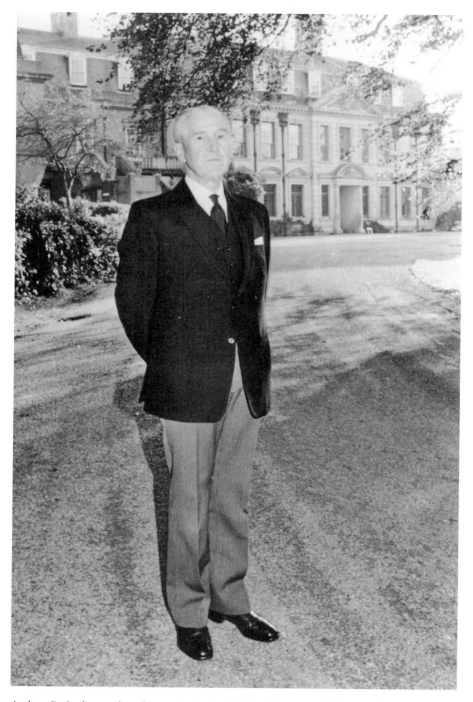

Arthur R. Inch, employed as a single-handed butler, around the time he retired from the Kleinwort family's service in 1980. (*Arthur R. Inch*)

learned in a few weeks at a special training school, but were the product of years of experience and of a steady progression up the domestic promotion ladder.

Even in the 1960s, when Peter Russell became butler to the Duke of Gloucester and later the Duke of Kent, he remembered the difficulty of keeping staff, particularly in the Gloucesters' country house. 'I took it to be the changing times. If things were bad in London, they were worse in the country. Who was going to cut themselves off from town life? It became difficult to replace staff.'[83] Peter himself entered private service after a spell as a batman/waiter in the 1950s when he was doing his National Service. He later became butler to the Chief Officer of the air base where he was stationed. Soon after leaving the Royal Air Force he went to an agency, Town and Country, near Sloane Square, to seek a post as a butler. He was told that the Duchess of Kent had a vacancy for an under-butler at Kensington Palace.[84] He took the post and thereby began his connection with the royal family. Yet, he, too, tired of the life in the 1960s and decided to accept a post with a large catering company in Essex. Not until the early 1980s did he revive his old skills by taking engagements as a contract butler.[85]

These, then, were the realities of servant life at the end of the twentieth century. In the large houses, staffs were much reducd and daily and contract workers had become an essential part of the domestic scene. The main growth area had become the households of the elderly and the affluent middle class, with their need for cleaners and for childcare providers. Admittedly, there were still large estates like Chatsworth, where longstanding, loyal servants were at work, but such examples were increasingly rare in a society governed by market forces and a growing sense of egalitarianism.

It is perhaps symbolic that Lynn Brittney, in her *Guide to Domestic Help* felt it necessary to warn employers of such potential dishonesties as the chauffeur who hired himself and his employers' car out for weddings when they were away and the housekeeper who purchased food and household articles out of her budget and then returned some of them to the shop in order to claim the refund for herself, or else she sold items to her friends.[86] Outside the pages of advice books there was also the case of the butler who faced a gaol sentence after selling his employer's Bentley car and hiring his own butler, while he pretended to be master of the house and entertained his friends from the public house.[87] However, even the Edwardians had complained of cooks who stole food from their mistresses and accepted bribes from tradesmen in return for placing orders with them.[88] Perhaps these later dishonesties were merely a sign that in the rapidly changing world of twentieth-century domestic service some old habits died hard.

HOTELS AND CATERING

The growing affluence of certain sectors of British society not only stimulated demand for domestic help but, coupled with an expansion in tourism, contributed greatly to the growth in the number and size of hotels and restaurants in the 1980s and 1990s. In the mid-1990s one estimate suggested that between 1979 and 1994 there had been almost a 27 per cent rise in the total of hotel and catering

After 1945 attempts were made to attract young people into the hotel and catering industry, by the issue of such publications as *Personal Service: Careers for Boys and Girls in the Catering Industry* (1946), from which this illustration is taken. (*TUC Library*)

jobs in the country.[89] That trend was predicted to continue into the new century.[90] The new posts included kitchen staff, chambermaids, cleaners, waiters and bar staff and some at least involved people who in earlier decades would have become private servants. The speed of the expansion in the hospitality sector is indicated by the rise in the number of chefs and cooks during the 1980s. At a time when the total population of Great Britain grew by about 2.5 per cent, the number of male chefs and cooks increased by 44 per cent, with around three-fifths of them working in hotels and catering, according to the 10 per cent sample of economic activity published in the 1981 and 1991 population censuses.[91] Among female chefs and cooks the expansion was far smaller – at about 13.4 per cent – but significantly only a little over two-fifths of the women worked in the hospitality industry. The rest were employed in schools, factory canteens and public institutions. The total number of waiters and bar staff likewise grew by 56 per cent in the 1980s, while the increase in the number of waitresses was only about 5 per cent. However, as with household cleaning, the casual, part-time nature of much of the work probably seriously under-estimated the true female contribution.

A survey of hotels and catering in the mid-1980s estimated that around two-thirds of the labour force was female, with three-quarters of them working part-time. It also concluded that the women's contribution tended to be 'ghettoised', so that, for example, chambermaids were mostly female. In the kitchens, too, women normally carried out the least skilled jobs.[92] Indeed, some leading chefs insisted that the members of their team should all be male, as they considered that women were unable to withstand the heat and the pressure that went with producing high quality dishes for a discerning and demanding clientele.[93]

Immediately after the end of the Second World War, efforts were made to expand employment in hotels and catering in order to promote tourism and to attract overseas visitors with their much-needed foreign currency. 'The work is full of interest', declared one promotional leaflet encouragingly, 'especially to those who are fond of preparing food, cooking it or helping people in personal ways.'[94] However, it was only in the final quarter of the century that changing attitudes and growing demand brought about rapid modernisation and expansion in the sector as a whole.

The calibre of staff employed in any hotel or restaurant was a major factor in establishing its reputation. Indeed, an account of the Grosvenor House Hotel in

London argued that in no other industry were staff-customer relations of greater importance. 'It is not, an exaggeration to say that the popularity of a hotel depends to a large extent on the quality of the personal service. In a luxury hotel this is especially important because one of the main qualifications of "luxury" is good room service.'[95]

That certainly applied to leading hotels like the Savoy in London, which prided itself upon its 'house-party atmosphere'. One of its directors claimed: 'We are the only hotel in London where every whim of the most exacting guests can be gratified at four in the morning as satisfactorily as at four in the afternoon.'[96] That meant employing a staff of over one thousand to attend to the needs of around five hundred guests. As Stanley Jackson declared in his highly flattering account of the Savoy, no hotel, 'however well-equipped and impressive, can function to perfection for twenty-four hours a day, year after year, without an enormous variety of gifted experts'.[97] When he wrote in the early 1960s, every floor was self-contained and was staffed by a housekeeper and a team of waiters, valets, chambermaids and cleaners.

In the 1980s and 1990s a growing number of hotels aimed to meet similarly exacting standards. They included Cliveden, which was opened in the Astors' former country house and sought to maintain much of the atmosphere of its illustrious past. One visitor to Cliveden in 1999 described it as offering 'the fantasy of country house luxury':

> Today's rich may no longer have staff living in their houses, but they are still paying servants to look after them – the only difference is that now they buy their services piecemeal. . . . When a butler in coat tails appeared on the gravel to take our bags, there was no requirement to check in; he simply took our coats and led us across the great hall, up sweeping stairs, to our room. . . . By the time we were inside four or five members of staff had volunteered to open doors and so forth.[98]

When she and her partner went to dinner, 'young men glided around the table. There was nothing to be done, beyond picking up our own knife and fork.' In the meantime, 'maids were upstairs turning down the sheets, drawing the curtains, and placing slippers and mats by the bed. At four o'clock in the morning, I called down to the butler's pantry for a sandwich. Ten minutes later a young man appeared with it; the cucumber slices had been freshly peeled.' The next day, as they drove away, they saw two gardeners standing on the verge, leaning on their rakes. 'As we passed, they doffed their caps.' This was, of course, service on the grand scale, which few people could afford to experience at £500 a night for two.

At the same time there was a growth of non-British speciality restaurants with their own characteristic cuisines, be they European or from the Far East. Most were staffed by nationals of the appropriate countries, whose working conditions were, on the whole, negotiated within their own ethnic communities.

For many of those working in the over-heated atmosphere of a kitchen, however, the attraction soon faded. The rigours of being on duty in these conditions for up to sixteen hours a day on occasion, led to a catalogue of illnesses, including bad backs, sore feet, dermatitis, varicose veins and high blood pressure.[101] Tempers grew short and many 'celebrity chefs' adopted a bullying approach towards junior members

Training to be a chef on a catering course at the South-East London Technical College, Lewisham Way, in 1973. (*London Metropolitan Photographic Archives*)

of their brigades. One top London chef resigned at the end of the 1990s after he had branded a kitchen worker with a hot knife. Earlier he had stated that Michelin stars were 'the only reason' he worked as a chef; to get three was 'the only thing that I've wanted in my life'. He had, some time before, been the youngest chef in Britain to be awarded two Michelin stars, but the constant striving for excellence had created a destructive intolerance towards others.[102]

Part of this tension could be attributed to the devastating effect which the loss of a Michelin star or the appearance of an unenthusiastic entry in *The Good Food Guide*, could have on a chef and on the owner or, the manager of the restaurant. In 1996-7 the proprietor of a highly rated hotel in Taunton described in his diary the care with which a new edition of *The Good Food Guide* was perused: 'The write-up was pretty up-beat . . . except for a couple of lines which suggested that ours was "classic, safe cooking" that lacked the "adventure of British provincial cooking".' The real blow came early in January 1997 with the arrival of the new *Michelin Red Guide*. This revealed that the hotel had lost its 'precious star', which it had first gained in 1984. 'The news is so fresh', wrote the owner in his diary, '. . . that the shock of it has not sunk in. I feel strangely numb.'[103] The chef immediately offered to resign and although this was not accepted a thorough post-mortem was conducted to find out what had gone wrong.

These were problems faced by workers at the upper end of the market. For the majority of hotel staff, however, the difficulties they experienced were not related to the winning of prestigious awards, but those associated with long working hours, poor pay and insecurity of tenure, in an industry plagued by fluctuating demand and seasonal variations. Many workers in seaside or other holiday resort hotels were recruited for a few months in the year only, as had always been the case, and might be expected to take on a wide range of duties if they were working in a small business. Typical of many were the Ullswater hoteliers who were looking 'for an energetic, outgoing personality to join us for the summer season, to help in all departments'.[104] Then there was the proprietor of a Devon hotel who wanted 'Seasonal staff . . . for small family run hotel. Housekeeping, restaurant and assistant to chef. Good sense of humour and thick skin essential.'[105] It is not clear if the 'thick skin' was needed to cope with the management or the guests, but many members of hotel staffs had to learn to accept with equanimity the arrogance and unreasonable demands of some customers. One worker from the north-west of England commented bitterly that she considered that she and her fellow workers should be better paid because 'of the unsociable hours we have to work, the snobs we have to put up with and the painted smiles we always have to wear!!!'[106] Another also disliked the long and unsociable hours, but most resented the fact that the majority of the public 'look down upon us and treat us like general dogsbodies'.[107] Such comments were similar to those made by domestic workers in private service over half a century earlier.

At the end of the twentieth century even the *Caterer and Hotelkeeper*, a trade journal, referred to the industry's poor labour relations, with 'chefs, waiters and other hospitality staff . . . four times as likely to get the sack as workers in other jobs. They are also the most likely to quit.'[108] The high turnover of employees was pinpointed in the mid-1990s by a regional study of the north-west which suggested over a quarter of those surveyed had had three or more jobs within two years. Many had moved voluntarily, but others had had to leave because they were made redundant.[109] One hotel group attributed its own high staff turnover to 'the large growth in the Leisure and Hospitality sectors', with workers presumably looking around in order to better themselves. In this particular group each hotel averaged about 150 bedrooms and staff numbers were divided between around one hundred full timers and ninety casual or occasional workers.[110]

Also indicative of the difficult labour relations in the industry was its resistance to trade unionism, although unionism was in any case hampered by the rapid turnover of employees and the large number of casual workers. Nevertheless, in 1985 Lord Forte, then head of a multi-million-pound hotel and catering empire, expressed a common attitude when he claimed that by 'natural process' his business had reduced union membership from 36 per cent to 3 per cent.[111] Within the industry as a whole, at that date, union members comprised around 6 per cent of the total workforce, one of the lowest proportions in any industry.[112]

A combination of part-time and casual labour, a high level of staff turnover, employer hostility to unionism and the large number of relatively small workplaces left most of the staff in a 'strait-jacket of low pay, poor conditions and overall insecurity'.[113] The widespread use of young people to fill part-time posts reinforced this. Students were thought likely to encourage younger customers with money to spend and were also highly flexible. As one hotelier put it, he felt free 'to ring them and say it's not very busy', so they need not come in. 'I don't feel guilty about it . . . if they want a night off they say to me "Can I swap tomorrow night?"'[114]

Young workers were also relatively cheap, even after the introduction of the National Minimum Wage, since the pay for 18 to 21-year-olds was set at just £3 an hour and for those under 18 no minimum was set. Few of these young, casual employees intended to make a career in catering. They were merely looking to earn some cash while they were at school or college.

Most hotels, however, adopted a mixed age strategy for part-time workers. Older females, including members of ethnic minorities, were recruited to carry out the duties of chambermaids, cleaners and waitresses, particularly for breakfasts. Youngsters were thought to be less reliable at getting up in the morning than older staff.[115] The young people would then work 'unsocial' hours in the evenings and at weekends, or

The skills of waiting at table being learnt on a catering course at the South-East London Technical College in 1973. (*London Metropolitan Photographic Archives*)

be expected to fill in as and when it was busy. A hotel general manager from the Manchester area described his own mixed-age policy in the late 1990s:

Food service is predominantly 16-19, bars 18-21, housekeeping and room attendants 25 plus and kitchen porters 40 plus.[116]

Training for casual or part-time workers was often rudimentary, not least because of the high staff turnover, and when it did take place it concentrated on basic food and hygiene issues, plus guidance on 'customer care' and sales techniques. The introduction of the National Minimum Wage boosted the pay of a number of adult females in the industry, although a few employers responded by charging for meals which had formerly been provided free, or by making an accommodation charge to those who lived in.[117] But for many non-resident part-timers there was a clear gain.

Despite this modest improvement, however, the pay and conditions of most workers in hotels and catering were still poor at the end of the century. Their position contrasted starkly with that of the small number of 'celebrity' chefs who not only commanded high salaries and great prestige, but might be able to secure lucrative television contracts and large royalties from the sale of books of recipes and reminiscences. On a broader front, the industry formed part of the important tourism sector and it provided growing employment opportunities for a number of people who might once have entered private service. That applied particularly to those in the kitchens and in the housekeeping department. One leading London hotelier even claimed that hotel housekeeping was 'home housewifery on a large scale'.[118] providing a further example of the changing face of domestic employment in the second half of the twentieth century. Also significant in that context was the banishing of the words 'servant' and 'maid' from the domestic vocabulary and their replacement by 'helper' and 'assistant'.

Undoubtedly, a greater spirit of egalitarianism existed in 2000 than had applied a century earlier, but in terms of cash rewards and even social status there still remained much to reform if those supplying these important personal services were to receive adequate recognition. Despite the fond hopes of reformers from the 1920s onwards, domestic work has remained largely the preserve of the untrained and poorly paid. Violet Markham's strongly expressed desire in 1955 that it would be reorganised 'as a skilled craft with status, hours and wages comparable with those in other occupations' was still very largely unfulfilled at the end of the century.[119]

NOTES

Some abbreviations used
ARC = Archival Resource Centre at the University of Essex
GFS = Girls' Friendly Society
Hansard = Debates in the House of Commons, unless otherwise indicated
IWMSA = Imperial War Museum Sound Archives
LMA = London Metropolitan Archives
MHM = Market Harborough Museum
NVA = National Vigilance Association
MRC = Modern Records Centre at the University of Warwick
PP = Parliamentary Papers
PRO = Public Record Office i.e. National Archives
SHOHT = Shugborough Hall Oral History Transcripts: Staffordshire County Council
TUCL = Trades Union Congress Library at the London Metropolitan University
URA = University of Reading Archives
YWCA =Young Women's Christian Association

ONE

1   Butler, *Domestic Service*.
2   Seebohm Rowntree, *Poverty*, pp. 14, 31. He estimated that only about two-thirds of the maids came from York homes because of the large demand for girls in the city's factories.
3   *Forty-first Annual Report of the Local Government Board for 1911*, PP. 1912-13, Vol. XXV, pp. xxvi, 175.
4   *Fifty-ninth Report of the Chief Inspector of Reformatory and Industrial Schools of Great Britain for 1915*, PP. 1916, Vol. XV, p.20.
5   *Domestic Servants' Advertiser*, 17 June 1913.
6   L. Rose, *The Erosion of Childhood*, p. 44.
7   Anderson, *A Rather Special Place*, p. 61.
8   Ibid., p. 62.
9   Burnett (ed.), *Useful Toil*, pp. 214, 216.
10 Noakes, *Town Beehive*, p. 11
11 MHM Oral History Transcripts, OR.46; Mullins &,Griffiths, *Cap and Apron*, pp. 7, 8-9.
12 MHM Oral History Transcripts, OR.46.
13 Minutes of the YWCA Women's Employment Department Committee 1902-1907 at MRC, MSS.243/131/2, 10 January 1907.
14 Asquith, 'In Front of the Green Baize Door' in Noel Streatfeild (ed.), *The Day Before Yesterday*, p. 101. *Hansard*, 5th Series, Vol. XXXI, 16 November 1911, col. 541.

15 E. Horne, *What the Butler Winked At*, p. 221.

16 Mullins & Griffiths, *Cap and Apron*, pp. 7, 18.

17 Loelia, Duchess of Westminster, *Grace and Favour*, p. 39.

18 Asquith, 'In Front of the Green Baize Door', *Day Before Yesterday*, p. 102.

19 *A Few Rules for the Manners of Servants in Good Families*, pp. 8-9, 15. A new edition of this pamphlet was published in 1901. I am indebted to Mrs Helen Harrison of Penzance for the 1895 edition of this work.

20 Asquith, 'In Front of the Green Baize Door', *Day Before Yesterday*, p. 103.

21 Ibid., pp. 103-4.

22 Dawes, *Not in Front of the Servants*, p. 32.

23 ARC, Oral History Transcript QD1/FLWE/93.

24 A. Thomas, Butler to the Principal, Brasenose College, Oxford, *Wait and See*, pp. 28, 31.

25 Loelia, Duchess of Westminster, *Grace and Favour*, p. 36.

26 Chorley, *Manchester Made Them*, p. 148.

27 Ibid., p. 126.

28 Mullins & Griffiths, *Cap and Apron*, p. 16.

29 Gorst, *Of Carriages and Kings*, pp. 30, 33.

30 King, *Green Baize Door*, p. 10.

31 Ibid., p. 11.

32 *General Report of the 1911 Census for England and Wales*, PP 1913, Vol. LXXVIII, pp. xxv-xxvi.

33 Mrs D. K. Dence, Great Bookham, Leatherhead, Surrey to the author, 19 October 1974.

34 Mullins & Griffiths, *Cap and Apron*, p. 1.

35 MHM Oral History Transcripts, OR.40. Mullins & Griffiths, *Cap and Apron*, p. 8.

36 Ibid., OR.40.

37 Mrs D. K. Dence to the author, 19 October 1974.

38 M. Thomas, 'Behind the Green Baize Door', in Noel Streatfeild, *Day Before Yesterday*, 91

39 IWMSA, 00693.

40 Ibid.

41 ARC, Oral History Transcript QD1/FLWE/156.

42 M. Thomas, 'Behind the Green Baize Door', in Streatfeild, ed., *Day Before Yesterday*, p. 88.

43 Dawes, *Not in Front of the Servants*, pp. 73-4.

44 Nowell-Smith, (ed.), *Edwardian England*, p. 146.

45 *Houseworker*, March 1948, at MRC, MSS.292/54.76/62a.

46 E. Horne, *More Winks*, p. 125.

47 *Ministry of Reconstruction: Report of Domestic Service Sub-Committee*, PP 1919, Vol. XXIX, p. 22.

48 E. S. Turner, *What the Butler Saw*, pp. 249-50. Mullins & Griffiths, *Cap and Apron*, p. 64.

49 *The Times*, 21 April 1914.

50 *The Times*, 21 May 1914.

51 *Lancet*, 19 August 1905, p. 546.

52 S. Jackson, *Savoy*, p. 39.

53 *The Times*, 21 April 1914.

54 S. Jackson, *Savoy*, pp. 47-8.

55 Walton, *Blackpool Landlady*, pp. 134-5.

56 *General Report of the 1911 Census of England and Wales*, p. xxvii.

57 *Report on the Twelfth Census of Scotland, 1911*, PP 1913, Vol. LXXX, pp. lxxi-lxxii.

58 *Hansard*, 5th Series, Vol. XXXI, 16 November 1911, col. 1122. See *Daily Mail*, 30 November 1911: 'Gag and Guillotine: How the Government Can Force the Servant Tax on the People'.

59 Dawes, *Not in Front of the Servants*, p. 117.

60 P. Horn, *Rise and Fall of the Victorian Servant*, pp. 184-5.

61 Minutes of the YWCA Women's Employment Department Committee 1902-1907, meetings on 16 November 1904, 18 January, 5 February, 15 February and 21 June 1905, at MRC, MSS.243/131/2. J Rutter, *Young Women's Christian Association of Great Britain 1900-1925*, p. 45.

62 *Fifty fifth Report of the Inspector of the Certified Reformatory and Industrial Schools of Great Britain for 1912*, PP 1912-13, Vol. XLVI, p. 196.

63 *The Astor Story*, TS of Lady Astor's autobiography in URA, MS.1416/1/6/86, p. 101.

64 Dallaston, *Around Foxton*, pp. 17-20.

65 Dawes, *Not in Front of the Servants*, p. 21.

66 *The Times*, 2 April 1914.

67 Woollacott, *On Her their Lives Depend*, p. 20.

68 Marwick, *Deluge*, p. 91.

69 Woollacott, *On Her their Lives Depend*, pp. 2, 18.

70 Braybon, *Women Workers*, p. 49.

71 Briar, *Working for Women?*, pp. 33, 38. Horn, *Women in the 1920s*, p. 6.

72 Quoted in P. Horn, *Rural Life*, p. 29.

73 *Hansard*, 5th Series, Vol. 105, 24 April 1918, cols. 1000-1001.

74 P. Horn, *Ladies of the Manor*, p. 202.

75 *Country Life*, 11 September 1915.

76 T. W. Turner, *Memoirs of a Gamekeeper (Elveden, 1868-1953)*, pp. 33, 117.

77 *Country Life*, 15 January 1916.

78 T. Humphris, *Garden Glory*, pp. 30, 91.

79 Sykes, *Nancy*, pp. 175-6. R. Harrison, (ed.), *Gentlemen's Gentlemen*, p. 140.

80 Sykes, *Nancy*, pp. 175-6.

81 *The Times*, 19 and 20 February 1915.

82 Firth, *Psychology of the Servant Problem*, pp. 19-20.

83 P. Horn, *Ladies of the Manor*, p. 203.

84 E. S. Turner, *What the Butler Saw*, p. 277.

85 L. C. Jackson, *History of the United Service Club*, p.118. *Country Life*, 20 March 1915.

86 S. Jackson, *Savoy*, p. 61.

87 *General Report of the 1911 Census for England and Wales*, p. cxvii.

88 IWMSA 00734.

89 R. Harrison, *Rose*, p. 22.

90 IWMSA 00693.

91 Woollacott, *On Her their Lives Depend*, p. 4.

92 IWMSA 00740.

93 Llewellyn Smith, (ed.), *New Survey of London Life and Labour*, Vol. II, p. 465.

94 *General Report of the 1921 Census*, pp. 98, 126.

95 See, for example, *The Times*, 18 February 1915.

96 Mrs Collier's Servants' Book was sent to the author by her son, Michael, in 1974.

97 Mullins & Griffiths, *Cap and Apron*, pp. 22-3.

98 *Daily Mail*, 8 November 1918.

99 Quoted in Braybon, *Women Workers*, p. 187. Briar, *Working for Women?*, pp. 45-6.

100 Braybon, p. 187. Strachey, *Cause*, p. 372.

101 Elliott, *Status of Domestic Work in the United Kingdom with Special Reference*

to the *National Institute of Houseworkers*, p. 6. P. Horn, *Women in the 1920s*, p. 17. Briar, *Working for Women?*, p. 58.

102   P. Horn, *Women in the 1920s*, p. 18.
103   *Labour Woman*, April 1919.
104   Braybon, *Women Workers*, p. 183.
105   *The Times*, 29 May 1919.
106   *The Times*, 15 March 1919.
107   *The Times*, 21 March 1919.
108   *The Times*, 26 March 1919.
109   *Labour Woman*, February 1919.
110   *The Times*, 19 March 1919.
111   Braybon, *Women Workers*, pp. 188, 212.
112   *Daily Mail*, 10 April 1923.
113   *Hansard*, 5th Series, Vol. 121, 28 November 1919, cols. 1003-1004.
114   Strachey, *Cause*, p. 372.
115   A. Thomas, *Wait and See*, p. 57.
116   *General Report of the 1921 Census*, p. 115.
117   *Daily Mail*, 11 April 1922.
118   E. S. Turner, *What the Butler Saw*, p. 278.
119   R. Harrison, (ed.), *Gentlemen's Gentlemen*, p. 140.
120   King, *Green Baize Door*, pp. 30-4.
121   Ibid., p. 34.
122   E. Horne, *What the Butler Winked At*, pp. 10, 258-60.
123   Ibid., p. 260.

TWO

1   Burnett (ed.), *Useful Toil*, 234-235. Gordon and Breitenbach (ed.), *World is Ill Divided*, pp. 140, 154.
2   Mrs M. Fugill of Barnehurst, Kent, in correspondence with the author, 30 August 1974.
3   See records of NUDW at MRC. For example, notes on a meeting to be held on 29 June 1938, concerning the organisation of domestic workers. This refers to there being 1 1/2 million domestic workers in the country. MSS.292/54.76/10. For the 1921 and 1931 figures see the relevant census reports.
4   Calculated from the relevant census reports. For details of the increase in the number of families between 1921 and 1931, see *1931 Census of England and Wales: Housing*, xviii.
5   *General Report of the Census of England and Wales, 1931*,152. *General Report of the 1911 Census of England and Wales*, PP 1913, Vol. LXXVIII, xxv.
6   Robinson, *Memories of Upper Bangor*, p. 34.
7   Llewellyn Smith (ed.), *The New Survey of London Life and Labour*, Vol. II, pp. 432, 438.
8   See, for example, notice in *The Times* on 10 December, 1937, reporting the deaths of Sarah Prentice, 'after 56 years' faithful service with Mrs Conway Thornton' and of Jane Burgess, 'for very many years the devoted housekeeper of the late Miss Alice Reynolds . . . and faithful friend of the family'. There are countless others in a similar vein from the inter-war years.
9   Miss G. J. Goff in correspondence with the author, September 1974.
10   Hall, *Canary Girls and Stockpots*, pp. 29-32.
11   Darcy, *Problems and Changes in Women's Work*, p. 73.
12   A. A. Jackson, *Semi-Detached London*, p. 49.
13   *General Report of the Census of England and Wales, 1931*, p. 152.
14   Robinson, *Memories of Upper Bangor*, p. 34.

15 H. Jones (ed.), *Duty and Citizenship*, p. 109.
16 Loelia, Duchess of Westminster, *Grace and Favour*, p. 149.
17 Ibid., pp. 201-3.
18 Field, *Bendor*, p. 169.
19 Tyack, 'Service on the Cliveden Estate Between the Wars' in *Oral History*, Vol. 5, No.1, p. 66.
20 SHOHT, R.73-044-0001; see also R.72-001-0001, information from Evelyn Bird.
21 Comments by Mrs Courtenay, SHOHT, R.73-044-0001.
22 Macmillan, *Winds of Change*, pp. 189-90.
23 R. Harrison (ed.), *Gentlemen's Gentlemen*, p. 107.
24 Caradog Jones (ed.), *Social Survey of Merseyside*, Vol. II, pp. 300-1.
25 Foley, *The Forest Trilogy*, pp. 105, 109. Winifred was born in 1914.
26 Ibid., pp. 129-30.
27 Ibid., p. 138.
28 Mrs Winifred Cardew in correspondence with the author, 15 July 1999. Mrs Cardew was born in 1908.
29 Gordon & Breitenbach (ed.), *World is Ill Divided*, p. 15.
30 M. Harrison, 'Domestic Service Between the Wars' in *Oral History*, Vol. 16, No.1, pp. 48-9.
31 Taylor, 'Daughters and mothers' in Clarke, Critcher & Johnson (ed.), *Working Class Culture*, p. 129.
32 Humphries and Hopwood, *Green and Pleasant Land*, p. 55.
33 Inch, *Reminiscences*, pp. 37-8.
34 Ibid., pp. 120-1 and Inch in correspondence with the author, November and December 1999.
35 Noakes, *Town Beehive*, pp. 30-3.
36 Ibid., p. 33.
37 *Home Office: Report on the Work of the Children's Branch, April 1923*, pp. 36, 48.
38 *Home Office: Fifth Report on the Work of the Children's Branch, January 1938*, pp. 90, 99.
39 Courtesy of Mrs Sheila Holland of Stanford-Le-Hope, Essex, on 9 and 21 February, 2000 in correspondence with the author.
40 Mrs E. Slade of Welling, Kent in correspondence with the author, 5 September 1974.
41 T. Jones, *A Diary with Letters 1931-1950*, pp. 285-6.
42 *Fiftieth Annual Report of the National Vigilance Association for 1934-35*, 6. These and other records of the NVA are preserved in the Women's Library at the London Metropolitan University.
43 NVA Records, Box 119, report on Mary Andrews from Treharris, 17 February 1933.
44 NVA Records, Box 119, comments by the Secretary of the GFS to the association concerning another Mary Andrews, 5 October 1933.
45 Stirling Women's Oral Project: Domestic Service, U3, born 1914.
46 B. Harrison, 'For Church, Queen and Family' in *Past and Present*, No. 61, pp. 125-6.
47 Typescript at MHM, OR.30.
48 Mullins & Griffiths, *Cap and Apron*, p. 9.
49 Ibid., p. 10.
50 NVA Records, Box 99, Employment Agencies, Reports on Medway's Domestic Agency, run by David Cohen, 1932. Ministry of Labour: Report to the Minister of Labour of the Committee on the Supply of Female Domestic Servants, pp. 23-4. At that date only 4.8 per cent of urban authorities had taken powers to

regulate domestic agencies.

51 Inch, *Reminiscences*, p. 77.
52 Milgate, 'Memories of a housemaid 1922-1930', typescript at MHM OR.37.
53 Ibid.
54 NVA Records, Box 99, The Fairbairn Agency Report on 20 August 1935.
55 *Report of the Ministry of Labour for 1938*, PP 1938-39, Vol. XII, pp. 13-14, 94.
56 Ministry of Labour to Local Education Authority, County Durham, 23 June 1932 and Report on Residential Home Training Centres: Recruitment and Placing of Trainees, 6 February 1932, both in LAB.2/1219/ETJ 1178/1932, PRO.
57 ARC, Oral History Transcript QD1/FLWE/391.
58 Humphries and Hopwood, *Green and Pleasant Land*, pp. 28-9.
59 Ibid., p. 29.
60 R. Harrison (ed.), *Gentlemen's Gentlemen*, pp. 43-4. Tyack, 'Service on the Cliveden Estate', *Oral History*, Vol. 5, No.1, p. 72.
61 R. Harrison (ed.), *Gentlemen's Gentlemen*, pp. 224-5.
62 E. S. Turner, *What the Butler Saw*, p. 287.
63 Balderson with Goodlad, *Backstairs Life*, pp. 11-12. Reminiscences at Market Harborough Museum, OR.30.
64 Correspondence between Mrs Viner and Lady Astor in Astor MSS at the University of Reading Archives, MS.1416/1/2/50, pp. 19, 20 November 1928 and MS.1416/1/2/53, 30 December 1928 and 12 May 1929. The Viners had been at Plas Newydd for over six years.
65 King, *The Green Baize Door*, pp. 40-1.
66 Ibid., p. 42.
67 Ibid., p. 57.
68 Mullins & Griffiths, *Cap and Apron*, p. 42.
69 ARC, Oral History Transcript QD1/FLWE/210.
70 Roberts, *Women and Families*, p. 53.
71 Foley, *Forest Trilogy*, pp. 140, 145.
72 Ibid., p. 149.
73 Hall, *Canary Girls and Stockpots*, p. 29.
74 Ibid., p. 29.
75 Mullins & Griffiths, *Cap and Apron*, pp. 29-30.
76 Cliveden Oral History Transcripts at Maidenhead Reference Library, BUT.91, Reminiscences of Noel Wiseman, agent at Cliveden from 1934.
77 Loelia, Duchess of Westminster, *Grace and Favour*, p. 46.
78 Lewis, *Private Life*, p. 111.
79 Ibid., p. 111.
80 SHOHT, R.73-044-0001.
81 Loelia, Duchess of Westminster, *Grace and Favour*, pp. 201, 204-5.
82 SHOHT, R.85-001-0001, Mullins & Griffiths, *Cap and Apron*, p. 39.
83 Astor, *Tribal Feeling*, p. 60.
84 Reminiscences at MHM, OR.30.
85 Ibid.
86 Mullins & Griffiths, *Cap and Apron*, p. 40.
87 Lewis, *Private Life*, p. 179.
88 Powell, *Below Stairs*, p. 94. The book was first Published in 1968.
89 R. Harrison (ed.), *Gentlemen's Gentlemen*, p. 146.
90 Mullins & Griffiths, *Cap and Apron*, p. 36.
91 Inch, *Reminiscences*, pp. 5-7.
92 Ibid., pp. 7, 49.
93 Ibid., p. 93.
94 Ibid., p. 96.

95 Lady Troubridge, *The Book of Etiquette*, p. 407.

96 Inch, *Reminiscences*, pp. 2, 79.

97 Ibid., p. 95.

98 SHOHT, R.87-005-0001.

99 Inch, *Reminiscences*, p. 91.

100 Powell, *Below Stairs*, p. 42.

101 Milgate, 'Memories of a housemaid 1922-1930', typescript at MHM OR.37.

102 Reminiscences at MHM, OR.30.

103 Powell, *Below Stairs*, pp. 38-9.

104 Noel, *Five to Seven*, pp. 79-89. Gathorne-Hardy, *Rise and Fall of the British Nanny*, pp. 72, 182-3.

105 Gathorne-Hardy, *Rise and Fall of the British Nanny*, p. 73.

106 Mullins & Griffiths, *Cap and Apron*, pp. 47-8.

107 Gathorne-Hardy, *Rise and Fall of the British Nanny*, p. 178-9, 184.

108 Powell, *Below Stairs*, p. 63.

109 Albert R. Butler of Winchcombe, Gloucestershire, in correspondence with the author, 27 August 1974.

110 R. Harrison, *Rose*, p. 21.

111 Ibid., pp. 32-3.

112 Ibid., pp. 63-4, 79-80.

113 Sambrook, *Servants' Place*, p. 45. SHOHT, R.73-035-0001.

114 SHOHT, R.84-0004-0001 and R.89-0004-0001.

115 Sambrook, *The Country House Servant*, pp. 209-10.

116 Ibid., p. 210.

117 SHOHT, R.73-035-0001.

118 ARC, Oral History Transcript QD1/FLWE/194.

THREE

1 *Ministry of Reconstruction: Report of the Women's Advisory Committee on the Domestic Service Problem*, pp 1919, Vol. XXIX, 8. Pamela Sharpe (ed.), *Women's Work*, p. 342.

2 Butler, *Domestic Service*, p. 114.

3 Ibid., pp. 114-16.

4 *Ministry of Reconstruction: Report of the Women's Advisory Committee*, p. 9.

5 *Report to the Minister of Labour of the Committee Appointed to Enquire into the Present Conditions as to the Supply of Female Domestic Servants*, 10 and 12. Hereafter cited as 1923 *Report on the Supply of Female Domestic Servants*.

6 Ibid., pp. 12-13.

7 *Royal Commission on Unemployment Insurance: Final Majority Report*, pp 1931-32, Vol. XIII, pp. 201, 203.

8 *Royal Commission on Unemployment Insurance: Minority Report*, pp 1931-32, Vol. XIII, p. 453.

9 Workers who had paid an appropriate number of contributions did not lose their benefit rights if they took up temporary domestic employment in private houses. *Hansard*, 5th Series, Vol. 245 (20 November 1930), col. 633. See also *Hansard*, 5th Series, Vol. 245 (2 December 1930), col. 2006.

10 Briar, *Working for Women?*, pp. 44-7.

11 Dawes, *Not in Front of the Servants*, p. 144.

12 *1923 Report on the Supply of Female Domestic Servants*, p. 29.

13 Briar, *Working for Women?* p. 59. Beddoe, *Back to Home and Duty*, p. 86.

14 *Ministry of Labour Gazette*, January 1922.

15 *Ministry of Labour. Second Interim Report of the Central Committee on Women's Training and Employment for the Period ending 31 December 1922*,

pp. 25-6. Hereafter cited as Second Interim Report.

16 'Summary of Action taken on Resident Domestic Service Outfits Scheme, May 6 - June 10 1921' in Markham MSS. 3/14 at the British Library of Political and Economic Science, London School of Economics. All the other Markham MSS. referred to are at this location.

17 *Labour Gazette*, May 1919.

18 *Second Interim Report*, pp. 5-6, 12.

19 Ibid., p. 17.

20 Briar, *Working for Women?*, p. 54. *Second Interim Report*, p. 18.

21 *Second Interim Report*, pp. 26-7. Lilian Barker, Executive Officer, CCWTE to L. V. Brock of the Ministry of Health in Markham MSS. 3/14, 15 November 1921.

22 *Second Interim Report*, p. 25.

23 Ibid., p. 35.

24 *Report of the Ministry of Labour for 1925*, pp 1926, Vol. XIII, p. 121. *Second Interim Report*, p. 19.

25 Draft letter from Violet Markham to Dr Macnamara, Minister of Labour, 13 October 1922, in Markham MSS. 3/15.

26 Ibid.

27 *Report of the Ministry of Labour for 1931*, pp 1931-32, Vol. XI, p. 42. The report noted that 'in nursery nursing' it proved easy to place trainees.

28 *Report of the Ministry of Labour for 1935*, PP 1935-36, Vol. XIII, p. 35.

29 *Report of the Ministry of Labour for 1938*, PP 1938-39, Vol. XII, p. 32.

30 Violet Markham to her sister, Geraldine Hole, 24 October 1937 in Markham MSS. 19/30.

31 See, for example, Sir George Murray to L. V. Brock, 19 November 1921, lamenting the fact that: 'On every side you hear of the difficulty of getting domestic servants, especially in the lower grades; and yet thousands of them are getting unemployment pay', in Markham MSS. 3/14. There were many similar complaints at this time.

32 Briar, *Working for Women?*, p. 58.

33 At the Home training centre in the Workington/Whitehaven area in 1925 it was proposed to hire sewing machines and possibly a gas boiler for laundry work. See LAB.2/1365/ED.730/18/29 at the PRO.

34 *Report of the Fifty-sixth Annual Trades Union Congress, 1924*, pp. 309-310 in TUCL.

35 Ibid., pp. 364-5.

36 *Hansard*, 5th Series, Vol. 205 (14 April 1927), cols. 600-602.

37 Ibid., col. 600.

38 *Hansard*, 5th Series, Vol. 175 (10 July 1924), col. 2484.

39 Ibid., Vol. 209 (27 July 1927), col. 1315.

40 Briar, *Working for Women?* p. 57.

41 *Hansard*, 5th Series, Vol. 240 (19 June 1930), cols. 555-556.

42 'Residential Home Training Centres. Recruitment and Placing of Trainees', para. 10 in LAB.2/1219/ET].1178/ 1932, PRO.

43 H. Jones (ed.), *Duty and Citizenship*, p. 112.

44 [Anon.] ed. *Men Without Work*, p. 260.

45 Ibid., p. 259.

46 Ibid., p. 260.

47 Report of YWCA Extension Work among Unemployed Women and Girls, *c.* 1933, in Unemployment Committee Minutes MSS.243/149, MRC.

48 *Ministry of Labour Gazette*, February 1929.

49 Ibid.

50 'Non-Residential Courses: Placing of Juvenile Trainees: Minute from District

Controller, North East' in ETJ.1379/31, PRO. The report related to the non-placement of trainees in the autumn of 1931 from the Gateshead, Sunderland and Blaydon centres. SeeLAB.2/1219/ETJ/1178/1932, PRO.

51 *Hansard,* 5th Series, Vol.245 (4 December 1930), col. 2406.

52 Correspondence between the Ministry of Labour and certain local education authorities in the depressed areas, 23 June 1932 in LAB.2/1219/ETJ.1178/1932, PRO.

53 Secretary to Coseley Urban District Education Committee to the Ministry of Labour, 25 June 1932 in LAB.2/1219/ET].1178/1932.

54 *Report of the Ministry of Labour for 1931*, PP 1931-32, Vol. XI, p. 39.

55 *Report of the Ministry of Labour for 1933*, PP 1933-34, Vol. XIII, p. 42.

56 Calculated from *the Annual Reports of the Ministry of Labour* for the relevant years.

57 *Report of the Ministry of Labour for 1935*, PP 1935-36, Vol. XIII, p. 34.

58 Calculated from the Records of the Centre at Ystrad, Rhondda, PRO, LAB.2/1365/ED.730/19/1929; courses ending 18 September, 12 November and 11 December 1928.

59 Quoted in P. Horn, 'Hunting the servants: The role of servant training centres between the wars' in *Genealogists' Magazine*, Vol. 26, no. 8 (December 1999), p. 299.

60 *Ministry of Labour Gazette*, May 1930. *Report of the Ministry of Labour for 1927*, PP 1928, Vol. XI, p. 29.

61 *Report of the Ministry of Labour for 1934*, PP 1934-35, Vol. X, 35. *Report of the Ministry of Labour for 1938*, p. 31.

62 Violet Markham to her sister, Geraldine Hole, 24 October 1937, in Markham MSS. 19/30.

63 Markham, *Return Passage*, p. 205.

64 Briar, *Working for Women?* p. 66.

65 *Are You Unemployed?* Leaflet in the TUCL, HD.6072. No publisher was given, but it was almost certainly produced by the Ministry of Labour.

66 *Residential Training Centres for Domestic Workers*, leaflet published by the Central Committee on Women's Training and Employment in the TUCL, HD.6072.

67 Mullins & Griffiths, *Cap and Apron*, p. 30.

68 Briar, *Working for Women?*, pp. 58, 67.

69 *Hansard*, 5th Series, Vol. 291 (21 June 1934), col. 575.

70 Ibid., Vol. 240 (18 June 1930), col. 490. ,

71 *1923 Report on the Supply of Female Servants*, pp. 42-3, 46. *Daily Mail*, 10 April 1923.

72 *1923 Report on the Supply of Female Servants*, pp. 25-30, 46-9.

73 *Report of the Ministry of Labour for 1937*, PP 1937-38, Vol. XII, p. 15.

74 Briar, *Working for Women?*, pp. 57-8.

75 *Report of the Ministry of Labour for 1934*, PP 1934-35, Vol. X, 16. *Report of the Ministry of Labour for 1931*, PP 1931-32, Vol. XI, p. 17. *Report of the Ministry of Labour for 1935*, p. 15.

76 *Report of the Ministry of Labour for 1937*, p. 14.

77 *Report of the Ministry of Labour for 1928*, PP 1928-29, Vol. VII, p. 23.

78 *Report of the Ministry of Labour for 1935*, pp. 16, 36.

79 *Report of the Ministry of Labour for 1925*, PP 1926, Vol. XIII, p. 34.

80 *Men Without Work*, p. 246. *Blackpool Gazette*, 28 April and 22 September 1934.

81 *British Boarding-House Proprietor*, June 1932.

82 *British Boarding-House Proprietor*, June 1932 and *Report of the Ministry of Labour for 1934*, PP 1934-35, Vol. X, p. 19.

83 Markham, *Return Passage*, p. 149. H. Jones (ed.), *Duty and Citizenship*, p. 157.
84 *Sixty-eighth Annual Report of Dr Barnardo's Homes for 1933*, p. 32.
85 Firth, *Psychology of the Servant Problem*, pp. 47-8.
86 B. Harrison, 'For Church, Queen and Family', in *Past and Present*, No. 61, p. 117.
87 *Report of the Work and Progress of the Girls' Friendly Society in 1926*, p. 61. These reports are hereafter cited as *Annual Report of GFS*, followed by the appropriate year.
88 Heath-Stubbs, *Friendship's Highway*, p. 34.
89 P. Horn, 'Training and Status in Domestic Service', in *History of Education Society Bulletin*, No. 65, p. 37.
90 Heath-Stubbs, *Friendship's Highway*, pp. 40-1. *Annual Report of GFS*, 1922, p. 46. Horn, 'Training and Status in Domestic Service', p. 38.
91 *GFS Magazine*, September 1931. Heath-Stubbs, *Friendship's Highway*, p. 193.
92 Heath-Stubbs, *Friendship's Highway*, pp. 193-4.
93 *Annual Report of GFS*, 1936, p. 35.
94 P. Horn, 'Training and Status in Domestic Service', p. 41.
95 *1923 Report on the Supply of Female Servants*, Appendix C, 41. Rutter, *The Young Women's Christian Association of Great Britain 1900-25*, p. 107.
96 Stokes, *Norland*, p. 18.
97 Gathorne-Hardy, *Rise and Fall*, p. 178.
98 Stokes, *Norland*, p. 22.
99 Gathorne-Hardy, *Rise and Fall*, p. 178.
100 Stokes, *Norland*, pp. 20-2. Gathorne-Hardy, *Rise and Fall*, pp. 178-9.
101 Gathorne-Hardy, *Rise and Fall*, p. 178.
102 Stokes, *Norland*, pp. 150-4.
103 'Mary Ann Gibbs', *Year of the Nannies*, p. 188. Gathorne-Hardy, *Rise and Fall*, p. 179.
104 Gathorne-Hardy, *Rise and Fall*, pp. 184, 185.
105 Middleton, *When Family Failed*, p. 279.
106 *Report of the Interdepartmental Committee on the Care of Children*, PP 1945-46, Vol. X, pp. 54-5.
107 *Home Office: Report on the work of the Children's Branch*, April 1923, p. 35.
108 L. Rose, *Erosion of Childhood*, p. 49.
109 *Sixty-second Annual Report of Dr Barnardo's Homes for 1927*, pp. 7-8.
110 Records of the Central London District School, Hanwell, for June 1926, LMA, CLSD.249.
111 Parish of Bermondsey: Service Register for those leaving the Shirley Schools, LMA, BBG.618/18.
112 Butler, *Domestic Service*, pp. 80-1.
113 Middleton, *When Family Failed*, p. 121.
114 Ibid., p. 257.
115 Mrs E. Slade of Welling, Kent, in correspondence with the author, 5 September 1974.
116 Stroud, *Thirteen Penny Stamps*, p. 199.
117 Ibid., p. 119.
118 *Report of the Interdepartmental Committee on the Care of Children*, pp. 69-70.
119 *Sixty-ninth Annual Report of Dr Barnardo's Homes for 1934*, pp. 15, 17, 19,35.
120 *Sixty-eighth Annual Report of Dr Barnardo's Homes for 1933*, p. 33.
121 *Sixty-fourth Annual Report of Dr Barnardo's Homes for 1929*, pp. 16-17. *Sixty-eighth Annual Report of Dr Barnardo's Homes for 1933*, p. 33. *Seventy-third Annual Report of Dr Barnardo's Homes for 1938*, pp. 39-40.
122 *Seventy-third Annual Report of Dr Barnardo's Homes*, p. 39.

123 J. Rose, *For the Sake of the Children*, p. 73.

124 Ibid., p. 73.

125 Ibid., p. 70.

126 Ibid., pp. 70-1.

127 Ibid., pp. 162, 201.

128 E. S. Turner, *What the Butler Saw*, p. 286.

129 *The Times*, 11 December 1937.

130 *The Times*, 19 May and 2 June 1936.

FOUR

1 Waterson (ed.), *Country House Remembered*, p. 145.

2 Duchess of Devonshire, *Estate*, pp. 132-3.

3 See, for example, *Gardeners' Chronicle*, 27 August 1927, recording that one head gardener had received a legacy of £600 from his former employer and another £150. Waterson (ed.), *Country House Remembered*, p. 142.

4 Festing, *Gertrude Jekyll*, pp. 137, 283-5,303.

5 Hamilton, Warden, 'Studley Agricultural and Horticultural College for Women' in *Women Workers Quarterly*, September 1913, Vol. XXIII, no. 2 in WAR.5/14/5, URA. See also *Prospectus of Studley College, Warwickshire for 1933*, 'Department of Horticulture', 12, detailing the careers of former students, URA.

6 *Gardeners' Chronicle*, 22 January 1938.

7 *Gardeners' Chronicle*, 14 May 1938, letter from S.M.R.M., Wokingham.

8 Waterson (ed.), *The Country House Remembered*, p. 146.

9 Ibid., pp. 152-3.

10 Ibid., p. 156.

11 *Gardeners' Chronicle*, 5 March 1938.

12 See, for example, an advertisement for a gardener in the Parks Superintendent's Department in the Borough of Tottenham in *Gardeners' Chronicle*, 29 January 1938. This offered a wage of £3 4s 6d a week, with superannuation to be deducted at 5 per cent. That was perhaps twice the money earned by a gardener in private service.

13 Willes, *Country House Estates*, p. 20.

14 Waterson (ed.), *Country House Remembered*, p. 158.

15 Letter from Lady Astor's secretary to W. Camm at Cliveden, 10 September 1928 and from Lady Astor to W. Camm, 15 November 1928, in MS.1416/1/2/42, URA.

16 *Gardeners' Chronicle*, 12 March 1927.

17 Eley, *Here is Mr Streeter*, p. 95.

18 Ibid., pp. 103-4.

19 Balderson with Goodlad, *Backstairs Life in a Country House*, 81. TS at MHM, OR.30.

20 Tyack, 'Service on the Cliveden Estate Between the Wars', p. 74.

21 Waterson (ed.), *Country House Remembered*, pp. 146-8.

22 Pearson, *Façades*, p. 337.

23 Gregory, *Gardener's Life*, pp. 21-2.

24 Ibid., pp. 16-17.

25 MHM Oral History Transcripts, OR.38.

26 Gregory, *Gardener's Life*, pp. 3, 8.

27 Eley, *Here is Mr Streeter*, pp. 89-90.

28 Ibid., p. 90.

29 Gregory, *Gardener's Life*, p. 6.

30 Ibid., p. 13.

31 Ibid., pp. 8-9.

32 ARC, Oral History Transcript QD1/FLWE/11.

33 Chorley, *Manchester Made Them*, p. 34.

34 Ibid., pp. 42-3.

35 *Population Census for England and Wales for 1911: Occupations*, PP 1913, Vol. LXXXVIII, xxv. *Population Census for England and Wales for 1921: Classification of Industries*, p. 201.

36 *Gardeners' Chronicle*, 18 June 1938.

37 *Gardeners' Chronicle*, 5 February 1938.

38 Mrs Hilda Rickard of Marldon, near Paignton, in correspondence with the author, 31 August 1974.

39 Waterson (ed.), *Country House Remembered*, pp. 157-8, 179.

40 Lewis, *Private Life of a Country House*, p. 42.

41 Ibid.,p.43.

42 Eley, *Here is Mr Streeter*, p. 103.

43 SHOHT R.90-001-0001 and R.89-006-0001.

44 Willes, *Country House Estates*, p. 22.

45 *Gardeners' Chronicle*, 5 January 1935.

46 *Gardeners' Chronicle*, 5 February 1938.

47 IWMSA,19669.

48 Tillyard, *Unemployment Insurance in Great Britain 1911-48*, pp. 48, 49, 158-9.

49 Tyack, *Service on the Cliveden Estate*, pp. 75-6.

50 Albert R. Butler of Winchcombe, Gloucestershire, in correspondence with the author, 27 August 1974.

51 Inch, *Reminiscences of a Life in Private Service*, p. 19.

52 T. Humphris, *Garden Glory*, pp. 30, 39-40, 91, 96.

53 Ibid., p. 116.

54 Ibid., p. 125-7.

55 Ibid., p. 128.

56 Ibid., p. 149-50.

57 Morgan & Richards, *Paradise out of a Common Field*, p. 224.

58 Waterson, *Servants' Hall*, pp. 195-6.

59 Letter from Mrs Margaret Camm, widow of the former Cliveden head gardener, to Lady Astor, 4 April 1929, pointing out that her late husband had never adopted such practices, MS.1416/1/2/52, ORA.

60 Gregory, *Gardener's Life*, p. 43.

61 SHOHT, R.89-006-0001.

62 Tyack, *Service on the Cliveden Estate*, p. 77.

63 Letter from Mrs Margaret Camm to Lady Astor, 4 April 1929, MS.1416/1/2/52, URA.

64 Cliveden Oral History Transcripts, MRL, BUT.91, Reminiscences of Mrs Spihnan, dairywoman.

65 Tyack, *Service on the Cliveden Estate*, p. 78.

66 Astor, *Tribal Feeling*, p. 65.

67 Cliveden Oral History Transcripts, MRL, BUT.91, Reminiscences of Mr Henderson, labourer and odd job man from 1928.

68 Lewis, *Private Life of the Country House*, pp. 35, 40. Willes, *Country House Estates*, p. 16.

69 *The Field*, 19 July 1928. *The Times*, 7 April 1934.

70 *Population Census for England and Wales for 1911: Occupations*, xxv. *Population Census for England and Wales for 1921: Classification of Industries*, p. 201. Thompson, *English Landed Society in the Nineteenth Century*, p. 341.

71 Lee, *Great Estates*, p. 14.

72 Cliveden Oral History Transcripts, MRL, BUT91, Reminiscences of Noel

Wiseman, assistant agent and agent at Cliveden.

73 Reminiscences of Noel Wiseman. Waterson (ed.), *Country House Remembered*, pp. 102, 108.

74 Waterson (ed.), *Country House Remembered*, pp. 105-6. Mursell, *Green and Pleasant Land*, pp. 52-3.

75 Tyack, *Service on the Cliveden Estate*, p. 77.

76 Willes, *Country House Estates*, p. 4.

77 Ibid., p. 10. Inch, *Reminiscences*, p. 21.

78 Inch, *Reminiscences*, p. 20.

79 *The Field*, 5 July and 6 September 1928.

80 Mursell, *Green and Pleasant Land*, p. 62.

81 Waterson (ed.), *Country House Remembered*, p. 174.

82 Ibid., p. 174.

83 Reminiscences of Mr Henderson, MRL.

84 Duchess of Devonshire, *Estate*, p. 82.

85 Comment by Maj. C. S. Jarvis in *Country Life*, 23 September 1939. Foyster & Proud, *Gamekeeper*, p. 87.

86 *Country Life*, 23 August 1924.

87 King, *Green Baize Door*, p. 35.

88 *The Field*, 9 August 1928.

89 T. W. Turner, *Memoirs of a Gamekeeper*, pp. 61-2.

90 Bryer, 'The Gamekeeper' in Noel Streatfeild (ed.), *Day Before Yesterday*, p. 216.

91 Waterson (ed.), *Country House Remembered*, p. 106.

92 Reminiscences of Noel Wiseman. Waterson (ed.), *Country House Remembered*.

93 *Country Life*, 29 September 1923.

94 Haggard (ed.), *I Walked by Night* by *The King of the Norfolk Poachers*, pp. 120-1.

95 *Country Life*, 28 August 1926 and 30 April 1927.

96 See 'Occupations' section of the 1911, 1921 and 1931 *Population Censuses* for England and Wales and for Scotland.

97 T. W. Turner, *Memoirs of a Gamekeeper*, pp. 146-7.

98 Foyster & Proud, *Gamekeeper*, p. 21, mentions that Foyster's father was a horseman on an estate farm; he had earlier been a keeper.

99 *The Field*, 16 February 1928.

100 Humphries & Hopwood, *Green and Pleasant Land*, p. 70.

101 Ibid., p. 70.

102 Mursell, *Come Dawn, Come Dusk*, p. 85.

103 Duchess of Devonshire, *Estate*, p. 103. Even in 1990 there were seven gamekeepers and three river keepers on the Chatsworth estate.

104 T. W. Turner, *Memoirs of a Gamekeeper*, p. 40.

105 *The Times*, 9 October 1999.

106 Humphries & Hopwood, *Green and Pleasant Land*, p. 66.

107 Waterson (ed.), *Country House Remembered*, p. 98.

108 Mursell, *Come Dawn, Come Dusk*, Preface by John Humphreys.

109 Duchess of Devonshire, *Estate*, p. 92.

110 Duchess of Devonshire, *House*, pp. 47-8.

111 Mursell, *Come Dawn, Come Dusk*, p. 41.

112 Foyster & Proud, *Gamekeeper*, pp. 44-5. See also Nudds, *Woods Belong to Me*, pp. 33-5.

113 Mursell, *Come Dawn, Come* Dusk, p. 43.

114 Foyster & Proud, *Gamekeeper*, pp. 50-1.

115 T. W. Turner, *Memoirs of a Gamekeeper*, p. 143.

116 Humphries & Hopwood, *Green and Pleasant Land*, pp. 71-2.

117 Ibid., p. 57.

118 Ibid., p. 58.
119 Ibid., p. 73.
120 Mursell, *Come Dawn, Come Dusk*, p. 95.
121 Ibid., p. 50.
122 Ibid., p. 52.
123 Ibid., p. 53.
124 Foyster & Proud, *Gamekeeper*, p. 73.
125 Mursell, *Come Dawn, Come Dusk*, p. 9. T. W. Turner, *Memoirs of a Gamekeeper*, p. 46.
126 Mursell, *Come Dawn, Come Dusk*, pp. 14-15.
127 Foyster & Proud, *Gamekeeper*, p. 124.
128 Duchess of Devonshire, *Estate*, p. 90.
129 Ibid., p. 82.
130 Reminiscences of Noel Wiseman. Waterson (ed.), *Country House Remembered*.
131 Mursell, *Green and Pleasant Land*, pp. 53-4.
132 *Gardeners' Chronicle*, 29 January 1927.
133 Mursell, *Green and Pleasant Land*, p. 53.
134 *Report of the Departmental Committee Appointed in November 1919 to Enquire on Land in Scotland Used as Deer Forests*, PP 1922, Vol. VII, p. 22.
135 *Country Life*, 23 December 1933. Imrie, *Keeper's Year*, p. 74.
136 *Country Life*, 7 August 1937.

FIVE

1 Calculated from *General Report of the Census of Population for England and Wales for 1931*, p. 152.
2 *Report of the Ministry of Labour Committee on the Supply of Female Domestic Servants*, p. 15.
3 Butler, *Domestic Service*, p. 37.
4 Powell, *Below Stairs*, pp. 78, 79.
5 Stirling Women's Oral Project: Domestic Service, Q.2.
6 Ibid., R.2.
7 Duchess of Devonshire, *House*, p. 60.
8 Letter to Lady Astor, 1 July 1932 URA, MS.1416/1/6/110.
9 ARC, Oral History Transcript QD1/FLWE/359.
10 Mrs Winifred Cardew to the author, 15 July 1999.
11 Mullins & Griffiths, *Cap and Apron*, p. 31. *General Report of the Census for England and Wales for 1931*, p. 152. *The Times*, 7 November 1952.
12 Mrs H. M. P. Gordon of London to the author, 25 September 1974.
13 Butler, *Domestic Service*, p. 16.
14 *Sixty-ninth Annual Report of Dr Barnardos Homes for 1934*, pp. 15, 35.
15 Lewis & Maude, *English Middle Classes*, p. 215. First published in 1949.
16 Dawes, *Not in Front of the Servants*, p. 131.
17 ARC, Oral History Transcript QD1/FLWE/210.
18 Butler, *Domestic Service*, p. 29.
19 Ibid., p. 29.
20 Dickens, *One Pair of Hands*, pp. 32, 65-8.
21 Mullins & Griffiths, *Cap and Apron*, p. 31.
22 *Mrs Beeton's Household Management*, pp. 10, 11.
23 Stirling Women's Oral Project: Domestic Service, R.2.
24 Ibid.
25 Winstanley, *Life in Kent at the Turn of the Century*, p. 163.
26 Powell, *Below Stairs*, p. 78. NVA Records at the Women's Library, Box 119, Report on Isabella Rogerson, 8 May 1931.

27 *YWCA Newsletter*, April 1920. Heath-Stubbs, *Friendship's Highway*, p. 25.

28 Miss G. J. Goff in correspondence with the author in 1974. Heath-Stubbs, *Friendship's Highway*, p. 25.

29 Miss G. J. Goff to the author, 1974.

30 Records of Domestic Workers' Guild: Hampstead and Area: Aims and Objects of the Guild: letter from Dorothy M. Elliott to Miss Nancy Adam, 30 December 1932; memorandum on the Organisation of Youth by Dorothy Elliott, 13 December 1933; and List of Fixtures for January 1933, at MRC, MS.292/54.76/4.

31 Organisation of the National Union of Domestic Workers: Organiser's Report for the five weeks ending 27 March 1939 and *Annual Report* for the year ending June 1939 at MRC, MSS.292/54.76/6.

32 Mrs E. Slade of Walling, Kent to the author, 5 September 1974.

33 Mrs E. Timms, Chadlington, Oxfordshire, to the author, 10 September 1974.

34 Dawes, *Not in Front of the Servants*, p. 128.

35 Powell, *Below Stairs*, p. 77. Robinson, *Memories of Upper Bangor*, p. 39.

36 Powell, *Below Stairs*, pp. 63, 73.

37 Dawes, *Not in Front of the Servants*, p. 131.

38 Gordon & Breitenbach (ed.), *World is Ill Divided*, p. 23.

39 Dawes, *Not in Front of the Servants*, pp. 125-6.

40 Ibid., p. 126.

41 MHM TS, OR.30.

42 Powell, *Below Stairs*, pp. 123-5.

43 Dawes, *Not in Front of the Servants*, p. 59.

44 MHM TS, OR.30.

45 SHOHT, R.87-008-0001 and R.87.005-0001, recollections of kitchen maid and stillroom maid at Shugborough in the 1920s and the beginning of the 1930s and Reminiscences of Mrs Lily Milgate at MHM, OR.37.

46 R. Harrison, *Rose*, p. 104. Tyack, 'Service on the Cliveden Estate' in *Oral History*, vol. 5, No.1, pp. 81, 82.

47 R. Harrison, ibid., pp. 104-5 and Tyack, ibid., p. 81.

48 Laurie (ed.), *Cricketer Preferred*, title page, p. 33.

49 Ibid., p. 13.

50 Tyack, 'Service on the Cliveden Estate' in *Oral History*, p. 66.

51 Duchess of Devonshire, *House*, p. 66.

52 Inch, *Reminiscences*, pp. 113-14.

53 Ibid., p. 112.

54 Balderson with Goodlad, *Backstairs Life*, pp. 51-2 and MHM TS, OR.30.

55 Balderson with Goodlad, ibid., pp. 68-71 and MHM TS, OR.30.

56 Mullins & Griffiths, *Cap and Apron*, p. 13.

57 E. Horne, *More Winks*, p. 58.

58 Powell, *Below Stairs*, pp. 87-8.

59 Noakes, *Town Beehive*, p. 42. See also King, *Green Baize Door*, p. 41.

60 MHM TS, OR.30.

61 A. Thomas, *Wait and See*, pp. 97, 100.

62 Inch, *Reminiscences*, p. 107.

63 Waterson (ed.), *Country House Remembered*, p. 173.

64 Inch, *Reminiscences*, p. 64.

65 Mullins & Griffiths, *Cap and Apron*, p. 17.

66 R. Harrison, *Rose*, pp. 106-7,205.

67 Winstanley, *Life in Kent*, pp. 218, 220.

68 *Mrs Beeton's Household Management*, p. 10.

69 Quoted in Taylor, 'Daughters and mothers – maids and mistresses: domestic service between the wars' in Clarke, Critcher and Johnson (ed.), *Working Class*

Culture, p. 135.

70 Davison, *Etiquette for Women*, p. 121.

71 Firth, *Psychology of the Servant Problem*, p. 20.

72 Mrs Alfred Sidgwick, 'The Professional Home-Maker. Another View of Domestic Service' in *Good Housekeeping*, September 1923.

73 Catalogue of *Domestic Services Exhibition*, 15-21 January 1938, at the TUCL, HD.6072.

74 *Newsletter of the National Union of Domestic Workers*, March/April 1949 at MRC, MSS.292/54.76/27, and *Report on the Post-War Organisation of Private Domestic Employment*, PP 1944-45, Vol. V, p. 19.

75 Darcy, *Problems and Changes in Women's Work in England and Wales, 1918-1939*, pp. 53-5, 72.

76 Llewellyn Smith (ed.), *New Survey of London Life and Labour*, Vol. II, pp. 429-30.

77 *Report of the Ministry of Labour Committee on the Supply of Female Domestic Servants*, p. 20.

78 *The Times*, 17 April 1937.

79 Ibid.

80 Taylor, 'Daughters and Mothers', p. 126.

81 Sambrook, *Country House Servant*, p. 222.

82 Mrs Winifred Cardew to the author, 15 July 1999.

83 Robinson, *Memories of Upper Bangor*, p. 38.

84 See correspondence dated 21 and 24 October 1926 on display at Dyrham Park, Gloucestershire, 1 April 2000.

85 Taylor, 'Daughters and Mothers', p. 133.

86 Powell, *Below Stairs*, p. 58.

87 *The Times*, 20 June 1928.

88 Minutes of the YWCA Industrial Law Bureau: see, for example, 26 January 1922, at MRC, MSS.243/139/3. *The Times*, 5 April 1928.

89 Taylor, 'Daughters and Mothers', pp. 130-1.

90 Firth, *Psychology of the Servant Problem*, pp. 20-1.

91 Notes sent to the author by Mrs Martin of Luton, 3 September 1974.

92 Daisy White of Purley in correspondence with the author, September 1974.

93 *Mrs Beeton's Household Management*, p. 11.

94 *Gardeners' Chronicle*, 15 January 1927.

95 *Catalogue of the Domestic Services Exhibition* at the TUCL, HD.6072.

96 London *Evening Standard*, 30 June 1938. See also 5 and 9 July 1938.

97 Balderson with Goodlad, *Backstairs Life*, pp. 9, 46.

98 Ibid., p. 42.

99 Inch, *Reminiscences*, pp. 96-9.

100 Ibid., pp. 83, 85.

101 Beddoe, *Back to Home and Duty*, p. 53.

102 Waterson (ed.), *Country House Remembered*, p. 184.

103 Ibid., pp. 190-1.

104 Festing, *Gertrude Jekyll*, pp. 227, 234, 301.

105 Waterson (ed.), *Country House Remembered*, p. 173.

106 Mullins & Griffiths, *Cap and Apron*, pp. 16-17.

107 Information provided by Mrs Mary Cocking in correspondence with the author, April 1999.

108 Duchess of Devonshire, *House*, p.64.

109 MHM TS, OR.30.

110 Duchess of Devonshire, *House*, p. 61.

111 Tyack, 'Service on the Cliveden Estate', p. 81.

112 *The Times*, 7 July 1925 and 17 June 1937, to quote two examples.

113 Sambrook, *Country House Servant*, p. 230.
114 Noakes, *Town Beehive*, p. 45.
115 Waterson (ed.), *Country House Remembered*, p. 197.
116 Ibid., p. 187.
117 Ibid., p. 193.
118 London *Evening Standard*, 28 June 1938. Lucy Sinclair, *Bridgeburn Days*, p. 221.
119 Middleton, *When Family Failed*, p. 259.
120 Quoted in Taylor, 'Daughters and Mothers', pp. 136, 138.
121 *The Times*, 17 April 1937.
122 Mullins & Griffiths, *Cap and Apron*, p. 18.
123 Inch, *Reminiscences*, pp. 43, 85, 93.
124 R. Harrison, *Rose*, p. 35.
125 Ibid., pp. 37-8.
126 Ibid., p. 88.
127 Rennie, *Every Other Sunday*, p. 51.
128 Duchess of Devonshire, *House*, p. 60.
129 Robinson, *Memories of Upper Bangor*, p. 39.
130 Dawes, *Not in Front of the Servants*, p. 121.
131 Records of the Training Centre at Ystrad, Rhondda at the PRO,LAB.2/1365/ ED.730/19/1929.
132 Dawes, *Not in Front of the Servants*, pp. 121-2.
133 C. Jones (ed.), *The Social Survey of Merseyside*, Vol. II, pp. 314-15.
134 *Labour Party: A Domestic Workers' Charter* at MRC, MSS.292/54.76/2. Charter in *Labour Woman*, February 1919. This charter concluded that no 'satisfactory arrangement of the domestic problem can ever be reached until the workers themselves have strong organisations to deal with their side of the matter'.
135 P. Horn, *Rise and Fall of the Victorian Servant*, p. 179.
136 Lewenhak, *Women and Trade Unions*, p. 181.
137 *Labour Woman*, August 1920. Horn, *Rise and Fall*, pp. 179-80.
138 *Labour Woman*, August 1920. Horn, *Rise and Fall*, p. 180.
139 Ibid.
140 P. Horn, *Rise and Fall*, p. 180.
141 *Daily News*, 27 January 1920.
142 Letter from National Domestic Union Edinburgh to Sir Walter Citrine, General Secretary of the TUC, 18 January 1937, reminding him that they had been in existence since 1919, at MRC, MSS.292/54.76/5. *Daily News*, 27 January 1920.
143 *What's Wrong with Domestic Service? We Want to Know What You Think*, pamphlet published by the Labour Party, 1930 in TUCL, HD.6072. Sheila Lewenhak, op. cit., p. 207.
144 *Labour Party: A Domestic Workers' Charter*, circulated at the National Conference of Labour Women, 2-4 June 1931 at MRC, MSS.292/54.76/2.
145 Dorothy M. Elliott, Hon Secretary of the Domestic Workers' Guild, Hampstead to Nancy Adam, Chief Woman Officer of the TUC, 30 December 1932, at MRC, MSS.292/54.76/4. *Report of the Sixty-fourth Annual Trades Union Congress for 1932*, p. 106, TUCL.
146 Letter from the Secretary of the Organisation Department of the TUC to Mr A. J. Smith, Hampstead Trades Council, 23 September 1937, MRC, MSS.292/54.76/5.
147 *Report of the Seventieth Annual Trades Union Congress for 1938*, p. 101, TUCL.
148 Ibid., pp. 73, 97.
149 *News Chronicle*, 14 December 1938. E. P. Harries, Secretary of the Organisation

Department of the TUC to Members of the National Union of Domestic Workers, 16 June 1938, at MRC, MSS.292/54.76/1. See also details of Miss Bezzant in MSS.292/54.76/10 and MSS.292/54.76/6.

150 Memorandum from E. P. Harries, Organisation Department, to Sir Walter Citrine, 28 June 1938 at MRC, MSS.292/54.76/1.

151 Dawes, *Not in Front of the Servants*, p. 150. *Annual Report of the National Union of Domestic Workers for the year ending 30 June 1939* at MRC, MSS.292/54.76/6 and *Organisation of Domestic Workers*, at MRC, MSS.292/54.76/7.

152 *Steps*. Charter for Domestic Workers drawn up by the NUDW; 1938, TUCL, HD.6072.

153 Report of the NUDW Organiser for the five weeks ending 27 March 1939, at MRC, MSS.292/54.76/6.

154 *Report of the Seventy-first Annual Trades Union Congress for 1939*, 138 in TUCL.

155 Minutes of the National Advisory Committee of the NUDW; 12 July 1939, at MRC, MSS.292/54.76/57.

156 Minutes of the National Advisory Committee of the NUDW; 7 June 1939.

157 *Report of the Seventy-first Annual Trades Union Congress for 1939*, p. 139. Memorandum from E. P. Harries to Sir Walter Citrine, 28 June 1938, at MRC, MSS.292/54.76/1.

158 'A Manager', *Behind the Swing Doors*, pp. 8, 11, 12, 13, TUCL, HD.9999.c.4b. 'Hotel and Catering Trades' in Llewellyn Smith (ed.), *New Survey of London Life and Labour*, Vol. VIII, p. 223.

159 Organisation of Domestic Workers at MRC, MSS.292/54.76/7.

160 Ibid. and report of correspondence with Miss Bezzant in July 1946. The report concluded: 'No further communication from Miss Bezzant and it is understood that she has now been placed in a post as Inspector of Approved Schools under the Home Office', at MRC, MSS.292/54.76/7.

161 Records of the National Union of Domestic Workers at the PRO, LAB.69/96. In 1951 the union's total membership was put at six males and fifty-nine females; in 1952 it was taken as fifty females only.

162 Minute from Miss D. Hunwicks, 30 August 1955 and endorsement on file: 'Ceased to Exist, 1954'. In her minute Miss Hunwicks stressed that 'the whole subject' was 'a delicate one'; at the PRO, LAB.69/96.

SIX

1 Johnson, *Emigration from the United Kingdom to North America*, p. 264. First published in 1913.

2 Minutes of the Employment and Emigration Department Committee of the YWCA, meetings on 16 July 1913 and 8 April 1914 at MRC, MSS.243/131/4. Carrothers, *Emigration from the British Isles*, for discussion of the fluctuations in policy with regard to assisted passages to Canada, Australia and New Zealand.

3 Johnson, *Emigration from the United Kingdom to North America*, p. 264.

4 *Daily News*, 27 January 1920.

5 *Report to the President of the Oversea Settlement Committee on Openings in New Zealand for Women from the United Kingdom*, PP 1920, Vol. XXII, pp. 4-5. See also *Report to the President of the Oversea Settlement Committee on Openings in Canada for Women from the United Kingdom*, PP 1919, Vol. XXXI, p. 4.

6 Johnson, *Emigration from the United Kingdom to North America*, p. 269.

7 Heath-Stubbs, *Friendship's Highway*, pp. 70-2.

8   Ibid., p. 70.

9   Johnson, *Emigration from the United Kingdom to North America*, p. 264.

10 Minutes of the Employment and Emigration Department Committee of the YWCA, meetings on 16 July 1913 and 8 April 1914, loc. cit.

11 Johnson, *Emigration from the United Kingdom to North America*, p. 265.

12 J. Rose, *For the Sake of the Children*, p. 83.

13 Ibid., p. 88. Parr, *Labouring Children*, pp. 126, 131 for the loneliness of domestic work on Canadian farmsteads.

14 J. Rose, ibid., pp. 90, 91. Parr, ibid., pp. 105, 115.

15 Parr, *Labouring Children*, p. 152.

16 Stokes, *Norland*, pp. 57-8.

17 Mitchell & Deane, *Abstract of British Historical Statistics*, pp. 50-51. From 1931 onwards there was net inward migration to Britain, but at no time after 1918 did emigration reach the levels achieved immediately before 1914.

18 Briar, *Working for Women?* p. 58.

19 *Report of the Oversea Settlement Committee for the year ending 31 December 1922*, PP 1923, Vol. XII, Pt. 2, p. 13.

20 Ibid., p. 14.

21 *Report to the President of the Oversea Settlement Committee on Openings in Canada*, p. 4.

22 *Report to the President of the Oversea Settlement Committee on Openings in Australia for Women from the United Kingdom*, PP 1920, Vol. XXII, p. 6.

23 Heath-Stubbs, *Friendship's Highway*, p. 75.

24 *Report of the Oversea Settlement Committee for the year ending 31 December 1922* p. 28

25 Ibid., pp. 20, 23. *Record of the Proceedings and Documents of the Imperial Economic Conference held in October and November 1923*, PP 1924, Vol. X, pp. 144, 145, 148. From 1 January 1924, the Canadian Government offered a rebate of £6 on the average 3rd class fare of about £16 to single, female household workers who settled on farms.

26 *The Times*, 10 November 1927.

27 Cecillie Swaisland, *Servants and Gentlewomen to the Golden Land*, p. 106. *GFS Magazine*, February 1929, for example, for advertisement of vacancies for children's nurses in Cape Province, Kenya and Rhodesia 'at £60 a year, free passages'.

28 J. Rose, *For the Sake of the Children*, p. 105.

29 Ibid., p. 106.

30 Ibid., pp. 108-10.

31 Minutes of the Employment and Migration Committee of the GFS, meetings on 7 October 1924 and 1 June 1928, 1/47 in GFS Archives. *Annual Report of the GFS for 1929*, p. 64. Heath Stubbs, *Friendship's Highway*, p. 196.

32 Minutes of the Employment and Migration Committee of the GFS, meetings on 26 February 1926, 7 December 1928, 10 January 1930 and 6 March 1931. *Annual Report of the GFS for 1935*, p. 58.

33 *Annual Report of the GFS for 1922*, p. 76.

34 Violet Markham to Dame Meriel Talbot, 7 and 13 December 1926 in Markham MSS. 3/15.

35 *Hansard*, 5th Series, Vol. 205, 14 April 1927, col. 634.

36 *Report of the Ministry of Labour for 1927*, PP 1928, Vol. XI, p. 25.

37 *The Times*, 3 and 12 December 1927 and 4 February 1928.

38 *The Times*, 12 December 1927.

39 *The Times*, 4 February 1928.

40 *The Times*, 12 December 1927.

41 *Annual Report of the Ministry of Labour for 1928*, PP 1928-29, Vol. VII, p. 40.

42 *Annual Report of the Ministry of Labour for 1929*, PP 1929-30, Vol. Xv, p. 45.

43 *Ministry of Labour Gazette*, May 1929. *Annual Report of the Ministry of Labour for 1932*, PP 1932-33, Vol. XIII, p. 39.

44 *GFS Magazine*, October 1929.

45 *Annual Report of the GFS for 1929*, p. 64. *Annual Report of the Ministry of Labour for 1930*, PP 1930-31, Vol. XV, p. 45.

46 *Hansard*, 5th Series, Vol. 241, 21 July 1930, col. 1762.

47 *Annual Report of the Ministry of Labour for 1930*, p. 45.

48 *Annual Report of the GFS for 1930*, p. 62.

49 *Annual Report of the Ministry of Labour for 1931*, PP 1931-32, Vol. XI, p. 40.

50 *Annual Report of the GFS for 1930*, p. 42.

51 *Annual Report of the GFS for 1932*, p. 60.

52 *Annual Report of the GFS for 1922*, p. 75. *Annual Report of the GFS for 1932*, p. 61.

53 Minutes of the Employment and Migration Committee of the GFS, meeting on 5 October 1934.

54 *Sixty-eighth Annual Report of Dr Barnardo's Homes for 1933*, p. 32.

55 *The Times*, 7 December 1927.

56 King, *Green Baize Door*, p. 52. Harrison, *Rose*, pp. 138-9.

57 King, *Green Baize Door*, pp. 72, 77.

58 Stokes, *Norland*, pp. 54, 60.

59 Waterson (ed.), *Country House Remembered*, p. 219.

60 Pay Roll no. 1 for Cliveden at Buckinghamshire Record Office, D.158/29. Harrison, *Rose*, p. 119.

61 R. Harrison, *Rose*, p. 119.

62 P. Horn, *Rise and Fall of the Victoria Servant*, pp. 99-100.

63 Ibid., p. 34.

64 *1911 Census of Population for England and Wales: Occupations*, PP 1913, Vol. LXXVIII, pp. xxii, xxv.

65 S. Jackson, *Savoy*, pp. 24, 34, 35, 126.

66 *1991 Census of Population for England and Wales: Occupations*, p. cxvii. *Memorandum by the Minister of Labour on the Procedure regulating the entry of Foreigners for Employment in Great Britain. Aliens Order 1920* (London, 1933), p. 4, in LAB.8/871 at the PRO.

67 *Memorandum by the Minister of Labour on the Procedure Regulating the Entry of Foreigners for Employment in Great Britain* (1933), pp. 4-5.

68 S. Jackson, *Savoy*, p. 194.

69 Information from the Museum of London on Restaurant Boulestin. Parkin & Hooker, *Salute to Marcel Boulestin and Jean-Emile Laboureur* (London, 1981), pp. 9-27.

70 *The Times*, 7 February 1939 and letter from 'British Waiter' in the *Daily Herald*, 2 July 1938.

71 *1931 Census of Population for England and Wales: Occupations* (London, 1934), pp. 148, 152-3.

72 *The Times*, 18 November 1938.

73 For details of the poor working conditions of British hotel staff at the end of the 1930s see, for example, 'Manager', *Behind the Swing Doors* (London pamphlet n.d. [*c.* 1938]) TUCL, HD.9999. c.46.

74 *Report of the Ministry of Labour for 1925*, PP 1926, Vol. XIII, p. 49.

75 London, 'British Immigration Control Procedures and Jewish Refugees 1933-1939' in Mosse et al. (ed.), *Second Chance*, pp. 489-91.

76 *The Times*, 10 November 1927.

77 See advertisements in *The Times*, 10 November 1927 and the *Post Office Trade Directory for London for 1935 and 1939*, in the London Metropolitan Library.

78 For reports on Mrs Kenning's agency see records of the NVA, Box 99, at the Women's Library.

79 Letter from Maatschappelijk Advies en Inlichtingen Bureau, Central Amsterdam, 13 February 1937 to Mr Sempkins, Secretary of the NVA concerning Mrs Bockling in Box 99 at the Women's Library.

80 The Revd. J. van Dorp to Mr Sempkins, NVA, 23 April 1937 in Box 99 at the Women's Library.

81 Minutes of the YWCA Social and Legislation Committee, meeting on 15 July 1920 at MRC, MSS.243/139/1.

82 Minutes of the Industrial Law Bureau Committee of the YWCA, meeting on 4 May 1931 at MRC, MSS.243/139/7.

83 Minute by R. A. Butler, 18 November 1937 in LAB.8/77 at the PRO. 'Admission of Aliens from Abroad for Employment as Domestic Servants in Private Households' in LAB.8/92 at the PRO.

84 Calculated from 'Note on procedure with regard to permits for foreign domestics', 9 November 1937 in LAB.8/77 at the PRO.

85 Ibid. Ministry of Labour circular on *The Aliens Order*, 1920, 2 November 1938 in LAB.8/82.

86 W. R. L. Blakiston, Ministry of Labour Divisional Officer for Employment and Insurance, London to V. A. Goddard at Headquarters of Ministry of Labour, 8 September 1938, in LAB.8/82.

87 Calculated from 'Note on procedure with regard to permits for foreign domestics',   9 November 1937 in LAB.8177.

88 Statistics in ibid.

89 *1931 Census of Population for England and Wales: Occupations*, pp. 152-3. There were 3,327 foreign male indoor domestic servants in 1931, of whom 1,029 came from Italy and 842 from France.

90 'Admission of Aliens from Abroad for Employment as Domestic Servants in Private Households' in LAB.8/92 at the PRO.

91 Schneider, *Exile*, p. 4.

92 Ibid., pp. 4-6.

93 Göpfert (ed.), *Ich kam allein*, pp. 17-18, 119-20.

94 Dora Frischmann's Registration Certificate at the Manchester Jewish Museum.

95 'Trades Union Congress: German and Austrian Refugees: Domestic Employment' in records of the NUDW at MRC, MSS.292/54.76/38.

96 Minutes of the National Advisory Committee of the NUDW meeting on 1 March 1939, at MRC, MSS.292/54.76/57.

97 E. N. Cooper to Mrs M. Ormerod, 8 September 1938 and E. N. Cooper to Miss Fellner, German Jewish Aid Committee, 7 September 1938. The German Jewish Aid Committee had initially pressed for this concession in July 1938. The correspondence is in HO.213/324 at the PRO.

98 *Hansard*, 5th Series, Vol. 346, 18 April 1939, col. 190.

99 'Note on the procedure and policy in regard to the admission of foreigners for employment in the United Kingdom', November 1938, section on *au pair* arrangements in LAB.8/871 at the PRO.

100 *Annual Report of the Ministry of Labour for 1938* in PP 1938-39, Vol. XI, p. 23.

101 Tony Kushner, 'Asylum or servitude?', p. 20.

102 Sir E. W. E. Holderness at the Home Office to S. L. Besso, Ministry of Labour, 22 December 1937 in LAB.8/77.

103 *The Times*, 24 March 1939.

104 *The Times*, 13 March 1939.

105 At a cabinet meeting on 16 November 1938, the Home Secretary noted that Jewish representatives were 'unwilling to give definite figures as to the number

of Jews admitted'. CAB.23.96, 227 at the PRO.

106 Note by Beatrice Bezzant of the NUDW 14 March 1939, at MRC, MSS.292/54.76/36. Minutes of the National Advisory Committee of the NUDW meetings on 25 August and 7 December 1938 at MRC, MSS.292/54.76/57.

107 E. P. Harries to Sir Walter Citrine, 29 August 1938 at MRC, MSS.292/54.76/36.

108 Nelly Marsh to Beatrice Bezzant, n.d. [c. 13 November 1938] at MRC, MSS.292/54,76/11. On 21 November 1938, a TUC deputation went to the Minister of Labour to ask for 'control of the entry of foreign domestic workers into this country'. *The Times*, 22 November 1938.

109 Minutes of the National Advisory Committee of the NUDW meetings on 11 January and 1 February 1939 at MRC, MSS.292/54.76/57.

110 Minutes of the National Advisory Committee of the NUDW meetings on 8 July 1941 and 9 December 1941 at MRC, MSS.292/54.76/57.

111 Tony Kushner, 'Politics and Race, Gender and Class', pp. 52-3.

112 IWMSA, 003816.

113 'Our English colleagues and us', TS magazine produced by Austrian refugees in Britain, in NUDW archives at MRC, MSS.292/54.76/36.

114 Rainer Kolmel, 'Problems of Settlement' in Hirschfield (ed.) *Exile in Great Britain*, p. 259.

115 IWMSA, 04588.

116 Mrs H. M. P. Gordon of London to the author, 25 September 1974. Kushner, 'Asylum or servitude?', p. 19.

117 Schneider, *Exile*, p. 22.

118 Josephs, *Survivors*, p. 137.

119 Kolmel, 'Problems of Settlement', p. 259.

120 *Mistress and Maid*, London, April 1940, anonymous leaflet issued by the Domestic Bureau and available in the Wiener Library, London, S.3b.

121 Josephs, *Survivors*, p. 139.

122 Douglas Biart to the author, 25 February and 1 March 2000.

123 B. Atkinson of Manningtree, Essex, 15 August 1939 in FO.371/241000 W.12043 at the PRO.

124 Central Training Sub-Committee: Domestic Bureau Correspondence, information on the Richmond Training Centre in YWCA Records at MRC, MSS.243/92/3. Letter from National General Secretary, YWCA to E. N. Cooper, Aliens Department: the Home Office, 20 January 1939, and his reply on 30 January 1939, also in MSS.243/92/3.

125 Letters from Mrs K. V. Harland to Miss Rattray at the YWCA, 1 and 22 April 1939 at MRC, MSS.243/92/3.

126 Reports on Trainees, 1939 and 1940 in YWCA Archives at MRC, MSS.243/92/4.

127 Reports on Trainees, 1939 and 1940 in YWCA Archives at MRC, MSS.243/92/4.

128 Sir E. W. E. Holderness of the Home Office to Maj. Gen. Sir H. Martelli, 4 July 1938 in HO.213/281 at PRO.

129 Capt. M. Jeffes, Passport Control Department to E. N. Cooper, Home Office, 5 June 1939 in HO.213/107 at PRO.

130 Schneider, *Exile*, p. 115.

131 Berghahn, *German-Jewish Refugees in England*, p. 119.

132 Segal, *Other People's Houses*, p. 78.

133 Ibid., pp. 80-1, 82.

134 IWMSA, 004296.

135 Meeting on Tribunals, 14 September 1939, comment by Lord Reading in HO.213/452 at PRO.

136 Schneider, *Exile*, p. 73.

137 Report on 'YWCA and Refugees', n.d. [*c.* July 1940] at MRC, MSS.243/92/3.

138 Berghahn, *German-Jewish Refugees in England*, p. 139. Kushner, 'An Alien Occupation' in Mosse et al. (ed.), *Second Chance*, pp. 572-3.

139 Schneider, *Exile*, pp. 70-1.

140 Ibid., p. 95.

141 Ibid., pp. 98, 127-8.

142 *Hansard*, 5th Series, Vol. 357,1 March 1940, col. 2410-2411 and *The Times*, 2 March 1940.

143 F. Lafitte, *The Internment of Aliens*, pp. 169-70.

144 Ibid., p. 171-2.

145 Ibid., p. 172.

146 Memorandum from Sir Nevile Bland, 14 May 1940 in FO.371/25189 W:7984 at the PRO.

147 *Hansard* (House of Lords), 5th Series, Vol. 116,23 May 1940, cols. 411-415.

148 *Hansard*, 5th Series, Vol. 362, 4 July 1940, col. 1016 and 11 July 1940, cols. 1319-1320.

149 IWMSA, 03822 for Biaria Heller and 003816 for Margot Pottlitzer.

150 IWMSA, 003816.

151 Kushner, 'An Alien Occupation', pp. 574-5.

152 Ibid., p. 575.

153 Ibid., pp. 576-7.

154 Kushner, 'Asylum or servitude?', p. 23. The Hon. Mrs Franklin of the Domestic Bureau to Beatrice Bezzant of the NUDW; 19 December 1938 in NUDW Archives at MRC, MSS.292/54,76/6. See also Kölmel, *Problems of Settlement*, pp. 259-60.

SEVEN

1 Marsh, *The Changing Social Structure*, p. 54.

2 *General Report of the 1951 Census of Population for England and Wales* (London, 1958), p.168. *Census of Population for England and Wales for 1951: Occupations* (London, 1956). *Census of Population for England and Wales for 1931: Occupations* (London, 1934).

3 *Census of Population for Scotland for 1951* (Edinburgh, 1956). The census estimated that the number of indoor domestic servants in Scotland had fallen by 46 per cent compared to 1931. (p. ix).

4 *Report on Post-War Organisation of Private Domestic Employment*, PP 1944--45, Vol. V, p.7. This report is hereafter referred to as the *Markham-Hancock Report*.

5 Mrs L. Buckley of Kettering to Violet Markham, 29 March 1946 in Markham MSS. 12/3.

6 Powell, *Below Stairs*, p. 154.

7 See *Ministry of Labour Gazette*, October 1951.

8 Summerfield, *Women Workers in the Second World War*, p. 31.

9 Robinson, *Country House at War*, pp. 12-13,46-8.

10 H. Jones (ed.), *Duty and Citizenship*, p. 150.

11 Waugh, *Put Out More Flags*, pp. 11-12,74. First published in 1942.

12 *The Lady*, 27 March 1941.

13 Robinson, *Country House at War*, p. 28.

14 T. Humphris, *Garden Glory*, pp. 101, 154, 157-8, 160, 161.

15 *The Times*, 6 August 1941. *The Lady*, 3 April 1941. *Country Life*, 8 February 1941.

16 *Census of Population for England and Wales for 1951: Occupations* and *Census of Population for Scotland for 1951*.

17 *Country Life*, 4 January 1941. T. W. Turner, *Memoirs of a Gamekeeper*, pp. 75, 78. Mursell, *Come Dawn, Come Dusk*, pp. 111, 113-14.

18 Mursell, *Come Dawn, Come Dusk*, p. 118.

19 *Censuses of Population for England and Wales and for Scotland*, 1931 and 1951.

20 Nudds, *Woods Belong to Me*, p. 60.

21 Inch, *Reminiscences*, pp. 115-16.

22 P. Horn, *Rise and Fall of the Victorian Servant*, p. 201.

23 R. Harrison, *Rose*, pp. 179, 186,203.

24 IWMSA, 11813.

25 Ibid.

26 Partridge, *Pacfist's War*, pp. 84, 91.

27 Summerfield, *Reconstructing Women's Wartime Lives*, p. 89, 307.

28 Pugh, *Women and the Women's Movement*, p. 274.

29 Balderson with Goodlad, *Backstairs Life*, p. 89.

30 Summerfield, *Reconstructing Women's Wartime Lives*, pp. 146,306.

31 Summerfield, *Women Workers in the Second World War*, pp. 34, 61.

32 Ibid, pp. 34-6. Briar, *Working for Women?* p. 75.

33 Thoms, *War, Industry and Society*, p. 47.

34 *Hansard*, 5th Series, Vol. 377, 27 January 1942, col. 566 and *Hansard*, 5th Series, Vol. 381, 21 July 1942, cols 1402-1403. Summerfield, *Women Workers in the Second World War*, p.49.

35 *Hansard*, 5th Series, Vol. 377, 27 January 1942, col. 377.

36 *The Times*, 15 February 1943.

37 Partridge, *Pacifist's War*, pp. 179, 181.

38 Quoted in Summerfield, *Women Workers in the Second World War*, p. 49.

39 *The Lady*, 20 February 1941.

40 *Hansard*, 5th Series, Vol. 383, 22 October 1942, cols 2072-2073.

41 Draft letter from Violet Markham to Ernest Bevin, n.d. [1943] in Markham MSS. 12/2.

42 *Hansard*, 5th Series, Vol. 377, 27 January 1942, col. 566.

43 *Report of the Royal Commission on Population*, Cmd. 7695 (London, 1949), pp. 182-3.

44 *The Times*, 20 February 1943.

45 *Hansard*, 5th Series, Vol. 403, 18 October 1944, col. 2402.

46 *Report of the Royal Commission on Population*, 185. See also Violet Markham draft letter to Ernest Bevin [1943] In Markham MSS., 12/2, section on home helps.

47 Hunt and Fox, *The Home Help Service in England and Wales*, SS.407 (London, 1970),
p. 3. E. S. Turner, *What the Butler Saw*, p. 294.

48 Mrs Mary Cocking of West Hoathly, Sussex, in correspondence with the author, 24 April and 5 May 1999.

49 Ibid., 24 April and 12 May 1999.

50 Letter from Mrs Sheila Chugg of Braunton Devon, to the author, 1 July 1999.

51 Ibid., n.d. [c. July 1999].

52 Violet Markham to Ernest Bevin, 19 April 1943, on 'Proposals for a Domestic Service Corps' in LAB.25/188, PRO.

53 Ibid.

54 Minutes from Miss Mary Smieton, 8 July 1943 and from Mrs A. C. M. Gulland, 7 July 1943 in LAB.25/189 at the PRO.

55 *Hansard*, 5th Series, Vol. 403, 18 October 1944, col. 2402. Elliott, *The Status of Domestic Work in the United Kingdom with Special Reference to the National Institute of Houseworkers* (Geneva, 1951), p. 7. Violet Markham to Mary

Smieton, 18 October 1943, in Markham MSS. 12/2.

56 Dorothy M. Elliott, ibid., p. 7.

57 'Memorandum on Post-War Britain of the Domestic Worker', produced
    by a Sub-Committee of Domestic Workers and TUC Women's Advisory
    Committee in Minutes of the National Union of Domestic Workers at MRC,
    MSS.292/54.76/57.

58 *Markham-Hancock Report*, pp. 3, 7-8,19.

59 See letter from Violet Markham to *The Times*, 15 January 1955.

60 *Markham-Hancock Report*, pp. 11-16,21. .

61 *Report of the Interdepartmental Committee on the Care of Children*, PP 1945-
    46, Vol. X, pp. 71,174. Briar, *Working for Women?* p. 85.

62 *Eighty-first Annual Report of Dr Barnardo's Homes for 1946*, (London, 1947),
    p. 13.

63 Information provided by Dr Barnardo's Homes. The Annual Reports of Dr
    Barnardo's Homes also confirm the decline in domestic servant or housecraft
    training in the post-war years.

64 J. Rose, *For the Sake of the Children*, pp. 200-1.

65 *The Times*, 2 February 1946. See also Violet Markham, typescript on 'Domestic
    Work', 22 January 1946, in which she referred to the 'alarming' effect on the
    birth-rate 'of the difficulties of making and keeping a home'. In Markham MSS.,
    12/9.

66 Lewis & Maude, *The English Middle Classes*, p. 256. First published in 1949.

67 See the *Population Census Reports for England and Wales*, for 1931, 1951 and
    1961.

68 Powell, *Below Stairs*, p. 156.

69 [Anon. ed.], *Mrs Beeton's Household Management*, p. viii.

70 P. Horn, *Rise and Fall of the Victorian Servant*, p. 202.

71 Waterson (ed.), *Country House Remembered*, pp. 193-4.

72 Stokes, *Norland*, pp. 105, 109-10.

73 *Newsletter of the National Union of Domestic Workers*, October 1950, at
    MRC, MSS.292/54.76/28.

74 Letter from Arthur R. Inch to the author, 15 December 1999.

75 Mullins & Griffiths, *Cap and Apron*, pp. 37-8.

76 In five issues of *The Lady* in January 1948 there were 159 domestic
    advertisements in all, including some for hotels and catering establishments. In
    the *The Lady* for 8 January 1959, there were 265 vacancies for private domestic
    staff advertised. There was a separate section for hotels and commercial
    premises. On 26 February 1959, 226 vacancies were advertised. Vacancies for
    mother's helps were mentioned, but the main emphasis was on cooks, nannies
    and occasionally, married couples.

77 Ellis (ed.), *Thatched with Gold*, p. 240. Violet Markham, TS on 'Domestic
    Work', (Markham MSS., 12/9), referred to women taking 'refuge in hotels and
    boarding-houses'.

78 Waterson (ed.), *Country House Remembered*, pp. 246-8.

79 Duchess of Devonshire, *House*, pp. 69, 74-6, 78.

80 Ibid., pp. 78-82.

81 Ibid., p. 78.

82 John, Duke of Bedford, *Silver-plated Spoon*, pp. 17-18, 180,203.

83 T. Humphris, *Garden Glory*, pp. 163, 164, 174.

84 Gregory, *Gardener's Life*, pp. 54-6, 58, 60, 62-3, 72.

85 Eley, *Here is Mr Streeter*, p. 127.

86 E. S. Turner, *What the Butler Saw*, p. 293. *The Times*, 8 February 1946.

87 Elliott, *Status of Domestic Work*, p. 9. The NIH was established under the
    Companies Act of 1929 as a company limited by guarantee and not having

share capital. See 'The National Institute of Houseworkers', extract from the *Ministry of Labour Gazette* for October 1951, in LAB.70/2 at the PRO.

88 *Training Scheme for Houseworkers: National Institute of Houseworkers* (London, n.d. [*c.* 1947]) at the TUCL, HD.6072.

89 Elliott, *Status of Domestic Work*, p. 21.

90 *The National Institute of Houseworkers Limited: Press Information* (1963) in LAB.70/2 at the PRO.

91 Elliott, *The Status of Domestic Work*, 17-19 and *Annual Reports of the Ministry of Labour and National Service* for 1948, PP 1948-49, Vol. XVII, pp. 46-7 and for 1949, PP 1950, Vol. XII, p. 38.

92 *The Employer and the Worker in Private Domestic Work*, issued by the NIH, n.d., at MRC, MSS.292/54.76/61. Elliott, ibid., pp. 12-14.

93 *Hansard*, 5th Series, Vol. 487, 27 April 1951, col. 803.

94 *Houseworker*, September 1948 at MRC, MSS.292/54.76/62a. See also *Houseworker*, January 1948, commenting that the Oxford centre was the smallest of those established.

95 'Institute Training: Experience of Five Years' Working, September 1947-August 1952' at MRC, MSS.292/54.76/ 62b.

96 *Houseworker*, January 1948.

97 *Plan for the Girl who Loves Housework*, leaflet issued by the NIH (n.d.) in Markham MSS., 12/10.

98 *Annual Report of the Ministry of Labour and National Service for 1949*, p. 38.

99 Elliott, *The Status of Domestic Work*, p. 16.

100 Ibid., p. 10.

101 NIH: 'Report on the Pre-Diploma Year', 12 June 1953, at MRC, MSS.292/ 54.76/62b.

102 Letter from Mrs S. Whiting (nee Chapman) to the author, 4 July 1999.

103 Letters from Mrs S. Whiting to the author, 4 and 11 July 1999.

104 Elliott, *Status of Domestic Work*, p. 17.

105 *The Times*, 7 November 1952, Marsh, *Changing Social Structure*, p. 147. *Annual Report of the Ministry of Labour for 1960*, PP 1960-61, Vol. XVIII, p. 34.

106 *Annual Report of the Ministry of Labour and National Service for 1949*, p. 38. NIH Ltd. 'Report on the London County Council Home Help Service', n.d. [*c.* 1949], in Markham MSS.,12/10.

107 Letter from Mrs S. Whiting to the author, 11 July 1999.

108 Mrs Kathleen M. Cripps, JP to Miss Nancy Adam, Chief Woman Officer of the TUC, 9 January 1949 at MRC, MSS.292/54.76/61.

109 *Hansard*, 5th Series, Vol. 487, 27 April 1951, cols. 803-806. *Sunday Pictorial*, 16 January 1949, under the heading 'Servant Scheme Waste of Money'. 'Report on the Cost of Training Students' by Dorothy Elliott, 22 March 1949, at MRC, MSS.292/54.76/62a.

110 *Hansard*, 5th Series, Vol. 509, 18 December 1952; written answer, col. 227.

111 *Manchester Guardian*, 26 September 1951, report headed 'Room for Economy'.

112 *NIH Annual Report*, June 1949 in Markham MSS., 12/10.

113 *The Times*, 10 July 1952.

114 *Annual Reports of the Ministry of Labour and National Service for 1952*, PP 1952-53, Vol. XlV, p. 39 and for 1953, PP 1953-54, Vol. XVI, p. 39.

115 *Annual Report of the Ministry of Labour and National Service for 1950*, PP 1950-51, Vol. XVI, p. 41. *Annual Report of the National Institute for Housecraft (Employment and Training) Limited for 1965-66*, pp. 12-13 in LAB.70/62, PRO.

116 *NIH: Progress Report to 16 January, 1954* at MRC, MSS.292/54.76/62b. *Annual Report of the Ministry of Labour for 1960*, p. 34.

117 Hunt & Fox, *Home Help Service*, pp. 3, 9-10. *Annual Report of the NIH (Employment and Training) Limited for 1964-65*, p. 13, at the TUCL, HD.6072. *Annual Report of the National Institute for Housecraft (Employment and Training) Limited for 1965-66*, pp. 12-13.

118 *Houseworker*, May-June, 1954.

119 Ibid.

120 *Houseworker*, September 1949.

121 *Annual Report of the NIH for 1964-65*, p. 14.

122 Miss M. Brodie, Executive Director, NIH to J. A. Doyle, Department of Employment and Productivity, Central Youth Employment Executive, 15 September 1970, PRO, LAB.70/9.

123 Miss M. Brodie to F. Pickford, Department of Employment, 16June 1972, PRO, LAB.70/11.

124 *Annual Report of the NIH for 1956-57*, 3-4, TUCL, HD.6072.

125 NIH, Memorandum to the Association of Education Committees, 20 August 1971, in LAB.70/11, PRO.

126 *Annual Report of the Ministry of Labour for 1959*, PP 1959-60, Vol. XVII, p. 49.

127 NIH (Employment and Training) Ltd. Points for discussion at an informal meeting on 13 January 1971, in LAB.70/10, PRO.

128 *Annual Report of the NIH for 1966-67*, pp. 7-12 listed some of the courses provided, TUCL, HD.6072.

129 *Annual Reports of the NIH for 1966-67*, p. 10 and 1964-65, p. 6.

130 The NIH (Employment and Training) Ltd. Points for discussion at an informal meeting on 13 January 1971, in LAB.70/10, PRO.

131 *Hansard*, 9 December 1971 in LAB.70/10, PRO. Letter from Robert Carr, Secretary of State for Employment to Baroness White, 17 January 1972, in LAB.70/11, PRO.

132 Miss M. Brodie, Executive Director, NIH to Sir William Alexander, Association of Education Committees, 29 August 1972. *Final Report to Directors of the NIH (Employment and Training) Ltd, 19 September 1972*, both in LAB.70/11, PRO.

133 *Hansard*, 9 December 1971, in LAB.70/10, PRO.

134 Meetings held on 19 and 21 June 1945. See Minutes in LAB.8/1208, PRO.

135 Minute by Mrs Gulland of the Ministry of Labour and National Service, 4 June 1946 in LAB.8/1208, PRO.

136 Minute from Mrs Gulland, 6 July 1946 in LAB.26/163, PRO.

137 Consultative Committee on Recruitment of Domestic Workers for Hospitals: Minutes of meeting held on 29 May 1946 in LAB.26/163, PRO.

138 *Annual Report of the Ministry of Labour and National Service for 1947*, PP 1948-49, Vol. XVII, p. 42.

139 Consultative Committee on Recruittnent of Domestic Workers for Hospitals: Minutes of meeting held on 29 May 1946 in LAB.26/163, PRO.

140 *Annual Report of the Ministry of Labour and National Service for 1947*, pp. 42-3.

141 *Annual Reports of the Ministry of Labour and National Service for 1949*, pp. 20-1 and for 1950, pp. 21-2.

142 *Hansard*, 5th Series, Vol. 413, 24 August 1945, col. 413.

143 Sir Alexander Maxwell to Sir Godfrey Ince, 19 November 1945 in LAB.8/92, PRO. See also Minute by Sir Godfrey Ince, 11 September 1945, concerning a meeting with Lord Rushcliffe and the latter's desire to bring over a domestic worker from Holland, in LAB.8/1171.

144 Violet Markham to Mary Smieton at the Ministry of Labour and National Service, 8 March 1946, in LAB.8/1171.

145 *Hansard*, 5th Series, Vol. 421, 11 April 1946, col. 2112. Letter from CM. Lead, Overseas Department of the Ministry of Labour and National Service, to Miss Nancy Adam of the National Union of Domestic Workers, 19 March 1949, MRC, MSS.292/54.76/37.

146 *Annual Report of the Ministry of Labour and National Service for 1949*, p. 22. *Annual Report of the Ministry of Labour and National Service for 1939-46*, PP 1946-47, Vol. XII, p. 209.

147 *Hansard*, 5th Series, Vol. 462, 8 March 1949, cols. 964-965.

148 *Hansard*, 5th Series, Vol. 414, 18 October 1945, col. 1365 and *Hansard*, 5th Series, Vol. 421, 11 April 1946, col. 2112.

149 *Annual Report of the Ministry of Labour and National Service for 1948*, PP 1948-49, Vol. XVII, 26. Letter from C. M. Lead of the Overseas Department of the Ministry of Labour and National Service to Miss Nancy Adam, of the NUDW, 31 December 1948, MRC, MSS.292/54.76/37.

150 C. M. Lead to Miss Nancy Adam, 31 December 1948, MRC, MSS.292/54.76/37.

151 Leaflet from Isobel Jay Ltd., International Employment Office, Hove, sent 9 June 1949 to Sir Walter Citrine at the Trades Union Congress, MRC, MSS.292/54.76/37.

152 See undated press cutting, MRC, MSS.292/54.76/37, noting that 'three million' German girls had 'no mathematical chance of getting a man at all' in their home country.

153 See undated press cutting (*c.* 1950) in MSS.292/54.76/37, MRC, MSS.292/54.76/37.

154 See cutting from the *Daily Mail* n.d. (*c.* 1952-53) in LAB.8/1905, PRO.

155 Waterson, *Servants' Hall*, pp. 200-1.

156 E.J. Toogood, Ministry of Labour and National Service to G.W.J. Cole, Councillor (Labour) British Embassy, 3 October 1956 in LAB.8/1905, PRO.

157 *Annual Report of the Ministry of Labour and National Service for 1950*, pp. 21, 28. 'Notes on the Scheme to provide a German Woman for resident domestic work in Great Britain' at MRC, MSS.292/54.76/37. 'Report on Private Domestic Workers Schemes, Germany and Austria', n.d. (*c.* 1954) in LAB.8/1905, PRO.

158 Minute on German P.D.W Scheme by Miss B.P. Boyes, 17 January 1952 and 'Report on Private Domestic Workers Schemes, Germany and Austria', both in LAB.8/1905, PRO.

159 Statement on the working of the German and Austrian schemes, 1954, in LAB.8/1905, PRO.

160 Dawes, 'The Dying Reign of the Pantry' in The *Daily Telegraph Magazine*, 6 July 1973, pp. 14-20.

161 Ibid., p. 16.

162 Dr Joyce Chalmers of Llangollen in correspondence with the author, 3 February 1999.

163 Mrs Helen Bell of Thatcham in correspondence with the author, 24 February 1999.

164 E.S. Turner, *What the Butler Saw*, pp. 295-6.

165 *Hansard*, 5th Series, Vol. 691, 16 March 1964, cols 976-977. One German *au pair* had five different places between April 1969 and January 1970; when her hosts asked her to leave, the first four invariably gave her just a few days' notice. Information and correspondence provided by Anne Jüssen, Frauen Museum, Bonn.

166 *Hansard*, 5th Series, Vol. 691, 16 March 1964, col. 976.

167 Briar, *Working for Women?* p. 111.

168 *Guardian*, 23 January 1993.

169 *Hansard*, 5th Series, Vol. 686, 16 December 1963, written answers, col. 150.
170 Patterson, *Dark Strangers*, pp. 82, 135-6.
171 Minute by Miss Hanson, Ministry of Labour and National Service, 14 October 1952, refers to taking 'the coloured women in small parties' in LAB.8/6, PRO.

EIGHT

1 'At your service' in *The Economist*, 14 December 1996.
2 Brittney, *Which? Guide to Domestic Help*, p. 10.
3 Young, 'It's not hard to find good help these days' in *The Times*, 25 September 1998.
4 Brittney; *Which? Guide to Domestic Help*, pp. 19-20.
5 *Guardian*, 6 February 1990.
6 Ibid.
7 Chris Arnot, 'Stark Vision' in *Guardian: Society*, 26 July 2000.
8 Alfred Sherman, 'In-house training and the domestic service dilemma' in *Guardian*, 9 January 1984. Rosie Cox, The Role of Ethnicity, p. 134.
9 Gregson & Lowe, *Servicing the Middle Classes*, pp. 140-1.
10 'Younger Mrs Mopps sweep back into rooms at the top' in *The Times*, 6 January 1997.
11 Brittney, *Which? Guide to Domestic Help*, p. 142.
12 Cox, 'Exploring the Growth of Paid Domestic Labour: a case study of London', forthcoming in *Geography*, p. 2. I am indebted to Rosie Cox of Coventry University for allowing me to see a copy of this paper ahead of publication.
13 Cox, 'The Role of Ethnicity', p. 138.
14 Pullinger & Summerfield (ed.), *Social Focus on Women and Men*, p. 28.
15 Gregson & Lowe, *Servicing the Middle Classes*, p. 50.
16 Ibid., pp. 96, 98-101.
17 Ibid., pp. 100-1.
18 *Guardian*, 6 February 1990. See also Nigella Lawson, 'Do you pay your Cleaner in Guilt' in *The Times*, 5 March 1997.
19 Brittney, *Which? Guide to Domestic Help*, p. 10.
20 Ibid., p. 23.
21 Matheson & Summerfield (ed.), *Social Focus on Older People*, p. 74. Brittney, *Which? Guide to Domestic Help*, pp. 30-3. *Oxford Times*, 11 February 2000.
22 'Paid to do the Dirty Work' in *Guardian*, 18 August 1992.
23 Mrs Sheila Whiting in correspondence with the author, 4 July 1999.
24 [Anon. ed.], *A People's Autobiography of Hackney*, p. 114.
25 Ibid., pp. 118-19.
26 Cox, 'Exploring the Growth of Paid Domestic Labour', p. 6.
27 'Nanny of the Year Award: 2000' in *The Lady*, 20-26 June 2000. Gregson & Lowe, *Servicing the Middle Classes*, p. 3.
28 William Weber in correspondence with the author, 18 July 1997.
29 Rachel Campbell Johnston, 'Life behind the green baize doors' in *The Times*, 11 July 1998. William Weber to the author, 25 August 2000.
30 Robin Young in *The Times*, 25 September 1998.
31 The Childcare Link was advertised in buses and other public places in 2000. *Need a Nanny? A guide for parents* (London: Department for Education and Employment, 1999). A list of member nanny and *au pair* agencies provided by the Federation of Employment and Recruitment Agencies was publicised on the Internet: www.fres.co.uk.
32 Details of Ivor Spencer's School were published on the Internet: www. ivorspencer.com/butler.htm.
33 Cox, 'The Role of Ethnicity', p. 137.

34 Gregson & Lowe, *Servicing the Middle Classes*, p. 196.

35 Ibid., p. 291.

36 *The Times*, 3 October 1998.

37 Mary Gold, 'Mrs Danvers' day has come' in *The Times*, 6 November 1999.

38 See *myhome* brochure (London, 2000) and Esther Addley, 'Are you being served', in *Guardian,* 16 March 2000.

39 Mary Gold in *The Times*, 6 November 1999.

40 Jane Shilling, 'In praise of housekeeping' in *The Times*, 27 September 1999.

41 Mary Gold in *The Times*, 6 November 1999.

42 *Guardian*, 7 March 2000.

43 Ibid.

44 Jane Ellison, 'Paying the price for nanny power' in *Sunday Correspondent*, 25 March 1990.

45 *The Times*, 19 January 1999.

46 Maureen Freely, 'We must do better than this' in *Guardian*, 20 January 1999. Gregson & Lowe, *Servicing the Middle Classes*, p. 5, note similar sensationalism in reaction to earlier cases involving nannies and their real or alleged mistreatment of their charges.

47 'Ministers to set up register for Nanny Agencies' in *The Times*, 17 January 2000.

48 *Need a Nanny?* p. 1.

49 *Hansard*, 6th Series, Vol. 327, 8 March 1999, col. 27.

50 Brittney, *Which? Guide to Domestic Help*, pp. 148-9 and information provided by the Home Office concerning *au pairs*, July 2000. *Hansard*, 6th Series, Vol. 326, 25 February 1999, cols. 629 and 634.

51 *Hansard*, 6th Series, Vol. 327, 8 March 1999, col. 27.

52 Cox, 'The Role of Ethnicity', pp. 135, 136, 140. *Hansard*, (House of Lords), 5th Series, Vol.597, No. 32, 8 February 1999, col. 8. *The Times*, 21 January and 17 February 1999.

53 *Hansard* (House of Lords), 5th Series, Vol. 597, No. 32, 8 February 1999, cols. 8-10. See also *Hansard* (House of Lords), 5th Series, Vol. 565, 3 July 1995, col. 934, concerning illegal immigration from Poland.

54 *Guardian*, 23 January 1993.

55 Information and correspondence kindly provided by Anne Jüssen of the Frauen Museum, Bonn, to the author, 14 December 1999. Anne is Adele's friend.

56 Lipman, *How Was It For You?*, p. 5-6.

57 Plimmer, 'She's mad, not bad, but I despair' in *The Times*, 12 June 1999.

58 Frean, 'Minimum pay threatens end of the *au pair*' in *The Times*, 21 January 1999. See also correspondence in *The Times*, 27 and 30 January 1999.

59 Frean, '*Au pair* minimum wage rules dropped' in *The Times*, 17 February 1999. *Hansard*, 6th Series, Vol. 326, 25 February 1999, cols. 633-634.

60 Brittney, *Which? Guide to Domestic Help*, pp. 149-50.

61 Cox, 'The Role of Ethnicity', pp. 139-40. Phizacklea (ed.), *One Way Ticket*, p. 98.

62 Anderson, *Britain's Secret Slaves*, pp. 43, 44.

63 *Observer Magazine*, 28 January 1990, pp. 19-20. *Hansard*, (House of Lords), 5th Series, Vol. 523, 28 November 1990, cols. 1039 and 1046.

64 *Hansard*, (House of Lords), 5th Series, Vol. 523, 28 November 1990, col. 1038. 'Foreigners Face Ban on Bringing in their Servants' in *The Times*, 21 August 1997. 'Foreign servants get right to quit "slavery"' in *The Times*, 10 February 1998.

65 *Hansard* (House of Lords), 5th Series, Vol. 592, 31 July 1998, written answer, cols. 131-132. 'Foreign servants get right to quit "slavery"' in *The Times*, 10 February 1998.

66 *Hansard* (House of Lords), 5th Series, Vol. 559,12 December 1994, written answer, col. 108.

67 [Anon.] *The Contract Clean-up*, p. 10, in TUCL, HD.6072.

68 [Anon.] *Taken to the Cleaners*, p. 33 in TUCL, HD.6072.

69 *Community Action*, No. 67 (November 1984), pp. 15-19 in TUCL, HD.6072.

70 *Statutory and Agreement-Based Provisions on Certain Aspects of the Organisation of Working Time in the Cleaning Industry. European Social Dialogue: Document Series* (Brussels, 1993), p. 17 in TUCL, HD.6072.

71 *Second Report of the Low Pay Commission. The National Minimum Wage: The Story So Far*, Cm.4571 (London, 2000), pp. 48-9. From October 2000 the minimum adult rate became £3.70 per hour.

72 *Guardian*, 26 July 2000.

73 *The Lady*, 11-17 January 2000. Brittney, *Which? Guide to Domestic Help*, p. 18.

74 Ivor Spencer's Internet site was www.ivorspencer.com/butler.htm.

75 See entry in Ivor Spencer's Internet site, June 2000.

76 *Guardian*, 28 December 1988.

77 'Butlers suffer as New Rich make poor Employers' in *The Times*, 26 July 1997.

78 *The Times*, 31 January 1998.

79 Robin Young in *The Times*, 25 September 1998.

80 R. Harrison (ed.), *Gentlemen's Gentlemen*, p. 243.

81 Arthur R. Inch in correspondence with the author, 15 December 1999.

82 Inch, *Reminiscences*, p. 116.

83 Russell, *Butler Royal*, pp. 181-2.

84 Ibid., pp. 24, 30-1.

85 Ibid., p. 204.

86 Brittney, *Which? Guide to Domestic Help*, p. 180.

87 'Butlers suffer as New Rich make poor Employers' in *The Times*, 26 July 1997.

88 P. Horn, *Rise and Fall of the Victorian Servant*, pp. 158-62.

89 Khan & Kirkham, *Behind the Painted Smiles*, p. 1.

90 *Second Report of the Low Pay Commission. The National Minimum Wage*, p. 45.

91 Calculated from the *1981 Census of Population of Great Britain: Economic Activity* (London, 1984), and *1991 Census of Population of Great Britain: Economic Activity*, Vol. 1 (London, 1994).

92 Byrne (ed.), *Waiting for Change? Low Pay Pamphlet No. 42* (London, July 1986), pp. 9, 16.

93 Dominic Bradbury, 'Sexism over the stove' in *The Times*, 6 March 1999.

94 *'Personal Service' Careers for Boys and Girls in the Catering Industry* (London: Ministry of Labour and National Service, September 1946), p. 4, in the TUCL, HD.9999CH.6.

95 Jones & Hewitt, *A.H. Jones of Grosvenor House*, p. 112.

96 S. Jackson, *Savoy*, pp. 261, 287.

97 Ibid., p. 144. Contarini, *The Savoy was my Oyster*, pp. 49, 55.

98 Decca Aitkenhead, 'At 4 a.m. I wanted a sandwich' in *Guardian*, 5 January 1999.

99 Advertisement in *Caterer and Hotelkeeper*, 11-17 November 1999.

100 Joe Warwick, 'Waiting for a proper job' in *The Times*, 16 January 1999.

101 'Labour Pains' in *Caterer and Hotelkeeper*, 19-25 August 1999.

102 *The Times*, 16 December 1999. See also the third leader in *The Times* for this date. Sabine Durrant on Gordon Ramsay, 'chef of the year' in *Guardian*, 10 July 2000, for another example of the volatile temperament and bullying attitude of one of the top chefs.

103 'King of the Castle but in fear of those Michelin men' in *The Times*, 9 January

1999.
104 *The Lady*, 20-26 June 2000.
105 *The Lady*, 23 February to 1 March 1999.
106 Khan & Kirkham, *Behind the Painted Smiles*, p. 27.
107 Ibid., p. 27.
108 *Caterer and Hotelkeeper*, 23 December 1999 to 12 January 2000.
109 Khan & Kirkham, *Behind the Painted Smiles*, pp. 23, 25.
110 Nichola Roskell, Group Personnel Manager of Paramount Hotel Group in correspondence with the author, 27 June 2000.
111 Byrne (ed.), *Waiting for Change?* p. 47.
112 Ibid, p. 47.
113 Ibid., p. 53.
114 *The Low Paid and the Minimum Wage* by the Low Pay Unit, Vol. 3 (London: Low Pay Unit, n.d. [*c.* 1999]), p. 20.
115 Ibid., pp. 17, 20.
116 Ibid., p. 17.
117 *Second Report of the Low Pay Commission, The National Minimum Wage*, pp. 45 and 47. *The Low Paid and the Minimum Wage*, p. 37.
118 Goring, *50 Years of Service*, p. 99.
119 *The Times*, 13 January 1955; letter from Miss Markham. See also Gregson & Lowe, *Servicing the Middle Classes*, pp.233-5.

BIBLIOGRAPHY

N.B. Only printed sources are given here. All manuscript and oral history material used has been detailed in the footnotes.

OFFICIAL PAPERS

Report of the Interdepartmental Committee on Care of Children (1945-46)

Home Office, *Report on the work of the Children's Branch, April 1923* (1923) and *Fifth Report on the work of the Childrens Branch, January 1938* (1938)

Hunt, A. and Fox, J. *The Home Help Service in England and Wales* (1970)

Ministry of Labour, *Annual Reports* (1924-25 to 1960-61)

Ministry of Labour, *Report to the Minister of Labour of the Committee on the Supply of Female Domestic Servants* (1923)

Ministry of Labour, *Second Interim Report of the Central Committee on Women's Training and Employment for the Period ending 31 December 1922* (1923)

Local Government Board, *Annual Report for 1911* (1912-13)

Second Report of Low Pay Commission, *The National Minimum Wage: The Story So Far* (2000)

Need a Nanny? A Guide for Parents (1999)

Report of Oversea Settlement Committee, for year ending 31 December 1922 (1923)

Reports of Population Censuses for England and Wales and Scotland (1901-1991)

Royal Commission on Population (1949)

Report on Post-War Organisation of Private Domestic Employment, Violet Markham and Florence Hancock (1944-45)

Reports to President of the Oversea Settlement Committee on Openings for Women in Canada (1919); in Australia (1920); and in New Zealand (1920)

Ministry of Reconstruction, *Report of the Women's Advisory Committee on the Domestic Service Problem* (1919)

Annual Reports of the Chief Inspector of Reformatory and Industrial Schools of Great Britain, for 1912 and 1915

Report of the Departmental Committee Appointed to Enquire on Land in Scotland, Used as Deer Forests (1922)

Royal Commission on Unemployment Insurance; Majority and Minority Reports (1931-32)

NEWSPAPERS AND JOURNALS

Blackpool Gazette, Houseworker, British Boarding-House Proprietor, Labour Woman, Caterer and Hotelkeeper, The Lady, Country Life, Lancet, Daily Mail, London Evening Standard, Daily News, Manchester Guardian, Domestic Servants' Advertiser, Ministry of Labour Gazette, Economist, Observer, The Field, The Times, Gardeners' Chronicle, YWCA Newsletter, GFS Magazine, Good Housekeeping, Hansard, Guardian.

BOOKS AND ARTICLES

A Few Rules for the Manners of Servants in Good Families (London, 1895)

Anderson, B. *Britain's Secret Slaves. An Investigation into the Plight of Overseas Domestic Workers* (Anti-Slavery International Human Rights Series, No.5, 1993)

Anderson, W. *A Rather Special Place. Growing up in Cardiff Dockland* (Llandysul, 1993)

Astor, M. *Tribal Feeling* (London, 1963)

Balderson, E. with Goodlad, D. *Backstairs Life in a Country House* (Newton Abbot, 1982)

Barnardo's, Dr, *Annual Reports of Homes*

Beddoe, D. *Back to Home and Duty, Women between the Wars, 1918-1939* (London, 1989)

Bedford, John, Duke of, *A Silver-plated Spoon* (London, 1959 edn)

Berghahn, M. *German-Jewish Refugees in England* (New York, 1984)

Braybon, G. *Women Workers in the First World War* (London, 1981)

Briar, C. *Working for Women? Gendered Work and Welfare Policies in Twentieth-Century Britain* (London, 1997)

Brittney, L. *The Which? Guide to Domestic Help* (London, 1998)

Burnett, J. (ed.), *Useful Toil* (London, 1974)

Butler, C.V. *Domestic Service. An Enquiry by the Women's Industrial Council* (London, 1916)

Byrne, D. (ed.), *Waiting for Change?* (Low Pay Pamphlet No. 42, London, July 1986)

Carrothers, W.A. *Emigration from the British Isles* (London, 1965 edn)

Chorley, K. *Manchester Made Them* (London, 1950)

Community Action, No. 67 (London, November 1984)

Contarini, P. *The Savoy was my Oyster* (London, 1976)

Contract Clean-up. An Outline of Trends and Conditions in the Contract Cleaning Industry (Greater London Council Economic Policy Group Strategy document no. 9, 1983)

Cox, R. 'The Role of Ethnicity in Shaping the Domestic Employment Sector in Britain' in Janet Henshall Momsen (ed.), *Gender, Migration and Domestic Service* (London and New York, 1999)

Cox, R. 'Exploring the Growth of Paid Domestic Labour: a case study of London', forthcoming in *Geography*.

Dallington, S. *Around Foxton. Memories of an Edwardian Childhood* (Wymeswold, 1991)

Darcy, G.H. *Problems and Changes in Women's Work in England and Wales, 1918-1939* (London University Ph.D. thesis, 1984)

Davison, I. *Etiquette for Women. A Book of Modern Manners and Customs* (London, 1928)

Dawes, F. *Not in Front of the Servants. Domestic Service in England 1850-1939* (London, 1973)

—, 'The Dying Reign of the Pantry', *Daily Telegraph Magazine*, 6 July, 1972.

Devonshire, Duchess of, *The Estate. A View from Chatsworth* (London, 1990)

—, *The House. A Portrait of Chatsworth* (London, 1982)

Dickens, M. *One Pair of Hands* (Harmondsworth, 1972 edn)

Eley, G. *And Here is Mr Streeter* (London, 1950)

Elliott, D.M. *The Status of Domestic Work in the United Kingdom with Special Reference to the National Institute of Houseworkers* (Geneva, 1951)

Ellis, J. (ed.), *Thatched with Gold. The Memoirs of Mabell, Countess of Airlie* (London, 1962)

Festing, S. *Gertrude Jekyll* (London, 1993 edn)

Field, L. *Bendor. The Golden Duke of Westminster* (London, 1986 edn)

Firth, V. *The Psychology of the Servant Problem* (London, 1925)

Foley, W. *The Forest Trilogy* (Oxford, 1992 edn)

Foyster, J. & Proud, K. *Gamekeeper* (Newton Abbot, 1986)

Gathorne Hardy, J. *The Rise and Fall of the British Nanny* (London, 1972)

'Gibbs, M.A.', *The Year of the Nannies* (London, 1960)

Girls' Friendly Society, Annual Reports of the

Göpfert, R. (ed.), *Ich kam allein. Die Rettung von zehntausend jüdischen Kindern nach England 1938-39* (München, 1997 edn)

Gordon, E. & Breitenbach, E. (ed.), *The World is Ill Divided. Women's Work in Scotland in the Nineteenth and Early Twentieth Centuries* (Edinburgh, 1990)

Goring, O.G. *50 Years of Service* (London, 1960)

Gorst, F.J. *Of Carriages and Kings* (London, 1956)

Gregory, B. *A Gardener's Life. Memories of Gardening on some of the Great English Private Estates* (privately printed n.d. [*c.* 1999])

Gregson, N. and Lowe, M. *Servicing the Middle Classes. Class, Gender and Waged Domestic Labour in Contemporary Britain* (London and New York, 1994)

Haggard, L.R. *I Walked by Night* by *The King of the Norfolk Poachers* (Ipswich, 1974 edn)

Hall, E. *Canary Girls and Stockpots* (Luton, 1977)

Harrison, B. 'For Church, Queen and Family: The Girls' Friendly Society', *Past and Present*, No. 61 (1973)

Harrison, M. 'Domestic Service Between the Wars: The Experiences of Two Rural Women', *Oral History*, Vol. 16, No.1 (spring, 1988)

Harrison, R. (ed.), *Gentlemen's Gentlemen. My Friends in Service* (London, 1978 edn)

Harrison, R. *Rose: My Life in Service* (London, 1975)

Heath-Stubbs, M. *Friendship's Highway* (London, 1935)

Hirschfield, G. (ed.), *Exile in Great Britain. Refugees from Hitler's Germany* (Leamington Spa, 1984)

Horn, P. 'Hunting the servants: The role of servant training centres between the wars', *Genealogists' Magazine*, Vol. 26, No.8 (December 1999)

—, *Ladies of the Manor* (Stroud, 1997 edn)

—, *Rural Life in England in the First World War* (Dublin, 1984)

—, *The Rise and Fall of the Victorian Servant* (Stroud, 1995 edn)

—, 'Training and Status in Domestic Service: The Role of the League of Skilled Housecraft, 1922-1942', *History of Education Society Bulletin*, No. 65 (May 2000)

—, *Women in the 1920s* (Stroud, 1995)

Horne, E. *More Winks* (London, 1932)

—, *What the Butler Winked At* (London, 1923)

Humphries, S. and Hopwood, B. *Green and Pleasant Land. The Untold Story of Country Life in Twentieth Century Britain* (London, 1999)

Humphris, T. *Garden Glory* (London, 1970)

Hunt, A. and Fox, J. *The Home Help Service in England and Wales*, SS.407 (London, 1970)

Inch, A.R. *Reminiscences of a Life in Private Service* (London, 1999)

Jackson, A.A. *Semi-Detached London. Suburban Development, Life and Transport, 1900-39* (Didcot, 1991 edn)

Jackson, Maj. Gen. Sir L.C. *History of the United Service Club* (London, 1937)

Jackson, S. *The Savoy. The Romance of a Great Hotel* (London, 1964)

Johnson, S.C. *Emigration from the United Kingdom to North America 1763-1912* (London, 1966 edn)

Jones, D.C. (ed.), *The Social Survey of Merseyside*, Vol. II (Liverpool and London, 1934)

Jones, H. (ed.), *Duty and Citizenship. The Correspondence and Papers of Violet Markham, 1896-1953* (London, 1994)

Jones, K. and Hewitt, T. *A.H. Jones of Grosvenor House* (London, 1971)

Jones, T. *A Diary with Letters 1931-1950* (London, 1954)

Josephs, Z. *Survivors. Jewish Refugees in Birmingham 1933-1945* (Warley, 1988)

Khan, S. and Kirkham, S. *Behind the Painted Smiles. A Report on Pay and Conditions in the Hotel and Catering Sector* (Greater Manchester Low Pay Unit, 1995)

King, E. *The Green Baize Door* (Bath, 1974 edn)

Kushner, T. 'An Alien Occupation - Jewish Refugees and Domestic Service in Britain, 1933-1948' in Werner E. Mosse et al. (ed.), *Second Chance. Two Centuries of German-speaking Jews in the United Kingdom* (Tübingen, 1991)

—, 'Asylum or Servitude? Refugee domestics in Britain, 1933-1945', *Bulletin of the Society for the Study of Labour History*. Vol. 53, Pt. 3 (1988)

—, 'Politics and Race, Gender and Class: Refugees, Fascists and Domestic Service in Britain, 1933-1940' in Tony Kushner and Kenneth Lunn (ed.), *The Politics of Marginality. Race, the Radical Right and Minorities in Twentieth Century Britain* (London, 1990)

Lafitte, F. *The Internment of Aliens* (Harmondsworth, 1940)

Laurie, K. *Cricketer Preferred. Estate Workers at Lyme Park 1898-1946* (Lyme Park Joint Committee, n.d. [c. 1981])

Lee, D. *Great Estates* (London, 2000)

Lewenhak, S. *Women and Trade Unions* (London, 1977)

Lewis, L. *The Private Life of a Country House 1912-39* (London, 1982 edn)

Lewis, R. and Maude, A. *The English Middle Classes* (London, 1953 ed)

Lipman, M. *How Was It For You?* (Oxford, 1989 edn)

Macmillan, H. *Winds of Change 1914-1919* (London, 1966)

Markham, V. *Return Passage* (London, 1953)

Marsh, D.C. *The Changing Social Structure of England and Wales, 1871-1961* (London, 1965)

Marwick, A. *The Deluge. British Society and the First World War* (London, 1965)

Matheson, J. and Summerfield, C. (ed.), *Social Focus on Older People* (London, 1999)

Men Without Work. A Report made to the Pilgrim Trust (Cambridge, 1938)

Middleton, N. *When Family Failed. The Treatment of Children in the Care of the Community during the First Half of the Twentieth Century* (London, 1971)

Mistress and Maid (anonymous pamphlet issued by the Domestic Bureau, London, April 1940)

Morgan, J. and Richards, A. *A Paradise out of a Common Field. The Pleasures and Plenty of the Victorian Garden* (New York, 1990)

Mosse, W. et al. (ed.), *Second Chance. Two Centuries of German-speaking Jews in the United Kingdom* (Tübingen, 1991)

Mrs Beeton's Household Management (London, 1923 edn and London, 1949 edn)

Mullins, S. and Griffiths, G. *Cap and Apron. An Oral History of Domestic Service in the Shires, 1880-1950* (Leicestershire Museums, Art Galleries and Records Series: The Harborough Series, No.2, 1986)

Mursell, N. *Come Dawn, Come Dusk. Fifty Years a Gamekeeper for the Dukes of Westminster* (Cambridge, 1996 edn)

—, *Green and Pleasant Land. A Countryman Remembers* (London, 1983)

Annual Reports of National Institute of Houseworkers

Annual Report of the National Vigilance Association for 1934-35 (1935)

Noakes, D. *The Town Beehive. A Young Girl's Lot. Brighton 1910-1934* (Brighton, 1995 edn)

Noel, D. *Five to Seven. The Story of a 1920s Childhood* (London, 1978)

Nowell-Smith, S. (ed.), *Edwardian England 1901-1914* (London, 1964)

Nudds, A. *The Woods Belong to Me* (Cambridge, 1998 edn)

Parr, J. *Labouring Children* (London, 1980)

Partridge, F. *A Pacifist's War* (London, 1978)

Patterson, S. *Dark Strangers. A Sociological Study of the Absorption of a recent West Indian migrant group in Brixton, south London* (London, 1963)

*People's Autobiography of Hackney. Working Lives,*Vol. II, 1945-77 (London, 1977)

Phizacklea, A. (ed.), *One way Ticket. Migration and Female Labour* (London, 1983)

Powell, M. *Below Stairs* (London, 1970 edn.)

Pugh, M. *Women and the Women's Movement in Britain 1914-1959* (Basingstoke, 1992)

Pullinger, J. and Summerfield, C. (ed.), *Social Focus on Women and Men* (London, 1998)

Rennie, J. *Every Other Sunday. The Autobiography of a Kitchenmaid* (London, 1955)

Roberts, E. *Women and Families. An Oral History 1940-1970* (Oxford, 1995)

Robinson, D. *Memories of Upper Bangor in the 20s and 30s* (Bangor, n.d. [*c.* 1999])

Robinson, J.M. *The Country House at War* (London, 1989)

Rose, J. *For the Sake of the Children. Inside Dr Barnardo's: 130 Years of Caring for Children* (London, 1987)

Rose, L. *The Erosion of Childhood. Child Oppression in Britain 1860-1918* (London and New York, 1991)

Rowntree, B.S. *Poverty. A Study of Town Life* (London, 1903 edn)

Russell, P. *Butler Royal* (London, 1982)

Rutter, J. *The Young Women's Christian Association of Great Britain 1900-1925. An Organisation of Change* (University of Warwick MA thesis, 1986)

Sambrook, P.A. *The Country House Servant* (Stroud, 1999)

—, *A Servants' Place. An Account of the Servants at Shugborough* (Staffordshire County Museum: Shugborough Estate, 1989)

Schneider, B. *Exile. A Memoir of 1939.* Erika Bourguignon and Barbara Hill Rigney (eds) (Columbus, Ohio, 1998)

Segal, L. *Other People's Homes* (London, 1965)

Llewellyn Smith, Sir H. (ed.), *The New Survey of London Life and Labour*, Vol. II (London, 1931) and Vol. VIII (London, 1934)

Statutory and Agreement-Based Provisions on Certain Aspects of the Organisation of Working Time in the Cleaning Industry. European Social Dialogue: Document Series (Brussels, 1993)

Stokes, P. *Norland 1892-1992* (Hungerford, 1992)

Strachey, R. *The Cause* (London, 1978 edn)

Streatfeild, N. (ed.), *The Day Before Yesterday* (London, 1956)

Stroud, J. *Thirteen Penny Stamps. The Story of the Church of England Children's Society (Waifs and Strays) from 1881 to the 1970s* (London, 1971)

Summerfield, P. *Reconstructing Women's Wartime Lives* (Manchester, 1998)

—, *Women Workers in the Second World War. Production and Patriarchy in Conflict* (London, 1984)

Swaisland, C. *Servants and Gentlewomen to the Golden Land. The Emigration of Single Women from Britain to Southern Africa 1820-1939* (Oxford and Pietermaritzburg, S. Africa, 1993)

Sykes, C. *Nancy. The Life of Lady Astor* (London, 1979 edn)

Taken to the Cleaners: The Lincolnshire Experience (SCAT for East Midlands NUPE/NALGO, November, 1988)

Taylor, P. 'Daughters and mothers - maids and mistresses: domestic service between the wars' in John Clarke, Charles Critcher and Richard Johnson ed., *Working Class Culture. Studies in History and Theory* (London, 1979)

Thomas, A. *Wait and See* (London, 1944)

Thoms, D. *War, Industry and Society. The Midlands 1939-45* (London and New

York, 1989)

Tillyard, Sir F. *Unemployment Insurance in Great Britain 1911-1948* (Leigh on Sea, 1949)

Annual Reports of the Trades Union Congress, for 1924, 1932, 1938 and 1939

Troubridge, Lady. *The Book of Etiquette* (London, 1931 edn)

Turner, E.S. *What the Butler Saw. Two Hundred and Fifty Years of the Servant Problem* (London, 1962)

Turner, T.W. *Memoirs of a Gamekeeper (Elveden, 1868-1953)* (London, 1954)

Tyack, G. 'Service on the Cliveden Estate Between the Wars', *Oral History*, Vol. 5, No.1 (spring 1977)

Walton, J.K. *The Blackpool Landlady. A Social History* (Manchester, 1978)

Waterson, M. (ed.), *The Country House Remembered. Recollections of Life Between the Wars* (London, 1985)

—, *The Servants' Hall. A Domestic History of Erddig* (London, 1980)

Waugh, E. *Put Out More Flags* (Harmondsworth, 1972 edn)

Duchess of Westrninster, L. *Grace and Favour* (London, 1961)

Willes, M. *Country House Estates* (London, 1996)

Winstanley, M. *Life in Kent at the Turn of the Century* (Folkestone, 1978)

Woollacott, A. *On Her their Lives Depend. Munitions Workers in the Great War* (Berkeley, California, 1994)

INTERNET WEB SITES

Federation of Employment and Recruitment Agencies, www.fres.co.uk

Ivor Spencer's School for Butler Administrators/Personal Assistants, www.ivorspencer.com/butler.htm

INDEX